...NSORED BY THE
...OWMENT FOR THE ARTS,
...ONAL FOLK ART FOUNDATION, AND
...GS AND MARY C. SKAGGS FOUNDATION

SPANISH TEXTILE TRADITION OF NEW MEXICO AND COLORADO

MUSEUM OF INTERNATIONAL FOLK ART

Compiled and Edited by Nora Fisher

MUSEUM OF NEW MEXICO PRESS /\/\/\ **SANTA FE**

Copyright © 1979 Museum of New Mexico Press
All rights reserved.
Printed in the United States of America.
Second Printing: 1984.

Library of Congress Catalog Card Number: 78–68065

ISBN 0-89013-113-9 (paperbound)

Museum of New Mexico Press
P. O. Box 2087
Santa Fe, NM 87503

Copy Editor: SARAH NESTOR
Designer: BETTY BINNS
Photographer: CRADOC BAGSHAW *(unless otherwise indicated)*
Compositor: BUSINESS GRAPHICS, INC.
Printer: LAND O' SUN PRINTERS, INC.

Museum of New Mexico Press
SERIES IN SOUTHWESTERN CULTURE

CONTENTS

FOREWORD

To mention weavings from the southwestern United States is to conjure up the image of Indian textiles. Apart from specialists, few persons are aware that a rich tradition with its own characteristics, introduced by the early Spanish settlers along the Rio Grande, developed parallel with that of the Native American.

This publication is the culmination of a project which was conceived in 1967 by the late E. Boyd, who was Curator of Spanish Colonial Art at the Museum of New Mexico, Santa Fe, from 1951 until her death in September 1974. The basis of the project was to gather information on Spanish weavings as distinct from Indian textiles of the Southwest in the collections of museums in the United States and to publish the data in a Union Catalogue, which would be a valuable tool for further research.

By 1969, a list of museum holdings had been compiled. Dorothy Boyd Bowen, Research Associate at the Museum of International Folk Art, undertook the field work which was funded by the International Folk Art Foundation. During a two-year period, 1,100 textiles from thirty-six public collections were examined and recorded. Thus, by 1969 the first phase of the project was complete.

It entered its second phase in 1975 when it was resumed by the staff of the Museum of International Folk Art, who broadened and deepened its scope by inviting eminent historians, anthropologists, and textiles specialists to contribute research articles. An additional 700 textiles were analyzed and recorded by Trish Spillman, Research Associate at the Museum of International Folk Art, under the capable direction of Nora Fisher, Curator of Textiles at the Museum of International Folk Art. Historical documents were perused, weavers were interviewed, dye samples and fibers were analyzed. All in all, nearly 1,000 Rio Grande blankets have been grouped according to design characteristics. In addition, over 250 other types of Rio Grande textiles and more than 500 Mexican textiles of the pre-1860 period were studied for comparative purposes. The museum is indebted to the International Folk Art Foundation and to the National Endowment for the Arts for funding the second phase of the research, a traveling exhibition of the textiles, and a highly illustrated publication.

The history of the study of southwestern Spanish textiles is an interesting one. An early writer on Navajo weaving, George Wharton James, included a short chapter in *Indian Blankets and their Makers* in 1914, in which he described Spanish weaving. He recognized the "Chimayó blanket" as a Spanish rather than an Indian product and listed the differences between the nineteenth century and the contemporary commercial Chimayó textiles. Most of the early twentieth-century interest in native textiles concentrated on the Navajo to the exclusion of the Spanish weaver, however. Much that got into print about the latter was on a popular and superficial level.

Dr. Harry P. Mera, Curator of Archaeology at the Laboratory of

Anthropology in Santa Fe from 1931 to 1951, first began to consider the problem of the "origin and history of Spanish-American harness-loom work" about 1910. At that time, these textiles were being attributed by prestigious museums to such nonexistent groups as "the Indians of Chemallo [Chimayó] Pueblo," or the "Trampas Pueblo Indians." During the following forty years he pieced together information from countless informants, documentary research, and careful analysis of textiles to compile the first clear statement regarding Spanish weaving in New Mexico and southern Colorado. Dr. Mera pointed out the vast differences between the twentieth-century Chimayó textiles and the nineteenth-century blankets, and proposed the term "Rio Grande blankets" for the latter. Weaving, of course, was never limited to Chimayó, as the older term, "Chimayó blanket," implied. Even as late as 1951, Mera still felt it necessary to defend the fact that these Rio Grande blankets were produced by traditional Spanish weavers rather than by Navajo or Pueblo, that they were distinctly unique in the Southwest, and that they were worthy of "equal treatment" by scholars. Although Dr. Mera's manuscript of 1947–1951 has never been published, his observations and conclusions have been the foundation upon which later students have built their research. This study is no exception.

What has emerged from the project under review is a comprehensive body of information about Spanish weaving in New Mexico and southern Colorado. The approach to the research has been twofold: an analysis of the historical, economic, and social aspects of the Spanish New Mexico culture as they affect the textile tradition, and an analysis of the stylistic and technical aspects of the textiles themselves. The fact that the authors of this publication disagree in some areas may be attributed, in part, to their dependence on different sources for their conclusions. Dr. Ward Alan Minge has confined his sources to the historical documents, while Dr. Joe Ben Wheat has drawn upon his long and firsthand experience as an anthropologist familiar with Indian as well as Spanish textiles. Marianne Stoller grew up in the San Luis Valley, and this intimacy adds warmth to her ethnohistory of the area. Nora Fisher brings a familiarity with textiles from many lands and years of experience as a Curator of Textiles, while Dorothy Bowen's background as an art historian was invaluable in her study of numerous collections. Trish Spillman's contribution is based on her experience as a weaver and her knowledge of natural dyes. Christine

Mather and Charlene Cerny have worked with contemporary Spanish craftsmen throughout northern New Mexico and have interviewed many persons who had been practicing their trade since the early 1930s. Their fieldwork and the oral histories they collected add a special dimension to this endeavor. Of special significance are the misconceptions that have been cleared up regarding the *colchas* from Carson, New Mexico, which, because of their religious content and stitch technique, were believed to be very old and solely Spanish. Their modern Mormon background went unrecognized. Accordingly, let no one be surprised to find that the results of this field investigation were included in a publication that lays heavy emphasis on the Spanish tradition.

Yet, although much new ground has been turned, the several authors recognize the need for further study. Surely, somewhere in Mexican Archives, records exist which could shed additional light on the subject. Also, the technology of dye analysis is still developing, and, in the future, more precise results can be expected in identifying a wider range of dyestuffs. While fiber samples were submitted to analysis, not all the results were readily available for assimilation into the body of information. Further study in this area is a particularly felt need. There is also room for a detailed study of the weaving and weavers of specific communities such as Taos, Abiquiu, and Las Trampas, as was done for the San Luis Valley by Marianne Stoller. The exploration and further definition of dyeing traditions would also be helpful, as would a complete listing of all recorded weavers of the eighteenth and nineteenth centuries. Information about the many weavers of the twentieth century should be compiled as a matter of urgency while firsthand accounts are still available.

This work makes no claim to being definitive. Rather, it should be considered a pioneering effort. Mention of some directions for further study only emphasizes the extent of research still to be done in piecing together the complex but fascinating history of Spanish textiles not only in New Mexico and southern Colorado but also throughout the vast area formerly under Mexican hegemony, which extends from Texas to California.

Yvonne Lange, Ph.D.
Director
Museum of International Folk Art

ACKNOWLEDGMENTS

This publication and its companion exhibition required the dedication of many persons. Tribute goes first to the late E. Boyd who conceived of the project and organized its initial research phase. Since the resumption of the project in 1975, the guidance and support of Yvonne Lange, Ph.D., Director, Museum of International Folk Art, Santa Fe, has been invaluable. Her assistant, Paul Winkler, was instrumental in coordinating the many phases of this undertaking.

We would like to thank the museums, universities, and private collectors who generously made their collections available for study. Thanks are also due to the following lenders to the exhibition inaugurated at the Folk Art Museum on July 2, 1978: Colorado Historical Society, Denver, Colorado; Mr. and Mrs. Larry Frank, Arroyo Hondo, New Mexico; Fred Harvey Fine Arts Collection, Phoenix, Arizona; International Folk Art Foundation, Santa Fe, New Mexico; Los Angeles County Museum of Natural History, Los Angeles, California; Lowe Art Museum, Coral Gables, Florida; Millicent A. Rogers Museum, Taos, New Mexico; Museum of New Mexico, Santa Fe, New Mexico; Al R. and Frank O. Packard, Santa Fe, New Mexico; School of American Research, Santa Fe, New Mexico; Spanish Colonial Arts Society, Inc., Santa Fe, New Mexico; Taylor Museum, Colorado Springs Fine Arts Center, Colorado Springs, Colorado; University of Colorado Museum, Boulder, Colorado; and University Museum of the University of Pennsylvania, Philadelphia, Pennsylvania.

We are indebted to the following scholars and specialists for the significant research contributions they made: Dorothy Boyd Bowen, Research Associate, Museum of International Folk Art, Santa Fe, who has contributed far more than her share to this project; staff members of the Museum of International Folk Art: Charlene Cerny, Curator of American and Latin American Folk Art, and Christine Mather, Curator of Spanish Colonial Art; Ward Alan Minge, noted historian and Chairman of the New Mexico State Commission of Public Records; Max Saltzman, Research Specialist, Institute of Geophysics and Planetary Physics, University of California, Los Angeles; Trish Spillman, Research Associate, Museum of International Folk Art, Santa Fe; Gail Tierney, ethnobotanist, Santa Fe; Marianne Stoller, Chairman, Department of Anthropology, The Colorado College, Colorado Springs; and Joe Ben Wheat, Curator of Anthropology, University of Colorado Museum, Boulder.

Special thanks for assistance with research are also owed to Michael Cox, Curator of Collections, History Division, Museum of New Mexico; Charlotte Mitchell, Santa Fe, and staff members of the New Mexico State Records Center and Archives: Myra Ellen Jenkins, Chief of the Historical Division and New Mexico State Historian, James Purdy, historian, and J. Richard Salazar, archivist, all in Santa Fe; and Fray Angélico Chávez, Archives of the Archdiocese of Santa Fe, Santa Fe.

Scholarly advice and assistance came from many persons. In particular, we would like to acknowledge the help of the following: Richard E. Ahlborn and Rita Adrosko, National Museum of History and Technology, Smithsonian Institution, Washington, D.C.; Nancy Blomberg, Natural History Museum of Los Angeles County, Los Angeles; Alfred Bühler, Museum für Völkerkunde, Basel, Switzerland; Maria Chabot, Albuquerque; Father Benedicto Cuesta, Santa Fe; Cynthia Davis, Heard Museum, Phoenix; Imelda DeGraw, The Denver Art Museum, Denver; Tom Dickerson, Glorieta; Dot Downs, Lowe Art Museum, Coral Gables; Carlos Elmenhorst, Antigua, Guatemala; Irene Emery, The Textile Museum, Washington; Jon T. Erickson, Heard Museum, Phoenix; Carmen Espinosa, Albuquerque; Bernard Fontana, University of Arizona, Tucson; Harold Gardiner, Daughters of Utah Pioneers, Salt Lake City; Philip C. Gifford, The American Museum of Natural History, New York City; Frances Graves, Ranchos de Taos; Marta Hoffman, Norsk Folkemuseum, Oslo, Norway; T. C. Jacobsen, Temple Square Museum and Information Center, Salt Lake City; Juanita Jaramillo, Taos; Katherine D. Jenkins, Berkeley; Irmgard W. Johnson, Mexico City; Joseph H. Jones, Phoenix Dye Works, Cleveland; Dena S. Katzenberg, Baltimore; Donald King, Victoria and Albert Museum, London; Concha Ortiz y Pino de Kleven, Albuquerque; Paul Kutsche, The Colorado College, Colorado Springs; Marge Lambert, Santa Fe; María T. Luján, Española; Kathleen Martin, Santa Fe; Rowena Myers Martínez, Taos; George McCrossen, Santa Fe; Dorothy McKibbin, Santa Fe; Laura Martínez Mullins, Santa Fe; Sarah Nestor, Santa Fe; Mable O'Dell, McIntosh, New Mexico; David Ortega, Chimayó; Hilda Pang, Indiana State University, Terre Haute; Lisbeth Ransjö, Santa Fe; Nora Pickens, Santa Fe; Allen Pittman, U.S. Department of Agriculture, Berkeley; María Teresa Pomar, Museo Nacional de Artes e Industrias Populares, Mexico City; Emma Powers, Española; Anne P. Rowe, The Textile Museum, Washington; Edwin M. Shook, Antigua, Guatemala; Marc Simmons, Cerrillos, New Mexico; Elmer and Winnie Shupe, Taos; Bronwen and Garrett Solyom, Honolulu; Tillie Gabaldón Stark, Santa Fe; Philip Stoiber, Heard Museum, Phoenix; Britt Story, Denver; Lonn Taylor, Dallas Historical Society, Dallas; Betty T. Toulouse, Laboratory of Anthropology, Museum of New Mexico, Santa Fe; Christa C. Mayer Thurman, The Art Institute of Chicago, Chicago; John Trujillo, Chimayó; Lois M. Vann, National Museum of History and Technology, Smithsonian Institution, Washington; Alan Vedder, Museum of International Folk Art, Santa Fe; Ed Wade, Peabody Museum of Archaeology and Ethnology, Cambridge; Sallie Wagner, Santa Fe; Wilfred Ward, U.S. Department of Agriculture, Berkeley; Alan Watson, Santa Fe; Michael Weber, History Division, Museum of New Mexico, Santa Fe; Kristina Wilson, Taos; María Vergara-Wilson, La Madera; Mrs. Charles H. Woodard, Colorado Springs; William Wroth, Taylor Museum, Colorado Springs Fine Arts Center, Colorado Springs; John and the late Dixie Yaple, Taos.

The museum also extends its deep appreciation to volunteers who assisted staff with work on the exhibition catalog and with mounting of the textiles themselves. The following persons generously donated their time: Anne Alexander, Tillie Armijo, Susan Bontecou, Leland Bowen, Peggy Bruce, Jean Cartwright, Kay Chiba, Barbara Gleye, Gretchen Goldstein, Mary Hall, Marguerite Kaiser, Mary Klare, Anne Kunz, Marjorie Levi, Lois Livingston, Robin Malone, Stella Pettus, Marion Rinehart, Dorothy Rudolph, George Spillman, Jennie Telcocci, Louise Venrick, Lynne Vesey, and Jane Watson.

Last, but certainly not least, the project could never have been completed without the patience and good will of two highly skilled secretaries: Lorraine Cook and Shirley Christensen.

Nora Fisher, Curator of Textiles
Museum of International Folk Art
Compiler and Editor

THE SETTING

CHRONOLOGY AND MAPS

1540	*Francisco Vásquez de Coronado explores the Southwest*
1598	*Colonization of New Mexico begun by Juan de Oñate*
1610	*Santa Fe founded under the direction of Governor Pedro de Peralta*
1638	*Trade invoice from weaving workshop of Governor Luis de Rosas indicates use of treadle loom in Santa Fe*
1680	*Pueblo Indians revolt and expel the Spaniards under Governor Otermín from Santa Fe*
1693	*General Diego de Vargas expels the Tano Indians from Santa Fe and reoccupies the old capital*
1696	*De Vargas overcomes Pueblo resistance*
1704	*De Vargas will details variety of textiles available in Santa Fe*
1776	*Fray Francisco Atanasio Domínguez inventories the Franciscan missions*
1790	*Census illustrates importance of weaving in Rio Abajo*
1807–1809	*Bazán brothers (master weavers) sojourn in Santa Fe*
1821	*Mexico achieves independence from Spain*
1821	*First wagons taken over the Santa Fe Trail from Franklin, Missouri*
1840	*Over 20,000 blankets exported from New Mexico south to Mexico, according to trade documents*
1846	*Mexican/American War is declared; Governor Manuel Armijo flees New Mexico and General Stephen W. Kearney occupies Santa Fe*
1850	*A formal territorial government is created for New Mexico*
1851	*Jean B. Lamy becomes first bishop of New Mexico*
1856	*The first coal tar (aniline) synthetic dye is discovered in England by William Henry Perkin*
1859	*The first Merino sheep introduced to northeastern New Mexico*
1862	*Confederate Army under General H. H. Sibley briefly occupies Santa Fe*
1876	*Colorado admitted to the Union*
1880	*Santa Fe Railroad constructed through New Mexico*
1912	*New Mexico becomes the 47th state of the Union*
ca. 1900	*Fred Harvey Company established*
1930–1931	*First Carson Colcha produced*
June 16, 1934	*The Native Market opens*
since 1941	*World War II; more women enter the weaving profession*
July 24, 1976	*Dedication of embroidery at church in Villanueva, N.M.*
Sept.–Oct. 1976	*Rio Grande Dyeing and Weaving Workshops sponsored by the Museum of International Folk Art*

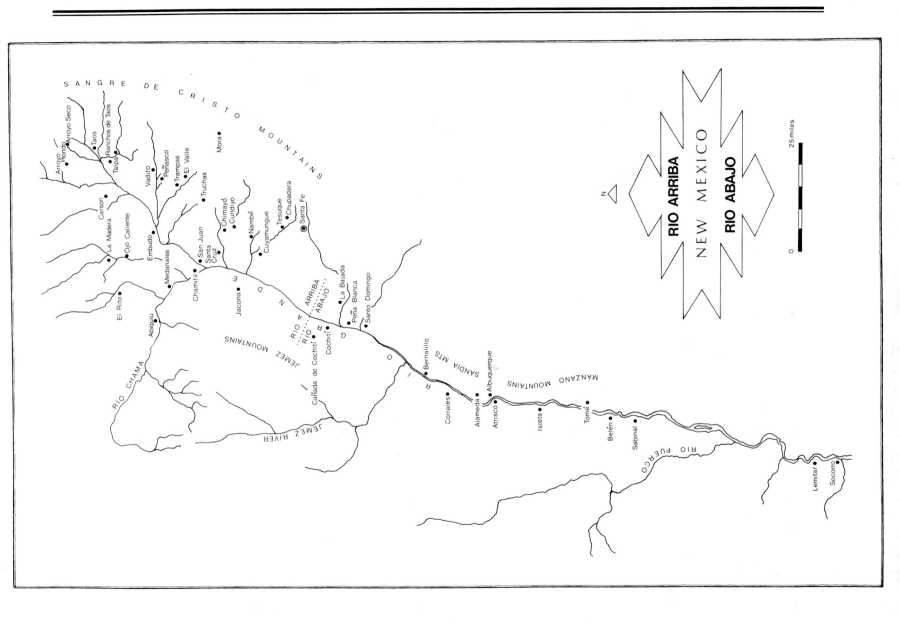

RIO ARRIBA
NEW MEXICO
RIO ABAJO

25 miles
0

N

SANGRE DE CRISTO MOUNTAINS

Arroyo Seco
Arroyo Hondo
Taos
Ranchos de Taos
Talpa
Vadito
Peñasco
Trampas
El Valle
Mora
Carson
La Madera
Ojo Caliente
Truchas
Chimayó
Cundiyo
Nambé
Tesuque
Chupadera
Santa Fe
Cuyamungue
El Rito
Embudo
San Juan
Santa Cruz
Medanales
Chamita
Jacona
Abiquiu
La Bajada
Peña Blanca
Santo Domingo
RIO CHAMA
JEMEZ MOUNTAINS
JEMEZ RIVER
Cañada de Cochití
Cochití
RIO ARRIBA
RIO ABAJO
R I O   G R A N D E
Bernalillo
SANDIA MTS
Corrales
Alameda
Albuquerque
Atrisco
MANZANO MOUNTAINS
Isleta
Tomé
Belén
Sabinal
RIO PUERCO
Lemitar
Socorro

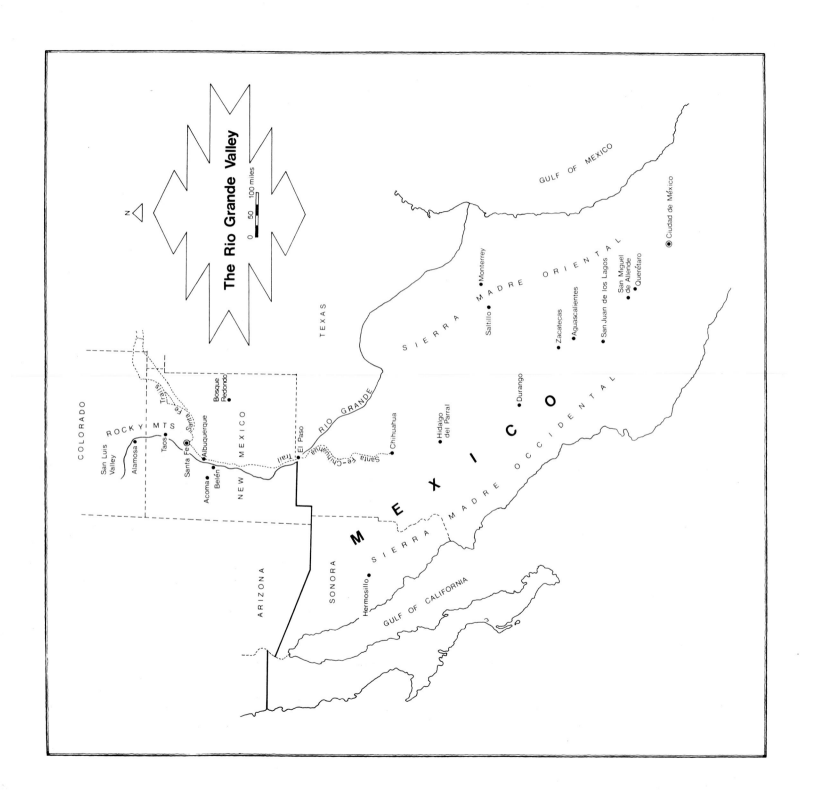

The Rio Grande Valley

N

0   50   100 miles

GULF OF MEXICO

Ciudad de México

SIERRA MADRE ORIENTAL

Monterrey

Saltillo

Zacatecas

Aguascalientes

San Juan de los Lagos

San Miguel de Allende

Querétaro

TEXAS

Durango

RIO GRANDE

Hidalgo del Parral

Chihuahua

COLORADO

ROCKY MTS

San Luis Valley

Alamosa

Taos

Santa Fe

Albuquerque

Bosque Redondo

Acoma

Belén

NEW MEXICO

El Paso

Santa Fe Trail

Santa Fe–Chihuahua Trail

M E X I C O

SIERRA MADRE OCCIDENTAL

ARIZONA

SONORA

Hermosillo

GULF OF CALIFORNIA

1 A BRIEF HISTORY OF SPANISH TEXTILE PRODUCTION IN THE SOUTHWEST

DOROTHY BOYD BOWEN

From the very first *churro* sheep which accompanied the Francisco Vásquez Coronado *entrada* into New Mexico in 1540, sheep, wool, and weaving have played an integral part in the development of Spanish Colonial culture in the American Southwest. Even though most of these small, long-fleeced *churros* perished, many others followed with Don Juan de Oñate in 1598. The early self-sufficient Spanish colonists also brought the knowledge of the treadle loom and the technology and dyes associated with it.[1] Much of their textile production was used locally for bedding, clothing, carpeting, and sacking, but wool was soon exported south to New Spain as a trade commodity both "on the hoof" and in the form of woven textiles.

By 1638 New Mexico Governor Luis de Rosas was operating a textile workshop in Santa Fe using both Indian and Spanish labor. A trade invoice from this shop which mentions 1,900 *varas* of *sayal* in nineteen pieces[2] (each piece presumably 100 *varas* long) is evidence that the European treadle loom was in use, for no Pueblo vertical loom could produce a length of nearly 100 yards. This record also proves that by 1638 the surplus of locally woven textiles was being exported on a commercial scale. This weaving tradition continued until the Pueblo Revolt of 1680.

At the same time the Pueblo Indians, settled along the banks of the Rio Grande, continued their pre-conquest textile tradition of weaving with cotton and other plant fibers primarily on the vertical loom, using their own dyes and designs. They soon learned to use the wool of the *churro,* as well as the indigo dye brought from Mexico by the Spanish, while keeping their own native looms. Sometime after 1650 the nomadic Navajos began to weave with the *churro* wool on a vertical loom similar to that used by the Pueblos, an adaptation which was to redirect their entire cultural development throughout the next three centuries.

After the reconquest of New Mexico by Don Diego de Vargas

Zapata Luján Ponce de León in 1694, sheep husbandry was resumed, with weaving again assuming a vital place in the general economy and in everyday life. Documents of the eighteenth century contain a number of references to the sheep industry and weaving in New Mexico. In 1701 a land grant refers to a tract on the Rio Grande near Bernalillo as "*Ancón del Tejedor*," or Weaver's Bend.[3] This seems to indicate a specialization of labor in which weaving was a full-time occupation. Other references imply steady production and trade of sheep and textiles south to New Spain via the trade fairs. Often sheep were not shorn until they reached Mexico City, where professional shearers took them in hand. Wool and sheep were then sold separately.[4]

One of the most important eighteenth-century trade fairs was at Saltillo in Mexico. Each September, textiles from Europe and Asia as well as from Mexico were offered in trade to New Mexican and Texan buyers.[5] Each autumn the Taos Fair in northern New Mexico attracted southern buyers from Chihuahua and Saltillo. The Chihuahua Fair was held in July, and the fair at San Juan de los Lagos in December.[6]

By 1777 New Mexico Governor Mendinueta noted a scarcity of livestock, including sheep, in New Mexico and blamed this trade for the shortage. Noting that looms were idle for lack of wool, he prohibited the export of livestock and wool.[7] In 1789 officials in Chihuahua advised New Mexico Governor Fernando de la Concha to prohibit slaughter of all female sheep of breeding age.[8]

Yet, the census records of 1790 indicate a thriving Spanish weaving industry on the Rio Abajo, where nearly one-third of the heads of family were involved in textile production, with fifty-five weavers, sixteen spinners, and thirty carders mentioned for Atrisco, Albuquerque, and Alameda alone.[9] Another twenty-six weavers and five carders are listed in towns south of Albuquerque, along the Rio Grande from Pajarito to just below Belén, with the tiny village of Tomé boasting seven weavers, two carders, and two tailors. Most surprisingly, however, this census lists only two weavers and one Comanche carder in the seventy-three households in Santa Fe.[10] Thus, weaving in the Rio Arriba apparently was in a sad state compared to weaving further south. Unfortunately, not a single documented example of this once prolific Rio Abajo textile industry has come to light, although evidence from nineteenth-century *guías* (cargo lists) gives a vague suggestion of its characteristics.[11]

Although only male heads of households are listed by occupation in the 1790 census, probably much of the carding, spinning, and weaving was done by other household members. Many of these weavers, carders, and spinners are listed as heads of large families with servants.[12]

The division of labor along ethnic lines is interesting. Thirteen of the thirty-eight carders in 1790 are classified as either *Genízaro* (Christianized Indian), Comanche, Navajo, Apache, or Indian. Of the sixteen spinners, only one is a *Genízaro*. Of the ninety-seven weavers, only four are *Genízaro* or Indian. Thus, nearly all weavers and spinners were either *mestizo* or Spanish, while almost one-third of the carders were Indians.

A description of the articles being produced was given in 1802 by New Mexico Governor Fernando Chacón, who noted that woven textiles included *bayetones* (baize, woven on narrow racks), long *frazadas* (blankets), *sarapes, bayetas, sayal* (sackcloth), and "*jergo*" (*jerga,* carpeting) dyed with *añil* (indigo) and *palo brasil* (brazil stick) which were imported "from the outer country," and with "*orines y yervas que conocen*" (urine and herbs which they know).[13] Chacón noted the lack of an apprentice system, official examinations for master-workmen, and *gremios* (guilds) like those found in New Spain, with their strict and explicit *Ordenanzas* (regulations).[14]

In an effort to upgrade the weaving done in the Rio Arriba, Spanish authorities arranged for the brothers Juan and Ignacio Bazán to teach weaving skills, including the spinning and weaving of cotton. They stayed in Santa Fe from 1807 to 1809.[15] A comment by Pedro Bautista Pino in 1812 reveals that these master weavers did indeed introduce "fine looms for cotton" and "taught many in a very little time."[16] Presumably the Bazáns brought the technical knowledge needed to execute the complex designs found in contemporary Mexican *sarapes,* particularly in those beautiful, fine garments now known as "Saltillo *sarapes*." Perhaps commercial dyestuffs such as cochineal, logwood, brazilwood, and fustic were introduced as well, although in New Spain dyers had separate guilds, and the art had reached a high level of specialization impossible to sustain in New Mexico.

The market for New Mexican textiles broadened with Mexican independence and the opening of the Santa Fe Trail, both of which occurred in 1821. New materials for weavers and embroiderers in the form of three-ply Saxony wool yarns dyed with cochineal, lac, natural yellows, and brazilwood, silk and cotton threads, cotton twill cloth for embroidery backing, and calico prints were but a few of the countless commodities that flowed steadily over the Trail. Numerous diaries and letters of travelers in the 1820s through the 1840s preserve a vivid record of these days on the Trail, and from them we see New Mexicans eager for eastern goods. In 1824, for example, Augustus Storrs took to Santa Fe woolen goods such as "super blues, stroudings, pelisse cloths, and shawls."[17] Some of these same woolen fabrics appear in Rio Grande and particularly Navajo blankets as bundled fibers (cloth which has been cut into strips and respun). In the Storrs Report, it is claimed that New Mexican citizens produce "twice the quantity of wool necessary to clothe their inhabitants."[18]

In 1831 Alphonso Wetmore noted the maintenance of a "good coach road from Santa Fe through El Paso, Chihuahua, El Bayo, Mapomis, Parras, Saltillo, and Monterrey to Matamoros" in Mexico.[19] Thus, the ambitious Yankee trader could travel the Santa Fe Trail from Missouri to New Mexico and find a trade route extending from Santa Fe deep into Mexico. The Chihuahua trade effectively ceased with the Mexican-American War, however.

Between the years 1830 and 1848 an organized caravan trade was conducted by Santa Fe merchants between New Mexico and California. New Mexican *sarapes, frazadas,* and *colchas* were exchanged for California horses, mules, a few Chinese silks, and other textiles.[20] A note in 1847 indicates that once in California, the caravan commonly broke up, with individuals trading blankets and other goods up and down the coast as far north as Monterey.[21]

The annexation of New Mexico by the United States in 1846 caused even greater traffic on the Santa Fe Trail by settlers from the East. Spanish weavers, meanwhile, continued to produce *jerga, sabanilla,* and *sarapes* for the local market as well as for trade. But in the late 1850s some changes were in the wind which would gravely affect the quality of their work. First, in 1856 the young English chemist William Henry Perkin accidentally discovered the first coal tar dye.[22] Within several years coal tar or aniline dyes and other synthetic dyes arrived on the New Mexico market to eventually replace the more durable natural dyes. Second, the first purebred Merino sheep arrived in 1859 in northeastern New Mexico.[23] The finer, short-staple kinky, greasy Merino fleece was impossible to hand-scour thoroughly and, therefore, to dye evenly. It was also difficult to spin by hand. By the early 1880s, the only area of New Mexico with much Merino blood was the northeast: Colfax, Mora, and San Miguel counties.[24] By the 1890s throughout most of New Mexico the coarse, wavy, long-staple *churro* wool was heavily contaminated by the Merino characteristics.

At the same time the coming of the railroad to New Mexico by 1880 brought cheaper commercial textiles which competed strongly for the local market, which was virtually all that was left to the Spanish weaver. Thus, in the last decade of the nineteenth century weaving became largely a home craft, with production limited to whatever the family and neighbors could use. Weaving of a higher quality persisted in the San Luis Valley of Colorado and in small northern New Mexico towns until as late as 1930.[25] The changes brought about in the twentieth century are treated in this publication, but for all practical purposes, the period of the Rio Grande blanket was over. In its place was something entirely different.[26]

2 EFECTOS DEL PAIS: A HISTORY OF WEAVING ALONG THE RIO GRANDE*
WARD ALAN MINGE

For more than 250 years, locally made textiles provided most of the clothing needed by the Spanish colonists along the Rio Grande. At first they had to rely heavily on New Spain and friendly Indians for supplies, but self-reliance was a matter both of habit and necessity. The mechanical advantages of the Industrial Revolution would not reach the sparsely settled northern frontier until relatively modern times. Meanwhile, the isolation of the Santa Fe colony, because of the great distances and rigors of travel, made any trading venture a ponderous and dangerous undertaking. The Spanish crown enforced trade restrictions, and monopolies in New Spain inhibited free and open trading. At times imported and manufactured goods were scarce and beyond the reach of the cash-poor New Mexican. Still, a ready market for regional produce could be found to the south, mainly in Chihuahua and the presidios in the northern provinces of New Spain where New Mexican sheep were needed to feed the troops.

Any trade across the eastern border of New Mexico with the United States was prohibited by Spanish authorities. This door to the east was opened in 1821, when Mexico declared her independence from Spain; and, as new trade developed, foreign goods became plentiful and more generally available. For twenty-five years, New Mexico prospered. Tools were welcome imports; and, as early as 1830, such manufactured articles as panes of glass made popular trade accessories to brighten New Mexican adobes long shut up for want of these materials as well as for protection.

The markets for native produce widened beyond El Paso del Norte and Chihuahua. New Mexicans drove sheep, hauled homemade goods, and transported some imports as far as Hermosillo and to settlements in Sonora and around Chihuahua—to towns such as Aguascalientes,

*Efectos del país: domestic production or manufacture, local production, produce of the country, manufactures of the country, local produce. Term first appears during the Colonial Period, and is commonly used during the Mexican Period.

Zacatecas, Durango, and San Miguel el Grande (de Allende). *Guías* (passports) of the early nineteenth century reveal that San Juan de los Lagos was a favorite destination, and that such faraway places as Michoacán, Sinaloa, and Mexico City attracted the New Mexican trader. To avoid the high tariff levied upon imported goods, the cargoes of native produce were declared as *efectos del país* to customs inspectors. Annual shipments included examples of the region's finest fabrics: *sarapes, mantas, jerga, sabanilla, frazadas, colchas,* and *sayal.* The popular demand for these items not only spurred production but also belied the traditional official opinion that New Mexican textiles were of no particular merit.

After 1846, when the United States took over from Mexico in Santa Fe, trade in eastern American commercial goods began to overshadow the traffic in native products. *Efectos del país* became identified predominantly with rural areas, while the mainstream of fashion was governed by increasing access to goods brought over the Santa Fe Trail. By 1900, railroads had replaced the old trade routes and regional dress and handwoven goods had virtually disappeared. One notable exception remained—the blankets woven by the Navajo Indians, who responded to the demands of the trading post operator, catering to the tourist trade.

/.\/.\/.\\

INTRODUCTION OF SHEEP TO THE
RIO GRANDE BY THE SPANISH

By the 1550s barely twenty years had passed since the conquest of the Aztecs at Tenochtitlán (later called Mexico City) before victorious Spaniards were exploring and subduing areas more than a thousand miles to the north in what is today New Mexico. Such enterprise created logistics which historians consider to be awesome even by today's standards. A very necessary element, in addition to food, was clothing for protection as well as survival; the manufacture of cloth from wool, cotton, and silk became a vital economic effort in the Spanish colonies early in the sixteenth century. By 1550, the inhabitants of Puebla were producing substantial amounts of silk goods, and all of New Spain, with

the earliest sanctioned mills located in Texcoco, was producing a surplus of woolen cloth on sophisticated treadle looms less than thirty years following the conquest.[1]

The rapid build-up of sheep and weaving industries in a country not completely explored and new to the Spaniards supplied the earliest expeditions with food and clothing. Coronado assembled 5,000 sheep, reportedly, for the 1540 exploration of New Mexico. They did not do well over the rough country, yet enough survived to feed the Spaniards, who carefully guarded this precious food bank.[2] Coronado's experiences may have influenced later exploring parties which did not include sheep. Chronicles of the separate expeditions made by Chamuscado-Rodríguez and Espejo (1581–83) make no mention of sheep. Castaño de Sosa (1590–91) took some cattle, goats, and oxen, as well as horses, but no sheep, apparently. At one point on the trail, in eastern New Mexico, the party killed an ox for food. They had only enough supplies to last to within a year or so of any contemplated settlement.[3]

In 1598, Don Juan de Oñate pledged under contract to take 4,000 sheep to New Mexico for use by the first Spanish colony in the area. Inspections and other delays, however, had dwindled his initial 4,439 ewes and rams to considerably below 3,000 by the time the expedition got underway. Other animals for the first settlement included 846 goats, as well as oxen, horses, and mules. A few settlers brought additional sheep which increased the main flock by 500 to a total of 1,000. With all the equipment assembled for the first colony, however, there were no looms—which leads one to conclude that these animals were intended mainly for food.[4]

The expedition came to New Mexico loaded down with foreign and domestic goods and clothing. Bundles of handspun woolen yarns might possibly have been used for weaving, but little emphasis is given to this type of supply in the inventories. Rather, there were numerous yards of ordinary cloth rolled into bolts or bundles, rolls of cotton goods, and others identified as Campeche cloth, Holland cloth, native and Chinese taffeta, London cloth, Chinese damask, and various types of native woolens, including native black baize. Ready-to-wear clothing, far more abundant than the yard goods, made up most of the luggage; apparently the colonists hoped soon to replenish both clothing and yard goods by trade with New Spain.[5]

Pueblo Indians and weaving

A discouraging revelation on the journey north was the general nakedness of the natives. Individual chroniclers expressed concern that they would not find Indians who were clothed and especially Indians who raised cotton and practiced weaving as a sign of high civilization. Above the Rio Grande and in New Mexico, however, they did find clothed Indians, who hopefully would become a ready labor force for the colony. Hernán Gallegos of the Chamuscado-Rodríguez expedition (1581–83) noted that there were many villages in whose houses they found cotton. "The natives wear Campeche-type cotton blankets, for they have large cotton fields." They found the Indian dress was entirely of cotton blankets fastened at the shoulder. These blankets were often of many colors, hand-painted and embroidered, "decorated with many figures and colors." Similar cotton material formed skirts for the ladies, who girded themselves with embroidered cotton sashes adorned with tassels.[6]

In 1581 Espejo described similar conditions among the natives: "The Indians spin cotton and weave cloth." They also prepared an agave material similar in appearance to linen. Cotton fields were noted in more temperate lowlands of New Mexico, and cotton cloth was found in great quantity among the Hopis. Here, Espejo reported receiving over 1,400 large and small pieces.[7]

Governor Oñate and the Spanish colonists lost no time in acquiring Pueblo Indian clothing for their own better protection against northern climes. The entire colony lacked foresight in this area of supplies, but this was remedied somewhat by the governor's steps to exact blankets, clothing, and food as tribute from the Indians. Oñate received permission to levy tributes of *efectos del país*, after the Indians rendered formal acts of obedience to the Spanish king. Such tributes could be assigned to individual Spaniards, especially when they received an *encomienda* grant. In theory, to avoid excesses or unfair treatment, the friars were to oversee these procedures.[8]

Oñate apparently ordered a blanket from every Indian household or each resident. His manner and demands were ruthless and led in part to investigations against him as early as 1601. According to a witness, there were perhaps a few more than 1,000 sheep and about 400 cattle among the settlers, which were being destroyed for food at the rate of seven animals per week. Oñate received around 2,000 blankets a year

from the Pueblos, according to other witnesses. Each blanket measured one and one-half *varas* long and nearly the same width. Further, the Indians supplied 500 dressed buckskins, 5,000 or 6,000 *fanegas* of corn and beans, and a number of fowl. These the governor distributed among the colonists.

Collecting these "gifts" got seriously out of hand at times. Desperate Spaniards were known to seize Indian donations by force "sometimes even when it is snowing, leaving the poor Indian women stark naked, holding their babies to their breasts."[9] Oñate martialed troops against the Jumanos Pueblos[10] for reneging on what was generally recognized as the "tribute of the blankets." The reluctant pueblo was fired upon and later Oñate hanged three Indians, including one of the interpreters. Another witness to these events described the Indians as poor people who "part with those things with much feeling."[11]

No weaving was accomplished during the Spaniards' first few years in New Mexico. Without help from Mexico, Fray Juan de Escalona wrote to the viceroy in October 1601, "the Spaniards face the prospect of going about naked like the Indians."[12] But despite the near collapse of the Oñate enterprise, royal aid and missionary effort gave the colony heart. Franciscans were successful in their arduous task of missionary work, converting, baptizing, and teaching the Indians rudiments of Christianity while also introducing them to Spanish agricultural techniques and animal husbandry.[13]

Sheep arrived slowly and in such few numbers that they could not be used for anything but food. In 1608, the viceroy of Mexico assembled a caravan for New Mexico in the Zacatecas area which totaled 500 horses, cattle, and sheep altogether. The following year he authorized a new governor, more colonists, nine more Franciscan missionaries, and supplies which included building tools, nails, farm implements, clothing, flour, and 200 oxen. Oñate turned over 1,000 sheep and goats to the new governor—probably a total for the entire colony. No list or inventory for these years included a loom, however, nor were looms designated as a needed supply item.[14]

Weaving of wool had not replaced the Indian cotton work by 1635. Fray Alonso de Benavides, *custos* for New Mexico missions, petitioned the king for relief in the form of personal tributes made by the Pueblos, among them cotton blankets. "It has been established by the first governors of New Mexico, and is being continued by order of the viceroy that each house pay a tribute consisting of a cotton blanket, the best of which are about a *vara* and a half square, and a *fanega* of corn.''[15] The Indians were being made to cultivate grain and raise cattle and sheep, apparently for wool. ''With the wool he [the friar] clothes all the poor, and the friar himself also gets his clothing and food from this source.''[16]

With the establishment of large mission centers between 1625 and 1640, sheep became more plentiful. The Pueblo Indians, abetted and taught by their friars, found themselves the envy of Spanish settlers by making articles of wool. Members of the Santa Fe *cabildo* (town council) claimed in 1639 that each religious owned from 1,000 to 2,000 sheep, while individual settlers were lucky to own 100 to 500, barely enough to feed their extended families. The friars were accused of exceeding authorized quotas of animals they could export to Mexico.

Such industry was difficult to control, because the colonists benefited as well. For example, the *encomenderos,* of which there were probably about fifty to sixty after 1640, were entitled to a *fanega* of corn and a cotton blanket annually from Indian households. Sometime during this period, the Pueblos started making stockings for the governor in Santa Fe, theoretically for redistribution to colonists; and, in 1660, the accounts showed: ''Senecú, 100 pairs; Socorro, 30 pairs; San Ildefonso, 262 pairs; San Juan, Santa Clara, Jacona, Pojoaque, Nambé, and Cuyamungué, a total of 280 pairs; Alomillo, 46 pairs; Santo Domingo, 156 pairs; Jémez, 360 pairs; Tano Pueblos, 165 pairs.''[17]

The church and the state each accused the other of exploiting the Indians. The friars argued that accumulating large flocks of sheep gave them a beneficial surplus in times of famine and allowed them to trade in New Spain for church furnishings and richer vestments. From their arguments emerges the real probability that each side was right about the other but, also, a great deal of information emerges about the status of weaving among the Indians. For example, a case involving physical abuse of Indians by a certain friar in the 1650s reveals that the Indians (Pueblos) wove both cotton and woolen *mantas.*[18]

The governors by and large sought personal gain at the expense, very often, of local inhabitants. One of the worst of these was Bernardo López de Mendizábal, who traded large amounts of Indian produce in New Spain. Most trading was in kind; in return for lavish imported furnishings and goods brought with him from New Spain, he accepted *mantas,* hides, piñon nuts, salt, and livestock. His trade caravans

transporting this material were legendary; in 1659 and 1660, he made two shipments worth an estimated 7,000 pesos and 12,000 pesos respectively. (One peso was roughly equivalent to one U.S. dollar.) The last consisted of 1,350 deerskins, 600 pairs woolen stockings, 300 *fanegas* piñon nuts, and ''quantities of leather jackets, shirts, breeches, salt, and buffalo skins.'' The same caravan employed ten new carts made in New Mexico, at least 160 oxen, and more than sixty pack mules.[19]

The clergy claimed heavy losses in livestock due to Governor López's policy making Indian service voluntary and paid. In other words, the missions could not afford to hire sufficient herdsmen and farmers and thus lost the services of many. The same regulation over mission labor was reiterated by Captain Don Dionisio Peñalosa Brizeñas Briceño y Berdugo in one of the few original documents to survive the Pueblo Revolt of 1680. His order, issued in 1664, stated that the friars were not to occupy the Indians in making *mantas,* stockings, or other things without his authority *(licenzia mía).*[20]

By 1680 and the Pueblo Revolt, sheep had become a desired addition to Pueblo culture. The Indians destroyed much in their anxiety to drive the Spaniards out, but inspection parties later found that they had been careful to preserve the animals, including sheep. Most of the Pueblos benefited, apparently—a great number of sheep were driven into the sierras of Cochití, above the pueblos of Santo Domingo and Cochití, and elsewhere. Then, except for the allied Indians who accompanied the defeated Spaniards to El Paso, all mission activities ceased until the next century.[21]

Some logistics of trade, the Pueblo Revolt of 1680, and the Spanish reconquest of New Mexico

With a few exceptions, local Spaniards did not exploit weaving commercially prior to 1680. Rather, they relied, perhaps too heavily, on the Indians and the factories in Mexico for materials and clothing which were supplied via the caravans. Haciendas had been established in the Rio Abajo (along the river valley below Bajada) to the south of the Tomé area, but sheep raising and wool production did not reach phenomenal heights until the next century. The Franciscan caravans, or military-escorted caravans under the supervision of the governors, brought the needed supplies from New Spain to the isolated region. Much to the distress of the colonists, these supplies went more often to the missions or to the governor's coffers than to the settlers. They had to petition the governor for permission to trade and on occasion conducted caravans and drove animals into New Spain illegally.

As noted previously, commerce was easily monopolized and exploited by the governor.[22] Records survive showing what steps were taken by individual governors in that direction. Governor Luis de Rosas established a workshop in Santa Fe where captured Apaches and Utes produced enough *efectos del país* to allow shipping the goods to Parral for sale and trade in 1639. Included in the list were 1,900 *varas* (about 1,600 meters) *sayal* (woolen cloth), 122 buffalo hides, 198 antelope skins, 79 jackets, 60 hangings, 46 drapes, 350 blankets, 126 painted blankets, 24 cushions, and 900 candles.[23] Governor López de Mendizábal employed Apache slave labor to produce enough goods for his caravans in 1659 and 1660.[24]

Legal or not, private trading expeditions were not the rule, but a Captain Cristóbal de Anaya made many trips. In January 1667, he was captured by inspectors as he was leaving New Mexico with eight wagons laden with goods. Cattle and sheep were also part of the caravan.[25]

Goods from the outside arrived via caravans officially assembled in New Spain. If not intended for the religious, they accompanied a newly appointed governor on the northward journey. Cattle, horses, and sheep made up the bulk of the trains; however, some European textiles and clothing came in this way. Official caravans also brought scarce commodities such as sugar, chocolate, and metals. From the very beginning, the New Mexico colony depended upon the viceroy in Mexico City for shipments of badly needed iron and iron tools. Iron was not abundant in New Mexico, and, as noted, individual colonists collected their own personal tools before making the expedition. No mention is made of looms or loom parts.[26]

After the disasters suffered during the Pueblo Revolt, surviving colonists took what sheep and cattle they were able to round up and depended upon them for food. One witness to the events stated that had they not been successful in taking these animals to El Paso the colony would have perished. Governor Antonio de Otermín gave some idea of the number of sheep around Santa Fe in his own brief report of the

affair. There were roughly a few more than 1,000 Spaniards in Rio Arriba (Bajada north) and somewhat over 2,500 persons altogether. Eight days before the rebellion, the governor had just repaired the *casas reales* (official accounting offices, buildings, and yards for gathering animals) to hold 1,000 persons, 5,000 sheep and goats, 400 horses and mules, and 300 beef cattle without crowding. The area was to protect most of the people and livestock then in the vicinity.[27]

Sheep did far more for the hardy colonists while they were in El Paso than to keep them from starvation. Within a year, the surviving flocks had multiplied so that some animals were sold in Parral. A few enterprising settlers had rescued all their wordly goods, leaving behind only buildings and other property. Largely because of their sheep and other animals, these few lived comfortably in El Paso, at least for a while. One such was Don Pedro de Chávez, an entrepreneur who operated a loom, weaving common cloth and *mantas* from the wool of his sheep. Trade from El Paso involved expeditions to Casas Grandes and Sonora where blankets, stockings, and other textiles were traded for cattle, corn, oxen, and other items.[28]

The serious business of regaining New Mexico and Santa Fe took Governor Don Diego de Vargas roughly five years, 1691–96. When he first arrived at El Paso, he found the colony neglected and depleted with scarcely 100 settlers, 70 horses, and about 600 sheep, most of these animals belonging to the mission. The presidio as well was poorly equipped with only 132 horses.

Despite these setbacks, however, he aroused the colonists with promises of rewards for supporting the grand project, and during the remainder of the reconquest he distributed booty and animals to those who marched with him in 1693 to Santa Fe. What were probably the first rewards occurred in December when the colonists stormed the capitol and seized 3,000 bushels of corn, a large quantity of wheat, beans, and other provisions. The Spaniards had brought a few supplies from El Paso but not enough to endure without replenishment. In April the following year, De Vargas attacked the rebellious Indians above Cañada de Cochití, capturing women and children, 70 horses, and more than 900 sheep. The horses and sheep, along with a large quantity of corn, he distributed in Santa Fe, "where the inhabitants were in need of supplies." In a similar way, more spoils were had from the pueblo of Jémez, but in 1696, nevertheless, the Spaniards faced starvation and began searching the mountains for wild animals.[29]

The following year saw the arrival of much-needed food and clothing, which De Vargas doled out to individual settlers on 1 May. Bolts of *paño* (roughly 1,500 *varas* of wool cloth) and *bayeta* (1,245 *varas* of flannel) to be made into clothing, 2,000 blankets, over 4,000 sheep, 180 goats, and some cattle constituted the shipment.[30]

Actually, most Spaniards were not much better off than their ancestors upon arrival in New Mexico 100 years earlier. Meanwhile, however, the Pueblos continued to raise sheep, and the friars hoped to restore normal life and industry as they returned to foster sheep raising and the production of wool.[31]

In splendid contrast to the above were the wordly goods of Don Diego José de Vargas Zapata y Luján Ponce de León y Contreras, accumulated in New Mexico. At the time of his death in Bernalillo on 8 April 1704 his wardrobe contained many articles of clothing, such as shirts, jackets, coats, vests, stockings, and drawers, most of them made from imported materials of silk, linen, lace, and velvet. The inventory was incredibly long and luxurious for life on a rough frontier. He had just spent 1700 to 1703 in Mexico City explaining the reconquest to authorities and clearing his reputation of slanders made by jealous officials. The viceroy reappointed him to a second term as governor of New Mexico; and, in the spring of 1703, he doubtless acquired and brought much expensive luggage to Santa Fe.

The inventory also included interesting *efectos*, significant because they comprised the handspun cloth which later became traditional. There were fifty-four yards of *sayal* (woolen cloth), *frazadas* (blankets), and possibly some of the stockings similar to those contributed by the Pueblos. Both *jerga fina* and coarse *jerga*, which later came to be used as a floor covering, had multiple uses in 1700 (Figure 1). Thirty yards of the material were unidentified as to purpose; twenty-seven sacks were of new *jerga*; and forty *mantas* (blankets) were described as coarse *jerga*. Two *colchones* (mattresses) appeared as blue and white striped, and two *colchas* had notably different characteristics than later ones—one was wool *de chino* (Chinese style?), red-lined in green linen; the other was blue cotton, also *de chino*. The inventory described bundles of silk, wool, three pounds of dyed *pita* (an agave fiber), and twenty ounces of *pita cartajena*. Most of these latter items were probably used for repairing clothing.[32]

FIGURE 1

Burros with jerga-wrapped burdens. Santa Fe, New Mexico, ca. 1866–67. Photo by Nicholas Brown. Museum of New Mexico. 10558.

∧∙∧∙∧∙∧

EIGHTEENTH-CENTURY TEXTILES

The death of De Vargas came at a turning point in New Mexico colonial affairs. The reconquest had been successful; the Spanish settlers were again establishing homes; and the missionaries returned to the pueblos. A single ingredient, however, was largely responsible for the permanency of the colony while at the same time it stimulated sheep raising and the wool industry. Governors could now issue grants of land, a dispensation which was found necessary to induce settlers to return. De Vargas rewarded his soldiers by distributing land, and he encouraged settlers to build homes and to plant. His successors issued so many grants that some of them overlapped and owners became confused over boundaries. Nevertheless, newly owned land supported enormous flocks of sheep, especially in the Rio Abajo which had access to plenty of food and water.

Sheep raising and economics

After the Pueblo Revolt, land grants encouraged settlement outside of Santa Fe. To the north Santa Cruz was founded as a Spanish *villa* in 1695; the Villa de Albuquerque followed in 1706. A common complaint from Santa Feans, found in the petitions to their governors, was that they did not own enough land to support their families or to raise herds. Those who sought grants in the Rio Abajo, however, soon developed into powerful sheep ranchers, with a ready market in El Paso, Chihuahua, and the northern presidios. Centers for sheep raising included Albuquerque, Atrisco, San Antonio, Tomé, San Fernando de los Silvas, Valencia, Los Padillas, Los Lentes, Pajarito, Sabinal, Belén, Los Chávez, Alameda, Bernalillo, Corrales, La Joya, Lemitar, Peralta, and Socorro, as well as others.[33]

New Mexicans found new and ready markets in Mexico to encourage sheep raising and some manufacturing of wool fabrics. Individual enterprise was not exactly encouraged by conditions such as restrictive travel laws, unfriendly Indians, or the great distance to these markets. But trading existed early in the century, the greater share going into Mexico.

In September 1683, the viceroy in Mexico City approved the establishment of the presidio at El Paso by New Mexico's Governor Cruzate. During the eighteenth century, the station became a gateway to Mexican presidio trade, while the civilian markets in El Paso and Chihuahua became trade centers. Local outlets for sheep and wool in New Mexico were more limited because most people had animals for food, and used the *zaleas* (sheepskins) for bedding, household purposes, and camping. According to some Albuquerqueans who had plenty for sale in 1744, there was little market for wool in New Mexico because the people made only a few *mantas* and some *sayal*. The owners were petitioning the governor for permission to sell sheared wool to a pair of buyers from Mexico, an aspect of this trade about which little information survives.[34]

Trade with foreigners was incidental, though the French tried to establish connections with Santa Fe from the Mississippi prior to the French and Indian War in 1763. Contacts with the French in 1723 resulted in some exchange of clothing and *bayeta*. The visit to Santa Fe in 1739 by Pierre and Paul Mallet was terminated by the viceroy in Mexico City, who reminded the officials that trade beyond New Mexico's borders was not tolerated by the king. On this occasion, there had been an exchange of clothing and other items.[35] The French continued a steady trade with the Plains Indians, the Comanches serving as agent to the Spanish colonists. This traffic was also considered illegal, and authorities in Santa Fe tried to prevent it from time to time. Foreign goods from the French did enter New Mexico via the Comanches and other tribes, however.[36] In December 1750, authorities detained four Frenchmen in the presidio at El Paso and confiscated their goods. The list ran mainly to foreign goods and included men's and women's stockings, ribbon, taffeta, buttons, linen, gauze, silk, thread, needles, and some clothing. The boxes also included some beaver hats and ammunition, the latter probably belonging to the Frenchmen.[37]

Frontier forts and other military settlements received new life as Mexican authorities sought protection for the rich mines and towns from fierce raids by Comanches. New Mexicans celebrated a treaty with the Comanches in February 1786, which not only saved this frontier from certain destruction, according to prevailing fears, but also protected the scattered haciendas in the Rio Abajo and lessened the risks to caravans and traders during the long drives south. Under these conditions, New Mexicans found themselves furnishing supplies to the Comanches as well as to the presidios that were meant to defend the rest of New Spain. The Camino Real ran from Santa Fe through El Paso and on to Chihuahua with branches to Altar, Tubac, Terrenate, and Fronteras (presidios in the province of Sonora); Janos, San Buenaventura, Carrizal, San Elizario, El Príncipe, La Junta de los Ríos Conchos y Norte, and San Carlos (in the province of New Vizcaya); and San Saba, Babia, Aguaverde, Monclova, San Juan Bautista del Río Grande, and Béjar at San Antonio, Texas (in the province of Coahuila). Though caravans reached these three provinces, they likely did not visit every presidio. Their sheep and *efectos,* however, were depended upon as supplies to all the garrisons.[38]

Few statistics survive to show to what extent individual New Mexicans traded into Mexico, apart from the annual caravan. Such trade was illegal without permit, but authorities seldom took aggressive steps to stop it. Indians also were known to make expeditions into Sonora for the purpose of trading.[39] Occasionally settlers attracted notice to this activity when they were captured by unfriendly Indians. Generally, merchants in Chihuahua monopolized trade coming from New Mexico, and merchants in New Mexico were known to hold a kind of monopoly over other less advantaged Spaniards and the poor Indian. This condition existed in 1782 when (as Fray Juan Agustín de Morfí described it) traders bought on credit the shearings of flocks from the Indians and then profited by three hundred percent during settlement of the debt.[40]

Authorities in Mexico and Santa Fe actually encouraged interior and exterior trade as a possible economic tonic to the northern frontier despite confusing prohibitions to the contrary. Settlers traded freely with the Pueblos; and, on occasion, governors encouraged similar exchanges with the Navajo and looked for ways to increase manufacture and trade of woven goods.[41] In 1778, Governor Juan Bautista de Anza sought a shorter and safer route between Santa Fe and Chihuahua for the encouragement of trade, but more pressing Indian problems diverted this project.[42] The governors usually did insist that New Mexicans receive a permit to leave the province. This was probably enforced, and it was one of the few controls a governor had over trade except for the *alcabala* tax, or duty on commerce.[43]

In 1788–89, authorities in New Spain, who described New Mexico as nigh poverty stricken, sought to encourage greater trade between Santa Fe and Chihuahua as well as other northern Mexican towns. To achieve this end the governor of New Vizcaya recommended to the viceroy in Mexico City the stimulation of sheep raising, the wool industry, and the cultivation of cotton. He offered suggestions on how to do it. The governor in Santa Fe should set up a center for weaving common cloth, *manta,* and *bayeta,* and for making hats, shoes, and saddles. Six craftsmen of each class should go to New Mexico from factories in Veracruz, Perote, and other places in order to start the weaving center. Also, they should take with them six *telares* (looms) for wool, six for *bayeta,* and six more for making *mantas.* And New Spain should send all the necessary tools for making hats and tanning, along with necessary dyes. All these people and supplies should collect in Chihuahua by January in time to enter New Mexico with the annual military supply train.[44]

Count Revilla Gigedo, an enlightened viceroy, agreed with proposals instructing the provinces to encourage more trade, to establish a weaving factory in Santa Fe, and to direct the New Mexicans not to kill off the females of their animals but instead to increase their herds and flocks. He cautioned, however, that New Mexicans would still be subject to the *alcabala* tax, a contribution which could not be waived without approval of His Majesty.[45]

Statistics on sheep for the Spaniards survive to some degree, though there are less for the Indians. Fray Morfí, for example, stated that most pueblos owned flocks of sheep in 1782 but neglected to say how many. In 1730, an inventory of goods belonging to the Indian Phelipe of Isleta Pueblo included unspecified numbers of goats, mares, and sheep. The same inventory listed bundles of dyed wool, a box with some loose cotton, and four bundles of spun cotton thread.[46] In 1744, the estate of Santo Domingo Indian, María Calabacita, contained 46 sheep, three to four years old and valued at two pesos each; 58 sheep, one or two years old and worth twelve *reales* each; 412 lambs worth two pesos each; and 11 castrated sheep worth two pesos each. She also had approximately 200 goats and kids.[47]

Nomad Indians were also assimilating sheep into their culture and diets. By the mid-eighteenth century, the Navajos traded in sheep and wool. At least in 1751, a resident of Bernalillo sold 350 sheep to a Navajo for the production of wool.[48] From time to time, the Spaniards made gifts of sheep for food to allied Indians identified as Comanches, Utes, Jicarillas, and Navajos. Other common articles on these lists were *escarlata* (red cloth), indigo dye, *cazos* (copper cooking vessels), bridles, corn, wheat, and tobacco.[49] Apaches, who enjoyed sheep as well, stole 400 or 500 from the pueblo of Acoma in 1799.[50]

Fray Francisco Atanasio Domínguez, appointed to make a visitation of the custody of the conversion of St. Paul in 1775, found the pueblos of New Mexico stocked with sheep which were used for food, hides, and wool, as well as for contributions to support the friars. Like Fray Morfí, he did not count the sheep in 1776 but rather indicated that most pueblos furnished the friars with lambs, wool, and other animals as tithes, obventions, and "first fruits"; and, in several cases, Indians took turns as shepherds for the convent flocks. Domínguez did not bother to find out how many sheep belonged to the Pueblos. In 1775, Fray Silvestre Vélez de Escalante found that the Hopis had "many flocks of sheep" and also harvested cotton. Cotton was raised elsewhere in the Rio Abajo, and Domínguez found the Indians planted that crop in the Isleta convent garden.[51]

Fray Juan Agustín de Morfí hardly amplified on this information in his "Geographical Description of New Mexico," written in 1782, except to verify the existence of extensive pastures, large flocks of sheep, and cotton raised generally where there was irrigation. Santo Domingo Indians harvested cotton which they "cultivate industriously." At Acoma and Hopi, there were many sheep (probably in contrast with many of the other pueblos), and he found abundant pastures all the way from Taos to Socorro. Finally, Fray Morfí pointed out that the inhabitants provided great quantities of mutton to the other provinces of New Spain.[52]

Most Spanish families in the province kept a few animals around for food, and if conditions permitted, they raised some for trading. The greatest commercial concentration of sheep existed in the Rio Abajo. A survey of estate settlements, property suits, and land rentals indicates that private flocks of 500 to 1,000 sheep were common, mostly as a mainstay for family economy. These were graded by years: one to two years of age and three to four years of age, the latter worth two pesos each. Other grades included lambs, pregnant sheep, and rams for breeding or castrating. According to Domínguez, friars at the various Spanish settlements farmed out flocks which belonged to the individual parishes. In many cases, these were given to the friar as offerings for masses and also to the church as donations. The parishes in Santa Fe, for example, farmed out over 1,000 sheep and yet purchased sheep for food to be used during celebrations.[53]

In 1790, all but a few *criadores,* or ranch owners, lived in the Rio Abajo, including the most illustrious names in New Mexico. In the northern census, Santa Fe had only three *criadores:* José Crespín, José Montoya, and Don Pedro Pino. The last had been born in Tomé.[54] In the Rio Abajo, on the other hand, at least sixty-four ranchers were listed according to location of residence, as follows:

Alameda
Antonio José Gonzáles, Spaniard[55]
Gerónimo Chaves, Spaniard
Five shepherds

Albuquerque
PLAZA 3
Santiago Armijo, Spaniard
Pablo Armijo, Spaniard
Francisco Candelaria, Spaniard

PLAZA 7
Comisionado Vicente Montoya, Spaniard

Five shepherds lived in Plaza 1, one in Plaza 2, one in Plaza 6, and one in Plaza 7

Sabinal
Gerónimo Naranjo, Spaniard
Two shepherds

Los Lentes
Comisionado Blas Lente, Indian

Ysleta
Cayetano Pojuida, Indian
Domingo Mariano Beitia, Mestizo

Atrisco
PLAZA 1
Comisionado Tomás García, Spaniard
Bertholo Padilla, Spaniard
Christoval García, Spaniard
Antonio García, Spaniard

PLAZA 2
Comisionado Diego Antonio Chaves, Spaniard
Pedro Antonio Chaves, Spaniard
Pablo Chaves, Spaniard
José María Chaves, Spaniard
Manuel Segundo Jaramillo, Spaniard

PLAZA 3
Francisco Antonio Chaves, Spaniard
Pedro Sanches, Spaniard
Jacinto Sanches, Spaniard

One shepherd in Plaza 1, and one in Plaza 4

Los Chávez
PLAZA 1
Comisionado Miguel Gabaldón, Spaniard

PLAZA 2
Comisionado Juan Chaves, Spaniard

PLAZA 4
Comisionado Juan Christóval Sanches, Spaniard

PLAZA 5
Mariano Sanches, Spaniard

PLAZA 6
Comisionado José Francisco Pino, Spaniard
Francisco Chaves, Spaniard
Balthasar Chaves, Spaniard

One shepherd in Plaza 2, two shepherds in Plaza 3

One shepherd in Plaza 5, one shepherd in Plaza 6

Los Padillas
Comisionado Tomás Chaves, Spaniard
Domingo Chaves, Spaniard
Santiago Chaves, Spaniard
José Antonio Padilla, Spaniard
José Antonio Baca, Spaniard
Manuel Antonio Varela, Spaniard
Two shepherds

Plaza de San Antonio
Teniente (Lieutenant) Don Vicente Armijo, Spaniard
José Armijo, Spaniard
Don Antonio Ruiz, Spaniard

San Ysidro de Paxarito
Don Lorenzo Gutierres, Spaniard
Pedro Mestas, Spaniard
José Marcos Ortis, Spaniard
One shepherd

Tomé
Christóval Gallegos, Spaniard
Juan Moya, Spaniard
Manuel Moya, Mestizo

Julian Sedillo, Mestizo
Four shepherds

Valencia
PLAZA 2
Manuel Aragón, Spaniard
Juan Aragón, Spaniard
Manuel Antonio Aragón, Spaniard
Domingo Chaves, Spaniard
Two shepherds in Plaza 1

Belén
PLAZA 1
Don Diego Antonio Sanches, Spaniard

PLAZA 2
Comisionado Don Miguel Antonio Baca, Spaniard
Juachín Castillo, Spaniard
Lucas Antonio Baca, Spaniard
José Antonio Padilla, Spaniard
Juan José Baca, Spaniard
Juan Dionisio Baca, Spaniard
Juan Domingo Torres, Spaniard
Barthole Pino, Spaniard

PLAZA 4 (San Antonio de los Trujillos)
Teniente Don Santiago Trujillo, Spaniard
Pedro Antonio Silva, Spaniard

PLAZA 5 (Nuestra Señora de Pilar)
Comisionado Juachín Torres, Spaniard
Xavier García, Spaniard
José Carillo, Spaniard

One shepherd in Plaza 2, one shepherd in Plaza 3, one shepherd in Plaza 4, three in Plaza 5

Shepherds appear to have had younger apprentices and other employees who did not qualify as shepherds for purposes of the census.[56]

As part of the viceregal efforts to improve conditions on the northern frontier, authorities in Mexico City proposed establishing an annual fair at a place convenient for New Mexicans to dispose of their goods. The proposal came in 1795; in 1802 New Mexico Governor Real Alencaster replied that New Mexicans preferred the promised fair to be located at El Paso. Sometime thereafter traders from the regional fair at Taos, held in July or August, began to form caravans linking with others from Rio Abajo for the journey to El Paso. The fair at Taos attracted many Indians who contributed to the *efectos* exchanged in El Paso during the "January Fair."[57]

A stimulant to trade occurred in 1796, when the viceroy eliminated the *alcabala* for New Mexicans for ten years. The great distance to settlements south of the Rio Grande was an unresolved drawback, however, as New Mexicans had started to take produce to Mexico City and even farther to Puebla. A report on economic conditions in New Mexico, dated 17 June 1805, stated that transportation costs raised the price of goods.[58]

Regional textiles in wool and cotton

Surviving inventories of estates and missions in the eighteenth century abound with information on imported cloth of all kinds. Later inventories indicate that craftsmen were producing weaving in wool and cotton which undoubtedly began to take on local attributes. They were not rated very highly by Spanish officialdom; but the common consumer in the form of presidio soldier, laborer, farmer, and Indian created a lively market.

A very early inventory (within a few years of the reconquest), of the estate belonging to Francisco Stefán de Rivera, dated 13 March 1726, contained a listing of goods which were probably all imported from Mexico or overseas. The most valuable articles were a *Colcha de Toluca* (bed covering) worth thirty pesos and a silk *rebozo*[59] worth eighteen pesos. Other foreign items ran to high prices. For example, red taffeta was valued at two pesos the *vara* (roughly 84 cm.), and blue serge from England was appraised at twenty *reales* the *vara*. The underpetticoats made of *sayal* could have been local produce. One was identified as imported and worth one peso, while the others, possibly made in New Mexico, were worth six *reales*. Obviously imported were bundles of silk—some of it black—and four *campeches* (logwood) "for thread." Remaining cloth included much linen. There was a *colchón*, or mattress, worth fifteen pesos, more *rebozos, mantas,* and other clothing.[60]

The inventory of women's goods belonging to the Indian Phelipe from the Isleta Pueblo, dated 7 January 1730, also showed imports—a shawl of Rouen linen and another of blue linen. But most of the items appeared to be made locally, in or near the pueblo; six dyed *mantas,*

seven embroidered *mantas,* two of wool, and one cotton *manta.* Two towels as well as two *sobremesas* (table coverings) were of cotton. Two boxes contained a "little cotton and two bundles of thread."[61]

The Indians primarily used domestic woven produce which they had made for that purpose or for trade. This was also now being practiced by the area's poorer Spaniards. During the *visita* of Governor Don Joachín Codallos y Rabal between 20 June and 20 October 1745, which was undertaken for the express purpose of hearing grievances, local people complained about the conditions under which these goods and services were exchanged. In Taos, Lieutenant Antonio Durán de Armijo owed the Indian interpreter, Esteban, along with other Indians, six pesos for weaving two *mantas* and cotton *sabanilla.* Other exchange goods complained of during the *visita* and also seemingly locally made included: woolen and cotton belts, boots and embroidered shoes, embroidered cotton *mantas,* a bundle of tansy, painted cotton *mantas,* a *frazada,* a dark brown woolen *manta,* woolen stockings, and a *colcha.* The Indian Joseph Valencia of the pueblo of Isleta asked the governor to help him collect eight sheep and two cows from Joseph Antonio de la Torre, resident of Rio Arriba, in debt for the *colcha.* Unless the *colcha* was imported, only one complaint involved foreign goods: four *varas* of Rouen linen.[62]

As the century progressed, more locally produced weavings appeared in wills and inventories, but these items were obviously utilitarian for the wealthier residents and not substitutes for imported clothing and luxuries. The estate of an Indian, María Calabacita, pueblo of Santa Domingo, in May 1744, had extravagant imported clothes. Her hat was red ribbed silk with feathers and gold embroidery; she had jackets of damask, covered with ribbons and lace; and there were six beautiful and valuable *mantas* (shawls), three embroidered and one painted. Two of the *mantas* appeared to be imported.[63]

The fact that some materials and workmanship were held to be of uncommonly high value is reflected in a legal suit in Santa Fe in 1764. Phelipe Tafoya, resident of Santa Fe, asked restitution for a rare *colcha* that Don Juan Joseph Moreno had borrowed from his wife six years before. The *colcha* had received bad treatment and needed cleaning. The parties described it as *fábrica de China bordado* (embroidered Chinese silk). The wife had hoped to sell it for necessary things.[64]

A number of wills and inventories which have survived from the

1760s reveal the extent of trade in foreign goods with Mexico and also indicate the gradual acceptance by the *ricos* of local weaving. The estate of Juana Luján in Albuquerque in 1762–63 held 300 to 400 sheep, iron tools from New Spain, a silver tray from Guadalajara and other silver dishes from Puebla, copper utensils, iron scissors, a wooden bed and its clothing, and, in addition, a *colchón* (mattress), a *colcha* (bed cover), two *sabanilla* (woolen sheets), and a *frazada* (blanket), all probably made locally. The same inventory also included clothing, remnants, and ninety bundles of wool or fleeces.[65]

When Juan Miguel Alvares de Castillo died in Fuenclara, Jurisdiction of Albuquerque, in 1765, he left a vast assortment of woven articles, only a fraction of which were probably made in New Mexico. There were 30 *varas* of *escarlata* (red cloth), 22½ *varas* of serge, 137 *varas* of *Ruan* (Rouen linen), a wide piece of *Bretaña* (linen), 6 pieces of lace, 15 *varas* of *sayal* (wool cloth), 5 ordinary *sombreros,* much ribbon, many pairs of woolen stockings, 18 scissors, 24 Puebla *sombreros,* 2 capes of ordinary cloth, 2 copper pots (one medium and one large), a *comal* (copper griddle), 39 *varas* of *bocadillo* (sheer linen cloth), 25 bundles of strands of spun silk, a mattress of *cotensio* (burlap material), two *sabanilla de Bramante* (linen sheets), an old *colcha,* embroidered serge, English shirts, silk stockings, and many items which seemed to indicate that Alvares de Castillo was a merchant or a trader. Included for local use were ten pounds of indigo dye, bundles of cotton, and sewing needles, but no imported tools for weaving. The inventory had another reference (common in this period) to *mantas de jerga,* which were likely woolen shawls as distinguished from those made of cotton. "Ordinary" materials were probably made in New Mexico.[66]

In 1767, Mariano Baca was imprisoned because of extensive debts involved in trading. The records show that more woven goods, sheep, and hides "in kind" than money exchanged hands. Some of the exchanged articles were *mantas,* embroidered shawls, *bayeta,* serge, ribbon, a *rebozo,* shoes, *sombreros,* and stockings. Baca's debts to Indians—Apaches and Navajos—involved sheep, hides, bridles, sugar, ribbon, *Ruan* (linen), and *escarlata* (red cloth). The declaration implied a more relaxed exchange of goods than existed ten or twenty years earlier.[67]

The estate of Matheo Joseph Pino was inventoried in Santa Fe on 7 December 1768. The inventory (though probably incomplete in the original document) listed jackets, coats, pants, and stockings—all imported—as well as sixteen *mantas de jerga* (again distinguishing these from the common cotton *mantas* being made by the Pueblos).[68]

Toward the end of the eighteenth century and later, *efectos del país* appeared more frequently and openly in inventories and wills as war donations[69] and donations to churches, in lists of government stores, and as part of the gifts to allied Indians. *Jerga fina,* a common, lightweight woolen material listed earlier, was identified as a floor covering sometime after 1750. References to *sarapes* showed up in great numbers. For example, war donations collected by Governor Lieutenant Colonel Don Fernando Chacón for shipment to Chihuahua contained about 900 *sarapes,* some *frazadas* (blankets), hides, Indian dresses, and dozens of pairs of stockings, both wool and cotton. Rather than ship to Chihuahua the *mantas* and other cotton goods made by the Indians, he had these traded or sold back to the Indians. In 1809, Governor Lieutenant Colonel Don José Manrique directed another campaign for war donations. Santa Feans primarily gave money, but the people of Rio Abajo gave at least several hundred *sarapes.* The list appeared without contributions from the citizens of Albuquerque and other key villages south of Alameda. In addition there were 33 *varas* of *jerga* (floor covering), a *manta de jerga* (woolen shawl), 12 *varas* of *sabanilla* (woolen sheeting), *frazadas,* stockings, hides, and *mantas.*[70]

Woven materials common to the military store and the Presidial Company in Santa Fe were primarily for uniforms, but some goods were meant for wives and dependents. Clothing of *bayeta* (flannel) was prevalent, as were yard goods of the same material, including a *bayeta azul* (blue flannel). *Bayeta* from New Spain came from Tlascala. *Indianas* (calicoes or domestic printed cotton) and *vermellón fino* (a red coloring matter)[71] were found among the imported goods. In 1815, the Santa Fe Company had in its inventory 30 *mantas de jerga* and 27 *mantas de Guangoche.*[72] During this same period, a soldier's possessions of woven goods might include *bayeta, mantas,* a *sombrero,* other clothing, and bedding, and more if he were married.[73] In 1817, the company store and granary stocked *elefanta* (braiding and silver cording), *Bretaña de Castilla* (linen), *indianilla* (calico), *indianilla inglaterra* (English printed cotton), *rebozos Guadalajarona* (head coverings), *rebozos finos Poblanos* (fine folk style head coverings), *coletilla de España* (Spanish coat material), silk, *satín amarillo* (yellow satin), *paño* (wool cloth), *bayetón de la tierra* (heavy coating fabric), pieces of *escarlata* and red *bayeta,* and odds and ends. Both *añil* (indigo) and *vermellón* were available. Except perhaps for the *bayeta* and *bayetón,* local produce was limited to *mantas,* hides, wool, stockings, and 556 sheep along with other animals. Clothing, tools, and food made up a large part of the inventory.[74]

Captain Don Facundo Melgares, New Mexico's governor from 1818 to 1822, made two appeals for public contributions; both times he accumulated materials woven locally. The first in 1818 was to support the military companies from Sonora-Nueva Vizcaya currently stationed in New Mexico. This account survives incomplete, but Socorro, Sevilleta, Belén, Tomé, Jemes, and Zía contributed *sarapes* and sheep. The latter were for food, most likely. For redemption of captives (possibly both Spanish and Pueblo) from the Comanches, the governor assembled money, tobacco, onions, sarapes, stockings, Indian dresses, one belt, and fourteen hides.[75]

Allied Indians—Comanches, Jicarillas (Apaches), Navajos, and Utes—received government gifts from time to time. Articles popular among them included not only the traditional beads, metal ornaments, buttons, and mirrors but also cooking utensils and iron tools of all kinds, harness, silver ornaments, bridles, and food. Dyes, wool, and cotton stuff were in demand—particularly *añil* (indigo) in large amounts and packets of *vermellón.* Many yards of red and blue *bayeta* material passed into their hands as gifts. Other woven imports appeared in the form of silk, serge, *cotense* (coarse brown linen), *chalón* (lightweight wool twill), *paño* (wool cloth), pieces of *bayeta* from Tlascala, gold and silver braiding, lace, pieces of blue woolen cloth from Querétaro, and some clothing. Around 1800, among the local produce given as gifts were the usual *mantas, mantas de 7/8 retejido* (pieces of coarsely woven material), and hides. Copper cooking pots of all sizes and coral and abalone shells for making jewelry were very popular.[76]

Thanks to the friars, churches and other public buildings were show places for the best of imported cloth; regional produce began to make inroads only by the end of the eighteenth century. In Fray Francisco Atanasio Domínguez' lists of furnishings belonging to Spanish churches, chapels, and Indian missions, the materials were, without exception, imported: metallic trimmings, satins, damasks, silk (ordinary, China, and Madrid), ribbons, lace and fringe, *bayeta* (black and red), linens, cottons, veils, gauze, velvets, lamé, embroidered

woolen bed covers, tapestries, and more. Altar cloths, clothing for the figures of saints, canopies, banners, vestments, and frontals—all were of imported goods. Domínguez, like other visitors from New Spain, could have overlooked ordinary materials; locally manufactured goods were barely mentioned in inventories. It was noted in 1776, however, that parishioners not only donated sheep, wool, and cotton but occasionally *frazadas* and *mantas* for support of the resident friars.[77]

Jerga (floor covering) appeared in a general inventory of the same churches in 1796. The "ordinary" altar cloths found in the Santa Cruz de la Cañada church were probably local weaving, as distinguished from those of fine linen with lace. Black woolen items appeared at San Estevan de Acoma, and Isleta's Mission of San Agustín had floor covering identified as *alfombra de jerga grande,* another small *jerga,* and a *guarda-polvo de jerga.* In the church at Senecú were four *jergas,* one very worn.[78]

In 1806, the inventories were made again and showed no radical changes from the earlier ones.

The Santuario de Esquipulas, a chapel at El Potrero de Chimayó, was built and furnished in the years 1813–16 entirely with *efectos del país.* Inventoried on 7 May 1818 by the official visitor Don Juan Bautista Ladrón del Niño de Guevara, the goods were identified as those belonging to the chapel and those donated by Don Juan Vigil to be sold. Woven goods that belonged to the chapel included twenty *varas* of *sayal,* six *sarapes,* a length of five *varas* of *sábana de sabanilla labrada* (embroidered handwoven wool),[79] and a new *colcha.* Vigil donated fourteen *sarapes,* twenty-four *varas* of *jerga,* seventeen *varas* of *sayal,* one *frazada atilmada azul* (decorated blue blanket), a *sobremesa* (tablecloth), and some stockings.[80]

In 1808, a donation similar to Juan Vigil's was made to Nuestra Señora del Rosario Chapel in Santa Fe. The greater part was produced locally, including sixteen *varas* of *manta* (woolen or cotton material), thirty-four woolen and cotton stockings, fourteen *varas* of *sayal,* six *varas* of *jerga,* twelve *sarapes* and an Indian dress, and two more *alfombras de jerga* (floor coverings), as well as several kinds of imported goods, hides, wax, candles, and more.[81]

Interesting *efectos del país* showed up in the expenses for refurbishing the town hall in Albuquerque. On 9 December 1814, officials were paying for the services of a carpenter and a tinsmith and, among other things, for twenty-six yards of *sabanilla de algodón* (cotton sheeting), *palo brasil* (brazilwood) to dye the *sabanilla,* and twenty-five yards of black and white *jerga.* Clearly, many of the common forms of New Mexican weaving had appeared in the open and were acceptable before the broader trade practices of the Mexican Period started in 1821.[82]

The craftsman

Until 1790, the New Mexican craftsman remained almost completely anonymous. Now and then a carpenter or blacksmith is identified by name, sometimes with additional biographical data in church records and judicial proceedings, but such instances are rare. On the other hand, many citations and descriptions of local produce belie their nonexistence. The census of 1790 tells us who the craftsmen were, what they did, their age and marital status, and whether they were pure Spanish, Indian, Black, or a mixture. Unfortunately, only the heads of households are listed by occupation, but due to the nature of the Spanish extended family, we can infer that all family members contributed in some way to the family economy, probably by carding, spinning, dyeing, and even weaving.

Weavers nearly dominate the list of various types of craftsmen, and all but two of these appear in the Rio Abajo area where the sheep industry was concentrated. Additionally, there were carders, spinners, and tailors.

The complete census for 1790 apparently did not survive, but information available on weavers indicates where most of that craft took place.[83] Again, it should be noted that the wool industry obviously centered in the Rio Abajo with greatest activity in Albuquerque.

As already noted, in 1788 and 1789 officials in Mexico City in the court of Viceroy Count Revilla Gigedo sought to improve economic conditions on the frontier by improving New Mexico's produce, especially weaving in both cotton and wool. Increased commerce in these items plus hides, animals, and farm produce would raise the level of the economy, according to their plans. A proposal was formulated to send master weavers along with the necessary tools to establish an *obraje* (weaving workshop) in Santa Fe. The viceroy also favored increasing the production of wool and cotton.

Craftsmen associated with weaving and processing wool, 1790

LOCATION	WEAVERS	CARDERS	TAILORS	SPINNERS
Valencia	3			
San Fernando de los Silvas	4			
Belén	9	4	1	
Tomé	7	2	2	
Los Padillas	2			
San Ysidro de Paxarito	1			
Atrisco	4	4		1
Ysleta		1		
Sabinal	1		1	
Los Chaves	11			
Los Lentes	2			
Alameda	4	2	1	
Albuquerque	47	24	3	15
Santa Fe	2	1	7	

The plans produced few results over the next fifteen years. In 1802, with what seemed like a lingering memory, the Commandant General of the Internal Provinces raised the entire issue again, probably spurred by enterprising merchants. Actually, New Mexico Governor Don Fernando Chacón tried to encourage local produce; he also reported that the Navajos had innumerable sheep and on their own worked their wool "with more delicacy and taste than the Spaniards." Navajo men and women were decently clothed and rarely seen without silver jewelry.[84]

Governor Chacón's response to the royal order directing a report on agriculture, industry, the arts, and trade presented a classic overview of New Mexican life. The extent to which the sheep industry had grown was clarified, as he reported that 25,000 to 26,000 sheep went yearly to the presidios and trade centers of the northern provinces. Once a year in November, 500 soldiers and militia escorted the goods to El Paso where the escort left the caravan and the traders proceeded to Sonora, Coahuila, Chihuahua, Durango, and the presidios.

In return, New Mexicans traded for many items missing at home. For the return trip, wagons were loaded with the finest cottons and woolen materials, *bayeta* from Querétaro, *sarapes, escarlata, chalones* (lightweight wool twill), and silks, as well as chocolate, sugar, soap, rice, spices, drugs, worked iron and tin, hardware, hats, hides of all kinds, cured skins, paper, some money, wagons, horses, and mules.

Internal trade existed but it was at a low ebb. Exchanges with the Indians (gentile nations) again reveals their competitiveness for horses, cooking pots, bridles, axes, lances, knives, scissors, all kinds of iron tools, *escarlata, sarapes, frazadas,* Indian dresses, *vermellón* and *añil* (indigo) dyes, mirrors, sugar, tobacco, corn, bread, and fruit. In exchange, the Spaniards received meat and hides.

Governor Chacón's concern, however, was that with an abundance of resources, including cotton, there were no master craftsmen or guilds in New Mexico. He explained that self-reliance and necessity caused the inhabitants to practice weaving, shoemaking, carpeting, tailoring, blacksmithing, and masonry. In all these crafts, he admitted they achieved a certain skill. The weavers turned out *bayetones, frazadas, sarapes, bayetas, sayal,* and *jerga,* in which they used natural dyes, indigo, and *palo brasil* (brazil sticks). From cotton, the inhabitants made *manta,* tablecloths, and stockings.[85]

The report requested that the viceroy in Mexico City contract with the Bazán brothers, Don Ignacio Ricardo and Don Juan, who were certified master weavers and tradesmen of the same guild, to live in Santa Fe where they would teach the weaving trade to the local youth. Looms and implements, salaries, horses, and a guide, along with two sons of Ygnacio Ricardo, were to be funded by the General Treasury of the Army and the Royal Treasury.

The Bazáns arrived in Santa Fe in 1807 with some of their equipment. The looms, whole or in part, apparently came with them; but Don Ygnacio Ricardo billed the treasury for equipment constructed to teach weaving. (The construction site was not given.) Additionally, there was a bill for working over five pieces of copper for the Bazán's use. Evidently the plan worked, as in 1809 the *alcaldes* of Santa Fe reported that the apprentices were producing without the maestro.[86] Another view of this project was given by New Mexico's Pedro Bautista Pino in 1812:

> A few years ago we saw introduced fine looms for cotton by an expert sent there by the government. He has taught many in a very little time. Although I call it fine this is in respect to that which was made before, for this fine cloth is coarse in comparison with the fine fabrics that we are accustomed to from China.[87]

The Bazán influence on New Mexico weaving and textiles was never fully reported. Because of their efforts and the resulting overall improvement, however, woven *efectos del país* doubtless earned a greater respectability.[88]

WEAVING AND TEXTILES IN THE MEXICAN PERIOD, 1821–46

The successful revolt of Mexico from Spain in 1821 opened trade that same year with the United States—after fifteen years of thwarted effort. Many enterprising traders had tried to reach Santa Fe. After Captain Zebulon Pike's arrest in 1805 by Spanish authorities, who had taken him to Santa Fe and later to Mexico City for questioning, his exciting descriptions caused others to try their luck at trading. The first to be welcomed in Santa Fe was William Becknell, who had left the Missouri with his party on 1 September 1821. On the prairie he encountered Spanish soldiers who escorted the party to Santa Fe, where they learned that the Spanish restrictive trade policies had ended after 16 September, the date of Mexico's independence. Becknell and his group were astounded at the ease with which they were able to sell their common goods at inflated prices, and from that year forward, the profits to be made from Santa Fe trade were irresistible in the United States. The wagon trains did not stop in Santa Fe but continued along the Camino Real to El Paso, Chihuahua, and points beyond.[89]

The excitement of these events in the United States, along with the cultural changes being introduced into New Mexico, overshadowed the local Mexican's response to the same trading opportunities. Trading was now open to all citizens on a competitive basis rather than controlled through the annual escorted caravans. Mexican authorities even went a step further to create embargos which protected *efectos del país,* and to encourage New Mexicans in internal trading by allowing those goods to be exchanged tax free. New Mexicans traded in both imports and local products but mostly in the latter which, though still considered inferior by Mexican authorities, achieved widespread acceptance and greater production than before Mexican independence.[90]

New heights in wool and cotton raising

Sheep raising continued to be concentrated in the Rio Abajo, though by 1830 more families throughout the frontier appeared to be raising sheep to take advantage of the trade. The census of 1822, though sketchy, shows 4,370 sheep belonging to the population of Albuquerque, not counting those in the vicinity—in Alameda, for example. In El Paso, there were 14,737 lambs and sheep. The Pueblo of Cochití had 914 goats and 270 sheep. On up north, Santa Cruz de la Cañada inhabitants owned 2,816 sheep.[91]

While sheep averaged 1,000 per owner, a few ranchers owned many more. A series of inventories in 1820 gives an insight into this ownership:

Santa Fe
José Francisco Baca—1,000 sheep
Ignacio Baca—370 sheep, 74 lambs
José Guadalupe Romero—1,030 sheep
Juan Rafael Ortiz—5,000 sheep
Diego Montoya—400 sheep
Pablo Montoya—5,000 sheep
Juan Antonio Cabeza de Baca—1,000 sheep

Albuquerque
Lucas Armijo—sheep not listed, much woven material of wool
Julián Armijo—sheep not listed, much woven material of wool
Vicente Armijo—1,000 sheep
Andrés Ortega—1,300 sheep
Juan Armijo—2,000 sheep[92]

Severino Martínez, who settled in Taos in 1804, counted 1,000 sheep in his last will and testament, dated 5 June 1827; in August of the same year, they had multiplied to 1,552.[93]

Though a good many persons would have liked to trade, the expenses of the undertaking were almost prohibitive. Families consequently banded together to provide resources for protection, wagons for freight, and employees for driving and herding, and they either gathered sheep on consignment from their owners or purchased them outright. In 1831, Don Ermenigildo Chávez took 12,000 sheep to Mexico City via Chihuahua and Durango.[94] At least 35,000 sheep left New Mexico in 1832, 30,000 of these belonging to Mariano Chaves from Los Padillas.[95] The crowning year was 1835, when New Mexicans drove approximately 80,000 sheep south. They all started in August, a few herds going to Chihuahua and Durango but most to Mexico City, a distance of 1,200 miles.[96] In 1837, at least 30,000 and in 1844, 40–50,000 sheep took to the trail with destinations of Mexico City, Chihuahua, Durango, Sonora, and Zacatecas. Don Antonio Sandoval drove 3,800 sheep to Puebla, about 1,500 miles.[97] But no other year equaled the 80,000 trailed in 1835.[98]

Josiah Gregg, a Santa Fe trader from 1831 to 1840, said that sheep raising was still a major industry while he was in New Mexico, but not as popular as in former times. The wealthy Spanish sheep merchant had become a myth. From hearsay he gathered that sheep had always been a principle article for exportation and that *ricos* profiting from this trade sent 200,000 head annually to southern markets and in good years as many as 500,000. According to Gregg, they purchased sheep from poor *rancheros* for fifty to seventy-five cents per head and realized a profit of one to two hundred percent. Gregg's sheep count is known to be exaggerated, however, as that number would have fed many more people than existed in the northern provinces.

Gregg described the sheep as small, producing "very coarse wool, and scarcely fit for anything else than mutton, for which, indeed, they are justly celebrated." The wool was inferior in quality and was produced in large quantity at very low prices. It was generally exchanged by the fleece and cost only three or four cents per pound.[99]

Sheep continued to be an economic staple for the Pueblos, Hopis, and Navajos, although Gregg reported that Pueblo textiles had fallen in quality.[100] According to Antonio Barreiro, who wrote in 1832, Navajos were raising many sheep, and a Navajo blanket was prized more highly than a *Saltillo*. Their weaving was outstanding, with many colors, and their *sarapes* were waterproof.[101] New Mexicans carried on trade for animals and *efectos del país* with the Indians. In addition, spoils of war between the Navajos and the Spanish often included both sheep and blankets. Throughout the Mexican Period, the Navajos raided along the Rio Grande, particularly in the Rio Abajo. Their primary booty was horses, but sheep ran a close second. Thus, Francisco Sandoval reported 130 sheep robbed from him by Navajos in 1829. A Mexican military expedition in 1835 recovered 4 prisoners, 14 horses, 6,604 sheep, and 109 cattle, all of which appeared in official campaign papers. Later in the same year, a Mexican reported to Santa Fe that the Navajos had taken 2,000 sheep and a herder from the vicinity of Lemitar, near Socorro. During the military campaign in 1836–37, Mexicans captured around 3,000 sheep from the Navajos; and, starting in 1838, these military campaigns began to report capturing Navajo *sarapes*. Despite peace treaty attempts, retaliations increased and spoils grew in volume. Governor Armijo returned with 1,000 pesos worth of *sarapes* in 1840, and military records showed an official count of 10,000 sheep captured in 1842. The campaigns of 1843 yielded 13,000 sheep. In 1844, the militia stationed at Pajarito retrieved 16,000 sheep which the Navajos had reportedly stolen. Both Navajo and Mexican raids continued in 1844, and all treaty attempts failed though many persons proposed trading by peaceful means.[102]

Trade with Pueblo Indians and friendly or allied Indian nations persisted; and, though little is recorded, there are indications from Gregg and other contemporaries that the Indians preferred locally produced *efectos*. Unlike the "better class" of people in Santa Fe, their dress did not become Americanized. Gregg observed that the dress of many of the Pueblos was assimilated in some respects by the "common Mexicans."[103] Production of cotton continued by the Pueblos and local Mexicans and was offered in trade and defense contributions, but the quantity had fallen because of imports from the United States. In 1825, production of native cotton was recorded at Alameda, Albuquerque, Valencia, Socorro, and Belén. In one of the last of these reports to survive, Sabinal harvested about eighteen *fanegas* of cotton in 1829. Gregg stated, too, that flax was "entirely neglected."[104]

Official gifts to allied Indians occurred annually and whenever an Indian party arrived in Santa Fe. These goods were made up largely of foreign imports and food. For the period 1825–27, Indians (variously listed as Comanches, Apaches, Navajos, and Utes) received hundreds of *varas* of red and blue *paño* (cloth), 1,000 *varas* of English woolen blanket cloth, 80 *varas* of *bayeta* of Castile, linen, *frazadas* (ordinary blankets), cashmere, shirts, shawls, *sombreros,* stockings, and many packages of *vermellón*. The many trinkets included buttons, rings, and mirrors. Practical articles and tools might include threads, knives, axes, bridles, scissors. Authorities prohibited sale of guns and ammunition to the Mexicans for the purpose of trading with Indians. Finally, the governor-commandant general arranged to give them food (bread and meat), tobacco, and sheep.[105]

Efectos del país

During the Mexican period *efectos del país* became the official nomenclature for taxation purposes to distinguish locally produced items from imports. In the sense that handwoven textiles fall into this category, they were treated by tax officials as *efectos*. For fifteen years starting with 1830, New Mexicans produced and traded an enormous volume of these distinctive goods.

The Santa Fe trade was barely a year old when authorities in Santa Fe descended on the merchant Pedro Armendaris for neglecting to pay taxes for trading with Chihuahua for the past three years. His goods were impounded and placed in the house of Francisco Ortiz where an inventory of October 1822 ran mainly to *efectos,* with a few imports, possibly some of them from the United States. Representative goods included:

> *Efectos:* 10 *sarapes atilmados corrientes* [ordinary *sarapes* with designs], 20 *reales* each [Eight *reales* equaled one peso or roughly one U.S. dollar.], 7 *sarapes de labor* [decorated *sarapes*], 7 *pesos* each; 3 large buffalo hides at 2 *pesos* each; 35 white elk hides at 9 *reales* each; 4 buffalo hides for camping at 1 *peso* each; 18 *colchas* at 8 *pesos* each; 9 dozen woolen stockings at 7 *pesos* per dozen; 47 *varas vayetón* [heavy cloth] at 3 *reales* the *vara;* 4 *frazadas atilmadas* [blankets with designs] at 5 *pesos* each; 6 more at 4 *pesos* each; 322 *varas jerga* at 2 *reales* the *vara;* 398 *varas* of *sabanilla;* 21 doors, salt, tobacco, sugar, chocolate, paper, numerous tools, and wagons.

> Imports: 65½ *varas lana* [wool] at 12 *reales* the *vara;* 1¼ *varas* Irish linen at 14 *reales* the *vara;* 8 *varas paño* [wool cloth] at 3 *pesos* the *vara;* 4 *tápalos grandes* [large shawls] at 6 *pesos* each; 6 fine kimonos at 6 *pesos* each; 11 of less quality at 5 *pesos* each; 12,100 needles; 11 *varas listón* [list cloth] at 1 *peso* the *vara;* 28 *varas* narrow list cloth [ribbon] at 6 *reales* the *vara;* 82 *varas Indianilla de Barcelona* at 18 *reales* the *vara;* 106¾ *varas* wide *Indiana Inglés* [English calico] at 11 *reales* the *vara;* 12 *varas* raw linen; and more.[106]

Clearly, markets in Mexico made trade in *efectos* an established and lucrative pursuit by 1821.

American trade goods reached a predictable variety after a few years, including printed cottons or calicoes, linens, and woolen articles which were appealing to Santa Feans and customers in other parts of Mexico. Of special interest were the goods transported by old hands like

Charles Bent, John Gentry, Jedediah S. Smith, William B. Giddings, Samuel Parkman, Isidor Robidoux, Solomon Hawk, John Scolly, Clifton Boggs, Josiah Gregg, and Jesse Sutton (partner with Gregg). Their wagons, though laden with yard goods, managed to carry stacks and boxes of window panes, tools, pins, needles, threads, combs, mirrors, soap, paper, writing sets, locks, shoes, stockings (silk, cotton, and wool), parasols, handkerchiefs, suspenders, gloves, razors, spittoons, knives, buttons, thimbles, candlesticks, and spices of all kinds. One trader shipped a gross of small stoves, and another declared 500 flintstones for Chihuahua in 1831. Among more unusual shipments were those of William B. Giddings, who took herbs and medicines and plants such as rhubarb.[107]

Yard goods and clothing formed the bulk of trade from the United States, however. Charles Bent arrived in Santa Fe in 1829 and continued on to Chihuahua and Sonora with several wagonloads of clothing and yard goods plus the usual accessories and tools. The entire shipment was made up of imported manufactured goods and clothing from the United States. And, as was often done, he included two unused, new wagons. The goods most frequently found in traders' manifests are cotton, silks, linens, woolens, flannel, serge, printed cottons, taffeta, quilting, pile cloth, list cloth, gingham, *bayeta* (in many colors), velvet, *cúbica* (fine wool), *merino negro* (fine black wool), cashmere, *mahón Inglés* (fine English cotton), *piel de diablo* (sturdy cloth), *coco negro* (black cotton), *mandarín, macedonia,* and *tejidos de jerquilla.* No machinery relating to the weaving trade appears on the manifests, but sometime in the 1830s there was a vermilion dye introduced. About ten pounds were shipped in 1834 and about seven pounds in 1835, the Mexicans using the familiar Spanish *vermellón* to describe it. In 1846, Eugene Leitendorfer brought to Santa Fe 100 pounds of *azul prusio* (Prussian blue), which may have been the first of this coloring matter in New Mexico.[108]

The native New Mexicans who drove thousands of sheep and hauled tons of *efectos del país* duty free into Mexico were a picturesque contrast with the foreign trade. *Efectos* were described officially as those homemade articles or produce of the country for which there existed a market. The owner of a wagon train might purchase some of his freight, receive part on consignment, or produce the articles himself. Aside from sheep, home woven goods comprised the bulk of this trade.

Other *efectos* included wool (valued at one peso the *arroba* or twenty-five pounds), *piñon* nuts (twelve *reales* per *fanega*), salt, buffalo hides (one–two pesos each), elk hides (four–six *reales* each), antelope hides (four *reales* to one peso each), bear hides (one–two pesos each), mountain lion hides, and beaver hides. The Indians no doubt produced, gathered, or hunted some of these. Some traders declared articles of clothing which were probably made by their wives or daughters—mainly gloves, a few dresses, and in one case, a child's wardrobe.

The enormous quantity and bulk of *efectos* produced in representative years for the Mexican Period are listed below along with valuations.[109]

Quantity and value of efectos *shipped to Mexico*

EFECTOS	1838	1840	1844	VALUE
Sarapes	952	6816		
Sarapes corrientes atilmados	1045	2350	1065	2 reales to 2 pesos
Sarapes atilmados	365	669	2092	1–2 pesos
Sarapes de labor	111	17		1–12 pesos
Sarapes atilmados corrientes				
Sarapes del gasto corriente				
Sarapes atilmados de gasto	8			
Sarapes corrientes de cobija				
Sarapes de colores	15			
Sarapes de vallos	2			
Frazadas	423	2451		
Frazadas corrientes	3685	7639	1065	2 reales
Frazadas cameras	103	147		1 peso
Frazadas de abrigo				
Frazadas atilmadas	570	137	19	1 peso
Frazadas de vallos	3			
Frazadas de Rio Abajo bordeadas				
Frazadas bordeadas		50		
Frazadas de labor	2	60		
Frazadas cuarterones		50		1 peso

Jerga (varas)	1779	1933	876	1–2 reales the vara
Jerga de sabanilla				
Jerga de tender				
Manta de jerga	1			
Manta			1	
Sayal, Sallal				1 real the vara
Sabanía, Sabanilla (vara)	110	295	313	1–2 reales the vara
Sábanas labradas				
Colchas	111	47	153	2–13 pesos
Colchones	9	2		
Concheyos, Conchello, Concheyes	11	19		1 real
Tilma	9	3	2	
Stockings (pair)	417	477	257	1–2 reales the pair
Tablecloths	2			3 reales each
Fajas de Indio				
TOTAL:	7844	20,934	4472	

In addition to 20,934 handmade textiles, traders declared 570 *arrobas,* or 14,250 pounds of wool and 1,049 buffalo hides in 1840. In 1844, they declared 2,056 buffalo hides. One manifest of 1838 describes a *colcha* embroidered with Castilian wool. *Mantas* and *sayal,* no longer popular trade items, were not being made, or they appeared under different names in the nineteenth century. Both might have been replaced by articles from the Santa Fe Trail trade just as local cotton, common to *mantas,* dwindled in production.

Not all records survived, nor did the manifests include weaving traded or used locally; therefore, these impressive figures are not complete, but a good indication of volume. Shipments went to Aguascalientes, California, Chihuahua, Durango, El Paso, Mexico City, Michoacán, Nueva Vizcaya, Puebla, San Juan de los Lagos, Sinaloa, Sonora, and Zacatecas. New Mexicans participated in fairs during these excursions, such as the fair at San Juan de los Lagos, where the major annual festival occurred during the first twelve days in December. Caravans departing from New Mexico in July and August reached San Juan before the end of November, even those driving sheep.

New Mexicans did not return with empty wagons. Rather, goods were exchanged for necessities and luxuries largely for home or personal use. Nearly every trader returned with *rebozos,* not made in New Mexico but universally used by females of all ages. These were identified generally from the region made: *rebozos saltilleros, de Santa María, Guadalajareños,* and categorized as silk or ordinary. Grocery items were brought back in quantity, such as sugar, rice, syrup, cooking oil, chocolate, sweetmeats, coffee, fruit, whiskey, and spices. Necessities included wax and wax candles, paper, thread, saddles, spurs, hats, boots and shoes, iron tools, certain material such as *bayeta* and printed cotton, and pounds of *carmesí* (cochineal) and indigo dyes.

Gregg was probably correct in his observation that the lower classes wore coarse woolen materials, *efectos del país.* "Coarse wool hats, or of palm leaf . . . , all of low crowns, are the kind generally worn by the common people." The Pueblo people wore blankets and Indian dresses, "as well as other woolen stuffs." The Mexican ladies wore shirts of ordinary wool, bound with a sash. Men wore short breeches, long stockings, and wool jackets with sleeves. Both men and women, Mexicans and Indians, wore cotton shirts or "chemises."[110] Lieutenant Colonel Emory made similar comments several years later, adding that the "better class of people" had beds, and the women were dressing like "American women."[111]

Contemporary inventories of estates give evidence of the traditional desire of the *ricos* to surround themselves with imports. The new republicanism introduced by Mexican independence did not change prevailing tastes in fashion. Among the *ricos,* Don Severino Martínez, past *alcalde* of Taos, upon his death in 1827 was representative of the ranchers having an abundance of material goods, animals, buildings, and land. The estate was made up of a mixture of imports and *efectos,* but the children placed a much higher value on items such as a gilded mirror and a cashmere shawl while assigning relatively little worth to *sarapes, manta, jerga, sabanilla,* and stockings. A *frazada atilmada* and a *colcha,* however, were appraised at six pesos each.[112] The estate of Lieutenant Colonel Blas de Hinojos (he had been a popular officer around Santa Fe) had nothing but imported goods when his will was executed in 1835. Governor Albino Pérez, killed during the 1837 revolution, owned fine uniforms but no local *efectos.* And finally, the property of wealthy Santa Fe merchant Mañuel Márquez y Melo contained no *efectos del país* except for some sacks made of *jerga* and a few buffalo and elk hides.[113]

Lieutenant Colonel Emory made this description of a wealthy home in Bernalillo, decorated with imports, in 1846:

The town of Bernalillo is small, but one of the best built in the territory. We were invited to the house of a wealthy man, to take some refreshments. We were led into an oblong room furnished like that of every Mexican in comfortable circumstances. A banquette runs around the room leaving only a space for the couch. It is covered in cushions, carpets, and pillows; upon which the visitor sits or reclines. The dirt floor is usually covered a third or a half with common looking carpet [*jerga*]. On the uncovered part is the table, freighted with grapes, sponge-cake, and the wine of the country.[114]

Susan Magoffin had the same experience with *jerga* in the home she and her husband shared while they were in Santa Fe, also in 1846. The walls were covered part way up with calico (commercial printed cotton) to protect the inhabitants from the whitewash. The floor "at the same end of the room is covered with a kind of Mexican carpeting; made of wool and coloured black and white only. In short we may consider this great hall as two rooms, for one half of it is carpeted and furnished for the parlour, while the other half has a naked floor, the dining table and all things attached to that establishment occupy it."[115]

Among the poorer people, *efectos del país* were the rule rather than the exception. A priest in Santa Fe had among his few earthly possessions a *colcha, frazada,* and *colchón* for bedding. Typical possessions of the soldiers, aside from their ammunition, might include *jerga*. All the rest of their clothing, shoes, and equipment were likely imports manufactured somewhere in Mexico, available from the commissary. When a citizen of the poorer class lay gravely ill in Santa Fe on 27 January 1830, he discussed the disposition of a wooden box with iron lock, a copper *cazo* (pot), two *colchones de sabanilla,* two *frazadas,* a *colcha,* and a *sábana de manta.* The estate amounted to little more than two horses and a mule with trappings, some clothes, two children, and a wife.[116]

The Mexican craftsman in New Mexico

Weavers of the Mexican Period remain anonymous although the improved quality of their product created a demand. Josiah Gregg noted that there were weavers of fine blankets and *sarapes* "curiously woven in handsome figures of various colors." Blankets of the finest texture, which sold for twenty dollars, he thought were imitations of Navajo *sarapes.* "There have been a few imitations of the *Sarape Sal-*

tillero—the blanket of Saltillo, a city of the south celebrated for the manufacture of the most splendid fancy blankets, singularly figured with all the colors of the rainbows. These often are sold for more than fifty dollars each." Gregg's statement implied that some local weavers did excel in their craft.[117] Indian-made *mantas* were still produced and exchanged but were largely overshadowed by imports of the United States-Mexican traders.

Reports of the 1822 census produced one of the few inventories of New Mexican looms in existence.[118] Albuquerque had 71, El Paso 131, Pueblo de Cochití had no looms in 1822 but had 14 in 1823, and Santa Cruz de la Cañada had 14. They received an evaluation of 10 pesos each (a common *sarape* brought 1 to 12 pesos), and those in Albuquerque were described as weaving cotton as well as wool. Little more survives of this census except an indication that Albuquerque had no *artesanos* (craftsmen),[119] El Paso had 681, and craftsmen in the rest of New Mexico remained uncounted.[120]

The New Mexican census in 1823 identifies a number of occupations related to the processing of wool and cotton. The Santa Fe quadrant known as Barrio de Torreón had five stocking knitters; Rio de Tesuque had nine—all female. The Barrio de Torreón had four female weavers and three shepherds, while the Barrio de San Francisco had three shepherds; a third barrio, that of San Miguel, had three; and the Barrio de Nuestra Señora de Guadalupe counted three more. Santa Fe had five tailors.[121]

A census in 1829 shows no industry beyond wool and agriculture and no craftsmen. Sabinal, population 207, raised about 18 bushels of cotton, 700 bundles of tobacco, and onions, chile, beans, wheat, and corn, as well as cattle and 309 sheep. The people of Abiquiu numbered 3,611 and made *frazadas, jerga* of all classes, *sabanilla,* and "in the winter some go to the states of Chihuahua and Sonora to trade these goods, others hunt buffalo, others trade with the Indians, and some guard their homes." The pueblos of Cochití and Santo Domingo had no industry other than farming, and the same was true for Peña Blanca, Cañada de Cohití, and Bajada. No weavers are mentioned.[122]

In 1841, Santa Fe had enough artisans to contradict its reputation as a sleepy town. In addition to 12 tailors and a spinner, those working on wool or cotton included over 200 seamstresses: Barrio de Guadalupe, 42; Barrio de San Francisco, 78; Barrio de San Miguel, 1; and Barrio de Torreón, 108.[123] Though weaving continued, it ceased to be recognized as a career in the Mexican censuses. This was probably due to the domestic orientation of the loom. The needleworkers or seamstresses evidently stayed in their homes where, in some cases, grandmothers, mothers, and daughters carried on the work. Peons and servants wove cloth on the household looms.[124]

/\/.\/\

AN OVERVIEW

Spanish settlers did very little trading of their own weaving before 1700. They used sheep primarily for food and relied on the Indians and caravans from New Spain for clothing and materials. The ascendancy of the sheep rancher and the shipment of sheep and other native produce to military and civilian markets in the northern provinces of Mexico shaped the economic destiny of New Mexico for many years. These *efectos del país* began to appear in several recognizable forms after 1750, but generally the woven goods were considered utilitarian and of poor quality. *Ricos* preferred imported goods over local weaving, which gained better acceptance, however, after the government contracted in 1807 with the Bazán brothers to teach the art in Santa Fe. Far surpassing their influence, the common market all over Mexico created a demand for Rio Grande textiles. Many New Mexicans, encouraged by favorable tax laws, turned to producing and trading *efectos del país* for a living. The large volume of woven goods created in New Mexico during the Mexican Period, especially in the years 1830 to 1846, established a genre of popular, regional art which is all but forgotten in our times.

3 RIO GRANDE, PUEBLO, AND NAVAJO WEAVERS: CROSS-CULTURAL INFLUENCE

JOE BEN WHEAT

The Basketmaker ancestors of the modern Pueblo Indians had been weavers for some time before the beginning of the Christian Era. Aside from the fine coiled and twined baskets from which their name derives, they were experts in non-loom techniques for the production of fur and feather blankets, highly decorative sandals, and fine sashes. Yucca, *apocynum,* and other plant fibers were used, as well as human and dog hair, rabbit fur, and the feathers of turkeys and other birds. Both mineral and plant dyes were used. By about A.D. 700, the back-strap loom had spread to the northern part of the Southwest, and the late Basketmaker-early Pueblo Indians were weaving cotton cloth.[1] By A.D. 1100, the wide vertical loom had been developed, and blankets and cloth of cotton and other plant fibers were being woven.

When the Spanish explorers first entered the Southwest in 1540, they were pleased to find the Pueblo Indians wearing clothing woven from cotton and decorated by dyeing, painting, and embroidery.[2] The most common garment was a small blanket woven wider than long, and worn wrapped around the body as a dress, or over the shoulders as a *manta* or blanket. One-piece shirts with a hole for the neck, kilts or breech cloths, and belts were also produced.

When the Spanish returned to settle in 1598, they brought with them the *churro,* the common sheep of southern Spain, to provide both food and wool for weaving. Within a few years, the Spanish had begun the production of wool cloth on locally constructed European-type treadle looms. By the 1630s,[3] wool cloth was being produced in Santa Fe workshops which exploited Indian as well as Spanish labor in spinning and weaving. It was not long before the Pueblo weavers adopted wool; and, except for the continuing use of cotton, primarily for ceremonial garments, wool became the predominant fiber in Pueblo weaving. The Spanish apparently introduced indigo dye at the same time. Indigo, combined with the natural dark brown and white wool of the *churro* sheep, provided a limited but pleasing array of colors for the Spanish weavers, with their treadle loom, and for the Pueblo weavers, who never abandoned their wide vertical loom. No documented blankets have survived from this early period (1600–1800), but it is likely that alternating stripes woven in indigo blue and natural-undyed brown and white wools constituted the primary decorative schemes of both groups of weavers, as was the case at a later date.

From the beginning, the Spanish colonists and their reluctant Pueblo subjects were surrounded by *Chichamecas,* semi-nomadic Indians. Most of these were Athabascans, the various Apache tribes. One of these Apache tribes, which inhabited the mountainous country northwest of Santa Fe, was first distinguished in 1626 by the missionary, Zárate Salmerón, as the *Apaches de Navajú.*[4] Four years later, in 1630, Benavides stated that the Apache de Navajú "are very great farmers, for that [is what] Navajú signifies—'great planted fields.' "[5] There is nothing to indicate that the Navajo were weavers at this time. By the middle 1600s, the Navajo were raiding widely, to Jémez, Acoma, and as far as Zuni, taking loot and prisoners, some of whom were incorporated into the burgeoning Navajo tribe. Other Pueblo Indians, in order to escape the rigors of Spanish domination, voluntarily exiled themselves to the Navajo.

Probably it was from some of these Pueblos that the Navajo first learned to weave, for they adopted, without change, the wide vertical Pueblo loom, together with the various techniques of spinning, dyeing, and weaving. It is almost certain that they learned these skills before the Pueblo Revolt of 1680, when the Spanish were driven from the Rio Grande Valley, for only ten years after the Spanish completed their reconquest of New Mexico in 1696, the Navajo were producing enough blankets and cloth not only for their own use but for a surplus which they traded with Pueblos and Spanish for other goods. This is clear from a letter written in August 1706, by Governor Cuervo y Valdez which states that "[The Navajo] *cultivate the soil with great industry . . . . Yet this is nothing new among these Apaches, for whenever they are sedentary they do the same things. They make their clothes of wool and cotton, sowing the latter and obtaining the former from the flocks which they raise.*" (Italics mine.)[6] The Rabal Documents state that by 1706 the Navajo were weaving wool and cotton cloth which they bartered to the Pueblos and Spanish, as well as baskets, buckskin, and other items.[7] Their clothing is stated to be like that worn by the Pueblos.

These early Pueblo-like garments consisted of the sash, woven in warp-faced weave, and the man's shirt and woman's one-piece dress, both normally woven in plain twill weave with diamond twill borders. By the middle 1700s, striped shoulder blankets for men, woven in a loose weft-faced plain weave, became the prototype for the Navajo chief blanket. The one-piece dress in twill weave, however, gave way to a two-piece dress which consisted of two small blankets in weft-faced plain weave, with brown wool center and indigo blue striped ends. Still later, red was added to the color scheme, but since the Navajo had no good red dye, the color was achieved by raveling Spanish or English commercial cloth and incorporating the raveled yarns into their own weaving.

The chief product of the Spanish looms in the Rio Grande Valley, aside from the coarse *sayal* (sackcloth) and the finer *sabanilla* (sheeting), consisted of *frazadas*—plain-woven common blankets used for bedding—and somewhat fancier blankets or *sarapes*—used as outer garments—woven in a tapestry weave. Unlike the Pueblo garments, Spanish blankets were longer than wide, and were usually composed of two long strips sewn together. In these early blankets, stripes may well have been the predominant and perhaps the only kind of decoration. In some existing striped blankets, particularly those using green, yellow, and red-brown natural dyes, with or without indigo, the rhythm of the color repeats is very complex. More common, and usually simpler, were the blankets decorated in panels of alternating blue and brown stripes separated by stripes of white.[8] This design style seems to have been taken over by most of the Pueblo weavers, and by the Navajo, who term it "the Mexican Pelt," clearly denoting its origin (Figure 1). Ironically, the pattern is frequently termed "the Moki Pattern," after the old Spanish name for the Hopi, who, of all the Pueblos, rarely wove that particular design.

Both Pueblo and Navajo weavers took over the *sarape*-type blanket, probably from the Spanish, since the Pueblos rarely wove such fabrics before the advent of the Spanish settlers. These, like the Spanish

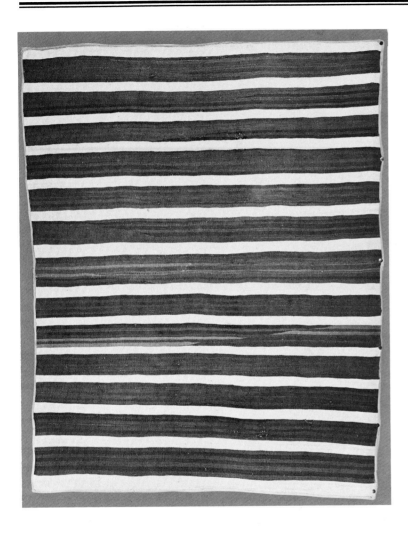

FIGURE 1

Navajo blanket in Rio Grande pattern of alternating brown, indigo blue, and white stripes—the so-called "Moki" pattern. Ca. 1860. Illinois State Museum. 808/929.

prototypes, were usually woven in weft-faced plain weave, that of the Pueblos remaining soft and loosely woven, while the Navajo developed a preference for a tightly packed weft-faced textile both in plain and twill weaves. Because of these differences in emphasis, it is usually easy to distinguish between Rio Grande, Pueblo, and Navajo textiles. Generally, Rio Grande blankets have a warp/weft ratio[9] of 5–7: 25–50 per 2.5 cm. (one inch), Pueblo blankets have a ratio of 3–5: 10–20 per 2.5 cm. (one inch), and Navajo textiles have a ratio of 6–12: 20–100 threads per 2.5 cm. (one inch).

Sometime before 1800, the Navajo had broken away from the simple stripe patterns and had begun to decorate their dresses and blankets with tapestry-woven designs, probably adapted from their basketry patterns, which consisted of rows of terraced triangles, often arranged so as to produce a zigzag stripe or used to form solid or hollow terraced diamonds. By alternating colors and size of these elements, it was possible to produce a very complex design appearance. Sometimes larger, stepped triangles were added in the corners of Navajo *sarapes*. By the early 1800s, the Navajo had clearly emerged as the premier weavers of New Mexico,[10] and partly as a result of the Spanish-Navajo economic competition, the Spanish, in 1807, engaged the services of two Spanish master weavers, the Bazán brothers, who were brought from Mexico City to Santa Fe to improve the quality of local Spanish weaving and to introduce a cotton weaving industry.[11] While little became of the cotton weaving enterprise, the production of wool blankets increased dramatically, many of them being of the more decorative kinds—the *frazadas atilmadas* or *labrado al gusto*. The designs of most of the fancy blankets featured simplified serrate

FIGURE 2

Rio Grande blanket with Navajo-type layout and corner decoration in serrate figures. Ca. 1850. American Museum of Natural History. 65/3322.

concentric diamond designs, figured grounds, and borders derived from the Saltillo *sarapes* of northern Mexico and probably introduced by the Bazán brothers about 1810 (Figure 2 and Plate 35). In a number of these Mexican influenced Rio Grande blankets, in a departure from the traditional Saltillo layout, the corners are decorated with triangular figures like those of Navajo blankets except that they are usually serrate rather than terraced. Furthermore, the Rio Grande weavers wove a number of blankets which in the 1830s, according to Gregg,[12] were imitations of the "*Sarape* Navajo," and which, because they were of the finest texture, sold for twenty dollars or more, while the common blankets sold for about two dollars apiece. In such blankets, which included central diamonds and corner quarter-diamonds, the figures were woven in the terraced style of the Navajo (Figure 3 and Plates 46 and 53).

Mexico won her independence from Spain in 1821 and opened her New Mexico border to trade with the United States across what later became known as the Santa Fe Trail. The flow of commerce which, prior to that time, had been from Chihuahua and farther south in Mexico, was reversed, and by 1826, trade from the United States had penetrated through New Mexico and far into northern Mexico. Commercial cloth of all kinds flowed into Mexico. The commercial yarns, and the wool cloth which had been raveled to supply colored wefts to Spanish and Navajo weavers and embroidery threads to the Pueblos, now came across the Plains. Perhaps because of the cheapness of the imported American cotton cloths, the New Mexican cotton industry did not develop, but the local wool industry seems to have expanded. If the Navajo were the dominant weavers in the early 1800s, it is clear that the Rio Grande weavers had achieved commercial dominance by 1840, for in that year, more than 20,000 Rio Grande

FIGURE 3

Rio Grande blanket with central diamond figure and corner triangles woven in Navajo terraced technique. Ca. 1850. University of Colorado Museum. WTXC–2.

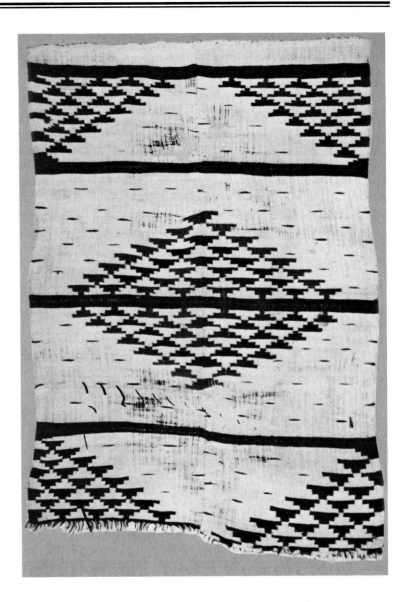

blankets were sold in northern Mexico, while only a few Navajo blankets were exported.[13] Within New Mexico, however, Navajo blankets were more sought after, often selling for fifty dollars or more, because of their high quality.[14]

From 1630 on, times of warfare and raiding by the Navajo, and counter-raids by the Spanish, had alternated with periods of peace and trade. Many *sirvientes* (Indian servants) were taken by both sides during the raids, servant trading by the Spanish being, in fact, one of the principal causes of the warfare.[15] Indian servants taken by the Navajo were simply incorporated into the tribe. Indian servants taken by the Spanish were frequently adopted into the family, but served the household in many ways, including the weaving of blankets (Plates 1, 2, and 53). Such blankets have come to be known as "slave blankets" because they usually incorporated both Spanish and Navajo elements. In this publication, these textiles are referred to as "servant blankets." Frequently, Spanish designs appear in layout and in individual design elements, in proportions, and occasionally in the use of a 2-ply warp. Most commonly, however, it is the use of dyes which were largely available only in the Rio Grande Valley (Plates 2 and 53), combined with Navajo loom-work, that led to the designation of a servant blanket. Navajo loom-work is indicated by the use of lazy lines—diagonal lines in the fabric which result from weaving the blanket one area at a time—and by the two-cord external selvedges which finish the ends and sides of Navajo-woven blankets. Such cords, when they appear on Rio Grande blankets, are the result of overzealous repair rather than original manufacture. Only four documented servant blankets are known[16]— two with a striped pattern, one woven in the wedge-weave technique (Plate 2), and a fourth containing terraced designs and madder dye (Plate 53); but many others are thought to be servant blankets

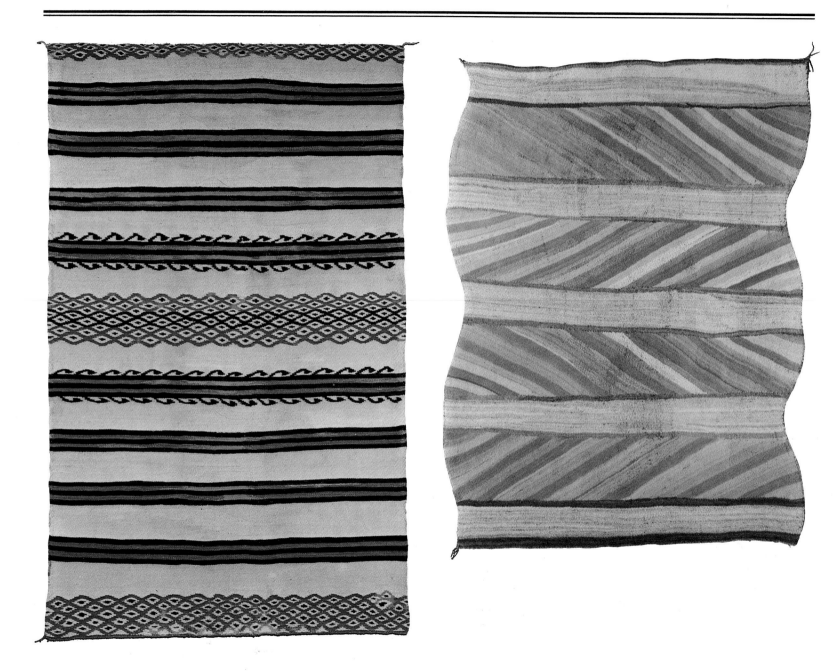

PLATE 1

Servant blanket, ca. 1860, one width, four-selvedged, 2.10 x 1.33 m. Warp: 1-ply handspun wool; weft: 1-ply handspun wool, light and dark undyed-natural and indigo. School of American Research, Santa Fe. T.189.

PLATE 2

Servant blanket, ca. 1876, one width, four-selvedged, 1.78 x 1.37 m. Warp: 1-ply handspun wool; weft: 1-ply handspun wool, natural-undyed grey and synthetic-dyed (UCLA, D–32–18, D–32–19, D–32–20, D–34–50). Probably woven by Guadalupe, Indian servant of Gaspar Gallegos, San Luis Valley, Colorado. University of Colorado Museum. 18088.

because of the character of their color schemes and patterns (Plate 1 and Figure 4).

Servant trading continued to be a cause of friction after the military conquest of New Mexico by the Americans in 1846.[17] Along with the territory, the Americans inherited the Navajo problem. By 1863, the situation had become critical, and American forces, under the command of Colonel Kit Carson, waged a classic guerilla war against the Navajo, burning their houses, destroying their crops, and killing their sheep. Defeated, the Navajo were exiled in 1863 to Bosque Redondo at Fort Sumner on the Pecos River far out in the arid plains of eastern New Mexico. Bosque Redondo was a turning point for the Navajo. Reduced to poverty and subjected to alien ideas and forces, their culture was changed in many ways. Their weaving depended more and more on U.S. Government supply of materials and on an increasing demand for

FIGURE 4

Navajo servant blanket (attributed) with a combination of Rio Grande and Navajo patterns and techniques, Rio Grande Valley dyes. Ca. 1860. Alfred I. Barton Gift, Lowe Art Museum. 57.169 (466).

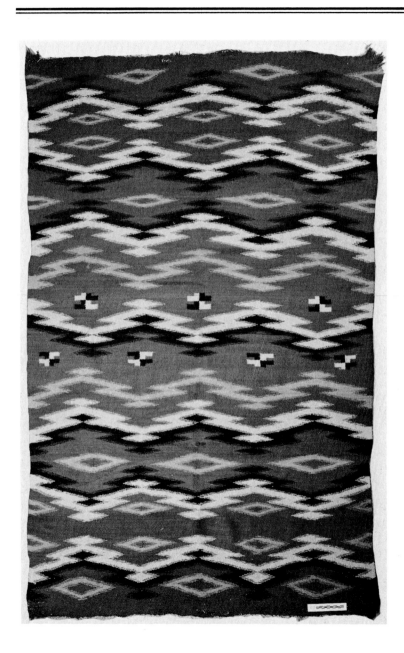

FIGURE 5

Navajo blanket *with Rio Grande-Saltillo serrate diamonds woven as zigzag stripes. Ca. 1880. The National Museum of Natural History, Smithsonian Institution. 394, 642.*

their fabrics by their captors. They were exposed more and more to the blankets woven by Spanish weavers in the Rio Grande Valley, with their simplified Saltillo designs. Four thousand Rio Grande blankets were authorized for distribution to them, and although only about a thousand were provided,[18] the new design style proved a stimulus to future weaving. When the Navajo returned to their home country in 1868, they took with them the Mexican-inspired designs—serrate diamonds, center-dominant motifs, and enclosing borders. By 1885, the Rio Grande design style, often rearranged, had become Navajo design style (Figure 5). By 1900, almost all Navajo weaving was commercial—rugs for American homes, pillow tops and runners, and souvenir blankets to supply curios for the increasing number of tourists to the Southwest.

The year 1900 also marked the end of Rio Grande weaving for use by the Spanish,[19] and saw the transition to weaving for the curio trade. Spanish looms began to turn out the Chimayó blanket. Tourists had come to expect Indian blankets from the Southwest, so Navajo design elements were mixed with old Spanish patterns. Even the Thunderbird design of the Great Lakes Indian tribes, and swastikas taken from Oriental weaving, were incorporated into Chimayó weaving. Many Chimayó fabrics were sold as products of the Pueblo Indians, but among the Pueblos, only the Zuni and Hopi continued to weave, and this in limited quantities, primarily for themselves. Beautiful fabrics continue to come from Spanish and Navajo looms, but the centuries-long era of weaving for themselves is ended.

4 SPANISH-AMERICANS, THEIR SERVANTS AND SHEEP: A CULTURE HISTORY OF WEAVING IN SOUTHERN COLORADO   MARIANNE L. STOLLER

The extraordinary project of surveying the entire history of Spanish textiles in the Southwest which was undertaken by the Museum of International Folk Art has resulted in an extensive study and description of the variety, styles, technical characteristics, tools, and artistic and historical origins of this textile tradition. It happens naturally, both as a function of the kinds of expertise other researchers have brought to the project and as a function of the data they have to study—the textiles themselves—that the people who produced and used those textiles fade into the background. Weavers' names have been lost, the circumstances under which they lived and worked lose the immediacy of experienced reality in the sweep of history and in the attention to their products.

This chapter, which is an ethnohistorical study of the weavers of the San Luis Valley of southern Colorado, attempts to add something of the human social and cultural dimension to the study of Southwest Spanish textiles.[1] Weaving certainly has technical and aesthetic dimensions, but it also has a cultural dimension, one that progresses through time and that is influenced by a variety of economic, technological, and social events. To some extent because it is a natural geographic area, but mostly because it was settled late in time and has a history somewhat different from that of northern New Mexico, the San Luis Valley can be isolated as a unit of study. The Valley was first settled by people from northern New Mexico of Hispanic cultural tradition, but their lives were strongly influenced by their relationships to Indians and Anglo-Americans, influences which seem to be accurately recorded in the history of weaving in the area as it will be reconstructed.

The following presentation is divided into four parts: 1) a brief general history of the San Luis Valley and Hispanic settlement in it; 2) an examination of the relationships of Indians and Hispanic settlers;

3) records of known weavers in the Valley; and 4) discussion of the cultural and social history of weaving and weavers, including the factors which led to the demise of the Hispanic textile tradition there. The textiles from the Valley have been incorporated into other chapters and are mentioned here only in relation to particular weavers.

/\/\/\/\

HISPANIC SETTLEMENT AND CULTURE HISTORY IN THE SAN LUIS VALLEY

The San Luis Valley in south central Colorado is the northernmost frontier of settlement by Spanish-Americans in the Southwest (see Map). These people, now often called Hispanos,[2] are the cultural descendants of the Old- and New-World-born citizens of Spain who began colonizing the Central and Upper Rio Grande River Valley at the end of the sixteenth century. The final penetration of Hispanic culture did not reach the headwaters of the Rio Grande—the San Luis Valley—until the middle of the nineteenth century. Politically, the area was no longer a part of Spain (severed by the Mexican Revolution in 1821 and the resulting Treaty of Cordova), or of her brief sovereign successor, the Republic of Mexico, but was well within the confines of the United States as established by the Treaty of Guadalupe Hidalgo in 1848 following the Mexican-American War. Until 1861, the San Luis Valley was a part of the U.S. Territory of New Mexico; in that year the Territory of Colorado was created by a Congress more versed in geometry than in cultural or physical geography, for it established a parallel boundary along 37°N that ignored both and placed the Valley in Colorado.[3]

The subsequent history of the two adjoining territories differs markedly. Unlike New Mexico with its village-dwelling Native American populations of Pueblo Indians and its two and one-half centuries' old Hispanic settlements, Colorado was very sparsely settled by "aboriginal" peoples who were, besides, largely nomadic in their way of life and thus not considered (by Anglos) to be in ownership of the land. Utes, some Apaches, Kiowas, Cheyennes, Arapahos, some Pawnees, and Comanches were the main Indian tribes who used the

natural resources of Colorado and occupied its mountains and plains. Consequently, with the discovery of gold along Cherry Creek near present Denver in the late 1850s, Colorado began to fill rapidly and in sizable numbers with Anglo-Americans (i.e., non-Hispanic Europeans).[4] Gold miners were followed by silver miners mixed with merchants, teamsters, preachers, and prostitutes. Very shortly came farmers and ranchers, accompanied by the flamboyant empire builders: land speculators, railroad builders, and politicians. In 1876 Colorado became a state, a status denied New Mexico until 1912 because the full panoply of Anglo economic expansion and cultural emissaries had proceeded much more slowly, at least partly because of its entrenched ethnic populations of Indians and Hispanos.[5]

In Colorado there was an entrenched population that preceded the Anglo onrush only in the San Luis Valley and a few oasis forts along the Arkansas River. The Comanches, Kiowa-Apaches, and Utes had periodically occupied the Valley, halting for more than a century attempts at Hispanic settlement north of the Taos Valley on the east side of the Rio Grande and the entire length of the Chama Valley on the northwest side. At least by the beginning of the Mexican Period (1821–46) the Valley was considered the special preserve of the Moache and Tabewache Utes, who encouraged trade with the Hispanos but very effectively discouraged settlement.[6] Population pressure was building in northern New Mexico, however, as were the political pressures brought by the opening of trade with the United States, the neglect by the Republic of Mexico of its Department of New Mexico, and the increasing economic strength of Anglo-American traders and their Hispano partners in the Department.

These forces prompted the awarding of two huge land grants, the traditional vehicles for settlement under Spanish and Mexican civil authority, in the San Luis Valley. The first grant was the Conejos or Guadalupe, given by Governor Francisco Sarracino to forty families in 1833 and revalidated to four of the same grantees on behalf of others in 1842.[7]

The second grant, the Sangre de Cristo, was given by Governor Manuel Armijo in 1843 to Narciso Beaubien, the sixteen-year-old son of Charles [Carlos] Beaubien,[8] and to Stephen Luis Lee, a transplanted-to-Taos Missourian and brother-in-law of Carlos Beaubien. The latter, a French-Canadian trapper and trader who became a Mexican citizen and married into a Taos Hispano family, became sole

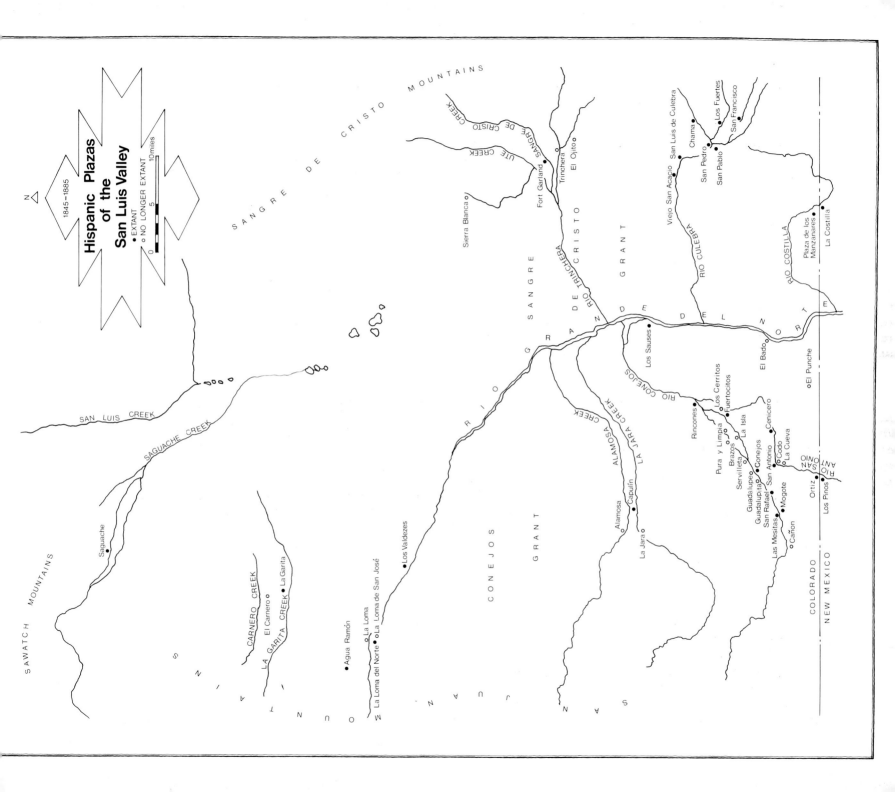

Hispanic Plazas of the San Luis Valley

1845–1885

• EXTANT
○ NO LONGER EXTANT

0   5   10 miles

N

SANGRE DE CRISTO MOUNTAINS

SAWATCH MOUNTAINS

SAN LUIS CREEK

SAGUACHE CREEK

CARNERO CREEK

LA GARITA CREEK

Saguache

El Carnero ○
La Garita ●

Agua Ramón ●

La Loma ●
La Loma del Norte ○
La Loma de San José ●

Los Valdezes ●

RIO GRANDE SANGRE

SIERRA Blanca ○

Fort Garland ○
Trinchera ●
El Ojito ○

SANGRE DE CRISTO CREEK

UTE CREEK

RIO TRINCHERA

RIO GRANDE DEL NORTE

SANGRE DE CRISTO GRANT

Viejo San Acacio ●
San Luis de Culebra ●
Chama ●
San Pedro ●
San Pablo ●
Los Fuertes ●
San Francisco ●

RIO CULEBRA

RIO COSTILLA

Plaza de los Manzanares ●
La Costilla ●

Los Sauses ●

El Bado ●

El Punche ○

RIO CONEJOS

ALAMOSA CREEK

LA JARA CREEK

Alamosa ●
Capulin ●
La Jara ○

CONEJOS GRANT

SAN JUAN MOUNTAINS

Rincones ●
Los Cerritos ●
Fuertocitos ○
La Isla ●
Pura y Limpia ○
Brazos ○
Servilleta ○
Guadalupe ○
Guadalupita ○
Conejos ●
San Rafael ●
San Antonio ●
Cenicero ●
Codo ○
La Cueva ●
Las Mesitas ●
Mogote ●
Cañon ○

RIO SAN ANTONIO

Ortiz ○
Los Pinos ●

COLORADO
NEW MEXICO

owner of this grant following the 1847 Taos Rebellion in which both his son and Lee were killed.[9]

The Conejos Grant was a community grant given to a group of people to settle, the Sangre de Cristo a private grant whose owner was expected to bring settlers in. The two grants together, the Conejos on the west side of the Rio Grande and the Sangre de Cristo on the east side, comprised around three million acres of land—all of the San Luis Valley within the tributary system of the Rio Grande. The entirety of the Sangre de Cristo Grant was confirmed under United States laws by an Act of Congress in 1861. The Conejos Grant was eventually totally denied by the U.S. Court of Private Land Claims in 1901.

Even though the lands had been granted and thus legitimately opened to settlement, the Indians didn't care how official the arrangements were. Oral history records give ample testimony to repeated attempts to colonize the area.[10] The Conejos Grant had to be revalidated, according to the claimants, because Navajo wars in the area prevented them from occupying it in the 1830s.[11] Although regranted and placed in their possession in 1842, the grantees still could not maintain settlement because of Indian harassment (which, in fact, continued through the 1850s). In 1848, according to a family document, Atanacio Trujillo, born in Ojo Caliente in 1801, a trapper, sheepman, and trader with the Utes, led a small group of settlers to found Rincones on the San Antonio River (see Map). They did not stay through the following winter, but returned in larger numbers in 1849 and were permitted to remain by virtue of "Tata Atanacio's" influence with the Utes.[12]

Also in 1849, on the Sangre de Cristo Grant at the present site of Garcia, Colorado, Beaubien settled permanent colonists.[13]

Settlement may have been attempted along the next river north—the Culebra—in 1850 at Viejo San Acacio[14] and was definitely started at San Luis de Culebra in 1851.[15]

The establishment in 1852 of Fort Massachusetts (six miles above present Fort Garland to which the fort was removed, and renamed, in 1858) provided sufficient assurance of security to attract settlers in larger numbers in the 1850s,[16] and *plazas* and the smaller *placitas* were founded in rapid order during the remainder of that decade on both grants. To all intents and purposes the Utes were removed from the San

Luis Valley in the early 1860s, so settlements continued to expand for another decade. All of the Hispano settlements known, together with their dates (when known) include:

Nineteenth-Century Hispano plazas in the San Luis Valley

CONEJOS GRANT AREA

Rincones (1848?; water right 1857)
Guadalupe (1854)
Guadalupita
Las Mesitas
Mogote (San Juan; 1849?)
Cañon
San Rafael (Paisaje; 1849?; water right 1856)
La Cueva
Codo
Ortiz (1871)
San Antonio
Los Pinos
Pura y Limpia
La Isla
Cenicero (Lobatos; early 1860s)
Los Sauses (1863)
Los Cerritos (1848?)
Fuertecitos (Espinosa)
El Brazo
Servilleta (1854)
La Jara (Capulín; 1867)
Alamosa (not the present town, but probably a *placita* in Alamosa Canyon)
Casillas
La Loma (1859; included here would be a cluster of settlements in the Del Norte area founded at different times in the 1860s and 1870s: La Loma, Loma, Del Norte, Lucero Plaza, and Ojo de San Francisco)
Los Valdezes (Seven Mile Plaza)
La Garita (1858)
El Carnero (1858)
San Luis (on Cottonwood Creek, north of La Garita)
Saguache (1866)

SANGRE DE CRISTO GRANT AREA

Plaza de los Manzanares (Garcia; 1849)
Plaza de Arriba (Costilla; 1849)

San Luis de Culebra (1851)
San Pedro (1852)
San Pablo
San Acacio (1853) (Viejo San Acacio)
San Francisco (1854)
Los Fuertes
Chama (1855)
Trinchera (1852–53)
Sierra Blanca (by 1869)
El Ojito
Fort Garland (1883) [U.S. Army, Fort Garland, 1858]

The distribution of the Hispanic settlements (see Map) shows a very characteristic pattern, apparently determined by their traditional mode of mixed pastoral and agricultural subsistence, their social custom of living in nucleated settlements for cooperative and defensive purposes, and the method of individual allotments of grant land. Beaubien, for example, gave 100 to 200 *varas* of land fronting on the river to each family he recruited to settle; the land extended back from the river to a point equidistant between it and the next river, making a long narrow strip approximately 182.88 m. (200 yards) wide and between 4.97 and 7.45 km. (8 and 12 miles) long.[17] Thus each family had a portion of irrigated land close to the river, some pasture in the river valley, and access to upland mesa land for grazing and woodcutting. In addition, settlers had woodcutting rights on the mountain lands, and, most importantly, the right of summer pasture for their flocks in the high mountain meadows. Settlements were mostly along the tributary streams of the Rio Grande: the Costilla, Culebra, and Trinchera on the Sangre de Cristo Grant and the San Antonio, Conejos, La Jara, Alamosa, and La Garita on the Conejos Grant (Los Sauses, Los Valdezes, and La Loma *plazas* are the only ones on the Rio Grande itself).

The Rio Grande, which bisects the flat Valley floor after it leaves the San Juan Mountains, provided a barrier as well as a boundary for the two grants and their settlements. The river enters a precipitous gorge a few miles above the present state line, emerging in a canyon where it was customarily crossed just above Pilar, New Mexico. Colonizers who were drawn to the Conejos Grant on the west side of the river

consequently came mostly from the Chama Valley: Abiquiu, El Rito, Ojo Caliente, Petaca, etc. Those whom Beaubien enticed to settle on his grant were mainly from Taos, Arroyo Seco, Arroyo Hondo, and Rio Colorado [Questa].[18]

Expansion of the Hispano settlements, and the founding of new ones, was slowed and/or halted very shortly by the end of the 1870s by the arrival of new immigrants—the Anglos. On the Sangre de Cristo Grant Hispano expansion was abruptly stopped when the grant was sold by Beaubien's heirs to William Gilpin and some partners in 1863. Gilpin *et al.* then set in motion a land promotion, development, and immigration scheme for the grant that involved London and Dutch banks and the English financier, William Blackmore, who was made famous (and suicidal) by his investments in Spanish and Mexican land grants.[19] The schemes never realized their promoters' dreams (few immigrants came and those mostly after 1900), but they had the effect of "freezing" the Hispano villages, stopping Hispano immigration (indeed, but for the objections of Blackmore and outcries of Costilla merchant Ferdinand Meyer, Gilpin would have tossed most of the Hispanos off the land as "squatters"), and restricting their rights of usage of mountain lands, a process still going on in Colorado courts.[20]

The Conejos Grant's inhabitants, both Hispanos already there and the Anglos who began to arrive in numbers in the 1870s, took out patents under the Homestead Act, etc., and in various other ways managed to acquire land titles. Anglo settlers—Civil War refugees and Mormon converts from the southern states, the accomplices and backwash of the mining booms, land seekers from the Midwest—filled in spaces left by Hispanos, largely in the northern (non-grant) area of the Valley and on its floor.[21]

The Denver & Rio Grande Railroad reached the Valley from the east over the Sangre de Cristo Mountains in 1877, founded the towns of Alamosa and Antonito, and pushed south to Española and west to Chama within the next few years. It not only made many material goods cheaper and more accessible and hence hastened the decline of traditional homemade Hispano arts and crafts,[22] but it also provided the means for commercial marketing of Valley products, chief of which became sheep, their wool, and meat. The Valley, however, had already been the scene of another kind of trade—that of Indian captives.

INDIAN CRIADOS, TRADE,
AND WEAVING

Commandering Indian labor was a part of the Spanish *encomienda* and *repartimiento* systems abandoned in New Mexico after the disastrous Pueblo Revolt of 1680. Taking its place was the practice of adopting Indian captives, preferably children, into Hispano families, Christianizing them, and using them as servants; this custom resulted in a class of people called *Genízaros,* Hispanicized Indians mainly from the nomadic tribes but also from the sedentary Pueblos. Very frequently there was intermarriage, and also interbreeding, between *Españoles* and *Genízaros* with the resulting children being absorbed into the Spanish family and given inheritance rights as well as full social and cultural Spanish suffrage. In the eighteenth century, whole communities were founded of *Genízaros,* usually placed in the "buffer" zones of settlement in the approaches to the Central Rio Grande Valley (one such *Genízaro* community was Abiquiu).[23] After the Republic of Mexico inaugurated the Plan of Iguala these people were given full citizenship rights and, to all intents and purposes, officially disappeared as a class, assimilated into the Hispano ethnic group. Yet the custom of acquiring Indian labor persisted—taking captives during raids, trading with Indian tribes for them, adopting orphaned Indian children or those placed by their parents who felt they could no longer care for them, etc. By the middle quarter of the nineteenth century the custom was becoming somewhat more rampant and vicious, as the demand for labor rose with the increasing *rico* class of Hispano and Anglo traders and merchants involved in traffic on the Santa Fe, Chihuahua, and Old Spanish Trails. The term Indian "slaves" is really a misnomer for Anglo minds because the southwest Spanish system never conceived of or treated these people as chattel. The word most commonly used for them in the San Luis Valley, *criado (-a),* meaning one who has been reared or educated as a servant, groom, or godchild, should be used in preference to "slave."[24]

Wheat has discussed the relationship and mutual influence of Pueblo, Navajo, and Spanish weaving traditions.[25] What follows here is an examination of the trade in *criados* between ca. 1830 and the 1860s and the possible relationship their labor and skills may have had to textile production in the San Luis Valley.

Scanty though the records are, it is obvious that the Valley was used intermittently previous to settlement, probably back into the eighteenth century, for summer pasturage for sheep and horses. It may well have been a "holding ground" for flocks destined for California via the Old Spanish Trail in operation between 1829 and 1848, for California horses and mules coming the other way, and perhaps also for Indian captives who were so much a part of that traffic, but there is little concrete evidence to support this conjecture. One arm of the Old Spanish Trail did go through the San Luis Valley.[26] Some of the early settlers from the Abiquiu area (the starting point for the annual caravans) had been involved in the Trail when it operated, and a rather large number of Indian "slaves" (both Ute and Navajo, but mainly the latter) appear in Hispano families in 1860, 1870, and 1880 censuses of the Valley.

Sheep—especially the woven blankets made of their wool—were the major westward-moving commodity on the Old Spanish Trail traffic to California.[27] The combined effects of a prolonged drought and secularization of the missions caused a major reduction in flocks there and a demand for blankets.[28] This suggests that both sheep raising and weaving were major industries in the Lower Chama Valley in the 1830s and 40s. Hafen and Hafen, quoting from Bancroft MS State Papers, provide some numbers:

> A trader caravan set out from New Mexico on October 27, 1833, and reached Los Angeles the day before Christmas. An attempt was made by California authorities to collect customs duties on the goods brought in, but the New Mexicans won exemption through a law of 1830. From records of the controversy we get a listing of woolen goods involved in the test case. There were 1645 *serapes,* 341 *fresadas,* 171 *colchos,* and 4 *tirutas* [sic].[29]

The same source quotes Duflot de Mofras, a Frenchman in California in 1841–42:

> Caravans travel once a year from New Mexico to Los Angeles. These consist of 200 men on horseback, accompanied by mules laden with fabrics and large woolen covers called *serapes,* jerzas [sic], and cobertones, which are valued at 3 to 5 piasters each. This merchandise is exchanged for horses and mules, on a basis, usually, of two blankets for one animal . . . . Returning caravans leave California in April in order to cross the rivers before the snow melts, taking with them about 2,000 horses.[30]

Blankets and horses (and even abalone shells) were also traded along the way to the Indians (mostly Utes and Paiutes) for furs and children.[31] Given the volume of traffic indicated by these and other reports cited in the same source, the weavers of northern New Mexico (including the Navajos?) must have been very busy. No doubt "slaves" were trained to be both sheepherders (the boys) and workers with wool (girls and women)—traditional tasks for these people according to consultants in the Chama River and San Luis Valleys.

Although the Old Spanish Trail traffic ended, coincident in time with the beginning of Hispano settlement in the San Luis Valley, traffic in Indian *criados* did not. Existing records make very clear that the settlers participated rather heavily in the traffic, particularly in the early 1860s when there was "open season" on Navajos who were being moved from their traditional homeland to Fort Sumner.[32]

Criados are found in quite a number of Hispanic households, and in those of early Anglo settlers such as Ute agent Lafayette Head, who moved from Abiquiu in 1854 and was agent of the Conejos Agency from 1858 to 1868.[33] The number of *criados* had appreciably increased by 1870, long after the Emancipation Proclamation of 1863. Enumeration from U.S. censuses for 1860, 1870, and 1880 provides total figures on ethnic groups in the Hispano areas of the Valley:

Ethnic composition of population in Hispano areas in the San Luis Valley[34]

YEAR	HISPANO	ANGLO	INDIAN	OTHER	TOTAL
1860	3215	59	22	2	3298
1870	4224	287	51	1	4563
1880	5550	2904	40	24	8518

Required to do a census of Indians in the Valley in 1865, Agent Head reported a total of 145, one hundred of whom were Navajo.[35] For example, there were eighty-eight Indian captives in Conejos County at this time, of which sixty-three were Navajo and forty-five of these were female. Head's census also reveals the source of these captives (i.e., from whom they were purchased); virtually all of the Navajos were

acquired from the Utes or from "Mexicans." The daughter of the Darío Gallegos family,[36] reported to have three *criados,* explains:

> The Utes would steal children from the Navajos, and vice versa, then they would sell the little Indians to the settlers in return for money, flour, groceries, and merchandise. The girls were trained in the duties of the house as domestics, while the boys had charge of the care of the stock—one of the principal occupations. The owners of these children treated them kindly, gave them a good home and brought them up as good Christians.[37]

Gibson also collected information on *criados* in the 1930s.[38] One report contains a short description of a "slave catching" expedition by the informant's father and uncles; the route leads to areas known to have been occupied by Navajos in the 1860s.[39]

That Navajos were the most desirable *criados* is further substantiated by a report that Hopis were "passed-off" as Navajos when, in 1866, eighty New Mexicans raided the Hopi village of Oraibi and took 558 head of stock and 11 captives whom they sold "as 'Navajo' slaves as far north as the Conejos settlements"![40]

As Smith pointed out, boys were trained to be herders; women and girls, in addition to being general household servants, are remembered for their abilities to work with wool.[41] While most of the recollections specify that Navajo women spent much of their time washing, carding, and spinning the wool, there is evidence that they also did some of the weaving. Age distribution of Indian females from Head's data reveals the following:[42]

Age of Indian female criadas in 1865 in the San Luis Valley

UNDER 10	10–19	20–29	30–39	40 AND OVER	TOTAL NUMBER
26	52	14	6	5	103

This suggests that since the females cluster in the mid-teens, they may have been old enough to have acquired skills in weaving before they were captured, although it is obviously impossible to ascertain this. Nor do we know what age they were taken captive. The majority of them, however, had been purchased in the 1860s, and the sharp increase in the number of Indians reported in the U.S. Census data between 1860 and 1870 (in many cases in the same household) supports the contention that they were old enough to have acquired traditional cultural skills before capture. Their youth in 1865 also indicates that the major part of their working years must have extended to the turn of the century and beyond. Indeed, the "last" Indian *criado* in San Luis died after 1970, according to informants.

Consultants in the Valley recalled Ute *criados* (of both sexes) as being exceptional leather workers; women in particular did the softening and tanning of skins. While it is difficult to say whether the Indians worked with wool as well as leather because they were *Indians* and brought some skills or aptitudes with them, or because they were *servants* and the preparation of these materials—needed in everyday Hispano life—was hard and time-consuming work, the evidence unquestionably points to their involvement with craft work.

Research on family histories, analyses of census data, and information from Valley informants, many of whom are in their seventies and eighties, reveals a striking coincidence: the presence of Navajo *criados* in the families of known weavers. This seems to be a "chicken and egg" proposition: did their labor make it possible for their Hispano masters and mistresses to do the fine weaving (as in blankets) that was so valued that it has survived until today in private and museum collections, or did the Indian women themselves do the weaving, with their master's name attached to it?

There are only two pieces of weaving from the San Luis Valley that are firmly attributed to Indian weavers. One of these (Plate 2), now in the collection of the University of Colorado Museum, is a very rare specimen—a wedge-weave blanket whose technical characteristics leave little room for doubt that it was woven on the vertical loom used by both Navajo and Pueblo weavers, not the treadle loom used by the Spanish. This textile belonged to the Gaspar Gallegos family of San Luis, and is said to have been woven by their Indian servant. Gaspar Gallegos, who was the son of José Darío and María Olofia [Eulogia?] Gallegos,[43] first appears in the 1880 census when he is listed as being six years old. Darío Gallegos started the first mercantile business in San Luis de Culebra, reportedly in 1857,[44] and became a wealthy merchant and rancher, owning some 26,000 head of sheep when he died in 1883. His son Gaspar recalled for Gibson that Darío also possessed a number of *criados*, at least five, of whom only one returned to her tribe after the

Civil War.[45] The 1870 census lists three Indians as servants in the Darío Gallegos household: Refugio (fifteen), Antonia (thirteen), and José A. (fifteen).[46] The 1880 census, however, lists only one, Guadalupe, then twenty (or twenty-five) years old, who was fondly remembered by the grandchildren of the household Combs interviewed.[47] Supposedly Darío Gallegos paid $100 for her.[48] It is she, a Navajo, who is said to have made this wedge-weave blanket.

The second piece of weaving attributed to Indian manufacture is in a private collection. Its stripe pattern, with the use of indigo, places it firmly in the Rio Grande Hispanic tradition of the last century. It appears to have been woven on the treadle loom, and is said to have been made by an Indian servant of Juan Antonio Baca.[49] The Bacas appear as residents of San Luis in the 1880 census with three Indian servants: Encarnación (twenty-eight), Guadalupe (sixteen), both listed as "step daughters," and Siriaco (eighteen).[50]

The census statistics show a decline in numbers of Indians by 1880, yet it is said that few Indian *criados* returned to their tribes after they were freed. In 1863, after the Emancipation Proclamation, a tragedy occurred: seven Navajo *criados* freed at Los Valdezes tried to make their way back to their New Mexico homes; six died of exposure, and the remaining one returned to his Hispano "family."[51]

County records in both Conejos and Costilla counties contain a number of affidavits of freedom of former *criados* dated in the late 1860s.[52] The two histories of individual families and their *criados* that are given above demonstrate some of the processes (marriage or liasons, with the children not carrying an ethnic label of Indian, and "trade" into the employ of another) by which these Indians were absorbed into the communities. The process was hastened when, as was frequently the case, very young children were captured or voluntarily placed with Hispano families for care, and they were literally adopted as sons and daughters.

∧∙∧∧∧
∙ ∙∙∙

HISPANO WEAVERS IN THE SAN LUIS VALLEY

A number of names of weavers have been collected from a variety of sources, both oral and written. It has been possible to substantiate

FIGURE 1

Rio Grande blanket, bands-and-stripes pattern with three-color beading, ca. 1860. 1.84 x 1.19 m. Warp: 2-ply handspun wool, weft: 1-ply handspun churro wool, natural-undyed white and brown and indigo. Said to have been woven by Juan Miguel Vigil, San Luis de Culebra, San Luis Valley, Colorado. Beryl G. and Charles H. Woodard Collection, Colorado Historical Society. E. 2018–3.

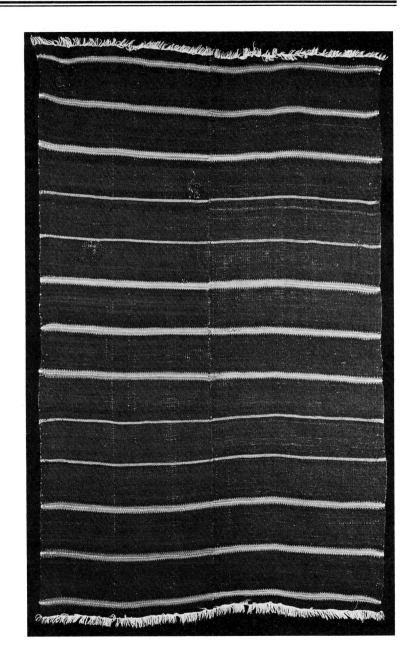

some but not all of them. The majority can be established as having lived and worked mainly in the last century, but some worked until the 1930s. There is good reason to believe that weaving activity had declined greatly by World War I, however. The weavers follow, arranged in approximate chronological order so far as the data permit.

María Olofia (Eulogia?) Gallegos: Mrs. Darío Gallegos of San Luis de Culebra; forty-four years old in 1880. A piece of *jerga* in the Woodard Collection (State Historical Society of Colorado, E.2018–51; Plate 64)[53] is said to have been made by her. Her son Gaspar reported that she wove 300 yards of this *jerga*.[54] It is handspun, single ply, 2/2 twill weave of natural dark and synthetic red colors. A piece of *sabanilla,* also in the Woodard Collection (E.2018–50), obtained from Vigil (Virgil) Pacheco in 1938 who said it was made by his grandmother,[55] is made of such finely spun 1-ply *churro* wool that Boyd says it could have been spun on a spinning wheel.[56] A wheel was indeed owned in this family.

Juan Miguel Vigil: said to have been among the first settlers of San Luis de Culebra.[57] In the Woodard Collection, E.2018–3 (Figure 1) is said to have been woven by Juan Miguel Vigil and repaired by Fred Vigil in 1945.[58] This blanket, which Boyd calls a "classic striped blanket," has handspun 2-ply *churro* warps and single ply wefts, of natural and light and dark indigo blue colors. Family history does identify Juan Miguel as a weaver, and also reports that Fred's wife, Fulgencia Gallegos, frequently bought and sold blankets ca. 1920s or so. Fulgencia was a granddaughter of Juan Antonio Baca.

Rumaldo Manzanares: of the Plaza de los Manzanares (García) is identified by author Olibama López Tushar as her mother's grandfather and the weaver of that settlement.[59] Rumaldo Manzanares came from

Abiquiu, New Mexico, in the fall of 1849, as one of the founders of that *plaza,* the earliest on the Sangre de Cristo Grant.[60] Tushar reproduced a picture of him.[61] If examples of his work survive, they are not known or described.

Juan José López: of San Antonio. Woodard, personally acquainted with this man, reported that he was born about 1855 (census records of 1880 list him living in the Los Pinos area, twenty-nine years old). He gave Woodard a very fine blanket, really a shawl, made when he was a young man.[62] Boyd identified the piece (E.2018–55) as being of commercially spun flax (warps) and wool and mohair wefts, commercially woven probably in a German or Czechoslovakian factory between 1900 and 1914.[63] No one else has identified this man as a weaver, although family history does so and also claims he was a full-blooded Navajo.

Juan Antonio Baca: of San Luis de Culebra; information on him has already been presented. Several informants report that he was a weaver, but the only known piece from his household is said by descendants to have been made by one of his Indian *criados.*[64]

Pablo García: three pieces in the Woodard Collection are attributed to Pablo García, who is identified as living in Ortiz and Conejos; in addition Boyd notes that the Museum of New Mexico "has a blanket made by an old man named García, weaving in the 1880s, from La Isla, near San Antonio."[65] The three pieces show an interesting range of styles and materials:

1. E.2018–29 is a simple stripe blanket of handspun 2-ply warps and 1-ply wefts and natural color *churro* wools, according to Boyd;[66] sometimes called *sarape del campo* or the "poor man's overcoat,"[67] such blankets were used by herders and servants, as robes in wagons, and for horses. Because of their utilitarian functions, few have survived in collections.
2. E.2018–1 (Plate 26) is a vivid striped blanket with small tapestry-woven motifs in the wide end bands; it is handspun of *churro* wool, and the colors are provided by undyed wools, natural dyes (?), and synthetic dyes. Because of this combination of color sources, Boyd feels the blanket could have been made any time "between 1885 and 1915."
3. E.2018–43 is of handspun yarns, a blanket with bands and striped designs which contains only synthetic colors. Woodard's notes say that all three examples were supposed to be about seventy-five years

old (E.2018–29, seventy-five to eighty years old) when he collected them in the late 1930s, but this seems unlikely for the last two examples with their synthetic dyes.

Félix Esquibel: of San Pablo. This blanket (Plate 3) of handspun, 2-ply warps and wefts is also from the Woodard Collection (E.2018–46). Boyd notes that it is an "exceptionally complicated adaption of Saltillo designs,"[68] and rather unusual in this collection of San Luis Valley textiles which has very few examples of Saltillo-inspired designs. The colors are both natural and synthetic, the latter apparently very bright when new. Woodard said it was seventy years old, again possibly a date too early.[69]

Informants agree that there were weavers in the large Esquibel family, but it has not been possible to corroborate Félix as one of them. A "Mrs. Esquibel" was identified as an excellent weaver when the WPA weaving project started in the late 1930s in San Luis. Pieces in private collections in the Valley are attributed to weavers in San Pablo y San Pedro, and one example also has certain Saltillo motifs in it; weaving activity is reported to have continued in this century, and other names are mentioned.

Francisco and Benima Barela: of San Luis. Listed in the 1880 census as twenty-three and nineteen years old, respectively. Second generation descendants, as well as other informants, report that they were weavers, but no pieces attributed to them have been seen (although some are said to exist in family possession in another state).

Emilia Gallegos Smith: of San Luis. The daughter of Darío and María Olofia [Eulogia?] Gallegos and sister of Gaspar, previously mentioned. Listed as four years old in the 1880 census, Mrs. Smith died in the 1950s. While no specimens of her work are known to exist, family reports of her weaving activity, as well as information from several others, are not to be doubted.

(?) Vialpando: of Chama (or LaValley?); grandson Ben Vialpando joined the WPA Weaving Project in San Luis in the late 1930s. It is said that Ben knew how to weave, having been taught by his grandfather, but did not know how to warp a loom.[70] No known pieces are identified as his work.

Librado and Epimenio García: of Mogote and Cañon Plaza.[71] Epimenio García was born in 1875 and died in 1947; Librado was some years older and died ten years earlier, in 1937.

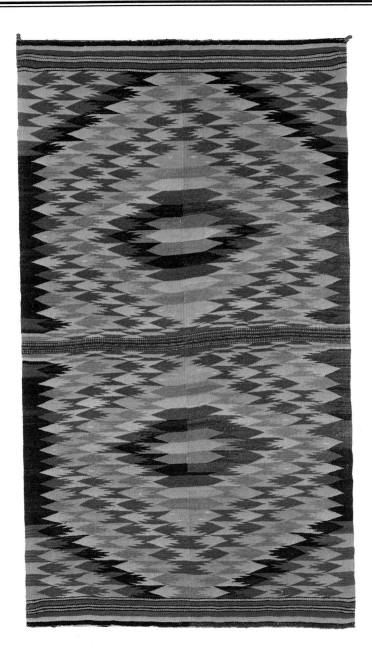

PLATE 3

Rio Grande blanket, 1885–1915, two widths seamed, 2.26 x 1.32 m. Warp: 2-ply handspun wool; weft: 1-ply handspun wool, natural-undyed white and brown and synthetic-dyed red, purple, green, orange, pink, and blue. Attributed to Félix Esquibel of San Pablo, San Luis Valley, Colorado. Beryl G. and Charles H. Woodard Collection, Colorado Historical Society. E.2018.46.

Family members mainly remember Librado as doing most of the weaving. The two brothers lived in adjacent houses and farmed together; they had horses and cows, but no sheep. Librado did not make his living from weaving, but wove in the winter months beginning work in October. He had a special little house for his loom which was so large that it barely fit in (after his death the loom was broken up for firewood by a family member). He wove to order, and made striped blankets of wool and rag rugs. The women of the two households helped card the wool and did some spinning, but he did most of the spinning. His niece, now in her sixties, remembers as a small girl tearing rag strips, sewing them end to end, and winding them in a big ball to be attached to his shuttle. Woven strips were sewn together with a carpet needle to make floor coverings. The only piece of Mr. Librado García's weaving seen was a rag rug with a wool warp, about 2.44 x 7.62m, but other pieces, including some wool blankets, are said to exist. Mr. García was still weaving in the 1930s.

Joe Martínez: of Saguache. Lived in this century. A rug using angora wool and synthetic dyes, now in the Saguache County Museum, was woven by him.

Mrs. J. J. Lovato: of Viejo San Acacio. Said by her family and others to have been a weaver, the only piece seen was woven in the 1930s of commercial yarns but in an old color scheme of blue bands with white and black stripes. It was her custom to make a blanket for each child and grandchild when they married. This is the only record so far obtained of a woman weaving blankets—except those done by the Indian women.

It is logical to assume that there were probably a number of other weavers in the San Luis Valley, Hispanos and perhaps more Indians, at least previous to the turn of the century. More weavers than those listed here have been mentioned by name in the research done, but either no documentary or genealogical information has been found on them so far, or the reports cannot be substantiated, or the leads have proved false. Among the names mentioned are Mrs. Daniel Chávez of the Saguache area; José Lovato of Chama; and Sánchez, Bernal, Luján, and Valdez all from the Chama, San Pedro, and San Pablo areas, as well as a male weaver (no name) from Viejo San Acacio. The Woodard Collection, as well as Rio Grande textile collections in other museums in Colorado and New Mexico, record pieces having been purchased in other Hispano *plazas,* in addition to those already mentioned: Las [Los] Sauses, Capulín, Lobatos [Cenicero], and Ft. Garland. Probably there were once weavers in those places, which were and are sizeable settlements, as well as in the northernmost *plazas* on the Conejos Grant, La Loma and La Garita.[72]

An example of a false identification is that of *Damián Durand* [Durán], named as a weaver in the Woodard MS (and repeated, erroneously, by Boyd, MS, and Stoller, 1977, p. 94). Damián Durán was a resident of Ortiz, a merchant, and one of the largest sheepmen in the area known for its wealthy sheep ranchers until the creation of the National Forest in 1908 drastically reduced mountain grazing land. Damián Durán appears in the 1880 census as thirty-eight years old, and he died in 1938 at the age of one hundred and seven, according to his son, Marcus, who is a mere ninety-five![73] He was born around Mora, New Mexico, moved to El Rito, and then to Ortiz sometime around 1870. He is said to have owned two Indian *criados* in Ortiz. Mr. Marcus Durán unequivocally denied that his father had ever been a weaver and suggested that since he had a general merchandise store in Ortiz, he most likely sold blankets made by others.

This same situation may account for other names reported in the Woodard MS, some of whom, such as Valdez of San Pablo, are known to have been merchants. The purveyors, in other words, have sometimes been confused with the manufacturers. It was noted earlier that Mrs. Fred Vigil in San Luis bought and sold blankets; because her husband's grandfather, Juan Miguel Vigil, was a weaver it would be easy to assume that her stock was of his manufacture. In fact, she bought from her neighbors, whose blankets had been made by various weavers. These confusions, naturally enough, often enter museum records—and create havoc for later researchers!

ᛉᛉᛉ

WPA WEAVING PROJECT IN THE 1930s

A number of people participated in the WPA Weaving Project, which was started in San Luis in 1935 by G. Madden Jones and run by Gladys Robinson (who joined it in 1936) from approximately 1938 until 1940, when funds ran out. The purpose of this project, funded through the Works Project Administration, was to revive weaving in the San Luis Valley, to provide employment for female heads of households and handicapped persons, and to teach a skill which might subsequently be income producing.[74] Some forty people are said to have worked in the project, but although it developed some younger skilled weavers, all were attracted into higher-paying jobs in Pueblo and Denver with the onset of World War II. The project relied on the skills of older people in the community, supplemented by Madden's and Robinson's knowledge, for these skills were rusty. Three women and two men are remembered as being excellent weavers—Mrs. Esquibel of Chama, Katarina Vigil and Faustina Bernal of San Luis, and Alberto Casías and Ben Vialpando. Mrs. J. J. Lovato of Viejo San Acacio acted as a consultant, since she was the only local weaver still actively productive. When the project started, it was found that knowledge was "piecemeal," that is, specialized. Some people knew how to card and spin, others to dye, and still others to weave (as Vialpando, who could weave but not warp a loom)—an interesting clue, perhaps, to earlier specialization.[75]

ᛉᛉᛉ

WEAVING IN THE SAN LUIS VALLEY

In relation to the ethnohistorical data so far presented, it is now possible to discuss weavers and weaving in the San Luis Valley in a broader socio-cultural context, and to present some additional material on those subjects. Some information will also be offered on the factors which contributed to the decline of the weaving tradition.

Study of the census reports of 1860, 1870, and 1880 shows that no individual is listed as having the occupation of "weaver." This is surprising since a variety of occupations are given—adobe-maker, herder, laundress, jeweler, freighter, fiddler, merchant, etc.—in addition to the most frequent ones for the Hispano population—farmer and rancher. Keeping in mind that the lack of listing may be due to the vagaries of the census-taker, it nonetheless would appear that weaving was not considered, and not carried on, as a full-time occupation by Hispanos. Many oral reports record the use of handwoven textiles by both Hispanos and Anglos into this century, for blankets and for floor coverings. Yet the reports of dealers who scoured the Valley in the 1920s and '30s for museums and private collectors, and an examination of family collections still in existence, show the presence of just about as many Navajo as Hispano textiles. The earliest known description of a Valley house interior, that of Nathaniel P. Hill in 1864, notes that the floors of a house in San Luis de Culebra were covered with cowhide, but that there were cushioned seats (most likely folded blankets) around the walls.[76] The only weaving he mentioned, however, was that of woolen blankets skillfully made by Navajos who lived "just over the Rio Grande . . . a wretched looking set."[77] It is clear that textiles of both Navajo and Hispano manufacture were used in the San Luis Valley and that weaving, even though it was not a full-time occupation, flourished there at least through the last century.

Although it is commonly claimed that weaving was primarily a man's occupation, the data show a number of women weavers. Tushar states:

> It was the men . . . who wove the *sarapes* on looms of their own manufacture. . . . They also wove the *sabanilla* for dresses and shirts, as well as for mattresses. Some also wove the woolen *tápalos* [shawls]. . . .
>
> Nearly all the cloth used was of wool which the housewife processed. The spinning and weaving of wool was usually done by each woman in her home, although on occasion there would be gatherings for this purpose. . . . The men wove the *sarapes, sabanillas,* and *tápalos* usually for those who could afford to pay; while the women wove for the use of their own families.[78]

This division of labor between the sexes seems to be well supported by the data presented here, with pieces of *jerga* and *sabanilla* attributed mostly to women and the blankets to men weavers. The exceptions noted are Mrs. J. J. Lovato, weaving probably only in this century and with commercial yarns, and the two Indian women who produced at least one blanket each.

The treadle loom is traditionally a man's machine; the looms were so heavy and cumbersome that they took a man's strength to operate them.[79] Blankets were heavier, and had to be more tightly woven than *sabanilla* or *jerga,* and perhaps this is why men were more likely to weave them. While few physical descriptions of them survive, it is possible that the Indian women, especially if they were Navajos, were markedly more robust than their Hispana counterparts, for the Navajo are generally a taller, heavier-boned people. Their work as servants certainly would have contributed to their developing considerable physical strength (it may be noted that in the 1880 census, several of these women are listed as laundresses—in the days before washing machines). Several of the Hispana weavers are described as being slight, small women, yet it is known that they were weavers.

No old looms from the Valley have been seen, and the only description of one—Librado García's loom—suggests that it was very large and heavy. Milled lumber was generally available in the Valley early, however, for sawmills were established by the 1870s.[80] Metal heddles and other parts may well have been available by the 1880s with the coming of the railroad. These two materials would both help reduce the strength needed to operate the loom. This is all conjecture, of course, because, heavy or light, it seems that many women and only a few men wove. In any case there is every reason, from the statements of Tushar and others, to believe that women wove mainly for home consumption and men for income-producing purposes.

The sexual division of labor was not only on these lines, but also apparently in the preparation of wool for weaving. Shearing the sheep and beating the wool to loosen dirt, etc., were said to be men's jobs. Washing and carding and spinning were almost always done by women (the report of Librado García's spinning is unusual), and preferably by servants if there were any. Spinning was a ladylike enough task—and one which could earn much neighborly approbation—so that mistress and servant alike engaged in it. The preparation of dyes was also said to be women's work. It is easy to see why female Indian servants were to be desired in weavers' households, and their presence there must be more than coincidence.

From the 1860s until the collapse of the sheep market in the early 1900s, there are clear differences of social status based on wealth in Hispanic communities in the San Luis Valley. Hispano merchants, cattlemen, and sheepmen formed a *rico* or *patrón* class (which also produced politicians) on whom quite a large number of other people were dependent for employment, especially as *partidarios* and herders. Another sizeable number of people were economically independent (if not very well off) on small land holdings, so long as they had grazing lands available. The lowest status was that of *criado,* servant, or *peon* (whether Indian or Hispano).[81] There was variation on east and west sides, which can be referred to the land grant histories: there were fewer *ricos,* and more indebtedness and dependence on the *ricos,* on the east side.

Weavers are found at all levels of the social spectrum with a predominance, however, at the top and bottom. That is to say, most of the known weavers were in *rico* or economically independent families and households, whether they were the wife of the *patrón* (for example, Mrs. Darío Gallegos) or the servant (Guadalupe Gallegos). Weaving, at least weaving of sufficient quality and aesthetic merit to have survived through time, was a highly regarded skill in the social world of the Hispanos. The reduction in economic success in the Hispano villages in this century, and the disappearance of a servant class, particularly the former Indian *criados,* may have contributed as much to the decline of weaving as did changes in the wool and the introduction of commercially manufactured textiles.

There is an interesting dichotomy between the western (Conejos Grant) and eastern (Sangre de Cristo Grant) sides of the Valley. Far more weavers have been identified from the eastern side—from San Luis and adjacent *plazas*—than from the western side. This may be the result of two factors. First, the Sangre de Cristo Grant was alienated into private land companies which restricted the amount of land that could be utilized by Hispanos, with the result that there were very few "sheep barons" on this side compared with the other, and, in general, less economic prosperity and participation in Anglo economics during the period ca. 1880 to 1941. Second, the railroad did not traverse these communities, coming no closer than Fort Garland, twenty miles from San Luis, and thus Anglo technology was not quite as accessible as in the communities around Conejos. These factors possibly led to the maintenance of home craft production for a longer period of time, involving a larger number of people. Genealogical histories from San Luis weavers seem to show fairly steady production with a slow

decrease up to the 1930s. In contrast, only one weaver can be documented from the Conejos area as producing into the 1930s.

The introduction of commercially woven cloth, which became increasingly cheap, accessible, and admired when the railroad arrived, almost totally replaced handwoven materials for clothing. The amount of weaving that was needed declined very rapidly. Even before the railroad, Hispano freighters *(fleteros)* had brought cloth back to their families and local stores carried yard goods like cottons, calicoes, and flannels.[82]

Vigil reports the costume of the early settlers: men wore buckskin suits or trousers of *jerga* (coarsely woven woolen cloth) and shirts of *sabanilla* (lighter and finer in weave); women wore skirts and blouses of *sabanilla,* a *rebozo* (of imported silk), and a wool shawl.[83] To this list Tushar adds an "overcoat" for men—the *tilma* or *conga* which was a short version of the *sarape,* and shawls *(tápalos)* of various weights for women; also, stockings, socks, and mittens were knitted of wool.[84] The preparation and sewing of buckskins was done by men, or, preferably, Indian servants, while women or servants did most of the weaving of *jerga* and *sabanilla.* It is estimated by informants that all of these woven items of clothing, except for the *tilmas* and *tápalos,* had been totally replaced even in everyday attire by 1900. Leather jackets continued to be used, and knitted sweaters were added to socks and mittens. *Tilmas* and *tápalos* of woven wool were still worn into the 1930s, especially by older people, so some reduced production of them must have continued, but they are reported to have gotten coarser and bulkier because of the changes in available wool. One consultant claimed that the wool got so bad that wearing a *sabanilla* shirt would have been a penance (because it was so harsh and prickly) and that the ewes would have followed the wearer around (because of the smell)!

Sewing machines became increasingly common after 1890, greatly facilitating the use of commercial textiles for clothing.

Most consultants in the Valley attribute the decline in home weaving to changes in the wool. Sheep raising became "big business" in the Valley as early as the 1870s when flocks of several thousand sheep are reported.[85] The Civil War and the hungry miners of Colorado provided a market in the '60s, too, and the number of miners swelled with the opening of mines in the San Juan Mountains. The coming of the railroad in the late 1870s permitted a greatly expanded market, although people still sometimes drove their sheep over LaVeta Pass to load them on the train at Cucharas.[86] As the decades progressed, flocks became larger and larger and the business was increasingly dominated by Anglo entrepreneurs who employed herders on *partido* contracts and controlled the shipping to midwestern and eastern markets for both wool and meat.

The native *churro* sheep of the Spanish colonists was an animal well adapted to the climate and vegetation of the semiarid Southwest, but it was a sparse wool and meat producer compared to other breeds.[87] Its wool was the long, fine, silky wool found in most Hispanic textiles of the nineteenth century (and mistakenly identified as Merino), but to the commercially minded, this was not enough. As early as 1837 Manuel Alvarez, a Spaniard who became a citizen of (New) Mexico and U.S. Consul in Santa Fe, petitioned for a grant of land on the eastern flanks of the Sangre de Cristo Mountains—the Ocaté Grant, promising to introduce Spanish Merino sheep to greatly improve the quality of sheep in the country. Although he was given the grant, there is no evidence that he did bring any Merino sheep in, a factor that was pointed out many years later when the grant was denied to his heirs and claimants.[88]

Merinos were introduced by Anglos, but Rambouillet became the major western sheep.[89] Lincolns were also brought in but their crimped wool—like the Merinos' neck "wrinkles"—made shearing difficult and the wool less desirable. Rambouillet gave a high wool yield, but the fibers were short and tight and very greasy. Crossbreeding of various kinds among these breeds was tried, of course,[90] but tariff protection under the Dingley Tariff of 1897 proved inadequate for domestic wool growers, and meat, not wool, became an increasing commercial concern for sheepmen.

The market took a new track at the turn of the century with the emphasis on meat—specifically lamb feeding. Previously, sheep had been managed from birth to maturity, pastured in the high mountain meadows in the summer and in the natural hay meadows of the Valley bottom along river courses in the winter. The discovery that lambs could be fattened and marketed a full year earlier on pea fields over the winter led to the rapid development of this market. Lambs were no longer

raised in such numbers in the Valley but many were shipped there from northern New Mexico in the fall, put on the pea fields, and shipped out to market in late winter.[91] Wentworth discusses this development; in the peak year, 1905–6, 400,000 lambs were shipped.[92] The land shortly became "peasick," and the practice declined. The sheep industry in the Valley never recovered its strength; it could not return to earlier practices of natural grazing because the creation of Rio Grande National Forest in 1908 severely restricted grazing land. A catastrophic blizzard in 1917 and a virus epidemic in 1918 put an end, to all intents and purposes, to the sheep industry in the Valley, whether for wool or meat.[93] The WPA Weaving Project in San Luis in the late 1930s often had to import wool, so little was locally available.[94]

These events strongly affected the fortunes as well as the weaving of the Hispano settlers. The rise of the sheep industry from the 1870s to the 1900s provided fortunes for a few Hispano growers, especially in the Ortiz Valley but in the Conejos area in general. Many men worked on *partido* contracts, and while this often led eventually to extreme indebtedness and loss of both their flocks and land, it provided much employment. Not a few Hispano ranchers competed very successfully with Anglo entrepreneurs such as Bond and Sargent. The shift to lamb feeding, however, greatly diminished Hispano participation in the market; the pea fields on the Valley floor were owned by Anglos, and not as many herders were needed to manage the flocks in fenced fields. With the curtailment of grazing rights on the old mountain grant lands, fortunes began to decline for Hispanos even before the feeding industry ended. Gradually, over the succeeding decades of this century, many Hispanos have become cattle ranchers.

Consultants in the San Luis Valley blame the Rambouillet for the decrease in weaving. The short, stubby fibers did not spin well, the greasiness required too much work to remove, and the resultant fabric was stiff, harsh, smelly, and oily, they say. This discouraged weavers and their clients. Long fibers were especially needed for strong warp threads, and weavers experimented with mohair and commercial cotton string. The shift to weaving rag rugs seems to have been more common on the western side of the Valley than the eastern. Rag rugs are reported for both the Conejos and Saguache areas as being favored and common, and were produced by both Anglo and Hispano weavers. While they were woven around San Luis, wool *jergas* seem to have persisted there much longer than they did elsewhere. The idea of loom-woven rag rugs is said to have been introduced in 1879 by the father of Mary Jane Cole, an immigrant family from the Midwest. This man built a loom and began weaving rag rugs: "People from miles away brought in rags and we made carpets for them."[95] This development appears to have marked the final stage of handwoven textiles for local use and functional purposes in the San Luis Valley.

In summary, the San Luis Valley of southern Colorado is the "last frontier" of settlement by peoples carrying the Spanish Colonial culture which developed over a three-hundred-year period of occupation in the American Southwest. Its history is relatively short—ca. 1850 to the present. The development of that culture in that area had scarcely thirty years to take root before there was a major migration of Anglo-Americans who bore a different language and culture, including a more industrialized technology and an economic system geared toward surplus production, commercialism, and mercantilism. Anglo migration, coupled with a different legal system for land and water, severely restricted—indeed halted—expansion of Hispano settlement. Initially joining the technological and economic aspects of the Anglo system—as merchants and cattle and sheep ranchers, particularly—Hispanos in many cases became a part of the new culture. With the collapse of the sheep market and land loss by grant adjudication, taxation, and sale, however, they were forced to retreat from full economic participation. Since the 1920s they have become an increasingly impoverished population, with out-migration to urban centers becoming common during and after World War II.

Weaving flourished in southern Colorado during the nineteenth century, but it diminished with the changes in types of sheep (and therefore wool) as the market changed, and with the increased availability and accessibility of manufactured textiles.

THE TEXTILES

DOROTHY BOYD BOWEN

In light of the foregoing historical and economic context, the textiles themselves will now be described, analyzed, and compared. To facilitate study the textiles have been grouped first according to type (blankets, yardage, *jerga,* and *colcha* embroideries), then within these categories according to design motifs, and finally further subdivided on the basis of materials (dyes and yarns) and fabric structure. Technical articles explaining the treadle loom, fabric structure, and dyes are in the appendices.

The first groups of textiles to be presented are those of the blankets (the *frazadas* and *sarapes*) and their prototypes, the Saltillo *sarapes.* What we have come to term the Rio Grande blanket was the most commonly produced and widely distributed of the nineteenth-century New Mexican Spanish goods. It was woven in the settlements and ranches along the Rio Grande and its tributaries for three centuries, and was a staple of the economy as well as a necessity for survival. As has

been shown, it was traded far south into Mexico, east into the United States, west to California, and in all directions to the Indians.

Rio Grande blankets were intended for wearing during the day and for bedding at night. More complex designs based on the Saltillo *sarape* do not have evidence of neck slits or wear at the center seam, which indicates that they were wrapped around the shoulders, unlike many Mexican *sarapes* which were woven with neck slits to be pulled on over the head. A description of San Miguel del Vado, New Mexico, in 1850 by Franz Huning illustrates textile uses. Most of the men wore blankets, "some of them very pretty, imported from Saltillo, Old Mexico," while the poor wore "jackets of homemade wool carpet."[1] Apparently, by the time photography was introduced about 1860, most of the Spanish citizenry had ceased to wear the blanket, but it was still in use for bedding. For another use see Figure 1, a photograph of about 1880 which includes an elderly man with a Saltillo-style Rio Grande blanket over his lap.

The typical Rio Grande blanket has the following physical

FIGURE 1

Photograph illustrating the use of a Rio Grande blanket over the lap of Jesús Rivera, ca. 1880–82. Photo by George C. Bennett. Museum of New Mexico. 15348.

characteristics. Designs include wide bands and zones of narrow stripes, later with Saltillo *sarape* motifs introduced. Colors are the natural-undyed white and brown *churro* wool, combined with natural-dyed yarns including a great deal of indigo, yellow, madder, tiny areas of cochineal, and much reddish to golden tan. The textiles were woven on the narrow treadle loom either in two widths or in one width with multiple center warps, in weft-faced plain weave or tapestry weave. Later examples have wefts of short-staple Merino wool brilliantly colored with synthetic dyes. Warp is normally 2-Z-spun-plied-S handspun wool, ca. 5-7/2.5 cm. (one inch) and weft is

1-ply Z-spun wool, ca. 25–40/2.5 cm. (one inch). Later examples may have cotton string warp, ca. 6–11/2.5 cm., and commercial wool wefts, ca. 30–40/2.5 cm. (one inch).[2]

What made the Rio Grande blanket unique? Was it different from blankets woven by the California Mission Indians, or later on the California ranches by Spanish and mestizo craftsmen, or in Spanish Arizona, or in Texas missions? Numerous references describe textile production in California, both at the missions and on the ranches and haciendas, but we know of no documented examples which approximate the Rio Grande blanket. The same holds true for Arizona, Texas, and northern Mexico. Yet, among the Rio Grandes, aberrant

Criteria used in dating nineteenth-century Rio Grande blankets

PERIOD	DYES	HANDSPUN YARNS	COMMERCIAL YARNS
Early: Pre–1860	Natural dyes, primarily indigo.	1- and 2-ply handspun, silky, coarse, long staple *churro* wool, evenly dyed. Handspun cotton may also appear.	3-ply natural-dyed "Saxony" yarn, 1800–1865.
Transitional: 1860–1880	Both natural and early synthetic dyes.	Some contamination with Merino wool by 1880.	Early "Germantown" yarn, 3-ply synthetic-dyed, 1864–1875, and later 4-ply synthetic-dyed.
Late: 1880–1900	Typically all synthetic dyes.	Most yarn is heavily contaminated with kinky, short staple Merino wool, unevenly dyed due to greasiness of wool.	4-ply synthetic-dyed wool yarn; 3- or 4-ply cotton string warp.

NOTE: This chart is intended as a general guide for the lay reader. Some textiles may have characteristics of two periods, and the dates of the periods must not be regarded as inflexible. For example, the late period might include twentieth-century pieces woven as late as 1930. For further definition of the commercial Saxony and Germantown yarns, see Fisher and Wheat, p. 196 ff. of this publication.

pieces do exist: eight handspun cotton blankets, other blankets with atypical stripe patterns, blankets with weft-ikat dyed yarns, and various late pieces. At this time many of these are assumed to be New Mexican, since they are more like than unlike the classic Rio Grandes, but this does not exclude the possibility that they could be representative of other geographic areas of Spanish weaving.

Another possible source of confusion is the Mormon weaving industry which grew in Utah in the 1850s and 1860s. Brigham Young brought a carding machine to Utah in 1848, and a carding factory opened in 1851 near Salt Lake City. By 1852 this factory was also engaged in weaving. In the mid-1860s the first Mormon wool mills were built in Parley's Creek Canyon, Utah, and others followed quickly. Mormon housewives carded, spun, dyed with local plant materials, and wove wool, flax, and cotton textiles, including blankets and rag rugs on the treadle loom.[3] Presumably much of their work was simply worn out by their large families, but the existence of such a thriving wool industry so close to the Rio Grande area, using similar dyes, wool, and looms, provokes speculation on the possibility of similar pieces being woven in both places.

The first group of blankets which will be presented includes only bands and stripes, the most simple designs which have been woven continuously from the beginning. The second group is the Saltillo *sarapes,* which are prototypes for most of the rest of the Rio Grande blankets. Following these are the Rio Grande blankets which include Saltillo design motifs, then the *Valleros,* the weft-ikat blankets, the cotton blankets, yardage (including *jerga*), the *colcha* embroideries, and finally the twentieth-century textiles.

6 BANDS AND STRIPES
TRISH SPILLMAN

Simple in structure, yet rich in design, the largest group of Spanish textiles is that of weft-faced plain weave blankets organized in bands and stripes. Bands are large sections of color, often containing interior groups of stripes separated by smaller sections of solid color, or stripes. Arranged in different combinations, these sections make up "band-and-stripe" blankets. (See Figure 3.) After a discussion of weaving techniques, the dyes and design qualities of each group will be outlined. The differences between Spanish and Indian striped blankets will be taken into account, as well as the use of the blankets as an economic trade item, and as everyday objects.

The large class of striped blankets can be separated into smaller groupings distinguished by weaving techniques, dyes, and materials: those of all natural wool (Figure 1); those of natural-dyed wool combined with the undyed light and dark wool; those of synthetic-dyed wool combined with the undyed light and dark wool; and those of synthetic-dyed wool of the later period.[1] There are, of course, natural-dyed blankets as late as the twentieth century, but these are usually Chimayó-style copies or revivals of the early blankets.

WEAVING TECHNIQUES

The majority of the band-and-stripe blankets were woven on narrow two-harness looms. When weaving in narrow widths on a two-harness loom, however, the weaver must constantly refer either to a pattern or to the first half of the blanket so that the two halves will be identical when sewn together. The difficulty of this task is clearly evident—many of the blankets are uneven, and one side of a blanket may pucker. A simple mistake throws the stripes off and results in an uneven pair of widths. For this reason, the double-woven technique is considered a more sophisticated but easier method than that of weaving two strips.[2]

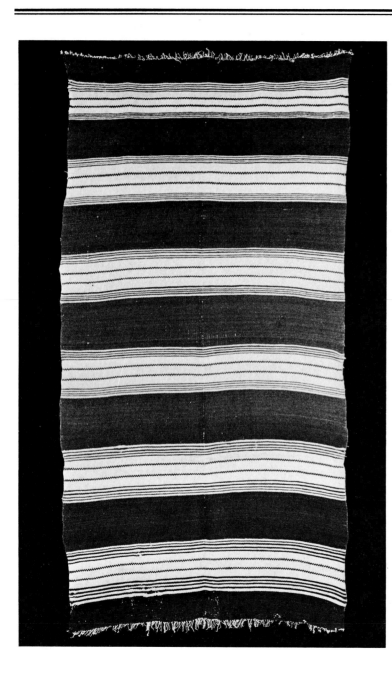

FIGURE 1

Rio Grande blanket, purchased in Chama Valley area
and known there as "old Taos blanket," 1830–60, one
width, 2.16 x 1.12 m. Warp: 2-ply handspun wool; weft:
1-ply handspun wool, natural-undyed white and brown.
Collections of the School of American Research in the
Museum of New Mexico. 26128/12.

When weaving an early blanket, approximately 70 cm., on the narrow loom, it was possible to make a single-width, 140 cm. blanket in one piece, double-woven, using two sets of warps. The warp sets are kept separate by the regulation of the tie-up of four harnesses. On a four-harness loom, the warp set for one-half of the width of the blanket would be threaded only on harnesses one and two, while that for the other half of the width would be threaded on harnesses three and four. The same weft shuttle alternates between the sheds formed by harnesses one and two and then three and four—thus weaving both halves at the same time. In effect, this technique turns a four-harness loom into a two-harness loom of twice the width. A close look at the center of these single-width blankets will reveal warps set closer together than in the rest of the blanket, creating a ridge directly down the center.[3] The actual weaving process is rather simple, but the tie-up of treadles is a bit complicated because one set of warps must be lifted and kept free from the other set of warps.

DESIGN ELEMENTS AND BLANKET REPAIRS

Design elements such as beading and ticking are all achieved in weft-faced plain weave simply by changing weft-color with successive passes of the shuttle (Figure 2). An elaborate use of ticking is seen in the blanket illustrated in Plate 10. This is a typical five-band striped blanket with the central band repeated at the top and bottom. The warp is light and dark undyed-natural handspun 2-ply wool. The piece is woven in a single width, double-woven technique. The coloring is rather unusual in that, in addition to indigo, the blanket contains a pink which is probably

FIGURE 2

a. Detail of beading typical of the San Luis Valley, achieved by alternating weft shots of brown, white, and blue. Rio Grande blanket, ca. 1870. International Folk Art Foundation Collection at the Museum of International Folk Art, a unit of the Museum of New Mexico. FA.67.43.1. *b. Ticking.* Achieved by alternating light and dark weft shots twice then reversing to dark and light. Rio Grande blanket, ca. 1870. Detail of textile in Plate 10. *c. Checkerboarding.* Small squares woven in same manner as ticking (Figure 2b) but continuing pattern until small checks are formed. Rio Grande blanket, ca. 1850. Detail of Plate 9.

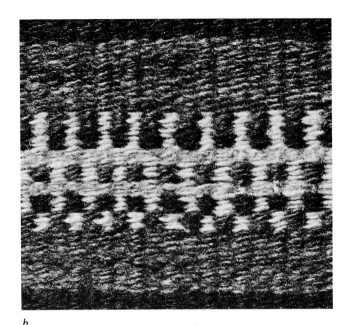

b

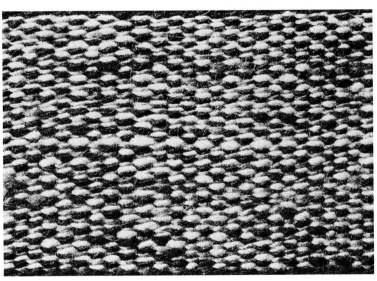

a

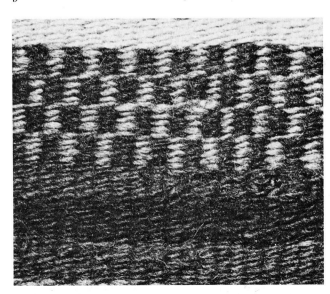

c

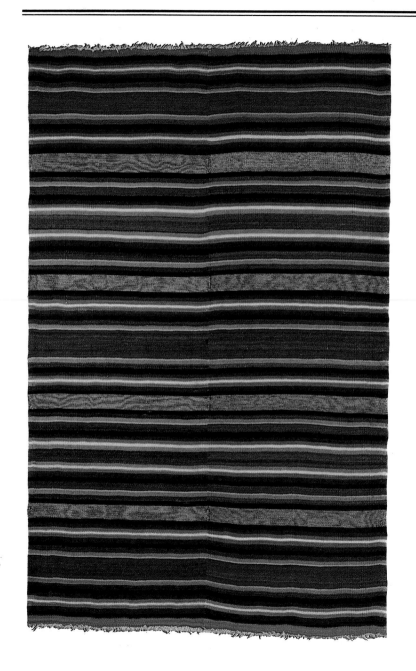

PLATE 4

Rio Grande blanket, ca. 1850, two widths seamed, 2.30 x 1.41 m. Warp: 2-ply handspun wool, except center cotton threads used as repair; weft: 1-ply handspun wool, natural-dyed with exception of 3-ply commercial red yarn added with a needle at a later date. Spanish Colonial Arts Society, Inc. Collection on loan to the Museum of New Mexico at the Museum of International Folk Art, Gift of Mr. and Mrs. John Gaw Meem, H. P. Mera Collection. L.5.62.90.

PLATE 5

Rio Grande blanket, ca. 1840, one width, 2.05 x 1.19 m. Warp: 2-ply handspun wool; weft: 1-ply handspun light and dark undyed-natural, indigo. Museum of New Mexico Collection at the Museum of International Folk Art, Gift of Miss Florence Dibell Bartlett, 2889.

PLATE 6

Rio Grande blanket, ca. 1850, one width, 1.99 x 1.28 m. Warp: 2-ply handspun wool; weft: 1-ply handspun wool, light and dark undyed-natural and indigo. Collections of the School of American Research in the Museum of New Mexico. 9474/12.

synthetic-dyed,[4] and a yellow faded to light tan that may be natural-dyed. Even though the pattern appears complicated, it is simple and achieved by merely alternating the shuttles to produce ticking.

Examples of beading are seen in Plate 4 and Figure 2a. Instead of the traditional white stripe, a mottled stripe is achieved by alternating weft shots of brown, white, and blue. According to Elmer Shupe,[5] this type of tricolor beading was done in the San Luis Valley of Colorado. The blanket seen in Plate 4 probably was made in that region around 1870.[6] It is all natural-dyed with the exception of the red stripe in the center.

The red is a commercial 3-ply yarn, added later when red became available and fashionable. Upon careful examination of this red stripe, one can see that a needle has split the warp threads, indicating that the whole red stripe was added with a needle at a later date. Curiously enough, the outer edges have also been rewoven. Such reweaving is a tremendous task—very time-consuming. The blanket is in excellent condition, and it is odd that the edges alone would have worn out.

Many Rio Grandes have been rewoven to some extent. Frequently entire end bands were eliminated, and the yarn was then used to reweave and repair worn areas in the blanket. Narrow stripes containing all the blanket's colors are usually found at each end of the blanket, as if the repair material was part of the planned blanket. Seldom does one find a blanket which does not show some evidence of time-consuming repairs. Much of this work was done by professional weavers who did reweaving,[7] but a great deal was probably done by the Spanish owners themselves. The great care taken to match the color and to recreate the original piece indicates that worn blankets were not just tossed aside or carelessly mended. When badly worn, they became stuffing for quilts. Luckily, many blankets have been found inside quilts and have been meticulously rewoven and restored.[8]

DYES AND WOOL

There were two categories of natural-dyed blankets in the early period, 1800s to 1860s: the indigo-dyed with light and dark natural wool, and a small, yet significant group of golden or red-brown, natural-dyed blankets. In about 1865 synthetic dyes became available. While the natural dyes were more stable than the early synthetics, the synthetics had the advantage of convenience. Unfortunately, the later blankets have altered in appearance because of the way in which the early synthetic dyes fade.

The quality of the raw wool also affects the dyes. The readiness with which wool fiber accepts dye depends upon the amount of grease or lanolin left in the wool. It is extremely difficult to hand-process and remove the excessive lanolin from the fine improved Merino wool; consequently, a coarse, lumpy wool results and produces uneven dyeing.[9] The wool itself is lifeless in comparison with the earlier soft, lustrous *churro* wool. Thus, when the inferior synthetic dyes were used on inferior wools, the resulting utilitarian blankets reflected not only the lower design standards but also the coarser materials used in the 1870s–1890s.

FIGURE 3

Five-band system. Drawing of a typical striped Rio Grande blanket with the central band (3) repeated in the two end bands (1 and 5). The stripes within band 2 are repeated in band 4. Drawn by Nora Pickens.

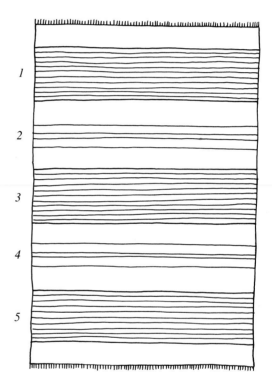

Indigo-dyed blankets

Indigo blue was used for a majority of early Spanish blankets—possibly because the imported indigo was readily available and cost less than other imported dye materials. Indigo, used as one of the main colors, generally indicates a blanket of high quality, not only in materials (mainly the wool), but also in design. Weavers seem to have excelled when they were limited by the few colors found in the indigo blankets. At first glance these early blankets may appear to be a

FIGURE 4

Typical wear pattern, Rio Grande blanket, pre-1860.
One width, 2.18 x 1.24 m. Warp: 2-ply handspun wool;
weft: 1-ply handspun wool, natural-undyed white and
brown and indigo-dyed blue. Collections of the School
of American Research in the Museum of New
Mexico. 9535/12.

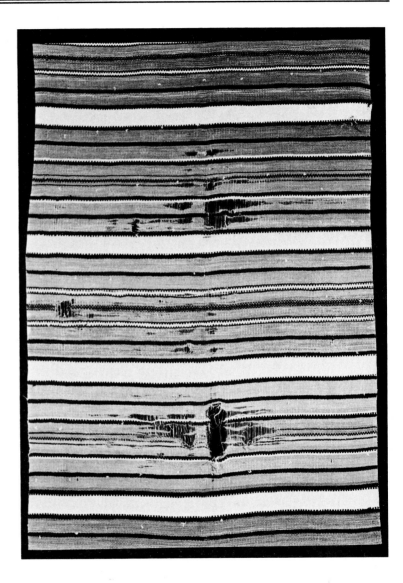

series of meaningless stripes in blue, white, and dark brown, but they are actually characterized by a rather complex design system (Plates 4, 5, 6, 7). After examining hundreds of these blankets, it becomes evident that initially there must have been a design source for the entire group. This does not mean that all the indigo blankets were a product of one workshop or *obraje,* but there was obviously a set of instructions or drawings to follow, or a blanket to copy or use as a point of reference in weaving them.

The design system of these early indigo-dyed blankets is based on a five- or seven-band layout. Each band section is composed of smaller stripes in varying widths, with the band repeated two or three times in the blanket. The center band usually repeats the two end bands, as shown in Figure 3. Here, in the typical five-band formula, bands two and four are alike. There are many variations to the five- or seven-band system. The individual probably felt free to weave his own interpretation of patterns, as long as he adhered to the basic formula.

As Plate 5 illustrates, a white stripe or band often begins the blanket, with other white stripes separating the bands throughout the blanket. A comparison of Plates 4 and 5 demonstrates different uses of white—in Plate 4 the white merely divides the bands, while in Plate 5 white becomes the field for stripes of indigo and brown. White is seldom used as a stripe within the dark bands, but it is sometimes used sparingly with indigo for design elements such as beading, ticking, and checkerboarding. Figure 2a–c illustrates these three design techniques which are used to break the monotony of solid stripes.

The Spanish indigo-dyed blankets were highly prized and given very hard use. As Figure 4 illustrates, wear patterns common to these textiles seem to indicate that they were often doubled lengthwise and thrown about the shoulders. The same typical wear pattern may have to do with the manner in which blankets were utilized for bedding.

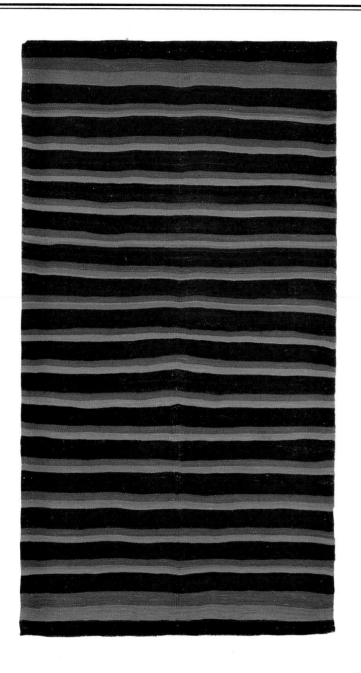

PLATE 7

Rio Grande blanket, *ca. 1840, one width, 2.23 x 1.25 m.*
Warp: 2-ply handspun wool; weft: 1-ply dark
undyed-natural and two shades of indigo. Museum of
New Mexico Collection at the Museum of International
Folk Art, Gift of Miss Mary M. L. Peck. A.60.4.1.

PLATE 8

Rio Grande blanket, *ca. 1850, one width, 2.50 x 1.46 m.*
Warp: 2-ply handspun wool; weft: 1-ply handspun wool,
natural-undyed and natural-dyed red-brown maybe a
red wood dye (UCLA D–34–60). Fred Harvey Fine Arts
Collection on loan to the Museum of New Mexico at the
Museum of International Folk Art. L.71.17.2.

PLATE 9

Rio Grande blanket, *ca. 1850, one width, 2.35 x 1.32 m.*
Warp: 2-ply handspun wool; weft: 1-ply handspun wool,
natural-undyed light and dark, natural dyes, red-brown
probably natural but unidentified, not brazilwood (UCLA
D–34–52). Spanish Colonial Arts Society, Inc. Collection
on loan to the Museum of New Mexico at the Museum of
International Folk Art, Gift of Mr. and Mrs. John Gaw
Meem, H. P. Mera Collection. L.5.62.70.

The Spanish were not the only ones to prize striped indigo-dyed blankets. There was much interchange of designs, materials, and dyes between the Spanish and Indian, and it would be foolish to isolate one development from the other. Of the Spanish striped blankets the indigo group most closely resembles highly traditional Navajo and Pueblo examples.[10] The Spanish indigo striped blanket is more complicated than the Pueblo striped blanket, however. The Indian blanket design formula is rigid, with regulated, repetitive stripes—usually alternating areas of dark indigo and undyed dark brown or black. These indigo stripes make up bands which are separated by narrow stripes of white.

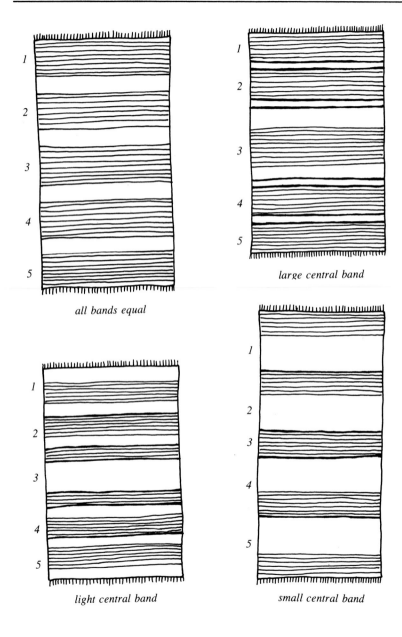

all bands equal

large central band

light central band

small central band

FIGURE 5

*"**Brazilwood**" band systems. See also the five-band system (Figure 3). Drawn by Nora Pickens.*

Occasionally, the Spanish adhered to this narrow striping pattern, but more often they broke the monotony of the design with patterned bands.

So-called "brazilwood-dyed" blankets

The double-width technique prevails in natural-dyed red-brown striped blankets (Plates 8, 9). Forty-four of the fifty-four red-brown blankets in U.S. museum collections are woven in this technique. The remaining ten were woven in two strips, then later sewn together. This very distinct group of blankets was previously thought of as the "brazilwood" group[11] because of the reddish or golden colors that predominate, which have always been attributed to the use of brazilwood dye. When a number of samples were analysed for dye content, however, no brazilwood was detected, though the red-brown in Plate 8 was apparently achieved by the use of a related red wood dye.[12] Max Saltzman has suggested that perhaps a tannin was used to produce the famed red-brown "brazilwood." It is to be hoped that some day the exact source of this distinctive color will be identified.

With the exception of three blankets, all in this group have four white stripes dividing the red-brown bands. Frequently the red-brown has faded to golden-tan, but the original color is visible between the weft threads. These blankets have a very rigid design system, being divided into almost equal sections, with the central section varying in width from the other four sections. The drawings in Figure 5 indicate the ways of varying the five-band "brazil" formula.

This is not to say that all the blankets within a band system are exactly alike. The bands are often divided in the same manner, but stripes and ticking vary within the bands. The stripes are much smaller and more complex than those in the majority of indigo-dyed blankets. The intricate beading, checkerboarding, and ticking are done with yellow, indigo, dark green, and dark undyed natural, the field color always being reddish or golden tan. Only a few textiles have broad areas of white, while most have a 5–8 cm. white stripe outlined with dark natural or dark indigo.

Technically, the blankets of the "brazilwood" group have much in common. The majority are done in the double-width technique; warps are 2-ply handspun wool—usually a light and dark mixture. The wool weft varies from soft and silky to a thicker yarn, but the wool is never the later coarse and lumpy hand-processed Merino. The first half of the blanket is repeated in the second half. The similarity in size, wool, designs, dyes, and the above technical aspects suggests that these blankets could easily have been production or workshop items.

The red-brown blankets do not show the wear areas common to indigo blankets, so it is possible that they were not worn or used in the same manner. Perhaps they were prized possessions then, as they certainly are today.

Synthetic-dyed blankets

A comparison of samples from the later (post-1865) period reveals that outside influences which affected the Spanish way of life resulted in simplified blanket design and new colors and materials. Many of the blankets, perhaps copying older patterns with new colors, are within the five-band formula (see Plates 11 and 12). In others (see Plate 13) the stripes are often random selections of color and size. Band elements are frequently repeated in a rigid format with little concern for variation or overall effect. Striped sections are often exact copies of portions of older blankets, but time and numerous washings have completely changed the character of these synthetic-dyed textiles. What sometimes remains of the synthetic-dyed colors are muted shadings of reds, oranges, and yellows—but often bright blues and greens survive only as silver-grey. There are certain colors which are typical of these synthetic-dyed blankets and may be said to characterize the late nineteenth century. Red is the dominant color. One group of blankets features reds, purples, and blues; a second group, reds, oranges, and yellows; and a third group, reds and a combination of bright pink, yellow-green, blue, bright yellow, yellow, and purple.

There are some beautiful striped blankets from each of the color and material groupings. Plates 11 and 12 illustrate red-orange-yellow synthetic-dyed blankets. These two pieces are highly traditional in that

over ▷

PLATE 10

Rio Grande blanket, ca. 1870, one width, 2.18 x 1.32 m. Warp: 2-ply handspun wool; weft: 1-ply handspun wool, natural-undyed light and dark, light-red unknown dye, probably synthetic (UCLA D–35–62). Spanish Colonial Arts Society, Inc. Collection on loan to the Museum of New Mexico at the Museum of International Folk Art, Gift of Mr. and Mrs. John Gaw Meem, H. P. Mera Collection. L.5.62.71.

PLATE 11

Rio Grande blanket, ca. 1895, one width, 2.18 x 1.24 m. Warp: 2-ply handspun wool; weft: 1-ply handspun wool, synthetic dyes. School of American Research, Santa Fe. T.606.

PLATE 12

Rio Grande blanket, ca. 1895, one width, 2.18 x 1.20 m. Warp: 2-ply handspun wool; weft: 1-ply handspun wool, synthetic dyes. School of American Research, Santa Fe. T.677.

PLATE 13

Rio Grande blanket, ca. 1930, one width, 1.95 x 1.22 m. Warp: 2-ply handspun wool; weft: 1-ply handspun wool, and possibly mohair. Synthetic dyes, possibly some natural dyes. International Folk Art Foundation Collection at the Museum of International Folk Art, a unit of the Museum of New Mexico. FA.75.38.1.

FIGURE 6

Rio Grande blanket, ca. 1925, reflecting traditional pattern of stripes, one width, 2.30 x 1.48 m. Warp: 4-ply commercial cotton; weft: 1-ply handspun wool and mohair, natural-undyed white and synthetic-dyed red, purple, violet, maroon, and yellow-orange. Courtesy of The Shalako Shop, Los Alamos, New Mexico; Mr. and Mrs. Edward B. Grothus.

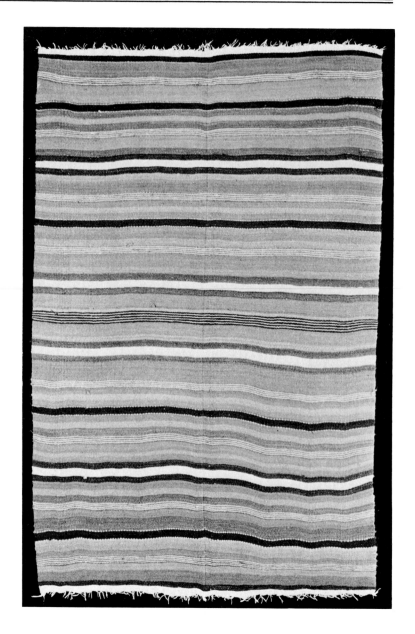

they still conform to the symmetrical band design system. Plate 13, on the other hand, provides a good example of random red-purple-blue stripes without an overall integrated design—there is no central band and the stripes appear to be haphazard in color.

In contrast to the lumpy, coarse wool found in the majority of the late blankets, the blanket in Figure 6, which survives in pristine condition, contains fine silky yarn. This is, in fact, a much later blanket, woven during the 1920s or 1930s and based on an older pattern.[13] The weft is of native goat's hair rather than wool, which makes it very soft and silky. There are five bands with four white stripes. The thin yellow and purple stripes create a nice play of color in relation to the red field and maroon stripes.

WEDDING BLANKETS AND UTILITY OR CAMP BLANKETS

Related to the band-and-stripe blankets are the so-called wedding and utility or camp blankets. A wedding blanket, of a very simple design and made primarily of extraordinarily fine, silky *churro* wool, is shown in Plate 14. According to tradition, these blankets were provided by the groom's family.[14] Small portions of colored yarns were quite often added later to give new life to both wedding and utility blankets. As illustrated, red is the favored color for the added decoration of dots and

FIGURE 7

Rio Grande utility blanket, ca. 1880, two widths seamed, 1.82 x 1.04 m. Warp: 2-ply handspun natural-undyed white and brown wool; weft: 1-ply handspun wool, natural-undyed white and brown, with 1-ply commercial synthetic-dyed red added later. Spanish Colonial Arts Society, Inc. Collection on loan to the Museum of New Mexico at the Museum of International Folk Art, Gift of Mrs. Laura Hersloff. L.5.63.3.

dashes and similar simple designs. Red linear circles were added later with a needle to the blanket seen in Figure 7. The wedding blanket, Plate 14, is typical in its simple pattern and allover white field with a dark brown stripe at the center.

Perhaps the scarcest blanket today is the one that was the most common a hundred or more years ago. Little remains of the blanket that was woven for the poorer people and used every day until, threadbare, it became a saddle blanket or stuffing for quilts and mattress ticking. As illustrated in Plates 15 and 16 as well as Figure 7, the utility blanket had no elaborate design, and only occasionally had a simple stripe to break the monotony of the overall natural brown blanket. Utility blankets were often woven from leftover wool which was neither white enough to be dyed or left in its natural state, nor dark enough to be used as a dark natural. Rather, a mottled effect was achieved with the light and dark mixed yarn, as seen in Plate 16.

A beautiful blanket, perhaps too good to be considered strictly a utility blanket, is seen in Plate 15—a textile with a dark, natural field and narrow indigo stripes.[15] A simple yet handsome piece!

Although little is documented concerning utility blankets, Mera states that "It is more than probable that if all the Rio Grande harness-loom blankets produced . . . could be known, . . . the utility type would outnumber the finer weaves as much as a hundred to one."[16] Given hard usage, primarily by herders, these common but pleasing textiles continued to be produced throughout the centuries and echo the much more elaborate band-and-stripe examples.

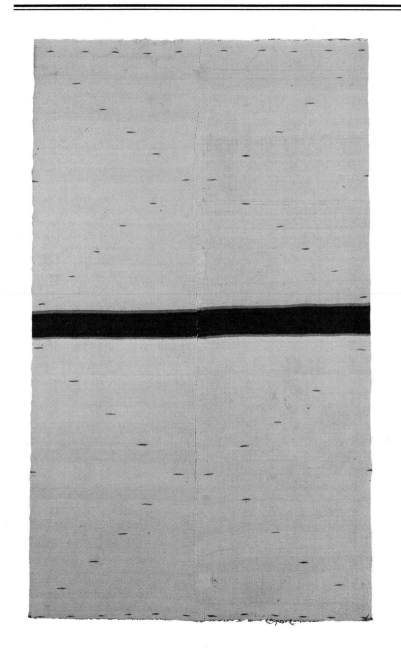

PLATE 14

Rio Grande blanket, ca. 1860, two widths seamed, 2.12 x 1.29 m. Warp: 2-ply handspun wool; weft: 1-ply handspun wool, dashes of indigo and commercial 3-ply cochineal added later. Museum of New Mexico Collection at the Museum of International Folk Art, Bequest of Charles D. Carroll. A.71.31.197.

PLATE 15

Rio Grande blanket, ca. 1860, one width, 2.17 x 1.19 m. Warp: 2-ply handspun wool; weft: 1-ply handspun wool, undyed-natural dark and indigo. School of American Research, Santa Fe. T.453.

PLATE 16

Rio Grande blanket, ca. 1876–90, two widths seamed, 1.95 x 1.12 m. Warp: 2-ply handspun wool; weft: 1-ply handspun wool, natural-undyed mottled brown, synthetic-dyed yellow and blue-red now faded to white, synthetic-dyed orange, probable Orange II discovered in 1876 (UCLA, D–32–17). School of American Research, Santa Fe. T.318.

7 SALTILLO SARAPES OF MEXICO

JOE BEN WHEAT

Saltillo *sarapes* are among the finest textiles ever woven. The intricacy and beauty of their design, the subtlety and richness of their colors, and the fineness of their weave have made them famous throughout Mexico and beyond. Ultimately, many of the design features of the Mexican Saltillo *sarape* were taken over by the Rio Grande weavers—the Spanish settlers of New Mexico.

During most of what may be termed their "classic period," from about 1700 to 1850, Saltillo *sarapes* were apparently used primarily by the Indians and mestizos of central Mexico and by all classes along the northern frontier. Because of the Spanish sumptuary laws, which prevailed until Mexico won her independence in 1821, European-style court dress was ordained for the ruling and upper classes of the capitals and other major cities.[1] In a burst of nationalism after 1821, Saltillo *sarapes* became a symbol of elegance, especially for the *charros*—the upper-class Spaniards who devoted much time, money, and energy to horse culture.[2] The *caballero's* fine horse, heavy silver-mounted bridle, spurs, and saddle, and richly embroidered and gadrooned clothing and *sombrero* were usually complemented by a highly decorative *sarape*—a Saltillo *sarape* if the wearer could afford it. In one way or another, the *sarape* became part of the everyday costume of most people of Spanish America, rich or poor.

Despite this fact, many details of its origin and development remain obscure, awaiting patient delving into the archives of Mexico and Spain. Nevertheless, enough is known that certain broad outlines are apparent. While a major part of the horse cult was carried from Spain to the New World, the *sarape* apparently was not, for there was no similar garment in Spain, where capes or cloaks were used instead. Most of the Indians from southern Peru through Central America, Mexico, and into the American Southwest with whom the Spanish came in contact, however, were weavers of native cotton and other plant fibers. One of the principal products of native looms was a rectangular *manta* or blanket, which served as clothing by day and bedding by night. Some of these rectangular fabrics had slits in the center, allowing them to be slipped over the head so that they became shirts or small ponchos with the sides open.[3] It appears reasonable that these native *mantas* and small ponchos became the model out of which the larger and more elaborate *sarapes* and ponchos developed.

As with the *sarape* in general, little is known of the details of origin and development of the famous Saltillo *sarape*. What is known leads to the Tlaxcalan Indians who lived in the mountainous area near present-day Puebla, Mexico. Like most of their neighbors, the Tlaxcalans were weavers in cotton and in *ixtle*—the fiber of the agave plant. Their loom was the narrow back-strap loom common to Middle America.[4]

Bitter enemies of the great Aztec Empire, the Tlaxcalans at first fought, and then became early allies of Cortés, and played a significant role in the Spanish overthrow of the Aztec regime. Because of their aid, they were given a favored status, and remained steadfast allies of the Spanish over the centuries. Spanish colonial policy, in general, was to exploit the raw materials of its colonies by having them sent back to Spain for manufacture and distribution. For example, cochineal shipped to Spain was a major product of Tlaxcala. Nevertheless, the Spanish did develop some industries for the maintenance of the colonists and the indigenous population. Weaving was, perhaps, the prime example of this development. Horses, cattle, and sheep were introduced from Spain. A small flock of the Royal Merino sheep were granted to Cortés, who confined them to his estate near Cuernavaca, but the common sheep of Spain, the *churro*, became the mainstay elsewhere, including the Tlaxcalan area. During the mid-sixteenth century, the Tlaxcalans produced handwoven woolen blankets for sale or trade.[5] The revolutionary treadle loom was introduced, and, by the last half of the sixteenth century, a major wool industry had been established in Tlaxcala.[6]

As the frontiers of Mexico were pushed northward, the Tlaxcalans were frequently recruited by the Spanish as colonists. Wherever the *Chichamecas*—the wild Indians—were a barrier to the settlement of new areas, the civilized Tlaxcalans were sent to tame them, to teach them the pursuits of agriculture and other arts of civilization. During the

last part of the sixteenth century, the mining districts of Coahuila and Nuevo León were being opened, and the native *Chichamecas,* the Guachichiles, resisted the intrusion. Viceroy Velasco II proposed that 400 Tlaxcalan families should colonize the area. Eighty of these families arrived at Saltillo in Coahuila in August, 1591, and were received by Francisco de Urdinola to begin their task.[7]

As usual, because of their special status, they were accorded certain privileges. They were given a separate *barrio,* or area, in Saltillo in which to settle, which was named San Esteban de Nuevo Tlaxcala. Special water rights were granted them, and their agriculture and grazing lands, the best in the area, were to be protected against encroachment by the Spanish settlers.[8] With them, they brought their weaving industry.

As other Spanish settlements were undertaken, small groups of Tlaxcalans from San Esteban were settled near the new Spanish towns. By 1598, a Tlaxcalan *barrio* was established in Parras. Still later, Tlaxcalans were settled around the lake district of Chihuahua and Durango. In San Esteban, there were some seventy looms used for the production of *sarapes*.[9] It was from the *barrio* of San Esteban that the Saltillo *sarape* came—Indian, not Spanish, even though Spanish sheep and Spanish treadle looms were used in its manufacture.[10]

One of the major problems in the study of Saltillo *sarapes* is to find the source of the design system employed on the finer and more intricate ones. From time to time, it has been suggested that Moorish designs, brought from Spain, formed the basis of Saltillo design. While serrate figures are employed in some North African weaving, especially in Tunisia, there does not appear to be, anywhere in the region, the combination of center-dominant serrate motif, vertically oriented structured background, and intricate border designs which characterize the Saltillo *sarape*.[11] Others have sought its origin in Chinese fabrics imported into Mexico via the Manila galleons, for use in Mexico and for transshipment to Spain;[12] but aside from the manner in which silk is used in late classic Saltillo *sarapes,* there is very little to suggest this source.[13]

While both Spain and China may remain as possible sources, there are others nearer at hand—the decorative motifs and the design systems employed by the Tlaxcalans themselves and by other indigenous peoples of Mexico. While almost nothing is known of pre-Columbian textile designs of the Tlaxcalans, historic Tlaxcalan *sarapes* feature serrate diamonds—some very intricate, some nested one within another as in the classic Saltillo *sarapes*. In the recent past, at least, similar design elements were used by the Otomí and other Indians of the mountain areas of central Mexico, people with whom the Tlaxcalans had contact. The Otomí frequently used serrate figures as center-dominant motifs in their weaving, and often used borders as well.[14] Aside from the Tlaxcala *sarape,* these textiles were all woven on back-strap looms and are mostly warp-faced fabrics.[15] The Tlaxcalan weavers, having made the transition from back-strap to treadle loom before they went to the Saltillo area, would have had little difficulty in adapting these design elements to the newer technique.

Throughout most of her history, Mexico's commerce was carried on by means of trade fairs. These fairs were held in various cities at different times of year, so that traders and merchants could attend them. Merchandise from China traveled from the port of Acapulco across Mexico to Vera Cruz for transshipment to Spain; but some of it was bought by merchants who, in turn, peddled it at the regional fairs or exchanged it for speciality products from the various regions. Products from Europe entered at Vera Cruz and were distributed from there. The great Saltillo fair was begun in the late seventeenth century,[16] and was held in September of each year. Merchants and traders from all over Mexico attended, and here they procured, among other things, the famous Saltillo *sarapes*.[17] These were, in turn, sold at the fairs at San Bartolomé, San Juan de los Lagos, and Chihuahua, along with other exotic items such as silk and porcelain from China, lace and linen from Belgium, and wool cloth from England, and domestic products such as Campeche cotton woven on treadle looms, cochineal from Oaxaca, *rebozos,* iron goods, and chocolate. The Chihuahua fair, held in December, was the exchange point for products from New Mexico and from other parts of the world.

New Mexico had its own trade fairs. In July or August of each year, at Taos, Pecos, and other places, the Utes, Comanches, Apaches, and Navajos exchanged buffalo robes, tanned skins, baskets, and blankets for goods supplied by the Spanish and the Pueblo Indians. In November, all of the people of New Mexico who wanted to attend the fair in Chihuahua banded together in a great caravan for mutual protection against the attacks of the *Chichamecas* through whose territory they had to pass. A military escort was usually provided.[18] The caravan included a large number of persons—individuals with a few home-produced articles to sell; representatives of the large haciendas, with hundreds of blankets and many *varas* of coarse cloth; and merchants with the varied produce gathered at the local fairs.[19] These articles were in great demand, particularly in the mining districts of northern Mexico. Other products from New Mexico included sheep, wool, salt, and *piñon* nuts. When the New Mexico settlers returned home, some brought *sarapes* from San Miguel el Grande (Allende) and from Saltillo, together with other goods acquired at the fair.

Weaving had been practiced by the Pueblo Indians in the Rio Grande Valley since prehistoric times. With Spanish colonization in 1598 came sheep and the treadle loom. While the Pueblo Indians continued to weave on their upright looms, the Spanish established workshops for the commercial treadle loom production of woolen goods such as coarse cloth and blankets, much of which was disposed of at the mining centers of northern Mexico.[20] Luxury fabrics were imported. After the settlement of lower New Mexico—the Rio Abajo—weaving flourished around Albuquerque, as demonstrated by the number of craftsmen listed in the 1790 census.[21] The once flourishing industry in Santa Fe and in the vicinity of Rio Arriba apparently declined. This decline, and competition from Navajo weavers, impelled the government at Santa Fe to request the service of master weavers from Mexico to improve the local production by instructing local weavers in better methods of spinning, dyeing, designing, and weaving, to meet the competition. The request was granted, and in 1807 the Spanish master weavers Don Ygnacio Ricardo Bazán and his brother, Don Juan, arrived in Santa Fe to upgrade the local weaving.

Within a few years, according to Pino,[22] Don Ricardo apparently had accomplished at least part of his mission—he had greatly improved the general level of spinning and weaving. Pino noted, however, that "Although I call this fine weaving, I do so with reference to that which was formerly woven."[23] Another goal of the Bazáns was to improve the designing of Rio Grande weaving. While we lack specific evidence at present, it appears most likely that a simplified version of the Saltillo design system was introduced at this time, for despite Boyd's disclaimer,[24] it is clear from Spanish sources that throughout the eighteenth century, the Mexican Saltillo *sarape* was recognized for the

PLATE 17

Saltillo **sarape,** *1750–1800, one width, 2.36 x 1.60 m.*
Warp: 3-ply handspun cotton; weft: 1-ply handspun wool,
natural dyes. Fred Harvey Fine Arts Collection on loan
to the Museum of New Mexico at the Museum of
International Folk Art. L.71.17.1.

beauty of its design and fine weave.[25] In any case, by the 1830s the Rio
Grande weavers were producing *sarapes atilmados de gusto,* that is,
fancy decorated *sarapes.*[26] Gregg, writing of the early days of the Santa
Fe trade (1831–40), notes that:

> The finer [Rio Grande blankets] are curiously woven in handsome
> figures of various colors . . . . [They make] imitations of the *Sarape*
> *Navajo* . . . [and] there have also been made in New Mexico a few
> imitations of the *Sarape Saltillero*—the blanket of Saltillo, a city of the
> south celebrated for the manufacture of the most splendid fancy
> blankets, singularly figured with all the colors of the rainbow . . . .
> What renders the weaving of the fancy blankets extremely tedious, is,
> that the variegation of colors is all effected with the shuttle, the texture
> in other respects being perfectly plain, without even a twill.[27]

The finer blankets of the Rio Grande weavers thus took as their
patterns the fine *sarapes* of the Navajo and those of Saltillo. While there
was considerable variation in the details of the Saltillo *sarapes,* many of
them were characterized by a layout which included a large and very
complex central diamond motif composed of concentric serrate bands,
with a background of solid color relieved by diagonal rows or a grid of
tiny figures (Figure 1), or one composed of vertically oriented serrate
figures and a figured border (Plate 17). Some *sarapes,* sometimes
thought to derive from San Miguel de Allende, have the central
diamond motif surrounded by, or replaced by a large round medallion
with a scalloped border (Figure 2). On other *sarapes,* generally thought
to be later, the central motif consists of a cluster or aggregate of four to
nine diamonds (Figure 3).

In the classic Saltillo *sarape,* each of the concentric bands
composing the central motif is decorated by minute figures (Figure 4).
The simplest of these figures consists of a line with serrations along one

FIGURE 1

Saltillo **sarape,** *ca. 1750, with serrate concentric diamond center on light ground, minute grid of tiny diamonds, and serrate zigzag borders, two widths seamed, 2.56 x 1.56 m. Warp: 1-ply cotton; weft: 1-ply handspun wool, natural-dyed reds, pink, blue, and green and undyed white. American Museum of Natural History. 65/4207.*

FIGURE 2

Saltillo **sarape,** *ca. 1775, with concentric diamond center surrounded by floral medallion on dark blue ground, vertically oriented zigzag and diamond stripes and border with "Saltillo leaf" (manita) arranged in diamond net frame, two widths seamed, 2.05 x 1.12 m. Warp: 2-ply cotton; weft: 1-ply handspun wool, natural-dyed blues and red and undyed white. American Museum of Natural History. 65/3364.*

FIGURE 3

Detail of Saltillo **sarape,** *ca. 1850, with cluster of four concentric diamonds on red ground with rows of dots, striped end borders, and figured side borders. Panhandle-Plains Historical Museum, Canyon, Texas. 1501/107.*

edge (Figure 4a). Opposed and offset serrations along a line produce a row of hourglass-shaped figures (Figures 4b), which may be joined at the apexes to make a net (Figure 4c) or woven in vertical and horizontal rows to fill an area. Another form of the serrate line consists of a thick stripe of zigzags (Figure 4d). Rhombs or diamonds of contrasting color are set in a solid-color band (Figure 4e) or placed in contiguous fashion to form a "diamond stripe" (Figure 4f). A double row of diamonds of contrasting colors produces an offset quartered diamond effect (Figure 4g). Tiny diamonds in clusters of four with alternating colors were sometimes used to form a band decoration (Figure 4h). Another figure used in rows to make a stripe, or in clusters to provide a diaper pattern, was the serrate leaf-shaped figure

FIGURE 4

Design elements of concentric diamond bands on Saltillo
sarapes *(drawn by Nora Pickens): a. Serrated line. b.*
Double serrate or "hourglass" line. c. "Hourglass" net.
d. Truncated zigzag stripe. e. Inset rhombs or diamonds.
f. Diamond stripe. g. Double diamond stripe with offset
color scheme. h. Clustered diamond stripe with
alternating color scheme. i. "Saltillo leaf" (manita)
pattern. j. Serrate diamond pattern.

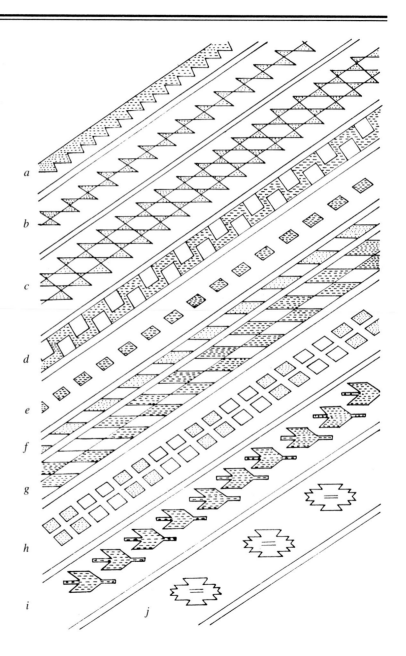

sometimes termed the "Saltillo leaf" *(manita)* (Figure 4 i). Combining two reversed "Saltillo leaf" *(manita)* figures base to base results in a serrate diamond figure (Figure 4 j). All of these figures are important, for they became part of the design vocabulary of the Rio Grande weavers.

In the Saltillo *sarape,* the warps are usually made of *ixtle,* linen, or cotton, and are very thin. The wefts, of handspun wool, are also very fine. The use of such threads produced warp counts of 15 to 20 per 2.5 cm. (one inch) and weft counts of 70 to 100 per 2.5 cm. (one inch). By contrast, the 2-ply wool warp and heavier weft used by the Rio Grande weavers resulted in warp counts of about 5 to 7 per 2.5 cm. (one inch) and weft counts of 25 to 50 per 2.5 cm. (one inch). Because of the relative coarseness of their materials, many of the design elements taken over from the Saltillo *sarapes* were enlarged and used along stripes or as separate and isolated figures, while the concentric bands of the central serrate diamond were either solid bands of contrasting colors or, more often, serrate lines, sometimes interlocking. Fewer bands were used than in Saltillo weaving. Frequently, in Rio Grande blankets, an additional diamond would be placed above and below the central diamond, but it was usually enclosed in the outermost band (Plates 37, 39–41).

The backgrounds of Saltillo *sarapes* frequently consist of rows of small dots which are so arranged as to produce both horizontal and diagonal lines parallel to the sides of the central motif (Figure 5 a). More common are vertically oriented stripes consisting of solid-color zigzag lines (Figure 5 b) or stripes that change color at each angle

FIGURE 5

*Design layout and patterns of ground figures and
borders (drawn by Nora Pickens): a. Sarape layout and
spaced dot ground. b. Vertically oriented solid-color
zigzags. c. Vertically oriented zigzags and diamonds,
color change at angles. d. Complex vertically oriented
zigzags and diamonds, quartered color pattern. e.
Vertically oriented diamonds with color change. f. Border
layout with diamond net and small figures. g. Side and
end border layout with concentric triangles and short
vertical zigzags.*

(Figure 5 c). Sometimes these are quartered (Figure 5 d). Usually,
these zigzag stripes enclose small serrate-edged diamonds (Figure 5 c).
Rarely there are vertical rows of diamonds, plain or halved, on a
solid-color ground (Figure 5 e). The Rio Grande weavers frequently
made use of the same elements, but, as with the diamond band motifs,
they were larger and coarser (Plates 35–41). In some blankets, only the
vertical background motifs were used, the central diamond being
omitted (Plates 43, 44, 45).

The borders of Saltillo *sarapes* were frequently composed of the
same elements as those used to ornament the concentric bands of the
center motif. Normally, both the ground color and the colors of the
decorative elements were the same as those used in the central motif,
contrasting with the ground color of the blanket as a whole. The
decorative elements were usually arranged to form a diamond net
(Figure 5 f), although some were laid out in vertical zigzags which
formed reciprocating triangles (Figure 5 g) or, along the end borders, in
short vertical zigzags (Figure 5 g). Following earlier custom, however,
many of the Rio Grande blankets lacked the wide borders, and end
borders consisted of simple stripes, even when they were woven in the
Saltillo manner, with a diamond center motif and serrate vertical
background. When side borders were woven, they were coarser than
those of the Saltillo patterns from which they derived, and consisted of
solid-color diamond nets, several concentric vertical zigzags in
contrasting colors (Plates 51, 54), vertical or diagonal rows of the

"Saltillo leaf" (Plates 35, 50, and 55), serrate diamond elements arranged in a diamond grid, or, occasionally, even a solid-color band. Very rarely, a figured end border would be woven, utilizing some variation of the diamond stripe. Deviating from the Saltillo pattern, Rio Grande blankets occasionally used triangular elements (actually quartered diamonds) in the corners, as did the Navajo, but they were usually serrated, as in the central diamond motif (Plate 46).

Subtle and harmonious color variations mark the Saltillo *sarapes*. The Tlaxcalan weavers of Saltillo had access to all of the commercial dyes of the time, and possessed the skills to use them.[28] Cochineal produced several shades of red, as did the tropical dyewoods. Indigo was used in several densities, and a variety of golds and yellows, together with black and white wools, completed the color palette. In New Mexico, many of these dyes either were not available or could be obtained only in limited quantities; and the mordants which allowed cochineal to produce a variety of reds were lacking or were not used.

Aside from indigo and limited amounts of cochineal and tropical dyewoods, local plants, long known to native Indian weavers and Spanish alike, were used for the simpler color schemes of the Rio Grande weavers. Strong reds were sometimes achieved by incorporating yarns raveled from commercial wool cloth—the famous "Bayeta"—or by using the 3-ply commercial yarns, which constituted a standard trade item in New Mexico from the earliest days.[29]

The Saltillo *sarape* spawned many copies over the centuries. Its fineness of weave, intricacy of design, and variegated colors kept it preeminent until about 1850, when it began a decline from which it never recovered. Meanwhile, the Rio Grande blanket, which took as its model the Saltillo design system, prospered, lasting nearly to the beginning of the twentieth century. What it lacked in fineness of weave, complexity of design, and range of color, it made up for in boldness and simplicity of design, and simple but harmonious color schemes. It was a worthy heir of the Saltillo tradition.

8 BANDS AND STRIPES WITH SALTILLO DESIGN ELEMENTS
DOROTHY BOYD BOWEN

A large group of blankets exhibit the same general design organization of bands and narrow stripes and, in addition, include bands of tapestry motifs taken directly from the Saltillo *sarape*. As has been shown by Dr. Wheat and Dr. Minge, the Saltillo *sarape,* as a status symbol for the *ricos,* was well known in eighteenth- and early nineteenth-century New Mexico. At least after the Bazán instruction in Santa Fe, probably earlier on the Rio Abajo, many New Mexican weavers possessed the skills needed to execute Saltillo designs in their blankets.

The inclusion of tapestry weave required that these pieces be woven either in two separate narrow widths on the narrow treadle loom, or, if woven in one width without a seam down the middle, on a wider loom.[1] Nearly all of the blankets with tapestry motifs consequently were woven in two widths until the late nineteenth century, when wider looms were introduced.

Figure 1 illustrates a number of these Saltillo motifs, with the descriptive terms that will be used. These terms are not related to the original Spanish designations, which are not reliably documented and would probably have varied regionally. For the purpose of design analysis, the Rio Grande blankets in this part of the study have been divided into groups according to motifs present, rather than according to materials used, as was done by Dr. Mera[2] and E. Boyd.[3] By means of this organization it is possible to show a continuity of design throughout two centuries as well as the effect new materials had on design in the late nineteenth and twentieth centuries.

Chevrons

The first and largest group of Rio Grande designs organized in bands with tapestry motifs includes three forms of the chevron: plain, stepped, and serrate. The plain chevron, found both early and late, is one of the

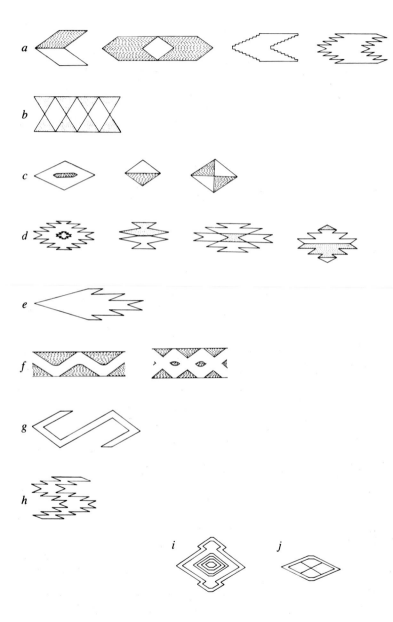

FIGURE 1

Saltillo motifs which appear in Rio Grande textiles
(drawn by Nora Pickens): a. Chevrons: Plain, Stepped,
Serrate. b. Diamond and Hourglass: Plain (may also be
Stepped or Serrate). c. Centered diamond; Bicolor
diamond; Four color diamond. d. Serrate diamond.
e. Leaf, manita, or palma. f. Meander or culebra,
interlocking meander. g. Horizontal "S." h. Serrate
zigzag column. i. Central concentric diamond. j.
Quadripartite diamond.

easiest tapestry motifs to execute. The angle of its sides depends on the proportion of the warp count to the weft count, and therefore varies.

The textile illustrated in Plate 18 is a fine example of plain chevron designs done with handspun 2-ply warp and 1-ply handspun *churro* wool weft. The natural dyes include light, medium, and dark indigo, rich green (indigo and yellow), pale yellow, light and medium golden tan, and natural brown and white. The brown may be overdyed. The five bands of chevrons are nicely balanced against a background of narrow stripes, and the two sides are well matched along the seam.

Another natural-dyed example in the Woodard Collection is said to have come from the Teofilo Trujillo family in the San Luis Valley, Colorado.[4] Trujillo is known to have moved to the Valley from Taos in 1864. He grazed his own *churros* north of the San Luis Lakes, but his ranch and sheep were wiped out by violent cattlemen in the early 1880s, at which time he moved to the village of San Luis.[5] As there is no record of his personally engaging in weaving, this blanket probably is simply made from his wool. It is woven of handspun *churro* wool, in natural-undyed brown and white and indigo. The bicolor chevrons alternate in the three colors to form a leaf pattern in six bands, the bands separated by zones of narrow blue and brown stripes. The piece is beautifully woven and the design well controlled.

Another natural-dyed piece with plain chevrons is illustrated in Figure 2. Here the chevrons are more complex, actually making a zigzag design, although they are still in bands separated by stripes. Plain chevrons also appear in synthetic-dyed pieces such as one owned by the Spanish Colonial Arts Society.[6] Here the design is not so well planned,

FIGURE 2

Rio Grande blanket, pre-1860, two widths seamed, 2.19 x 1.34 m. Warp: 2-ply handspun wool; weft: 1-ply handspun wool, natural-undyed light and dark, indigo, and faded red (synthetic-dyed?), and commercial 3-ply wool yarn, cochineal and pale green. Spanish Colonial Arts Society, Inc. Collection on loan to the Museum of New Mexico at the Museum of International Folk Art. Gift of Mr. and Mrs. John Gaw Meem, H. P. Mera Collection. L.5.62.80.

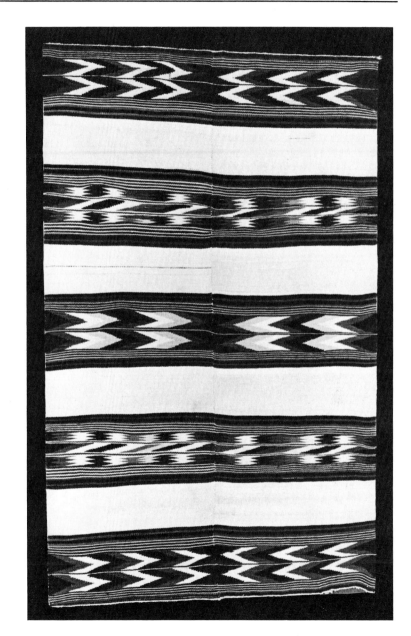

and the chevrons form flat diamonds. The warp is dyed cotton string and the weft handspun 1-ply wool with synthetic dyes. E. Boyd assigned this blanket to the San Luis Valley, ca. 1890.

The stepped chevron is thought to be related to Navajo designs,[7] although the Spanish weavers apparently adopted it early. Many of the blankets in this group are skillfully woven, with well-controlled designs. A fine example with natural white and brown and indigo is at the Lowe Art Museum.[8] The weaver used two bands of double stepped chevrons, separated by stripes with a broad zone of stepped diagonals at the center. It is woven in two pieces and was dated by Mera as 1860–70.

An interesting design based on the stepped chevron but more directly related to the Navajo "chief blanket" is found in Plate 19.[9] Woven in two widths with handspun natural-undyed white and brown and indigo wool, it originally had six bands of stepped chevrons forming diamonds at the center seam. The bands are separated by zones of blue and brown stripes.

The stepped chevron, like the plain chevron, continued as a design element into the late synthetic dye period. Five of these appear quite similar in design.[10] They are all woven in two widths with handspun 2-ply wool warps and handspun 1-ply wool wefts, and with synthetic dyes including (in various combinations) red, yellow, and green, in some blankets also pink, purple, orange, brown, and blue. The blue in one blanket may be indigo.[11] The blankets have from three to seven bands of divided stepped chevrons forming diamonds at the center seam, separated by zones of narrow stripes. None has a reliable

PLATE 18

Rio Grande blanket, pre-1860, two widths seamed, 2.12
x 1.54 m. Warp: 2-ply handspun white wool; weft: 1-ply
handspun wool, natural-undyed light and dark,
natural-dyed pale yellow, green, golden tan, and light,
medium, and dark indigo. From the Collections of the
Millicent A. Rogers Museum, Taos, New Mexico. BL65.

PLATE 19

Rio Grande blanket, pre-1865, two widths seamed, 2.12
x 1.28 m. Warp: 2-ply handspun light wool, weft: 1-ply
handspun light and dark natural and indigo dye. Design
is related to the Navajo "chief blanket." Museum of
New Mexico Collection at the Museum of International
Folk Art, Gift of Mrs. Edgar L. Rossin. A.64.69.4.

PLATE 20

Rio Grande blanket, pre-1865, two widths seamed, 1.74
x 1.20 m. Warp: 2-ply handspun light wool; weft: 1-ply
handspun churro wool, dark and light natural and indigo
dye. Museum of New Mexico Collection at the Museum of
International Folk Art, Gift of Alfred I. Barton.
A.65.67.1.

provenience, but all were probably woven in 1880–1900. These
may well have been done in the same place, perhaps some by the
same weaver.

The serrate chevron can be seen as one unit of the common serrate
zigzag columns in the backgrounds of many Saltillo *sarapes.* The Fred
Harvey Fine Arts Collection includes a fine example of this style.[12]
Woven in two pieces with handspun 2-ply wool warps and 1-ply wool
wefts, it has two indigo and natural white bands of serrate chevrons and
a central band of six-point Saltillo leaves, separated by zones of stripes
and beading. The warp ends have been trimmed and tucked back into
the web.

Plate 20 illustrates another fine piece with handspun indigo and
light and dark natural *churro* wool wefts and 2-ply wool warps. Here,

FIGURE 3

Rio Grande blanket, *1880s, two widths seamed, 2.3 x
1.34 m. Warp: 2-ply handspun wool; weft: 1-ply
handspun wool with synthetic-dyed red, yellow, and green
and natural-undyed light and dark wool. Spanish
Colonial Arts Society, Inc. Collection on loan to the
Museum of New Mexico at the Museum of International
Folk Art. Gift of Mr. and Mrs. John Gaw Meem, H. P.
Mera Collection. L.5.62.66.*

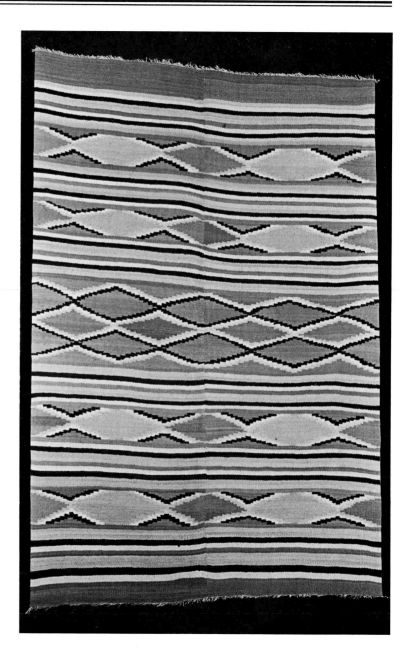

the serrate chevrons have become more like the Saltillo zigzag columns,
but they are still separated into bands rather than taking over the entire field.

With the use of synthetic dyes the serrate chevron continued to
appear. The blanket shown in Plate 21 with synthetic-dyed pink, red,
orange, and yellow, and dark undyed handspun wool, is very similar to a
piece in the Museum of the American Indian which is of synthetic-dyed
red, green, orange, and natural-undyed brown and white handspun
wool.[13] Both are woven in two widths with 2-ply wool warps and 1-ply
wool wefts. Both have three bands of serrate chevrons with tiny
hourglass figures separated by zones of wide colored stripes. A blanket
at the Museum of New Mexico is similar to both of these in material,
dyes, and design, except that the chevrons are double in the center band
and five instead of three bands of serrate chevrons are used.[14] The
textile shown in Figure 3 is also woven of these materials with five
bands of serrate chevrons turned to form diamonds. None of these
blankets has a documented provenience, but they may be dated by
materials to the 1880s or 1890s.

Diamond-hourglass bands

Three fairly early pieces have diamond and hourglass bands which,
when done in indigo and natural-undyed brown and white, allows a
pleasing play of positive and negative images.[15] These three blankets
are so similar in structure, materials, and design as to suggest a regional
style or perhaps the same shop. None has a documented early
provenience, unfortunately. A fourth blanket, also woven in two widths

with handspun 2-ply wool warps and handspun 1-ply indigo and natural-undyed white and brown wool wefts, has four bands of the stepped hourglass-diamond motifs with two bands of Saltillo leaves, separated by bands of narrow stripes.[16] According to Charles Woodard, this blanket was made in Los Sauses, Colorado. Marianne Stoller points out that if this is true, the blanket must post-date 1863.[17] A fifth blanket resembles these pieces except that it contains a small amount of synthetic-dyed (?) red commercial yarn used in the centers of alternate diamonds.[18] If this is an early synthetic dye rather than a natural one, the blanket was woven in the early 1860s.

The textile in Plate 22 is a particularly unusual stepped diamond-hourglass blanket in that it contains natural-dyed tan and cochineal red as well as natural-dyed yellow, green, and indigo and natural-undyed white and brown. All handspun wool, it is similar in design to an example at the Lowie Museum.[19]

Another group of blankets, represented by Plate 23, is done in mostly natural dyes and handspun yarns with bands of serrate diamond-hourglass motifs separated by bands of stripes. Four are virtually identical to each other in structure and materials,[20] except that two include unfaded synthetic-dyed (?) red 3-ply commercial wool yarn used as centers in the white diamonds. These probably were done in the same place at the same time, ca. 1865–70. An example at the Field Museum is similar.[21]

The blanket in Plate 24 is similar in structure, materials, and design to these but contains 4-ply commercial red yarn, which is probably synthetic-dyed, in the centers of the diamonds in one row. If this is a synthetic-dyed Germantown yarn, it would place the blanket in the late 1870s.

Illustrated in Plate 25 is a beautiful blanket woven in Conejos, Colorado, with handspun *churro* warp and weft, indigo, natural-undyed white and brown, and possibly synthetic yellow, orange, yellow-orange, red-purple, and a dull red. E. Boyd believed that this piece might contain the elusive and unproven chokecherry dye, or *capulín* (the "dull red"). Unfortunately, we have not been able to submit samples of this piece for dye analysis, and chokecherry has not been found in any fibers analyzed by Max Saltzman for purposes of this study. In any case the blanket is representative of a transitional period between natural and synthetic dyes, perhaps in the 1870s, in the San Luis Valley.

Three other later pieces are related in design.[22] The serrate diamond-hourglass design even carried over into the late nineteenth century, as shown by the textile in Figure 4, which has cotton string warp and handspun coarse, lumpy wool weft dyed with synthetic red,

over ▷

PLATE 21

Rio Grande blanket, ca. 1880, two widths seamed, 1.90 x 1.20 m. Warp: 2-ply handspun wool; weft: 1-ply handspun wool, natural-undyed light and dark and synthetic-dyed pink, red, orange, and yellow. Museum of New Mexico Collection at the Museum of International Folk Art, Gift of Miss Florence Dibell Bartlett. MNM 2837.

PLATE 22

Rio Grande blanket, ca. 1860s, two widths seamed, 2.23 x 1.18 m. Warp: 2-ply handspun light wool; weft: handspun 1-ply wool, natural-undyed light and dark, cochineal red (UCLA D–67–75), indigo, and natural-dyed tan, yellow, and green. Alfred I. Barton Gift, Lowe Art Museum. 60.220.032.

PLATE 23

Rio Grande blanket, ca. 1860s, two widths seamed, 2.36 x 1.37 m. Warp: 2-ply handspun light and dark wool; weft: 1-ply handspun wool, natural-undyed light and dark and indigo, and 3-ply commercial wool yarn, probably cochineal-dyed red. Los Angeles County Museum of Natural History, William Randolph Hearst Collection. A–5141–12.

PLATE 24

Rio Grande blanket, late 1870s, two widths seamed, 2.70 x 1.22 m. Warp: handspun 2-ply light and dark wool; weft: handspun 1-ply wool, natural-undyed light and dark, indigo, and commercial 4-ply synthetic-dyed red wool yarn. Alfred I. Barton Gift, Lowe Art Museum. 60.220.033.

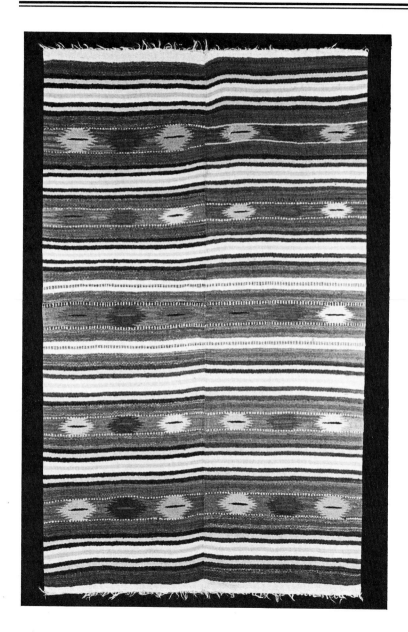

FIGURE 4

Rio Grande blanket, ca. 1890s, two widths seamed, 1.80 x 1.07 m. Warp: 4-ply commercial cotton; weft: handspun 1-ply wool, natural-undyed light and synthetic-dyed red, green, purple, pink, yellow, orange, and light green. School of American Research, Santa Fe. T.440.

green, purple, pink, yellow, orange, and green. Since the colors are largely unfaded, the blanket clearly shows the bright, garish combinations possible with synthetic dyes. The motifs are larger and proportioned differently owing to the Merino wool and cotton string warp.

Another late piece from the San Luis Valley is illustrated in Plate 26. Said to have been woven by Pablo García of Conejos, Colorado, [23] this piece has been dated by E. Boyd as 1885–1915. While still woven with *churro* wool, it contains perhaps eight synthetic dyes (the green and purple may be natural but this has not been proven). The weaver has used carded natural brown, which is more common in Navajo textiles. The design is five double bands of diamond-hourglass motifs.

The serrate diamonds appear throughout the nineteenth and into the twentieth century, although, as time goes on, they are not always well controlled by the weaver.

The "Saltillo leaf"

Another common and beautiful Saltillo motif is the leaf, or *manita* ("little hand"). Here, again, are six nearly identical pieces woven with handspun natural-undyed white and brown and indigo wool, with 2-ply warps and 1-ply wefts.[24] One of these has a small amount of 3-ply commercial unfaded synthetic-dyed (?) red wool yarn,[25] while the piece in Figure 5 appears to have a bit of commercial 3-ply cochineal (?) red wool yarn. These could both be cochineal, but they have not been tested. Again, it is likely that these were done in the same place, if not

FIGURE 5

Rio Grande blanket, probably 1860s, two widths seamed, 2.37 x 1.36 m. Warp: 2-ply handspun white wool; weft: 1-ply handspun wool dyed with indigo, natural-undyed light and dark wool, and 3-ply commercial cochineal red wool yarn, used only in the small rows of diamonds in the center band. Collected in 1910 in Taos, New Mexico. American Museum of Natural History. 65/3316.

by the same weaver, and probably in the 1860s. The piece in Figure 5 was collected in Taos in 1910; the others have no provenience. All feature five white bands of colored leaves separated by zones of narrow colored stripes. In two identical blankets, the center band has serrate diamonds in place of the leaves.[26]

A beautiful indigo and natural blanket showing skillful and effective use of the "Saltillo leaf" is reproduced in Plate 27. The leaves flow regularly across five tapestry bands, which are separated by zones of regular stripes. The design is rhythmically controlled and is an outstanding example of the New Mexican weaver's adaptation of a single Saltillo element to his own materials.

Other late pieces with "Saltillo leaves" show the continuity of the design. Plate 28 illustrates a fine example, with three rows of leaves in each of four zones, separated by zones of narrow stripes. The warp is 2-ply handspun *churro* wool, with 1-ply handspun synthetic-dyed weft.

One of the finest contemporary weavers, Teresa Sagel,[27] has used this traditional "Saltillo leaf" and the five-band design system to produce a masterpiece in natural dyes which she entitled "October Leaves" (Plate 73). The rich yellows, golds, and browns were obtained from *cota (Thelesperma* spp.), a native herb, mordanted variously with alum, chrome, tin, and iron, the pale cream from apple leaves and alum. A soft, lustrous commercial wool yarn has been used (2-ply for warp, 3-ply for weft). To obtain different subtle shades the weaver dyed white, light grey, and darker grey yarns with the natural dyes. Thus an old pattern can still challenge the modern weaver and stimulate the eye of the beholder.

PLATE 25

Rio Grande blanket, *ca. 1870s, two widths seamed, 2.34 x 1.16 m. Warp: 2-ply handspun light wool; weft: handspun* churro *wool, natural-undyed light and dark, light indigo, synthetic-dyed (?) yellow, orange, yellow-orange, blue-red, and dull red. Supposed to have been woven in Conejos, Colorado. Beryl G. and Charles H. Woodard Collection, Colorado Historical Society. E.2018.15.*

PLATE 26

Rio Grande blanket, *1885–1915, two widths seamed, 2.18 x 1.25 m. Warp: handspun 2-ply light and dark* churro *wool; weft: handspun 1-ply* churro *wool, natural-undyed dark and carded brown, synthetic-dyed (?) red, green, yellow, blue, purple, blue-red, pink, and red-orange. Said to have been woven by Pablo Garcia, Conejos, Colorado. Beryl G. and Charles H. Woodard Collection, Colorado Historical Society. E.2018.1.*

PLATE 27

Rio Grande blanket, *pre-1860, two widths seamed, 2.18 x 1.25 m. Warp: 2-ply handspun light and dark wool; weft: 1-ply handspun wool, natural-undyed light and dark and indigo. Museum of New Mexico Collection at the Museum of International Folk Art, Gift of Alfred I. Barton. A.65.67.3.*

Meander line or *Culebra*

The meander line is used in six blankets, four of which contain indigo and natural-undyed brown and white handspun wool.[28] One of these four also includes a 1-ply handspun faded red wool weft as well as 1-ply wool warp, which is atypical.[29] It is woven in one piece, yet has a typical Rio Grande selvedge and no lazy lines, so does not appear to be Indian. It might possibly be Mexican. The meander in each blanket appears in bands which are separated by zones of narrow stripes.

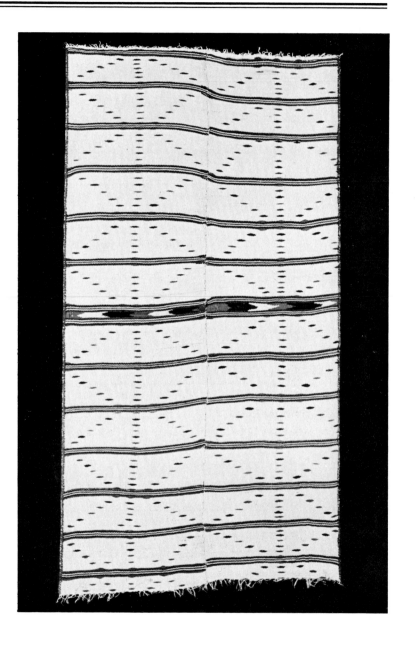

FIGURE 6

Sarape, Oaxaca, Mexico, pre-1860, two widths seamed, 2.77 x 1.35 m. Warp: 1-ply handspun white wool; weft: 1-ply handspun wool with natural-undyed dark and light and dark indigo. American Museum of Natural History. 65/3370.

FIGURE 7

Rio Grande blanket, pre-1860, two widths seamed, 2.14 x 1.09 m. Warp: 2-ply handspun wool; weft: 1-ply handspun churro wool, natural-undyed light and dark, indigo, and cochineal; also, bundled strips of cochineal and cochineal "fuzz" spun with white weft in several places. Museum of New Mexico Collection at the Museum of International Folk Art. A.64.76.1.

A later example of the meander motif is in the Taylor Museum.[30] The design is typical, but the materials include cotton string warp and synthetic red and purple dyes, as well as natural-undyed handspun white, carded grey, and brown wool wefts. Martha Tilley, formerly of the Taylor Museum, has dated this blanket in the 1890s.

Three other natural-dyed blankets exhibit an interlocking meander in bands.[31] One contains small amounts of commercial 3-ply unfaded purple yarn, perhaps a hue of cochineal.[32]

Miscellaneous motifs

Several fine pieces with miscellaneous Saltillo motifs are worthy of mention. The blanket illustrated in Plate 29 has two shades of indigo as well as natural-undyed brown and white handspun wool wefts, with 1-ply Z-spun wool warp. Four bands of stepped diamond-hourglass motifs, separated by striped zones, two wider bands of stepped chevrons, and a central band of blue stepped diamonds and stepped chevrons combine in a handsome, skillfully woven design.

A slightly later piece which contains synthetic orange dye as well as natural-dyed yellow, indigo, and natural-undyed white and brown wool is reproduced in Plate 30. Woven of handspun 2-ply wool warp and 1-ply wool weft, the design consists of five bands of serrate interlocking chevrons and diamonds and leaves separated by wide bands of stripes. This blanket is a beautiful example of the complex designs achieved by the weavers in the late 1860s.

Dots and dashes

A number of blankets contain many extra-weft dots and dashes. They appear to be based on *sarapes* commonly attributed to Oaxaca, such as the example in Figure 6. The dots appear in Saltillo *sarapes* as well, but seem to dominate the Oaxaca pieces. The blanket in Figure 7 is typical of this group: the white field is divided into bands by narrow stripes, and colored dots or dashes have been added in a diamond lattice pattern in the white areas. This is a rare piece in that it contains bundled cochineal strips as well as 1-ply handspun cochineal wool. Other colors are brown and indigo; wool is *churro*.

A particularly fine example owned by the State Historical Society of Colorado was obtained from the Valdez family of San Pablo, Colorado, in the San Luis Valley.[33] Woven with handspun *churro* warp and weft, the colors are limited to natural-undyed white and brown and light indigo. The dots are arranged to form diamonds and chevrons in wide white bands, separated by brown and white bands of beading which form narrow vertical stripes.

Dots and dashes are a dominant form of embellishment in another group of blankets which will be discussed later: the eight known cotton blankets supposed to be from nineteenth-century New Mexican looms. Since these cotton blankets appear to be a product of the Rio Abajo, it is possible that the dot-and-dash embellishment may be typical of this area. Minge has cited documents of 1838–44 which include "*Frazadas de Rio Abajo bordeadas,*" literally translated "embroidered blankets from the Rio Abajo," which may be similar to the one illustrated in Figure 7.[34]

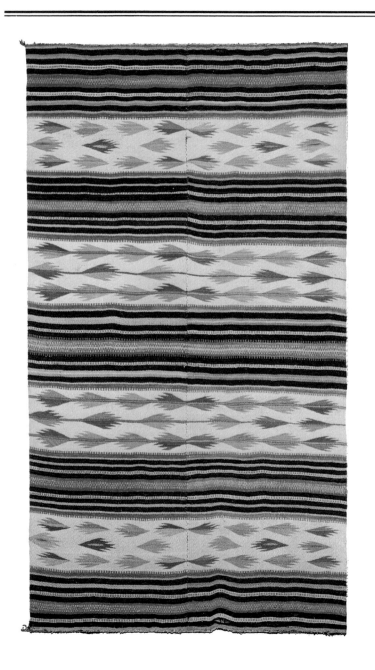

PLATE 28

Rio Grande blanket, ca. 1870, two widths seamed, 2.25 x 1.26 m. Warp: 2-ply handspun light and dark wool; weft: 1-ply handspun churro wool, natural-undyed light and dark, synthetic-dyed orange, purple, yellow, red, and dark blue-grey. Spanish Colonial Arts Society, Inc. Collection on loan to the Museum of New Mexico at the Museum of International Folk Art, Gift of Mr. and Mrs. John Gaw Meem, H. P. Mera Collection. L.5.62.78.

PLATE 29

Rio Grande blanket, pre-1860, two widths seamed, 2.04 x 1.34 m. Warp: 1-ply handspun light wool; weft: 1-ply handspun wool, natural-undyed light and dark, and dark and medium shades of indigo. Los Angeles County Museum of Natural History, William Randolph Hearst Collection. A.5141–19.

PLATE 30

Rio Grande blanket, ca. late 1860s, two widths seamed, 2.27 x 1.33 m. Warp: 2-ply light and dark handspun wool; weft: 1-ply handspun wool, natural-undyed light and dark, natural-dyed indigo and yellow (UCLA D–33–23), and three synthetic-dyed oranges (UCLA D–32–12, 13, 14). Spanish Colonial Arts Society, Inc. Collection on loan to the Museum of New Mexico at the Museum of International Folk Art, Gift of Mr. and Mrs. John Gaw Meem, H. P. Mera Collection. L.5.62.68.

9 SALTILLO DESIGN SYSTEMS
DOROTHY BOYD BOWEN

We come now to the categories of Rio Grande designs which are the most complex, and which often are mistaken for Mexican textiles by the layman. These patterns, for the most part, are based directly on the center-dominant Saltillo plan, which has been discussed by Wheat. Rather than the repetitive horizontal organization of the blankets shown in Plates 18–30, these Rio Grande designs emphasize the central area and often also the four corners of the blanket. The individual design elements are similar to those in Figure 1 of Chapter 8.

"Lightning" pattern

The "lightning" pattern apparently was a standard design used in hundreds of blankets. Four identical examples have appeared in this study,[1] typified by the blanket in Plate 31 which has an allover zigzag

pattern in indigo, brown, and white handspun wool. Plate 32 illustrates a variation in indigo and white; Plate 33 shows another exceptional variation in natural-dyed yellow, green, two tans, and natural-undyed brown and white.

The blanket in Figure 1 is also a synthetic-dyed repetition of the "lightning" pattern done before any trace of Merino wool appears, perhaps in the 1870s. A still later adaptation of the "lightning" design to Merino wool as well as to synthetic dyes is shown in Plate 34. The angles of the design have increased with the different thread count ratio of Merino weft and cotton warps, but the bright colors give an idea of the original appearance of the faded blanket seen in Figure 1.

Basic Saltillo patterns in Rio Grande blankets

Perhaps the largest group of early Rio Grande designs is based directly on the Saltillo *sarape* (Plate 17), with its large serrate concentric

PLATE 31

*Rio Grande blanket, pre-1860, two widths seamed, 2.21
x 1.40 m. Warp: 2-ply handspun light and dark wool;
weft: 1-ply handspun wool, light and dark natural-undyed
and indigo. Spanish Colonial Arts Society, Inc. Collection
on loan to the Museum of New Mexico at the Museum of
International Folk Art, Gift of Mr. and Mrs. John Gaw
Meem, H. P. Mera Collection. L.5.62.97.*

diamond lozenge, its field of vertical zigzag columns, diamond grid, or
serrate diamond columns, and its picture-frame borders which are
embellished with tiny dots or meanders or hourglass motifs. While the
Saltillo *sarape* had countless subtle variations in design, including
central scalloped round medallions instead of the diamonds, it was
basically the center-dominant diamond on an elaborately patterned
field, with decorative side borders and end bands, which impressed
New Mexican weavers. The classic Mexican Saltillo *sarapes* reached
their zenith before the advent of synthetic dyes, and many of the finest
Rio Grande "Saltillo" patterns are done with indigo, "brazil," tiny bits
of cochineal, and natural-undyed dark and light *churro* wool. These
blankets do not show the same wear patterns as the striped blankets, and
many are in excellent condition except that the commercial 3-ply
cochineal yarn seems to disintegrate.

The blanket depicted in Plate 35, because of its high thread count
and unusually subtle colors, more closely resembles Saltillo prototypes,
and is perhaps the finest Rio Grande blanket discussed in this
publication. It has unusually fine handspun 2-ply wool warps and 1-ply
wool wefts dyed with light and dark indigo, natural-dyed yellow, and
golds. Although the intricate pattern has been skillfully handled, the
weaver made several mistakes in the pattern at one end, which were
faithfully duplicated when weaving the matching side. Several inches
are now missing from one end, and perhaps some from the other, but the
borders obviously were limited to the sides rather than extending
completely around the field. Although this exquisite piece was acquired
in Alcalde in 1923, it appears to have been woven by a master craftsman
at some point between 1800 and 1860. Judging from the high technical

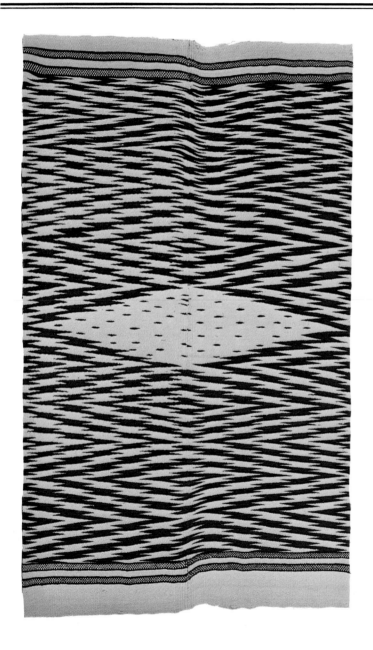 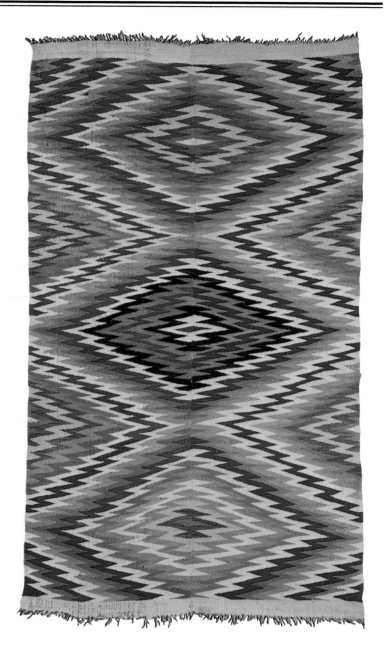

PLATE 32

Rio Grande blanket, pre-1860, two widths seamed, 1.91 x 1.16 m. Warp: 2-ply handspun wool; weft: 1-ply handspun wool, natural-undyed light and dark indigo. Fred Harvey Fine Arts Collection on loan to the Museum of New Mexico at the Museum of International Folk Art. L.71.17.3.

PLATE 33

Rio Grande blanket, pre-1860, two widths seamed, 2.15 x 1.28 m. Warp: 2-ply handspun light and dark wool; weft: 1-ply handspun wool, natural-undyed light and dark and natural-dyed yellow-green, yellow, tan, and red-tan. From the Collections of the University Museum of the University of Pennsylvania. NA 4989.

PLATE 34

Rio Grande blanket, ca. 1880s, two widths seamed, 1.87 x 1.25 m. Warp: 3-ply commercial cotton; weft: 1-ply handspun wool, natural-undyed white, synthetic-dyed red, green, yellow, and purple. From the collection of Al Packard. L.77.87.1.

quality, it could even be related to the Bazán brothers' instruction in 1807–9. Whether this reasoning applies or not, an unusually early date for this piece is indicated. The two blankets which are shown in Plate 36 and Figure 2, while not quite so fine as the blanket seen in Plate 35, seem to have certain motifs in common with it. Both are woven of handspun dark and light *churro* warp and weft dyed with indigo, while the blanket in Figure 2 has small areas of 3-ply cochineal commercial wool yarn. In the piece in Plate 36, next to the side borders, the weaver has used serrate chevrons similar to those found in Plate 35. Also, the organization of the bicolor serrate diamonds on a white field is similar in Plates 35 and 36. The isolation of the central diamond in a separate zone is seen in both Plate 36 and Figure 2, and the side borders in the two textiles are identical. These two blankets could easily have been woven by the same person, perhaps someone familiar with the work of the weaver of the blanket in Plate 35.

FIGURE 1

Rio Grande blanket, ca. 1870s, two widths seamed, 2.20 x 1.46 m. Warp: 2-ply handspun wool; weft: 1-ply handspun wool dyed with synthetic red, orange, and green and light and dark natural-undyed wool. Museum of New Mexico Collection at the Museum of International Folk Art. A.8.56.4.

The fine blanket shown in Plate 37 is a somewhat later example of the direct adaptation of Saltillo *sarape* designs by Rio Grande weavers. The vertical zigzag columns in the background, which are greatly enlarged in comparison with the Saltillo prototype, will be discussed later with the blankets which lack central lozenges.

The handsome *sarape* in Plate 38 is representative of the majority of these elaborate pre-1860 "Rio Grande Saltillos." The natural-undyed handspun brown and white *churro* wool combines with indigo dye and a bit of 3-ply commercial wool yarn (cochineal and a natural-dyed orange) to form a well-controlled complex allover design with a central concentric serrate diamond, serrate zigzag columns over the field, and a curious meander form in the side borders. This same form persists into the late nineteenth century. Another excellent example is shown in Plate 39.

Plate 40 illustrates a fine blanket containing both handspun wool (indigo, natural-undyed light and dark) and 3-ply commercial yarn (synthetic-dyed blue, green, violet, gold, and blue-grey and cochineal dark and light red). The commercial yarn wefts are paired to match the coarseness of the handspun wool. The warp is 2-ply handspun wool. While the design is quite similar to the blanket in Plate 39, the synthetic dyes and an abundance of commercial yarn suggest a slightly later date, perhaps 1870, when cochineal and indigo would still have been available.

The textile in Plate 41 was woven perhaps two decades later, ca. 1890–1900, yet the pattern, though simplified in the border areas, is basically the same as in the early indigo pieces. Here commercial cotton

FIGURE 2

Rio Grande blanket, pre-1860, two widths seamed, 2.09 x 1.10 m. Warp: 2-ply handspun white wool; weft: 1-ply handspun wool dyed with indigo and natural-undyed light and dark wool, and 3-ply commercial cochineal red wool yarn used sparingly. American Museum of Natural History. 65/3318.

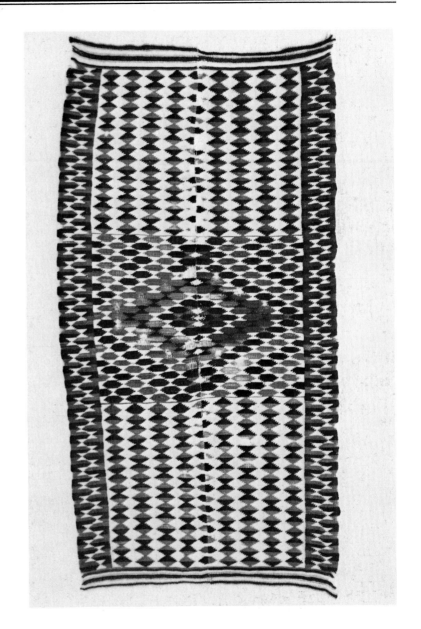

string warps (10/2.5 cm.) and all synthetic-dyed commercial wool weft (32/2.5 cm.) combine to produce a lightweight blanket which was the immediate forerunner of the twentieth-century Chimayó textiles produced for the tourist and curio market.

An interesting late piece, collected in 1897 and supposedly woven in Chimayó by either the Martínez or Vigil family, is shown in Plate 42. Woven entirely of 4-ply synthetic-dyed commercial wool yarn wefts with cotton string warps, this blanket appears to be a direct link between the complex old Rio Grande patterns and the simplified designs of the twentieth-century Chimayó textiles. Since the colors are still largely unfaded, this is representative of the color sense of the weavers of this period.

Basic Saltillo without central lozenge

One common variation on the Saltillo pattern is illustrated by Plate 43. Here the borders, end bands, and serrate zigzag columns are similar to blanket designs in the previous group, but the central concentric diamond is missing. Woven entirely of handspun natural-undyed white and brown and indigo wool wefts and 2-ply handspun brown wool warp, this piece is nearly identical in design and materials to two blankets at the Los Angeles County Museum.[2]

Two other blankets are nearly identical to these pieces except that they lack side borders.[3] The colors are limited to indigo, white, and brown.

PLATE 35

Rio Grande blanket, ca. 1800–1830, two widths seamed,
1.98 x 1.29 m. Warp: 2-ply handspun churro wool; weft:
1-ply handspun churro wool, natural-undyed light,
natural-dyed pale yellow, gold, and light and dark
indigo. Spanish Colonial Arts Society, Inc. Collection on
loan to the Museum of New Mexico at the Museum of
International Folk Art, Gift of Mrs. Laura Hersloff.
L.5.63.4.

PLATE 36

Rio Grande blanket, ca. 1830, two widths seamed, 2.22
x 1.16 m. Warp: 2-ply light and dark handspun wool;
weft: 1-ply handspun wool, natural-undyed light and dark
and indigo. Museum of New Mexico Collection at the
Museum of International Folk Art, Gift of Alfred I.
Barton. A.65.67.2.

PLATE 37

Rio Grande blanket, pre-1860, two widths seamed, 1.95
x 1.09 m. Warp: 2-ply handspun wool; weft: 1-ply
handspun wool, natural-undyed light and dark and
indigo, and commercial 3-ply wool yarn, cochineal.
International Folk Art Foundation Collection at the
Museum of International Folk Art, a unit of the Museum
of New Mexico. FA.67.16.1.

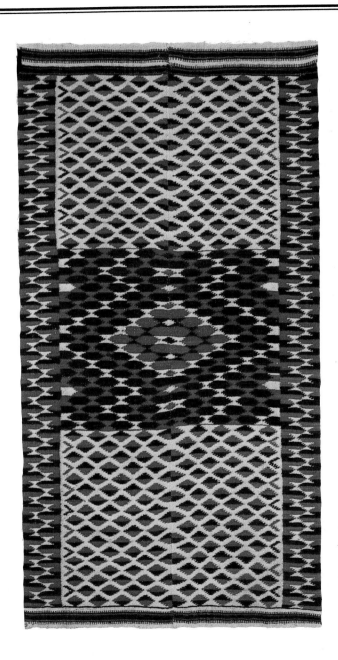

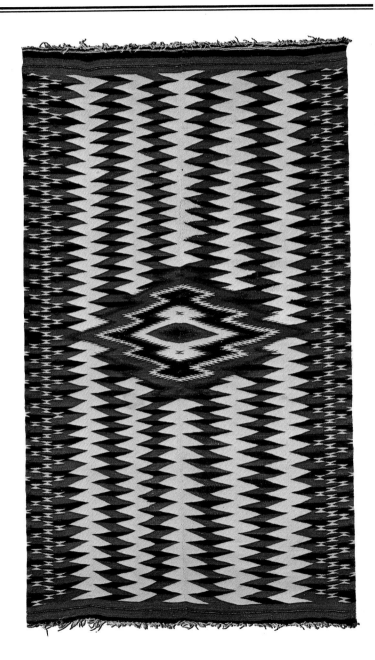

PLATE 38

Rio Grande blanket, *ca. 1830–60, two widths seamed, 2.15 x 1.24 m. Warp: 2-ply handspun white wool; weft: 1-ply handspun wool, natural-undyed light and dark and indigo, and 3-ply commercial wool yarn, cochineal and natural-dyed yellow (UCLA D–32–15, 16), and natural-dyed pale orange. Spanish Colonial Arts Society, Inc. Collection on loan to the Museum of New Mexico at the Museum of International Folk Art, Gift of Mr. and Mrs. John Gaw Meem, H. P. Mera Collection. L.5.62.85.*

PLATE 39

Rio Grande blanket, *pre-1860, two widths seamed, 2.20 x 1.21 m. Warp: 2-ply handspun white wool; weft: 1-ply handspun wool, natural-undyed light and dark, and indigo, and paired 3-ply commercial wool yarn, cochineal. Los Angeles County Museum of Natural History, William Randolph Hearst Collection. A–5141–212.*

PLATE 40

Rio Grande blanket, *ca. 1870, two widths seamed, 2.34 x 1.22 m. Warp: 2-ply handspun white wool; weft: 1-ply handspun wool, natural-undyed light and dark and indigo, and 3-ply commercial wool yarn, synthetic-dyed blue, green, violet, gold, and blue-grey, and dark and medium cochineal (UCLA D–34–54, D–34–55). Spanish Colonial Arts Society, Inc. Collection on loan to the Museum of New Mexico at the Museum of International Folk Art, Gift of Mr. and Mrs. John Gaw Meem, H. P. Mera Collection. L.5.62.84.*

PLATE 41

Rio Grande blanket, ca. 1890–1900, two widths seamed,
2.19 x 1.09 m. Warp: 4-ply commercial cotton; weft:
4-ply commercial wool yarn, white and synthetic-dyed
red, yellow, purple, green, and black. Museum of New
Mexico Collection at the Museum of International Folk
Art, Gift of Mrs. Hatton L. Clark. A.60.21.3.

PLATE 42

Rio Grande blanket, obtained 1897, two widths seamed,
1.76 x .95 m. Warp: 4-ply commercial cotton; weft: 4-ply
commercial wool yarn, white, synthetic-dyed red, black,
yellow, green, purple, blue, pink, and dark red.
Supposed to have been woven by the Vigil or Martínez
family, Chimayó. Collections of the School of American
Research in the Museum of New Mexico. 45314/12.

PLATE 43

Rio Grande blanket, pre-1860, two widths seamed, 2.60
x 1.36 m. Warp: 2-ply handspun brown wool; weft: 1-ply
handspun wool, natural-undyed light and dark and
indigo. Alfred I. Barton Gift, Lowe Art Museum.
65.050.127.

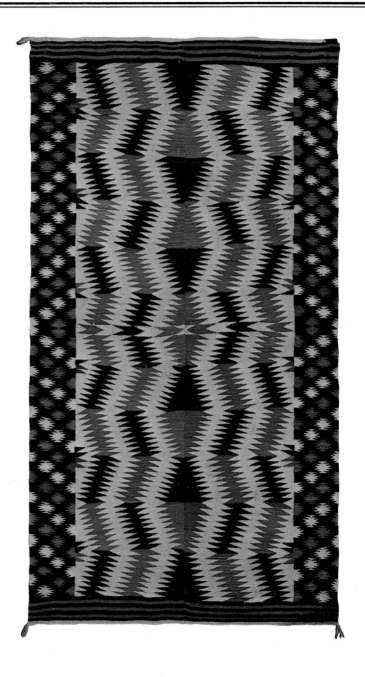

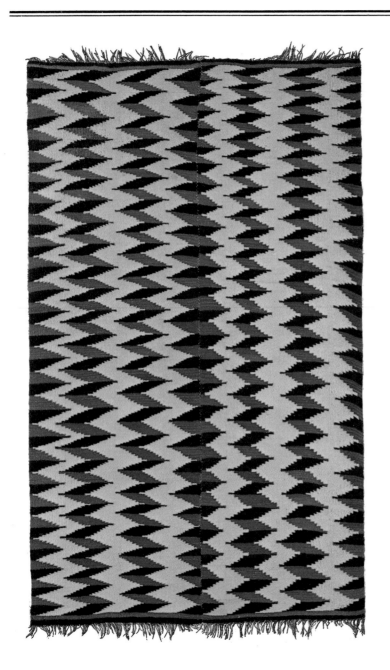

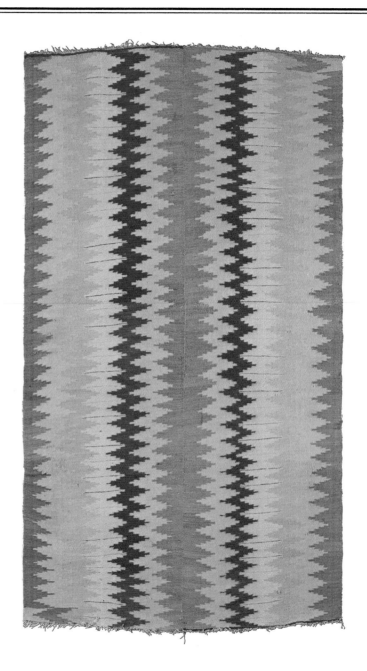

PLATE 44

Rio Grande blanket, ca. 1860s, two widths seamed, 2.07
x 1.23 m. Warp: 2-ply light and dark handspun wool;
weft: 1-ply handspun wool, natural-undyed light and dark
and indigo. Spanish Colonial Arts Society, Inc. Collection
on loan to the Museum of New Mexico at the Museum of
International Folk Art. L.5.70.6.

PLATE 45

Rio Grande blanket, 1890s, two widths seamed, 2.13 x
1.17 m. Warp: 2-ply handspun light wool; weft: 1-ply
handspun wool, natural-undyed white and synthetic-dyed
brown, yellow, red, green, pink, and blue. Taylor
Museum, Colorado Springs Fine Arts Center. 5074.

Plate 44 depicts another less complex example woven entirely of handspun wool. The natural-undyed white and brown and indigo zigzag columns vary in width and the design is not so well controlled as in the former pieces. This overall zigzag design is directly related to the background of the textile in Plate 37.

The blanket in Plate 45, perhaps woven in the 1890s, shows the continuity of the zigzag column design into the 1890s. Woven with handspun synthetic-dyed wool, the pattern really has been reduced to the Saltillo background, without central diamond and borders. This is a system picked up by Navajo weavers, who tended to make the zigzag columns less regular and balanced.[4]

Central diamond with corner slashes

A standard Rio Grande design system which is derived originally from Mexico features a strong central diamond with quarter diamonds in each corner of the blanket, with end bands. This was common in natural-dyed pieces such as those in Plates 46 and 47. Both are done in handspun *churro* wool with indigo and natural wool. The latter is atypical in that it contains no natural white wool and has an unusually

high warp count (10 to 11/2.5 cm. as opposed to 6 to 7/2.5 cm.). The division of this blanket into wide bands is similar to designs found in Oaxacan *sarapes.* Corner slashes have been omitted from the design.

A slightly later piece woven in Los Pinos, Colorado, with both indigo and synthetic-dyed red and pink, is shown in Figure 3. Here the central diamond is an approximation of the Saltillo *sarape* center, and the white field is covered with rows of serrate diamonds and dashes. The corners echo the central lozenge. It is a beautiful transitional piece, perhaps woven between 1865 and 1875.

Figure 4 illustrates a later piece with all synthetic dyes and handspun wool warp and weft. Here the central diamond is in a separate zone, similar to Oaxaca patterns, while the corner slashes are elaborately serrated.

Three late pieces based on this design are nearly identical.[5] All have handspun wool warp and weft dyed with synthetic dyes and backgrounds of strong horizontal stripes. One of the blankets was acquired from the Velarde family of Farisita, which is twenty miles west of Walsenburg, Colorado.[6] This suggests that the other two were also from Farisita, and probably from the same loom. The blanket shown in Figure 5 features a complex stepped central lozenge; the corner patterns echo the stepped diagonals of the center. The greasy Merino wool seems to have taken the dye unevenly, but it is tempting to speculate that the weaver intended this in the diagonal areas.

Central concentric diamond

Another popular Rio Grande design is based on the Mexican Saltillo central concentric diamond, but instead of having a vertical or grid field as do most Saltillo *sarapes,* here the center diamond has been echoed by diagonals (often serrate or composed of Saltillo motifs) over the entire field. The first group of these blankets has end bands but no side borders. Most contain synthetic dyes, many have cotton warps, and all have 1-ply handspun Merino wool wefts. A typical blanket is shown in Plate 48, with 2-ply handspun wool warp and 1-ply handspun wool weft in natural-undyed white and synthetic red, orange, turquoise, and purple dyes. Woven in two widths in a complex serrate concentric diamond pattern, it would surely have been dazzling in an unfaded state.

PLATE 46

*Rio Grande blanket, pre-1860, two widths seamed, 2.6 x
1.19 m. Warp: 2-ply light and dark handspun wool; weft:
1-ply handspun wool, natural-undyed light and dark and
indigo. Spanish Colonial Arts Society, Inc. Collection on
loan to the Museum of New Mexico at the Museum of
International Folk Art, Gift of Mr. and Mrs. John Gaw
Meem, H. P. Mera Collection. L.5.62.73.*

PLATE 47

*Rio Grande blanket, pre-1860, two widths seamed, 2.19
x 1.26 m. Warp: 2-ply handspun wool; weft: 1-ply
handspun wool, natural-undyed brown and indigo.
Collection of Mr. and Mrs. Larry Frank. L.77.105.1.*

PLATE 48

*Rio Grande blanket, 1875–85, two widths seamed, 2.20
x 1.35 m. Warp: 2-ply handspun wool; weft: 1-ply
handspun wool, natural-undyed white, synthetic-dyed red,
orange, turquoise, and purple. Museum of New Mexico
Collection at the Museum of International Folk Art, Gift
of Clay Lockett. A.66.41.1.*

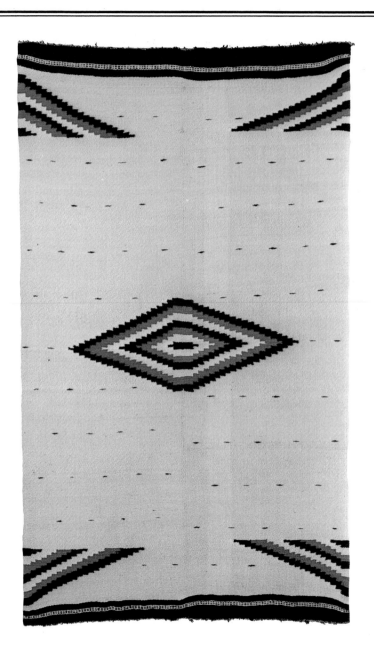

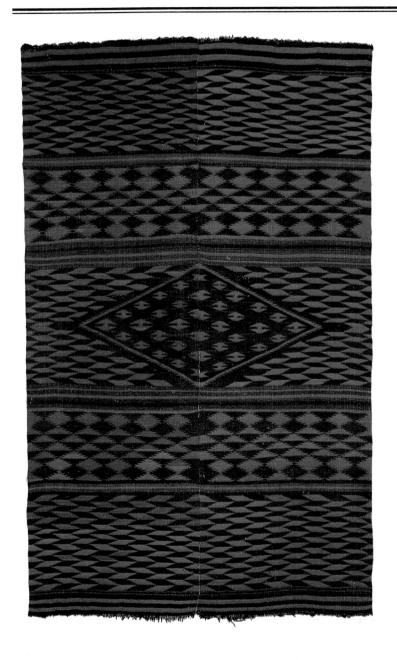
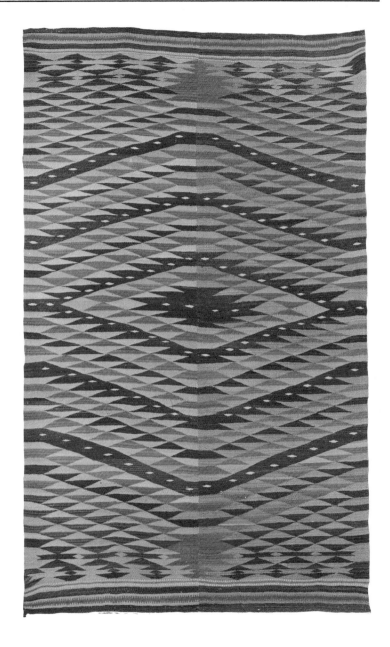

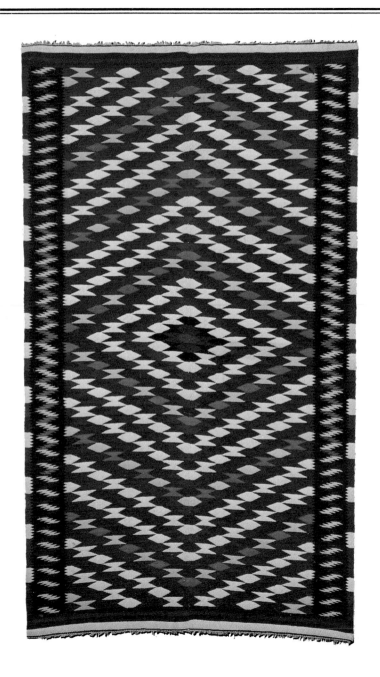

PLATE 49

*Rio Grande blanket, ca. 1880s, two widths seamed, 2.06
x 1.17 m. Warp: 4-ply commercial cotton; weft: 1-ply
handspun wool, natural-undyed light, and 4-ply
commercial wool yarn, synthetic-dyed dark red, red,
orange-red, purple, green, and yellow. School of
American Research, Santa Fe. T.438.*

PLATE 50

*Rio Grande blanket, 1880s–1890s, two widths seamed,
2.20 x 1.31 m. Warp: 2-ply handspun light wool; weft:
1-ply handspun wool, natural-undyed light, synthetic-dyed
red, purple, yellow, green, orange, and pink. Museum of
New Mexico Collection at the Museum of International
Folk Art, Gift of the Historical Society of New Mexico.
A.5.56.40.*

A smaller blanket in this design group, which appears to be a copy
of an older natural-dyed one, is illustrated in Figure 6. Perhaps intended
for a child, it is woven of lumpy handspun wool warp and weft, with
natural-undyed light and dark and a blue which seems to be synthetic.
Another small blanket in similar colors and materials is in the
collections of the School of American Research.[7]

The addition of side borders to the concentric diamond field design
is found in a large group of Rio Grande blankets, many of which are
done with both cotton string warp and commercial wool yarn weft.
Since this combination allows for a finer thread count and more intricate
detail, many of these blankets are quite complex and expertly woven.
The greater expense of commercial materials over the local handspun
wool could have restricted it to use by a skilled craftsman producing
primarily for sale rather than by a housewife weaving to keep her family
warm. An excellent example of the former is illustrated in Plate 49, in
which the colors of the commercial yarn remain vibrant and the close set
of the cotton warp allows for tiny, detailed work.

A second fine specimen produced with handspun 2-ply wool warp
and 1-ply wool weft with synthetic dyes is shown in Plate 50. The
diagonals here are formed with hourglass motifs and the side borders

with colored chevrons arranged in a zigzag pattern. Two diagonal bands
are striped horizontally, a common decorative device of the 1880s and
1890s which might be related to the American flag design. Here,
although the individual motifs may be derived ultimately from Saltillo,

over ▷

FIGURE 3

*Rio Grande blanket, ca. 1865–75, two widths seamed,
2.10 x 1.15 m. Warp: 2-ply handspun light and dark
wool; weft: 1-ply handspun wool, natural-undyed light
and dark, indigo, and synthetic-dyed pink and red.
Supposed to have been woven in Los Pinos, Colorado.
Beryl G. and Charles H. Woodard Collection, Colorado
Historical Society. E.2018.10.*

FIGURE 4

*Rio Grande blanket, 1880s–90s, two widths seamed,
2.13 x 1.07 m. Warp: 2-ply handspun wool; weft: 1-ply
handspun wool, natural-undyed white, synthetic-dyed red,
yellow, pink, green, purple, and blue-green. Taylor
Museum, Colorado Springs Fine Arts Center, Gift of
Alice Bemis Taylor. 2279.*

FIGURE 5

*Rio Grande blanket, perhaps 1880–95, probably woven
in Farisita, Colorado, two widths seamed, 2.20 x 1.29 m.
Warp: 2-ply handspun wool; weft: 1-ply handspun wool
dyed with synthetic red, orange, yellow, green,
blue-green, and greyed purple. Spanish Colonial Arts
Society, Inc. Collection on loan to the Museum of New
Mexico at the Museum of International Folk Art, Gift of
Mr. and Mrs. John Gaw Meem, H. P. Mera Collection.
L.5.62.89.*

FIGURE 6

*Rio Grande blanket, date unknown, one width, 1.08 x
.69 m. Warp: 2-ply handspun wool; weft: 1-ply handspun
wool, natural-undyed light and dark, probably synthetic
blue dye. School of American Research, Santa Fe. T.319.*

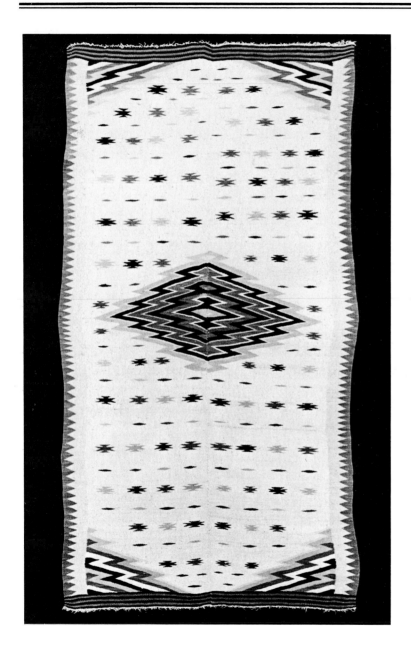

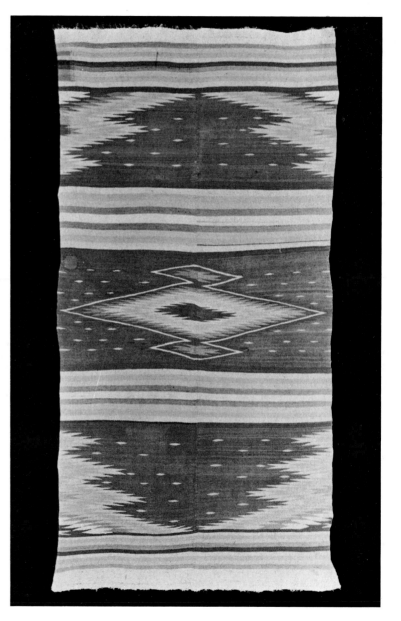

PLATE 51

Rio Grande blanket, *ca. 1865–70, two widths seamed,
2.25 x 1.16 m. Warp: 2-ply handspun light wool; weft:
1-ply handspun wool, natural-undyed light, indigo (UCLA
D–33–39), and carded pink (probably cochineal and
white carded together), and commercial 3-ply wool yarn,
two shades of cochineal (UCLA D–33–34, 35) and
synthetic-dyed purple, blue-green, and pink. (UCLA
D–33–33). Spanish Colonial Arts Society, Inc. Collection
on loan to the Museum of New Mexico at the Museum of
International Folk Art, Gift of Mr. and Mrs. John Gaw
Meem, H. P. Mera Collection. L.5.62.83.*

PLATE 52

Rio Grande blanket, *1880–1900, two widths seamed,
2.04 x 1.36 m. Warp: 2-ply handspun wool; weft: 1-ply
handspun wool, natural-undyed light and dark,
synthetic-dyed red, dark red, orange, and turquoise.
Spanish Colonial Arts Society, Inc. Collection on loan to
the Museum of New Mexico at the Museum of
International Folk Art, Gift of Mr. and Mrs. John Gaw
Meem, H. P. Mera Collection. L.5.62.79.*

PLATE 53

Rio Grande blanket, *ca. 1875, one width, 1.50 x .56 m.
Warp: 2-ply handspun light and dark wool; weft: 1-ply
handspun wool, natural-undyed light and dark,
natural-dyed yellow, indigo, grey, light yellow-red, and
two shades of red-brown identified as a madder-like plant
(UCLA D–32–3, D–32–4). Woven in Abiquiu, New
Mexico, by a Navajo servant for a child's bed. Museum
of New Mexico Collection at the Museum of International
Folk Art, Gift of the Historical Society of New Mexico.
A.5.57.10.*

FIGURE 7

Rio Grande blanket, ca. 1890s, two widths seamed, 1.92 x 1.26 m. Warp: 2-ply handspun wool; weft: 1-ply handspun wool, Merino, natural-undyed light and dark and synthetic-dyed red and blue-green. Collections of the School of American Research in the Museum of New Mexico. 45320/12.

they have become integrated to form a regional style which has been attributed by E. Boyd and others to Peñasco, in northern New Mexico.

Three other blankets bear mention because of their similarity to each other. All are done with handspun faded synthetic-dyed wool weft; the first two have handspun wool warp (Figure 7),[8] while the last has cotton string warp.[9] In each one the central diamond is complex and extends well into the side borders, which contain serrate zigzag columns. The three blankets could well be products from the same weaver, who probably worked in the 1890s in northern New Mexico.

Miscellaneous diamond designs

A number of Rio Grande designs are based on the diamond but do not fit into any of the previous design categories. An outstanding blanket of this type is Plate 51, with a complex, well-woven center-dominant design which is largely unfaded. The white wefts, carded pink wefts, and dark blue-green indigo over yellow wefts are handspun wool, while the purples and turquoise are 3-ply commercial wool with early synthetic dyes. Two 3-ply reds have been identified by Saltzman as 3-ply commercial yarn with cochineal dye, which most likely places this blanket in the 1860s. The use of carded pink (probably cochineal red and white) is unusual in Spanish weaving, though it is common in Navajo textiles. The design is unusually detailed and includes a thin white horizontal pin striping which is not typical of early Rio Grande designs but appears later in twentieth-century work.

The second example of diamond designs, shown in Plate 52, has handspun wool warp and weft and synthetic dyes. The design consists of large stepped zigzag columns which meet to form stepped diamond columns. While still complex compared with twentieth-century pieces produced for the tourist trade, the design is certainly more simple than the one discussed above.

A servant blanket

Plate 53 illustrates the only Rio Grande textile which has been proven by Max Saltzman to contain a madder-like dye (not *Rubia tinctorium,* but related to it). Natural-undyed dark brown and white and natural-dyed yellow, grey, indigo, yellow-gold, and dark and medium red-brown ("madder") combine to form a stepped design with a center diamond and corner quarter-diamonds. The overall feel of the pattern is Navajo, but the loom and warp are Spanish.

This is one of only three documented servant blankets. According to Jaramillo family tradition it was woven by a family servant for the bed of a small boy, Venceslao Jaramillo.[10] Born about 1873, Venceslao was raised by his grandmother, Doña Manuelita Lucero Gallegos of Abiquiu, until he was enrolled in boarding school at age seven. His nurse was described by his family as a "big, fat Navajo maid" named Juliana.[11] Juliana, who is listed in the 1860 United States Census in the household of Don Pablo and Manuela Gallegos of Abiquiu, would have been born about 1840.[12] The blanket, then, was probably woven about 1875 by Juliana. This clear example of cross-cultural influence illustrates Wheat's description of Navajo design elements (the stepped terraces) appearing in a blanket which is technically Spanish in materials and construction.[13] Furthermore, the stepped terrace central diamond and corner quarter diamonds woven with natural-dyed handspun wool are found in at least four other blankets in this study. They may also be assumed, therefore, to come from the Abiquiu area.[14] The Abiquiu settlers, as Stoller so capably points out, had long preferred Navajo servants for work with wool.[15] This blanket is a beautiful example, then, of the result of the servant/master relationship.

NORA FISHER

Brilliantly colored, flamboyant, and characterized by eight-pointed stars, the *Vallero* blanket has been described as "the last fling of native weaving."[1]

The *Vallero*-style Rio Grande blanket derives its name from the small village of El Valle in the canyon east of Trampas. There in that village, "local residents tell of a crippled girl named Patricia Montoya, for whom her family made a loom with hand pedals instead of foot pedals. She is known to have woven during the 1890s, and is credited with the introduction of the eight-pointed star as a motif. In point of fact, these had appeared many years earlier when indigo and cochineal dyes were still in use."[2]

Indeed, as *Valleros* exist in large numbers, one woman could not have woven all of them. Furthermore, a number of these textiles contain 3-ply yarns which would date them about 1865–70, and dye analysis has verified that some of the blankets utilize cochineal-dyed weft, which confirms the date indicated by the yarns (Plates 54 and 55).[3]

The fifty *Valleros* studied in conjunction with this project have many traits in common. Almost all were woven in two widths seamed at the center; all except one exhibit strong vertical emphasis in the side borders; all are colorful; all contain eight-pointed stars. Approximately half of the pieces studied have handspun warps and wefts, while the other half contain a variety of commercially prepared yarns. There are a number of *Vallero* types, by far the most popular of which is the five-star, with a star in each corner and one at the center (Plate 57). Among the five-star pieces there is a wide range of blankets containing both hand and commercially prepared yarns, and some seven distinct design varieties. All of the five-star *Valleros* utilize synthetic dyes exclusively, however, and appear to be relatively late in date, post-1880, with one textile inscribed *1904*. Among them there is one blanket which appears to have been purchased from Patricia Montoya's

PLATE 54

Rio Grande blanket, *1865–70, two widths seamed, 2.30 x 1.16 m. Warp: 2-ply handspun wool; weft:1-ply handspun wool, natural-undyed light and dark, indigo and 3-ply commercial wool, red (cochineal, UCLA D–32–7), synthetic-dyed red-orange (UCLA D–32–6), synthetic-dyed purple (UCLA D–32–1). International Folk Art Foundation Collection at the Museum of International Folk Art, a unit of the Museum of New Mexico. FA.67.43.3.*

family and may, indeed, have been woven by her (Figure 1). As is typical of a number of the five-star examples, the stars in this piece are encased in octagonal frames, there is strong vertical emphasis at all four sides, and the Saltillo-style diamond is almost obscured by the large central star. The textile, typically synthetic-dyed, is completely composed of late commercially prepared yarns, 4-ply cotton warps, and wool wefts which cannot predate 1875.

One could analyze *Vallero* blankets according to the placement of stars in the composition, but no coherent groups surface. As H. P. Mera suggested, it makes more sense to categorize the *Valleros* according to the nature of the materials used: commercial 3- or 4-ply wefts, single handspun wefts, and handspun versus commercial warps.[4] When one does this, the blankets containing the earlier 3-ply wool wefts stand out, carefully composed and brilliantly colored (Plates 54, 55, 56). Viewing these pieces, one can understand how spectacular they were to those who saw them for the first time. The power of these finely woven textiles certainly explains the ensuing popularity of the *Vallero* style.

In certain ways these three early *Vallero* blankets show quite close affinity to the Saltillo-style Rio Grandes. Except for the presence of stars, the textile illustrated in Plate 56 is a Saltillo-style blanket, similar to pieces such as those illustrated in Plates 49 and 51. The textile shown in Plate 54, with its corner diamonds and strong zigzag side borders, and the blanket in Plate 55, with its background of Saltillo-style flowers, are similar to the Rio Grandes illustrated in Plates 28, 35, 44, and especially 51.

FIGURE 1

Rio Grande Vallero *blanket, ca. 1890–95, two widths seamed, 2.08 x 1.28 m. Warp: 4-ply commercial cotton; weft: 1-ply handspun wool, synthetic-dyed green, orange, and blue, and 4-ply commercial wool, synthetic-dyed red, light and dark pink, green, yellow, blue-green, and tan. Apparently purchased from the family of Patricia Montoya of El Valle. Museum of New Mexico Collection at the Museum of International Folk Art. A.8.56.3.*

Furthermore, as has been noted, natural dyes are present in these early *Vallero* blankets. The textile in Plate 54 illustrates the concurrent use of the natural and early synthetic dyes. Here, though attention is focused on the central star framed by a diamond, there is a myriad of stars in the field, twenty-eight to be exact, with eight half-stars at the sides. The warps are 2-ply handspun wool, the weft is both handspun and early (ca. 1865) 3-ply commercial yarn. The piece contains a cochineal-dyed red wool weft, as well as unidentified synthetic-dyed red-orange and purple. Considering the presence of the 3-ply yarns and cochineal, the piece, which is extremely fine, professionally executed, with an unusually high warp and weft count and two exactly matched halves, can be positively dated 1865–70.

How did the star come to be a characteristic motif of this large group of Rio Grande blankets? H. P. Mera noted: "In connection with the eight-pointed *Vallero* star, it may be of interest to know that a study of the subject has not yet disclosed a satisfactory origin for this figure nor has it been found, as far as known, on any other Southwestern or Mexican textile dating from a time prior to its appearance [on] the *Vallero* type."[5] Yet, with the thriving Santa Fe Trail trade, and the presence of all manner of imported textiles, it makes sense to look toward eastern North America for design sources.

The eight-pointed star, a simple symmetrical geometric motif, has known popularity in a number of cultures throughout history.[6] During the nineteenth century in the eastern United States, it was extremely popular in a number of textile forms. Joe Wheat has noted, "These look suspiciously like American quilt patterns brought in by the American settlers,"[7] and they also recall the Jacquard-woven coverlet patterns and the American flag. In quilt patterns well over one hundred star forms have been separately defined and described, and stars "far outnumber all other designs."[8] The *Vallero* star, composed of diamonds in alternate contrasting colors, is identical to the simplest of the quilting stars, "an eight-pointed star known as the *Star of LeMoyne*" (Figure 2).[9] The eight-pointed star also appears with some frequency in the Jacquard-woven coverlets of the American Midwest and eastern seaboard.[10] Though the *Vallero* star is usually the two-color LeMoyne star, there are a few exceptions, the most notable of which is illustrated by the central star in Plate 54. This star, divided by an X-shaped form, had to have been inspired by the Jacquard-woven coverlets, a motif of which is illustrated in Figure 3. During the decades following the acceptance of New Mexico as a territory of the United States in 1848, many New Mexican-made objects reflected the American flag. Abstract versions of the flag were painted on Pueblo Indian pots. A Navajo blanket depicting the American flag was photographed in 1873 while it was being woven.[11] Certainly, the *Vallero* star is eight-pointed while the star of the flag is five-pointed, yet coverlets based on an American

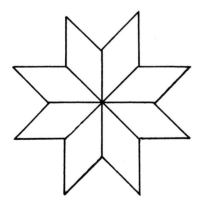

FIGURE 2

The LeMoyne star, *simplest and most popular of the American quilt stars. Adapted from Carrie Hall and Rose G. Kretsinger,* The Romance of the Patchwork Quilt in America, *p. 54. Drawn by Nora Pickens.*

over ▷

PLATE 55

Rio Grande blanket, 1865–70, two widths seamed, 2.19 x 1.23 m. Warp: 2-ply handspun wool; weft: 1-ply handspun wool, natural-undyed light and dark, and 3-ply commercial wool, red (cochineal, UCLA D–34–56), light-blue, brown, blue-grey; 4-ply commercial wool, blue-red, bright blue, purple. Spanish Colonial Arts Society, Inc. Collection on loan to the Museum of New Mexico at the Museum of International Folk Art, Gift of Mr. and Mrs. John Gaw Meem, H. P. Mera Collection. L.5.62.98.

PLATE 56

Rio Grande blanket, ca. 1870, two widths seamed, 2.19 x 1.24 m. Warp: 2-ply handspun wool; weft: 1-ply handspun wool, natural-undyed light, 3-ply commercial wool, red and brown-red (synthetic-dyed, UCLA D–34–58, D–34–59), dark blue, orange, green, and 4-ply commercial wool, light blue, yellow, purple. Fred Harvey Fine Arts Collection on loan to the Museum of New Mexico at the Museum of International Folk Art. L.70.3.39.

PLATE 57

Rio Grande blanket, ca. 1880, two widths seamed, 2.26 x 1.20 m. Warp: 2-ply handspun wool; weft: 1-ply handspun wool, natural-undyed dark; red, pink, orange, purple, green, synthetic-dyed. Taylor Museum, Colorado Springs Fine Arts Center, Gift of Alice Bemis Taylor. 5087.

PLATE 58

Rio Grande blanket, ca. 1900, one width, 1.85 x 1.22 m. Warp: 2-ply handspun wool; weft: 1-ply handspun coarse wool, natural-undyed light and dark, synthetic-dyed red and yellow. Museum of New Mexico Collection at the Museum of International Folk Art. A.71.20.1.

patriotic theme used the symmetrical eight-pointed rather than the five-pointed star.[12] The eight-pointed star, as an American symbol, also appears in quilt patterns.[13] The asymmetrical five-pointed star is a difficult geometric form to cut, even more difficult to weave as a pattern. The symmetrical eight-pointed star is, on the other hand, easy to create either with scissors or on the loom. The textile illustrated in Plate 56, with its stars, red and white stripes, and overall red-white-and-blue color scheme, reflects the American flag.

Not only are the textiles illustrated in Plates 54 and 55 early, as evidenced by the presence of cochineal dye, early 3-ply yarns, and Saltillo-style motifs, but also certain details of Plates 54 and 55 might perhaps indicate that these pieces were prototypes of the *Vallero* style. Plate 54 incorporates an atypical central star, as well as a profusion of stars in the field—possibly an indication of the weaver's enthusiasm for a new motif. Plate 55 illustrates a tiny Saltillo-style diamond surrounded by stars which are uneven in proportion and awkwardly drawn. It is as if the weaver were reluctant to banish the Saltillo-style, and also unable to easily construct symmetrical stars in tapestry weave. The piece shown in Plate 56 seems to be slightly later in date. It contains no cochineal and illustrates a complete Saltillo-style blanket, with only two carefully constructed stars.

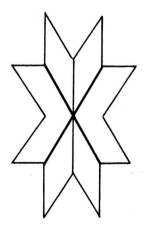

FIGURE 3

Star from a woven coverlet. Adapted from Carleton L. Safford and Robert Bishop, America's Quilts and Coverlets, *Plate 386. Drawn by Nora Pickens.*

FIGURE 4

"Tree of Life" pictorial weaving. John R. Trujillo, Chimayó, ca. 1960, one width, 1.84 x .87 m. Warp: 2-ply commercial wool; weft: 4-ply commercial wool, synthetic-dyed blue, black, tan, red, and grey and undyed white. From the collection of Dr. and Mrs. Zigmund W. Kosicki, Santa Fe.

FIGURE 5

Vallero-*style blanket, John R. Trujillo, Chimayó, 1977, one width, 2.11 x 1.36 m. Warp: 2-ply commercial wool; weft: 4-ply commercial wool, undyed white and synthetic-dyed orange, grey, gold, black, brown, red-brown, and grey-blue. From a private collection, Santa Fe.*

The *Vallero* form, with its many variants, spread and gained great popularity. Some of the later pieces, stylized and laid out in a grid, are strongly reminiscent of seamed quilt squares.

As evidenced by the blanket in Plate 58, some *Vallero* textiles are pictorials. The design is simple, with four eight-point stars and a yellow horse in the center of the brown field. The Spanish Colonial Arts Society owns another pictorial acquired near Taos, probably woven by the same person, which depicts a yellow elk.[14] This was woven on a wide loom in one piece, perhaps around 1900. Pictorials have been woven in occasional Mexican Saltillo *sarapes* and Navajo blankets at least since the first half of the nineteenth century, and it is curious that more Rio Grande Spanish weavers did not attempt it. Presumably, the weaver of these two Rio Grande pictorials would have been familiar with the Navajo "cow blankets" of the 1880s and 1890s, although the early Navajo animals are usually more geometric than those seen in Spanish textiles.

Mena describes several pictorial *sarapes* woven at San Miguel de Allende in Old Mexico. One, woven in 1877 by Ezequiel Garcia for Pope Pius IX and supposed to be now in the Vatican, depicted a physical likeness of the Pope in the center with the pontifical arms at the corners. Other San Miguel *sarapes* mentioned by Mena depicted a tiger *(tigre)*, landscapes, emblems, and other portraits. A factory in Guadalupe (state of Zacatecas), produced such pictorial designs as George Washington and the American flag and a portrait of General Calles, President of the Mexican Republic. Mena reported that such designs were woven in by free hand, copied from a pattern placed beneath the warp.[15] Several nineteenth-century Mexican pictorial *sarapes* were located in museums in the course of this study.

We have no early natural-dyed examples of Rio Grande pictorials, but the twentieth century has seen some very fine Spanish pictorial weaving, as represented not only by Plate 58, but also by the work of John Trujillo (Figure 4). The *Vallero*-style blanket, not as popular today as the pictorial, "largely died out about 1900" with the advent of the "Spanish-American and Pan-Indian" style of the Chimayó blanket.[16] Yet, as illustrated by another Trujillo blanket (Figure 5), it is still being woven today. Indeed, it is one of the few traditional forms of the Rio Grande blanket to have been retained by the commercial-scale Chimayó-style Spanish weavers. For this reason, the *Vallero* style might be considered transitional between the earlier Rio Grande style and the twentieth-century Chimayó style.

11 WEFT IKAT BLANKETS
NORA FISHER

Λ/\/\/\/\ Among some 2,000 Southwest Spanish textiles studied in conjunction with this project, there is an unusual group of blankets, all exhibiting handspun indigo-dyed wool weft ikat (Plates 59 and 60). Though there is a great deal of variation within this group, there is general agreement that, considering the quality of the yarns, weaving, and dyeing, these pieces are all early in date, a safe range being 1800–1860.

Ikat, a word of Malay origin now commonly used as an English term, describes a resist-dyeing process that takes place before the loom is set up for weaving. Warps, wefts, or both sets of elements are grouped according to a predetermined pattern, wrapped, and bound. They are then dyed, at which point the binding resists the dye, producing a pattern in the yarn that will eventually appear in the finished textile.

The technique of ikat is known and practiced throughout the world. It was highly developed at an early date in Indonesia; however, it is also found in elaborate forms and variations in Japan, China, India, Afghanistan, throughout the Arabic world of North Africa, in Europe, and in pre-Columbian Peru and present-day Guatemala. In all cases warp ikat, being the earlier and simpler form, is far more common than the comparatively rare weft ikat.[1] A weaver normally makes up a warp before weaving. To pattern that warp by bind-and-dyeing before putting it on the loom doesn't involve many extra steps. The weft, however, is not normally arranged as a unit before weaving. To separate the made-up weft into logical groups, to bind-and-dye it, and then to set up a system whereby the weft will be reeled back into the fabric in a logical order to form the desired pattern is a technically advanced and complicated procedure. Warp ikat occurs throughout Central and South America. During the pre-Columbian era it was practiced in Peru and probably also in Central America. The warp ikat of Mexico, for

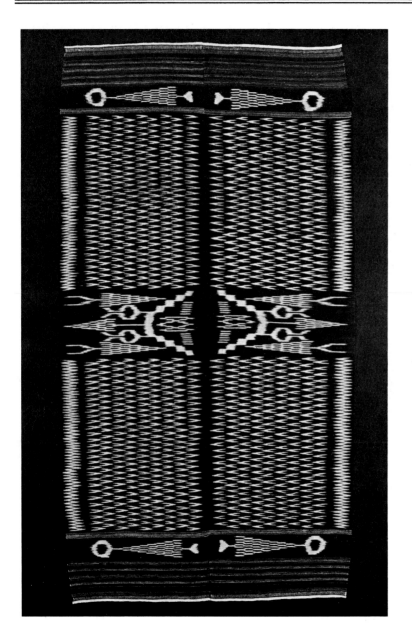

FIGURE 1

Weft ikat blanket, ca. 1800, two widths seamed, 2.36 x 1.30 m. Warp: 3-ply wool(?), weft: 1-ply handspun wool, natural-undyed white, indigo-dyed blue ikat. Fred Harvey Fine Arts Collection on loan to the Museum of New Mexico at the Museum of International Folk Art. L.70.3.37.

example, is well known to us in the form of the extremely fine silk rebozos. Weft ikat, however, was not commonly used in this hemisphere. The major exceptions to this are pieces from Guatemala (Figure 5) and a small, aberrant group of Spanish blankets from the southwestern United States.[2]

How has it come to be that a group of technically advanced weft ikat blankets are isolated in the southwestern United States?

It has never been known just what effect the Bazán brothers had on the weaving of the Santa Fe area and the Rio Arriba. It has been postulated that they introduced ikat, but that seems unlikely.[3] In the first place, the Bazáns apparently represented the mainstream of the Mexican treadle-loom weaving industry. Furthermore, weft ikat is extremely rare in Mexico. In her exhaustive study of Saltillo *sarapes,* Katherine Jenkins never saw weft ikats related to the pieces under discussion.[4] Irmgard Johnson, in consultation with a number of others in Mexico City, has stated that the pieces cannot be Mexican. According to her, certain design elements in the blankets pictured in Plate 60 and Figure 1 are related to the Mexican textile tradition. (She undoubtedly refers to the Saltillo-type central diamond.) She feels, on the other hand, that the Smithsonian example which was formerly attributed by Boyd to the Bazáns (Figure 2) does not fit into the Mexican blanket styles. In concluding she states, "So far as I know—and this is the crucial factor—there is no weft ikat in Mexico. I have never seen a Mexican blanket exhibiting . . . weft ikat."[5] The Bazáns were weavers from Mexico City. Though trade guilds do not seem to have been formally set up in the Rio Grande area, they were very strong in Mexico, governing every aspect of textile production. Weaving and dyeing guilds were separate. The Bazáns were weavers, not dyers. Would they have

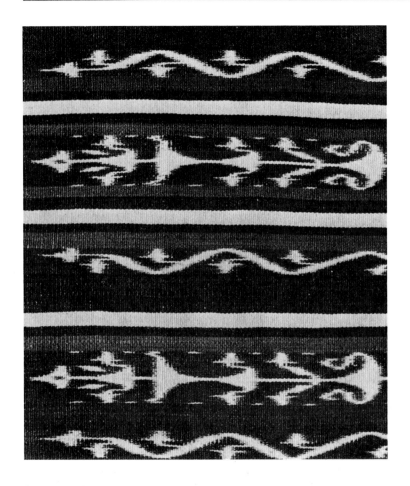

FIGURE 2

Weft ikat blanket, ca. 1800, collected ca. 1910 in "Chemayo, New Mexico." One width, 2.79 x 1.43 m. Warp: 1-ply handspun wool; weft: 1-ply handspun wool, ikat-dyed indigo on white wool. The National Museum of History and Technology, Smithsonian Institution. 357–437.

brought a non-Mexican dyeing tradition to the Rio Grande area? It is highly unlikely.

The first indication that weft ikat blankets had been woven in New Mexico came in 1958 from a specimen given to the Spanish Colonial Arts Society by Mabel O'Dell (Figure 3). Mrs. O'Dell, famed throughout the southwestern states for her careful work in textile cleaning and reweaving, has always kept a stock of ragged New Mexican blankets for use in matching yarns. An ikat blanket which is Rio Grande (Figure 3), being typical in all aspects—texture, warp count, and warp yarn make-up (2-Z-spun-plied-S)—appeared among the ragged textiles. Though she had not seen ikat before, Mrs. O'Dell recognized the piece as Rio Grande and, realizing that it was unusual, presented it to E. Boyd. E. Boyd looked for related pieces and soon found the extremely elaborate, carefully executed example that belongs to the Smithsonian (Figure 2). This piece, woven with wefts of fine short-staple kinky yarn, is harsh and unlike the Rio Grandes in texture; unlike the Rio Grandes, the warp is single Z-spun. Yet, the catalogue at the Smithsonian stated that the piece was purchased in "Chemayo [sic], New Mexico," around 1910. In response to E. Boyd's enthusiasm and writings,[6] and through the careful exhaustive survey work of Dorothy Bowen, nine other weft ikat blankets have turned up.

Although all of these textiles seem to come from the southwestern U.S., with New Mexico, Rio Grande, Mexico, and Chimayó mentioned as sources, the provenience is always vague with no documentation beyond the dealer or donor. One piece, however, has a more specific provenience: "collected: village of Carachic [sic], Chihuahua-Tarahumara, Mexico."[7] This piece, containing three bands of zigzag weft ikat and woven in one width, superficially resembles the textile illustrated in Plate 59. Thinking that this might be a real lead, I have contacted a number of individuals. So far, however, we have had only negative responses, from Jon Erickson at the Heard Museum and Bernard Fontana in Tucson.[8] No one has seen a Tarahumara textile of this type.

Though this is a coherent group of textiles, all indigo-dyed weft ikat, there are variations among the group, and no two pieces can be said to have been woven in one workshop. Besides weft ikat, the pieces have in common single Z-spun wool wefts and a predominance of paired warps at the centers of the single width textiles. Nine of the

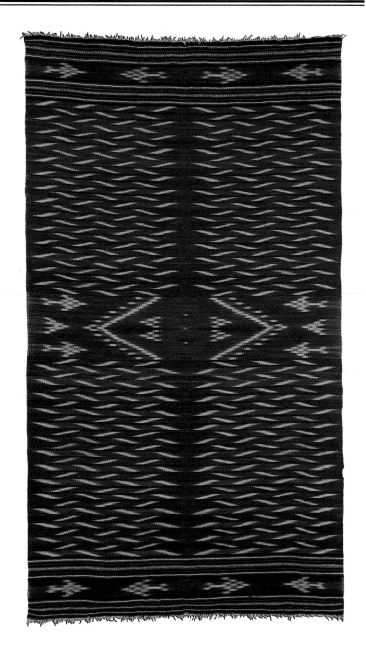

PLATE 59

Ikat blanket, ca. 1800, one width, 2.04 x 1.26 m. Warp: 1-ply handspun cotton; weft: 1-ply handspun cotton, natural-undyed white, 1-ply handspun wool, indigo and natural-undyed light, ikat dyed. International Folk Art Foundation Collection at the Museum of International Folk Art, a unit of the Museum of New Mexico. FA.64.21.1.

PLATE 60

Ikat blanket, ca. 1800, one width, 2.27 x 1.28 m. Warp: 1-ply handspun cotton plus an unidentified plant fiber; weft: 1-ply handspun wool natural-undyed light and dark, blue (indigo) and white ikat, dark blue-green natural-dyed. Frank Packard Collection on loan to the Museum of New Mexico at the Laboratory of Anthropology. 36329/12.

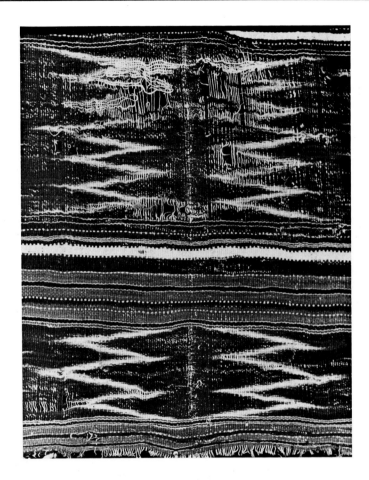

FIGURE 3

Detail of Rio Grande weft ikat blanket, ca. 1860, one width, 1.92 x 1.16 m. Warp: 2-ply handspun wool; weft: 1-ply handspun wool, natural-undyed light and dark and indigo-dyed ikat. Spanish Colonial Arts Society, Inc. Collection on loan to the Museum of New Mexico at the Museum of International Folk Art, Gift of Mabel O'Dell. L.5.60.48.

eleven were, indeed, woven in one width and, from the paired warps at the center, it would seem that they were double-woven—a technical feat! Sizes of these textiles range from 1.92 m. to 2.79 m. in length and 1.05 m. to 1.47 m. in width. One piece incorporates handspun cotton in the weft (Plate 59), while another has cotton mixed with unidentified plant fiber in the warp (Plate 60). One textile includes red (cochineal-dyed?) and white ikat, and appears to have been woven four-selvedged, presumably on a vertical loom.[9]

There are two basic ways of handling ikat design. The simplest of these involves dyeing the yarns in rectangular blocks and then pulling the ikat-dyed elements out of line to form a pattern. The usual resultant motif is an "arrowhead" type of form,[10] an extention of which is a zigzag (Figures 3 and 4). More complex is the practice of tying the yarns in specific pattern blocks which produce elaborate designs in the woven textile. We can refer to these two forms of ikat as either "pulled" or "blocked." Both types are illustrated in the eleven southwestern Rio Grande pieces. Pulled ikat, with the resultant zigzag motifs, occurs in six of the pieces (Figure 3), two of which include only three simple bands of ikat (Plate 59). The more complicated blocked ikat is illustrated in three pieces (Figure 2), while the remaining two pieces illustrate a combination of blocked and pulled ikat (Plate 60 and Figure 1).

With a craft such as weaving the simplest explanation is always the most probable one. In this case there seems to be no simple explanation. As Alfred Bühler claims in a recent letter, however, these pieces seem to be American.[11] And, indeed, when one surveys the full range of ikat throughout the world, it becomes obvious that the southwestern Rio Grande ikats are closely allied to the ikats of Guatemala (Figure 6, compare Figure 1 to Figure 5).[12] Certain motifs, such as those referred to by the names *pinetto* and *jarro* (Figure 6) in Guatemala, occur frequently there and are reflected in the pieces from the southwestern United States (compare Figure 1 to Figure 5).[13] In Guatemala all forms of ikat abound: warp, weft, and double ikat. Ikat is locally known by the name *jaspe*, which means "spotted or variegated in appearance."[14] Weft ikat is extremely common in Guatemala, as Lila O'Neale points

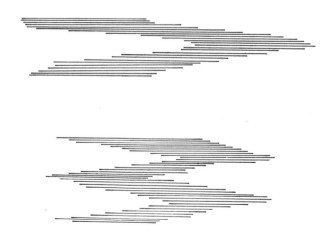

FIGURE 4

The ikat arrowhead and zigzag motifs. Drawings adapted from the textiles shown in Plates 59 and 60. Drawn by Nora Pickens.

FIGURE 5

Detail of Guatemalan weft ikat shawl. Totonicapan, Totonicapan, Guatemala. International Folk Art Foundation Collection at the Museum of International Folk Art, a unit of the Museum of New Mexico. FA.77.3.4.

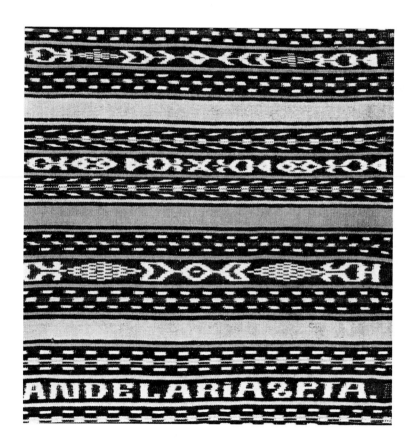

out when she notes that ikat wefts are simpler to dye than the warps and describes a nine-year-old boy binding weft for ikat dyeing.[15] I have consulted Edwin Shook and Carlos Elmenhorst concerning the possibility of Guatemalan origins for a number of these pieces. Because texture and scale are so important, however, it is almost impossible to identify textiles through photographs, so we will not be receiving a final opinion on this matter in the near future.[16]

Without doubt, there is a direct link between Chimayó, New Mexico, the stated place of origin of these textiles, and Guatemala—specifically Esquipulas in southwestern Guatemala. The Santuario at Chimayó, built and furnished between 1813 and 1816, was dedicated to Our Lord of Esquipulas.[17] The cult seems to have come fairly directly to New Mexico from the Guatemalan source;[18] its importance throughout the Rio Grande area is reflected in the fact that

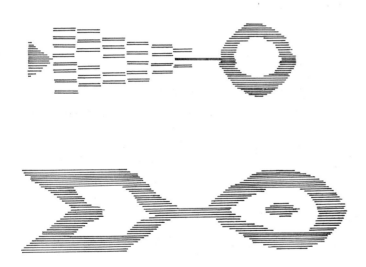

FIGURE 6

Additional weft ikat motifs of Guatemala and New Mexico. Drawings adapted from the textiles shown in Figures 1 and 5 of this chapter. Drawn by Nora Pickens.

the altar screen at Ranchos de Taos as well as three other works by the artist, Molleno, were dedicated to Our Lord of Esquipulas.[19] Bernardo Abeyta was responsible for building the Santuario and for dedicating it to Our Lord of Esquipulas. Though it is clear that Abeyta was involved in extensive trading operations,[20] little is known about the extent of his devotion to the Guatemalan cult which he introduced at Chimayó.[21] Was the cult of Esquipulas accompanied by Guatemalans—specifically weavers? Hopefully, patient delving in archives and church records will turn up some concrete data.

A simple suggestion made by Alfred Bühler in his recent letter may lead in the future to an explanation of the phenomena of these eleven southwestern ikats. Dr. Bühler asks: "Was there a change in loom type? When did the treadle loom make its appearance in this area?"[22] Weft ikat is easier on the treadle loom. The long treadle loom warps are harder to arrange, bind, and dye than the warps that would be used for the back-strap, horizontal, and vertical looms indigenous to this area. Might there have been an individual, skilled in ikat weaving, who, when working with the new loom and long warps, transferred his skill in ikat and the ikat designs from the warp to the weft of the treadle loom woven fabrics? Though not specifically documented, it is clear— throughout Guatemala, Mexico, and the southwestern United States from perhaps 1550 until 1800—that there was a shift from the indigenous back-strap loom to the treadle loom of European origin.[23] If it could be documented, this theory might explain the close relationship between the Guatemalan and New Mexican weft ikats, and it would certainly explain the high degree of skill illustrated by certain of these isolated weft ikats from the southwestern United States (Figures 1 and 2).

We may never know all the answers. But there are clues that point to highly probable—extremely simple and logical—types of explanation. There are rich sources for further study in the archives and church records of New Mexico, the weaving of northern Mexico, and perhaps the weaving of Guatemala. Other related textiles doubtless will turn up, and with them, some further clues. Indeed, if enough information were to surface we might even be able to prove that certain of the weft ikat blankets from the southwestern United States predate the early nineteenth-century Bazán brothers—that other craftsmen, perhaps Guatemalans, influenced Rio Grande weaving.

A curious group of early blankets containing 1- or 2-ply handspun cotton weft and either 2-ply handspun cotton or wool warp has been attributed by various authorities to the Rio Grande Valley.[1] So far at least seven, possibly eight, of these blankets have been located.[2] Although there is wide variation in design, structure, and technical details, none of the textiles contain synthetic dyes and none contain commercially spun cotton. All were collected in New Mexico.

One beautiful piece (illustrated in Plate 59) contains bands of 1-ply indigo weft-ikat-dyed wool with wide white bands of 1-ply handspun cotton. The warp is 1-ply handspun cotton. This blanket has many technical and structural similarities to the other weft ikat textiles and can be presumed to have the same origin—probably not New Mexican, perhaps Guatemalan.

Of the remaining cotton blankets, five feature dots and dashes in geometric patterns which include diamonds, Xs, and horizontal S-forms, all of which are found in eighteenth- and nineteenth-century

Oaxacan *sarapes* (Figure 6, Chapter 8) and which were borrowed often by Rio Grande weavers.[3] One of the most simple of these designs appears in Figure 1, with 1-ply handspun cotton and handspun natural-dyed wool wefts. These same materials are found in the blanket illustrated in Plate 61, which has been found to contain lac. Cochineal usually appears only in commercially manufactured and dyed yarns. The blanket in Plate 61 is rather a maverick in design, and may well be an attempt by a New Mexican weaver to imitate an Oaxacan textile.

PLATE 61

Rio Grande cotton blanket, ca. 1820–50, two widths seamed, 2.43 x 1.12 m. Warp: 2-ply handspun cotton; weft: 1-ply handspun cotton, undyed, and 1-ply handspun wool, light and dark indigo and lac. Spanish Colonial Arts Society, Inc. Collection on loan to the Museum of New Mexico at the Museum of International Folk Art, Gift of Mr. and Mrs. John Gaw Meem, H. P. Mera Collection. L.5.62.74.

140

◁ *preceding page (right)*

PLATE 62

Rio Grande cotton blanket, *ca. 1820–50, two widths seamed, 2.34 x 1.14 m. Warp: 2-ply handspun wool; weft: 1-ply handspun undyed cotton, 3-ply paired commercial wool yarn, natural-dyed dark indigo, yellow, cochineal, and three shades of green. Taylor Museum, Colorado Springs Fine Arts Center, Gift of Alice Bemis Taylor. 3773.*

Two cotton dot-and-dash blankets which closely resemble each other are in the collections of the Taylor Museum (Plate 62).[4] Both have 2-ply handspun wool warp and weft of 1-ply handspun cotton and 3-ply paired natural-dyed commercial wool yarn. Such extravagant use of commercial wool yarn is rare in New Mexican weaving until the 1880s, when 4-ply synthetic-dyed yarns were commonly combined with commercial cotton warps. Particularly unusual in the Taylor blankets is the use of commercial indigo-dyed yarn; indigo-dyed handspun wool is normally the rule, even when commercial yarn of other hues appears in quantity in the same textile. The three shades of green here are also atypical of Rio Grande weaving. In addition to dots and dashes, the design of these two blankets includes bands of stepped chevrons which in neither textile is balanced or well executed. In the blanket in Plate 62, the weaver has made noticeable mistakes in pattern and has not adequately controlled the straightness of the selvedges.

The fifth of the dot-and-dash cotton blankets, at the Museum of Northern Arizona, bears a Fred Harvey tag which reads "Native cotton raised Lemitar, N.M."[5] On the basis of this bit of provenience, E. Boyd tentatively linked Lemitar, about sixty miles south of Albuquerque on the Rio Grande, with archival records of Joaquín Alejandro Bazán, son of Don Ignacio Ricardo Bazán. Joaquín Bazán apparently lived at Tomé and at Belén, where he was buried in 1871.[6] The chronology of Joaquín's life, ca. 1807–71,[7] meshes well with that of the materials in these five dot-and-dash cotton blankets and it is indeed tempting to

postulate that he or his pupils wove them along the Rio Abajo in the 1820s to 1860s.[8]

A sixth blanket, in the collections of the Lowe Art Museum, is similar in materials and structure to the above five blankets but the design is the familiar five-band stripe pattern without tapestry motifs.[9]

The history of cotton weaving along the Rio Grande begins with the Pueblo Indians.[10] Minge has cited numerous references to locally produced cotton in wills and legal records of the seventeenth and eighteenth centuries. He concluded that cotton was probably produced wherever irrigation was available along the Rio Abajo. Local cotton is mentioned in various forms: as bundles, thread, cotton sheeting (*sabanilla de algodón), mantas,* and *colchas.*

Although cotton as a weaving material was largely supplanted by wool by 1800, a letter from New Mexico Governor Fernando de Chacón in 1803 that describes the agricultural products of New Mexico mentions cotton *mantas* for shirts with "twisted thread closer and stronger than that of Puebla," as well as cotton tablecloths and stockings.[11] The context of the statement implies that the weavers were Spanish, not Indian. By 1808 Fray Josef Benito Pereyro of Santa Clara stated that the only Pueblos still weaving cotton *mantas* for blankets, *cotones* (cotton cloth), and *tilmas* (Indian dresses) were Laguna, Acoma, and Zuni.[12]

The mission of the Bazán brothers to promote a thriving cotton industry has been described in this publication by Minge and Wheat. Apparently, from the above cited records, some cotton weavers were already at work in New Mexico when the Bazáns arrived. Since cotton is a product of a warm climate, the probable settlement of Don Ignacio Ricardo Bazán on the Rio Abajo is logical—he would have preferred to be close to a ready source of materials. He was a native of Puebla, Mexico, which was famous for its fine cottons.[13]

Minge found records of cotton produced in 1825 at Alameda, Albuquerque, Valencia, Socorro, and Belén, and in 1829 at Sabinal. He also cites the 1822 Mexican Census, which records seventy-one looms in Albuquerque that were used for cotton weaving as well as for wool. Minge has concluded that the Santa Fe Trail trade of the 1830s and 1840s discouraged the local production of cotton and that quantities diminished throughout the remainder of the nineteenth century.

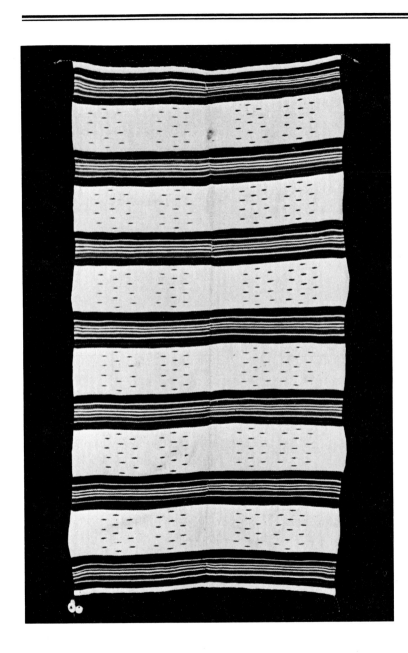

FIGURE 1

Rio Grande cotton blanket, ca. 1820–50, two widths seamed, 2.06 x 1.10 m. Warp: 2-ply handspun cotton, weft: 1-ply handspun undyed cotton, 1-ply handspun wool, indigo, cochineal, and natural-undyed brown. Fred Harvey Fine Arts Collection on loan to the Museum of New Mexico at the Museum of International Folk Art. L.70.3.36.

In conclusion, the six cotton blankets described above were probably woven along the Rio Abajo between Alameda and Socorro, eighty miles to the south, between 1820 and 1850. They are most likely related in some way to the influence of Don Ignacio Ricardo Bazán or his son Joaquín Alejandro Bazán and are about the only group of surviving Rio Grande textiles which can be linked to the Rio Abajo. Since most of these blankets include dot-and-dash designs, one is tempted to speculate whether other wool dot-and-dash blankets may also be representative of the elusive Rio Abajo weaving tradition.

13 YARDAGE
NORA FISHER

Bayeta, bayetón, sayal, and sabanilla are Spanish names for varieties of simple yardage woven on the treadle loom in New Mexico.[1] It is difficult to describe these fabrics, and we cannot be sure exactly who wove them. The citation of 1638 concerning the production of sayal would lead us to believe that yardage may have been woven in a workshop.[2] On the other hand, it has been discovered that in the San Luis Valley men generally wove blankets, while women were employed in the home, weaving lightweight yardage fabrics for the family's use.[3] The truth may lie somewhere in between.

As will be seen, sabanilla, which continued in wide use until a much later date, is today the best known and most easily described of all these fabrics. Bayeta, bayetón, and sayal are, on the other hand, known to us primarily through the documents. And, due to the fact that fabric names change quickly with fashion, it is difficult to ascribe specific meanings to these terms. Sayal, "a coarse woolen cloth used for wagon covers, tents, sacks, and horse blankets,"[4] was the first of the yardage fabrics to be mentioned in the documents pertaining to New Mexico. As we have seen, the extent of its production in the Santa Fe area proves that the Spanish treadle loom was used in New Mexico as early as 1638.[5] Fortunately, quite an explicit seventeenth-century description of sayal exists in a communication from Rome dated 1688 which decrees the color and quality of the fabric to be used for the habit of the Franciscan Order in Mexico. The fabric was to be of natural untreated, undyed, mixed white and black wool, overall grey in color.[6] Knowing that the fabric was woven of crude wool, we can assume that sayal was probably plain-woven.[7] As the English translation, sackcloth, would indicate, it was probably quite harsh in quality and taken from the loom without the addition of any particular finishing process. On the other hand, *bayeta* and *bayetón,* both of which were definitely being woven in New Mexico in 1812,[8] were apparently finished by being fulled (cleansed and thickened) or napped after having been taken from the loom. *Bayeta,* commonly referred to in English as baize, felt, or flannel was "the homespun woolen of the eighteenth century."[9] Happily, small fragments of this fabric may indeed have survived.[10] *Bayetón,* known in English as blanket cloth or coating fabric, was heavier in weight than *bayeta,* but similar in quality. We can assume that both of these napped fabrics were either twill- or plain-woven and, certainly, tighter in weave than *sayal.*

Sabanilla, the diminutive in Spanish of *sábana* (sheet), is a term that can certainly be applied in New Mexico to white wool handspun, handwoven sheeting, or yardage, usually plain weave though occasionally twill-woven.[11] Apparently *sabanilla* differed from *bayeta* and *bayetón* in that it was not a fulled fabric, and from *sayal* in that it was much softer and finer than the crude sackcloth.

Sabanilla had many uses, the most common of which were clothing, mattress ticks, and the backing fabric for the wool-on-wool *colcha* embroideries. Owing to the hard wear given to the everyday clothing, there are no documented surviving examples of garments; only the descriptions remain, some of them quite colorful.[12] Many pieces of *sabanilla* have, however, survived and been preserved as parts of mattress ticks and backings for embroideries. Figure 1 illustrates a mattress tick of twill-woven *sabanilla.* This sacklike form is meant to be stuffed with loose unspun wool or straw, then stabilized by tying the sack together at intervals through the provided holes. The tick, due to the sparse furnishing of the homes, was a common object, presumably used in every Spanish New Mexican home. Vivid descriptions of the yearly, almost ritual, cleaning of these mattresses and related articles of bedding have been preserved for us.[13] The example shown in Figure 1 is an extremely fine and elegant version of the common mattress tick. Not only is the fabric a fine twill weave, but the tie holes are embroidered in buttonhole stitch with plied yarns in blue and red, presumably dyed with indigo and the very valuable cochineal. As will be seen, *sabanilla* was the perfect cloth for use as the ground for the fully covered New Mexican wool-on-wool *colcha* embroideries.[14] Indeed, it may be that this type of *colcha* embroidery died out due to the increasingly scarce

supplies of *sabanilla.* With the availability of imported fabric yardage and perhaps with the establishment of nearby woolen mills in Colorado, eastern New Mexico, and Utah, the production of all of these locally woven yardage fabrics came to an end.[15]

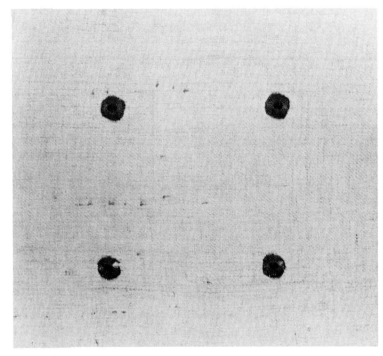

FIGURE 1

Detail of mattress tick, nineteenth century. Two widths seamed, sewn together at sides and ends, with an additional two widths to make a bag-like mattress cover, 1.96 x 1.25 m. Warp and weft: 1-ply handspun natural-undyed white wool, 2/2 twill weave. Holes and edges embroidered, buttonhole stitch, red and blue. Fred Harvey Fine Arts Collection on loan to the Museum of New Mexico at the Museum of International Folk Art. L.71.17.9.

TRISH SPILLMAN

Another common, inexpensive, multipurpose textile produced by the colonial northern New Mexicans was *jerga*. The word *jerga* is of uncertain origin, possibly from the French *serge* or the Portuguese *xerga* meaning serge or sackcloth (mourning clothes). Documents of the eighteenth century refer to it variously as *jerga, gerga, herga,* and *zerga*.[1] Used by the Spanish it meant a "thick, coarse cloth" which was used for clothing, packing material, and floor covering. Today the term *jerga* generally means handspun lengths of twill-woven plaids and checks used for floor covering. In rural contemporary New Mexico, however, its meaning seems to extend to include any type of floor covering, such as factory carpets, linoleum, or contemporary rag rugs.

The importance and various uses of *jerga* are listed in historical documents. In an inventory of the belongings of Governor de Vargas, 20 April 1704, various types of *jerga* are mentioned: *varas de jerga, costales de jerga* (bags or sacks made from *jerga*), *arpilleras de jerga* (sackcloth or coarse linen made from *jerga*), and locally woven *mantas de jerga*.[2] Several nineteenth-century sources indicate that *jerga* was used to fashion warm, cheap clothing for the poor. In 1812 Pino mentioned "black and white striped frieze used for carpets as well as for clothing by poor people."[3] In 1850 Franz Huning described "jackets of homemade wool carpet" worn by the poor in San Miguel del Vado, New Mexico.[4]

In 1825 the United States government sent Benjamin H. Reeves, George C. Sibley, and Thomas Mather to survey the Santa Fe Trail and trade with the Kansas Indian tribes for the right of way. Sibley's Santa Fe diary of 1825–26 records his order of 120 yards of "coarse woolen stuff . . . 6 yards Herga for wrapper, 19 yards Herga, 11½ yards Herga,

FIGURE 1

Group of U.S. Army officers in studio with **jerga** *carpeting. New Mexico, ca. 1867–70. Museum of New Mexico, 56281.*

[and] 9½ yards wrapping Herga."[5] It is also listed throughout the eighteenth and nineteenth centuries with the *efectos del país* (domestic production) as defense donations and trade items.[6]

Jerga was used as floor covering in government buildings, churches, and private homes. Susan Magoffin described her Santa Fe home of 1846, in which

> at the same end of the room [the floor] is covered with a kind of Mexican carpeting; made of wool and coloured black and white only. In short we may consider this great hall as two rooms, for one half of it is carpeted and furnished for the parlour, while the other half has a naked floor, the dining table and all things attached to that establishment occupy it.[7]

The floors of colonial New Mexico were of packed earth smoothed and sealed with ox blood. The *jerga* was then placed directly upon the earthen floor (Figure 1), or, as John Yaple in Taos recalls, a layer of straw or similar material was used under the *jerga* as a protective cushion.[8] Dr. Alan Minge, whose collection of *jerga* surpasses that of any museum, suggests that "*yerba de la víbora*," or snakeweed, was used under the dirt on ceilings to repel varmints and insects. That type of material might have been used under the *jerga*—partly as a cushion and partly to deter mice.

A more contemporary use of a twill fabric identical to New Mexican *jerga* was found in Spain in 1963.[9] This interesting textile (Figure 2) was purchased at a country fair in Arzúa, northern Spain, and was then used as a blanket on top of the saddle, rather than underneath. It is homespun red and black wool woven in one-inch twill checks, with two separate pieces bound together on two sides by a handmade braid of the same wool. A comparison between this piece woven in Spain and a piece of *jerga* woven in New Mexico (Figures 2 and 3) reveals obvious similarities. A reference to the production of *jerga*-like fabric in Spain is found in *Popular Weaving and Embroidery in Spain* by Mildred Stapley. She refers to a blue-and-white checkered pattern from La Mancha that closely resembles *jerga*.[10] Scraps of linen and wool were woven in rag rugs in patterns of plaids, zigzags, and lozenges. Apparently the combination of white linen and dark wool was quite common in Spain, but without the availability of linen in the colonies, natural white handspun wool was substituted. This light and dark

PLATE 63

Jerga, ca. 1850, two widths seamed, 1.93 x 1.33 m. Warp and weft: 1-ply handspun natural-dyed wool. Spanish Colonial Arts Society, Inc. Collection on loan to the Museum of New Mexico at the Museum of International Folk Art, Gift of Mr. and Mrs. John Gaw Meem, H. P. Mera Collection. L.5.62.95.

PLATE 64

Jerga, ca. 1880, one width, 4.83 x .65 m. Warp and weft: 1-ply handspun wool, dark natural and synthetic red. Said to have been woven by Mrs. Darío Gallegos, San Luis, Colorado. Beryl G. and Charles H. Woodard Collection, Colorado Historical Society. E.2018–51.

combination, as seen in Figure 3, is the most common type of early *jerga* produced in New Mexico.

Jerga yarn is a thick handspun coarse wool, natural or dyed. The structure of this twill fabric leaves the warps and wefts equally exposed to wear. The blanket is a tightly woven fabric, a cross section of which reveals at least three threads; in contrast, the *jerga* cross section shows only one thread. It is curious that a fabric of a single thickness would be placed on the floor. It was used, however, in areas where traffic was less constant, so that years of service or durability were not of great concern.

The rugs were not discarded, however, for like the blankets, the *jerga* would be recycled until mere fragments remained. Many of the lengths left today have been patched with various other *jergas,* either matching the original *jerga* or in a pattern coming from a completely different one. Most of the blankets show reweaving.

The *jerga* is not generally found to be rewoven but, rather, patches have been found applied on top of the worn area. In view of the use and abuse that *jerga* has received, it is amazing to have examples that are still in good condition to study and enjoy.[11]

Since *jerga* is twill woven, the method of weaving it differs from that used for blankets. The warp is not covered, the beating is not as hard, and the movement of the feet on the treadles is more complicated.

Plain weave blankets require only two harnesses and treadling of two foot pedals, while twill weave *jerga* requires four harnesses and the use of four treadles. A distinct pattern of foot treadling is required to weave the common twill of *jerga;* a break in the pattern results in a change in direction of the twill. *Jerga* was inexpensive compared with blankets because it was a looser weave, using less wool, physically less strenuous and time-consuming to produce, and employed cheaper dyes and fibers. In the late 1880s there was a gradual change from handspun wool warps to commercial cotton warps, and apparently also from the

FIGURE 2

Detail of Spanish textile resembling Rio Grande **jerga, northern Spain,** *ca. 1930, 95 x 73 cm. Warp and weft: 1-ply handspun wool, synthetic-dyed red and black, twill weave. International Folk Art Foundation Collection at the Museum of International Folk Art, a unit of the Museum of New Mexico. FA.63.13.34.*

FIGURE 3

Detail of Rio Grande **jerga,** *brown and white, most common type, ca. 1850, two widths seamed, 1.51 x 1.29 m. Warp and weft: 1-ply handspun natural-undyed white and brown wool, twill weave. Spanish Colonial Arts Society, Inc. Collection on loan to the Museum of New Mexico at the Museum of International Folk Art. L.5.PROP.*

twill weave to the plain weave. The large plaids were seldom woven as matching widths, but the same colors used throughout gave the finished textile a unified appearance.

The weaving of *jerga* was commonplace, and patterns varied from a simple twill which may well have been woven by older children to complex patterns which required the knowledge of expert weavers. One such complex pattern, found occasionally, is the diamond or partridge eye *(ojo de perdiz)* (Figure 4), for which the warp is threaded through the harnesses in a pattern different from that of the fabric of the plain

twill *jerga*. The treadling is also different. Much more pattern concentration is necessary when weaving any *jerga*, and especially the partridge eye variation. Nearly all examples show evidence of weaving mistakes, which are easily made.

The choice of colors for much of the *jerga* is rather startling when compared to the colors found in the blankets. Picture a whole room in tiny red and green checks that vibrate like contemporary optical art! Red is a favorite color for later *jerga*—red with shocking pink, blue, orange, or brown. With the exception of the natural light and dark *jerga* and a few pieces containing natural dyes, every sample of *jerga* contains red. It is very possible that the inexpensive dyes were commonly used in

FIGURE 4

Detail of Rio Grande **jerga,** *"diamond" or* ojo de perdiz *twill weave, 1870–90, 38 x 37 cm. Warp and weft: 1-ply handspun wool, natural-undyed brown and synthetic-dyed red. Museum of New Mexico Collection at the Museum of International Folk Art. A.77.72.2.*

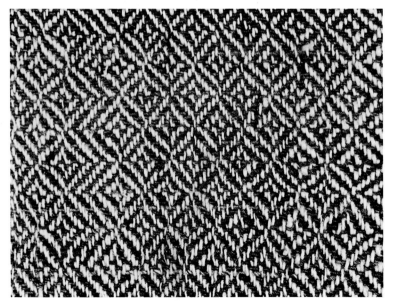

FIGURE 5

Rio Grande **jerga,** *with two types of weft—1-ply undyed white and carded undyed grey handspun wool and synthetic-dyed rags, plain weave, post-1860, 3.64 x .85 m. Warp: commercial 4-ply cotton string. Collection of Dr. and Mrs. Ward Alan Minge, Corrales, N.M.*

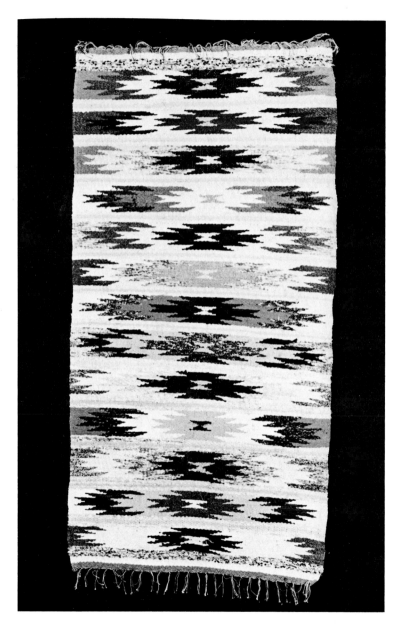

FIGURE 6

New Mexican **rag rug,** *woven by Ruth Vigil, Española, 1972, 1.56 x .82 m. Warp: synthetic-dyed commercial cotton; weft: strips of fabric. International Folk Art Foundation Collection at the Museum of International Folk Art, a unit of the Museum of New Mexico. FA.72.56.1.*

jerga; expensive imported dyes were saved for blankets and *colchas,* while ordinary dyes, possibly from native herbs and plants, were also used in *jerga.*

One *jerga* of exceptional beauty apparently employs the natural dyes not often found in these textiles (Plate 63). If *jerga* was always as inexpensive as indicated by wills and trade documents, it is possible that with a bit more money a patron could request special dyes. Not only are these dyes unusual for *jerga,* but the condition of this textile indicates that it was a special piece originally as it is now. Plate 64 is also an example of *jerga* in excellent condition—it was woven by María Olofia Gallegos of the San Luis Valley, who is said to have woven 300 yards of *jerga.* It is single-ply diagonal twill of dark natural and synthetic reds.[12]

Mention should be made of *jerga* woven with strips of rags for weft. It may be speculated that the earliest introduction of rags woven in *jerga* happened by accident.[13] Perhaps one weaver used a light and dark natural wool *jerga* with handspun wool. When the strip was almost the desired length, there was not enough handspun left to finish it, so cloth was cut or torn into strips and used as weft. How much easier and more economical to use strips from existing rags than to card and spin wool! In some pieces of *jerga* it is hard to tell the difference between the handspun wool and the strips of material. A perfect example is the striped light and dark *jerga* from Dr. Minge's collection (Figure 5)—part is handspun wool and part uses rags.

Today there is an interesting revival in rag rugs. No longer do we see a mere random selection of various rags woven into long strips; rather, there is a very careful selection of color and the introduction of tapestry-weave design. Figure 6 shows a weft-faced rag rug with Saltillo design elements, and a contemporary use of bright colors.

15 COLCHA EMBROIDERY
NORA FISHER

Today *colcha* embroidery is by far the most popular of the traditional New Mexican Spanish textile arts. "The stitching of geometric and floral motifs in elaborate design patterns [as Stoller says] certainly must represent the highest creative achievements in the arts by Hispano women . . . . *colcha* says 'life is . . . good and joyous.' "[1]

This embroidery form is currently so popular that the word *colcha* has become emotionally charged, each individual insisting on his or her own personal definition of the term. In fact, *colcha* in Spanish means "bed covering." What with common usage in both Spanish and English, the use of the term "*colcha* stitch," and several extant types of *colcha* embroidery, however, the word *colcha* is almost beyond definition.[2] For this reason we use it here only as a modifier: *colcha* stitch, *colcha* embroidery.

Though there are many types of *colcha* embroidery—the early Spanish wool-on-wool and wool-on-cotton examples and a myriad of twentieth-century variants—these textiles are all New Mexican in origin and are all characterized by the use of wool embroidery in *colcha* self-couching stitch (Figure 1). There has been a great deal of speculation about how this stitch came to be used in New Mexico, excluding almost all other stitches. Chinese and Spanish origins have both been postulated.[3] Yet, examining the admirable nature of the stitch, there is really no need for such speculation. In the first place, it is very economical. In her recent survey of *colcha* embroidery Marianne Stoller has stated: "I would conjecture that . . . [an] appeal of the stitch is its efficiency in execution—probably faster for covering a large area than any . . . other kind of stitch would be—and modern *colcha* workers I talked with repeatedly emphasized this virtue of the stitch."[4] It also saves yarn; in fact it is probably more economical than any other stitch in providing a full, luxurious covering on the front, with little

153

FIGURE 1

The colcha *self-couching stitch which utilizes the same yarn for both the laid and tacking (couching) elements. After Irene Emery from "Wool Embroideries of New Mexico: Some Notes on the Stitch Employed." Sampler by Lisbeth Perrone, photo by Art Taylor.*

a

b

FIGURE 2

Details of wool-on-wool colcha *embroidery, illustrating: a. economy of yarns with very small stitches showing on the reverse and full coverage of the ground, with the nearly invisible seam indicated by an arrow. b. textural effects achieved by the use of the* colcha *stitch. Both are details of the textile illustrated in Plate 66.*

waste of embroidery yarn on the reverse (Figure 2a). Secondly, though no less important, the *colcha* stitch provides an interesting texture (Figure 2b), and it is free flowing. As Jacqueline Enthoven has said, "The joy . . . is that it is flexible; it enables . . . one to react spontaneously to the demands of the design."[5] It is not surprising that *colcha,* or a very similar stitch, is known to the world of embroidery, although by many names: *Convent Stitch, Laid Oriental Stitch, Figure Stitch, Deerfield Stitch, Bokhara Couching, Romanian Couching,* to list only a few. Emery points out that "no matter what the name, the stitch has obviously been somewhat widely known and used through the centuries."[6] There is no need to search for its origins in either Europe or the Orient—an embroiderer is above all a practical person who makes use of the stitch that suits the occasion. It would seem that many peoples have discovered its economies and joys.

There are two principal types of New Mexican *colcha* embroidery. In the first, a handwoven, handspun, plain weave, woolen ground is fully covered with couching stitch embroidery. This type will be referred to as "wool-on-wool *colcha* embroidery" (Plates 65–68). The second type employs a cotton ground with wool *colcha* embroidery motifs sparsely applied: it will be called "wool-on-cotton *colcha* embroidery" (Plates 69–70).

The earlier and rarer of the two forms of *colcha* embroidery, the wool-on-wool embroidery, is technically distinctive. The ground fabric is *sabanilla*, white, handwoven, balanced, plain weave of handspun wool, with a count that ranges from twelve to twenty-two yarns per 2.5 centimeters (one inch), and a typical loom width of about 76 centimeters (thirty inches).[7] Three seamed panels of *sabanilla* make up the backing fabric of the typical wool-on-wool embroidery. Side selvedges of the *sabanilla* are intact, while the ends are cut, turned, and hemmed. This backing is fully covered with *colcha* stitch embroidery. The covering, in fact, is so complete that it is very difficult, at times impossible, to detect the seaming of the *sabanilla* ground (Figure 2a). The embroidery yarn for these pieces is generally a single (Z-spun) handspun wool yarn, which is most often silky, long-staple wool used paired or doubled. A commercially prepared yarn occasionally is used for wool-on-wool *colcha* embroidery, notably the 3-ply (3-Z-spun-plied-S) red yarn in Plate 65. The wool-on-wool embroideries are frequently finished on all four sides with a simple woolen fringe.

over ▷

PLATE 65

Wool-on-wool colcha *embroidery, 1800–1850. 2.03 x 1.42 m. Ground fabric: white balanced plain weave, handspun wool (Z-spun), 21 per 2.5 cm. Embroidery: colcha couching stitch; handspun wool (Z-spun-paired); white,* brown, undyed-natural; blue, yellow, green, natural-dyed; commercially-spun wool (3-Z-spun-plied-S), red cochineal-dyed (UCLA D–32–10). Collected from a Mr. Chávez, Capulín, San Luis Valley, Colorado. Spanish Colonial Arts Society, Inc. Collection on loan to the Museum of New Mexico at the Museum of International Folk Art, Gift of Mary Cabot Wheelwright. L.5.58.41.*

PLATE 66

Wool-on-wool colcha *embroidery, 1790–1850. 2.25 x 1.71 m. Ground fabric: white balanced plain weave, handspun wool (Z-spun) 22 per 2.5 cm. Embroidery: colcha couching stitch; handspun wool (Z-spun-paired); white, natural-undyed; tan, dark and light blue, yellow, dark blue-green, all natural-dyed. Fred Harvey Fine Arts Collection on loan to the Museum of New Mexico at the Museum of International Folk Art. L.70.3.38.*

PLATE 67

Wool-on-wool colcha *embroidery fragment, 1750–1825. 1.68 x 1.31 m. Ground fabric: white balanced plain weave, handspun wool (Z-spun), 16–20 per 2.5 cm. Embroidery: colcha couching stitch; handspun wool (Z-spun-paired); white, brown, natural-undyed blue, blue-green, green, light green, yellow, and bright yellow, natural-dyed. Museum of New Mexico Collection at the Museum of International Folk Art, Gift of the Historical Society of New Mexico. A.5.54.9.*

PLATE 68

Wool-on-wool colcha *embroidery, 1790–1850. 2.16 x 1.55 m. Ground fabric: white balanced plain weave, handspun wool (Z-spun), 19 per 2.5 cm. Embroidery: colcha couching stitch, crossed and looped stitches; handspun wool (mostly Z-spun-paired); white, brown, natural-undyed; tan, blue, green, yellow, natural-dyed. International Folk Art Foundation Collection at the Museum of International Folk Art, a unit of the Museum of New Mexico. FA.67.43.4.*

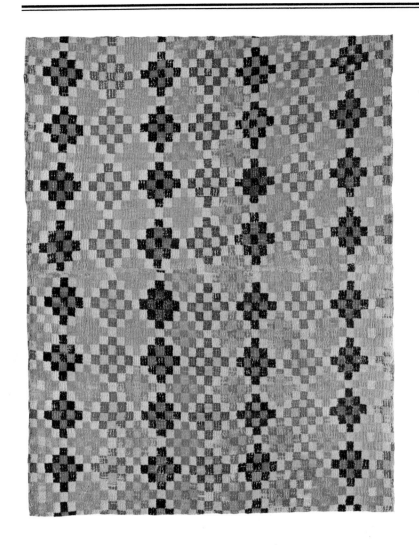

Colors used for the wool-on-wool embroideries vary from piece to piece, but there is consistent use of the light and dark natural undyed wool. Indigo, in varying shades, predominates as a dyed yarn. All of the other dyes appear to be natural, including a tan, a yellow, and varying shades of green, blue-green, and light-green, all presumably obtained by over-dyeing natural-dyed yellow with indigo. There is one bright red appearing in these textiles, the 3-ply yarn illustrated in Plate 65. This has been analyzed by Max Saltzman, and identified as cochineal.[8] Other dyed yarns from the same textile were analyzed for dye content, but no positive identification resulted. The tan is not brazilwood, not *cañaigre*, not mountain mahogany, not logwood, not any of the dyes that seemed to be logical suspects.[9]

Design sources for the wool-on-wool *colcha* embroideries are many and varied. A rather curious but very popular design is illustrated by Plate 67—small checks are arranged to form diagonals in the finished composition. This textile is thought to be one of the earliest *colcha* embroideries known.[10] Considering its soft texture and the wonderful combination of extremely fine yarns in a range of tans, greens, blues, and natural-undyed wool, this piece may possibly date from the mid-1700s. There are three closely related early textiles[11] and a whole series of later synthetic-dyed pieces which fit with the wool-on-wool group and are also based on this checkered pattern.[12] A number of the synthetic-dyed examples contain embroidery yarn that consists entirely of scraps of commercial wool knitting yarn. The ground fabrics are pieced from cotton feed sacks. These textiles, which date between 1900 and 1910, clearly illustrate how ideally suited the *colcha* couching stitch is for working out the simple geometric pattern.

For the most part, however, the wool-on-wool *colcha* embroideries are not stark and geometric; they are characterized instead by elaborate curvilinear floral patterns. Design sources for a number of these patterns can easily be detected. A zigzag repeat found in several of the wool-on-wool pieces (Figure 3 and Plate 68) is closely related not only to certain of the Saltillo-style Rio Grande blankets (Plates 43–45), but also to Mexican Saltillo *sarapes* (Plate 17), and to a Mexican embroidery in the collection at the Museum of International Folk Art.[13] Three pieces, including those shown in Figure 4 and Plate 68, display the heraldic double-headed eagle, symbol of the Hapsburgs.[14] The Maltese Cross clearly forms the central motif of the textile illustrated in

FIGURE 3

Detail of wool-on-wool **colcha** *embroidery illustrating the traditional zigzag motif. 2.57 x 1.37 m. Ground fabric: at least two widths seamed. White balanced plain weave, handspun wool (Z-spun). Embroidery: colcha couching stitch, handspun wool (Z-spun-paired), light and dark natural-undyed and indigo. Collected in Los Valdezes, San Luis Valley, Colorado. Museum of New Mexico Collection at the Museum of International Folk Art. Gift of Mary Cabot Wheelwright. Gift of the Historical Society of New Mexico. A.5.54.10.*

FIGURE 4

Wool-on-wool colcha embroidery illustrating a stylized, heart-shaped version of the Carmelite arms superimposed on a double-headed eagle. 1.43 x 1.07 m., two widths seamed. Ground fabric: white balanced plain weave, handspun wool (Z-spun). Embroidery: colcha couching stitch, chain stitch; handspun wool, natural-undyed white and brown, natural-dyed blue, tan, yellow, and over-dyed natural brown. Spanish Colonial Arts Society, Inc. Collection on loan to the Museum of New Mexico at the Museum of International Folk Art. L.5.57.41.

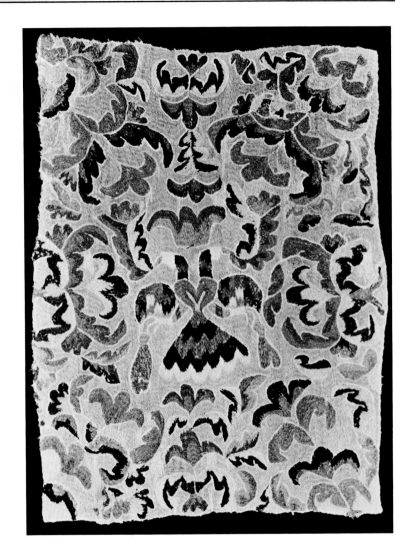

Plate 68. Less obvious, and pointed out by E. Boyd, is the fact that the three double-headed eagles known from the wool-on-wool embroideries (Figure 4, Plate 68, and note 14) incorporate a heart-shaped motif as the body of the eagle.[15] This closely resembles atypical renderings of the arms of the Confraternity of Our Lady of Carmel that were drawn on the title page of the *Book of Accounts* in Santa Cruz, New Mexico, by Father Francisco Campo Redondo around 1760 (Figure 5).[16]

Other sources for the designs of these embroideries include painted Indian chintz fabrics, the design of which is directly reflected in both the overall composition and the individual elements of these textiles. The heavy rounded leaf forms in Plates 65, 66, and 68 are closely related to the leaves in the chintz fabrics of the Coromandel Coast of India as seen in the "curled and scroll-like" leaves illustrated in Figure 6.[17] It is worthwhile to compare the embroideries and painted fabrics and note the positioning of the flowers in relation to the stems, as well as the characteristic way in which the flowers extend into one another. Shown in Figure 7 are details of the *colcha* embroideries and chintz fabrics which clearly illustrate similarities in design, including the fact that the curvilinear stem which runs the whole length vertically through the textile illustrated in Plate 65 is closely related to the famous flowering-tree chintz motif.[18]

How could far-off India have had an influence on isolated New Mexico? Indian fabric design, in fact, affected textile design throughout the world. According to John Irwin and Katharine Brett, "From 1600 to

FIGURE 5

An atypical heart-shaped rendering of the Carmelite arms superimposed on the Hapsburg double-headed eagle as shown on the title page of the Book of Accounts XXIV, *Confraternity of Our Lady of Carmel, Father Francisco Redondo, 1760–80, Santa Cruz, New Mexico. Archives of the Archdiocese of Santa Fe.*

FIGURE 6

Indian chintz fragment. Coromandel Coast, made for the European market, 1700–25. 35 x 14.5 cm. Harry Wearne Collections, Royal Ontario Museum, Toronto, 934.4.64, Neg. 62.AA.221.

1800—India was the greatest exporter of textiles the world had ever known, and her fabrics penetrated almost every market of the civilised world."[19] Of all the Indian fabric names, "chintz carries the strongest overtones, for its importation not only revolutionised taste and fashion but challenged the economic stability of western nations and provoked such passionate political controversy that even the survival of governments was at stake."[20] Extremely elaborate and refined examples of these painted fabrics are known to us today, but the great bulk of

a

b

FIGURE 7

Similarities of New Mexican colcha *embroidery and*
East Indian chintz designs. Curved stem forms: a.
chintz, b. colcha *embroidery. Flower forms: a. chintz, b.*
colcha *embroidery. Drawings of the chintz fabrics*
adapted from John Irwin and Katharine B. Brett, Origins
of Chintz, *Plate 144 and p. 69, Figure 29. Colcha motifs*
are details of Plate 65. Drawn by Nora Pickens.

exported chintz fabrics were "cheap expendable wares which have largely disappeared."[21]

We know from the documents that a great many fabrics were imported to New Mexico from New Spain.[22] Chintz, so widely exported throughout the world, has been known by many names. *Pintados*—its name in Portuguese—[23]is a fabric type found in the New Mexican import lists. Calicoes, fabrics commonly used for chintz painting, were of Indian origin, named for the seaport of Calicut on the southwest coast of India. Also listed in the documents are *carrancia fino de la India, percal,* and *guinga,* or gingham. Among all the Indian fabrics, however, "*indianas* was one of the most common cloths imported into New Mexico."[24] *Indianas* is defined as chintz, painted Indian cotton fabric of the Coromandel Coast. *Indianas* is the same as *indianilla,* a fabric mentioned in New Mexican church inventories of the period—although church authorities considered it unsuitable, it was used for altar frontals.[25]

No one has been able to document the exact routes by which these imported fabrics reached New Mexico. It is likely, however, that they came by way of the Manila Galleon, from the Philippines to Acapulco and thence north. "The viceroyalty of New Spain [William Schurz says] . . . was the principal market for the cargoes of the Manila Galleons."[26] Chinese porcelains dating from 1644 to 1722 have been excavated in the Palace of the Governors and in the New Mexican Spanish missions. Though these pieces may have been brought in as heirlooms, they do give us concrete evidence that Manila Galleon exports arrived in New Mexico at an early date.[27] The galleons, which operated between the Philippines and Acapulco from 1565 until 1815, carried a good deal of porcelain, but the bulk of the cargo was in the form of easily transported textiles. The textiles were, in fact, so popular that it was said in 1720 that "the Chinese goods form the ordinary dress of the natives of New Spain."[28] These textiles did not come just from China, however; according to Schurz "some merchandise that had been brought three fourths of the way round the world entered Mexico through Acapulco."[29] Included were "Flemish laces and 'many other kinds of European goods.'"[30] Though Indian fabrics were illegally imported at an earlier date, trade with India was officially banned until 1789 when the port of Manila was opened to Europeans. At that time "Indian cottons came to hold a place second only to the silks of China in the cargoes of the galleons."[31] So indeed, though the history is not completely authenticated, directly imported chintz fabrics may well have influenced *colcha* embroidery design, particularly between 1700 and 1815.

How were these wool-on-wool *colcha* embroideries used? Where and when were they made? A Mexican *exvoto* illustrated by Carrillo y Gariel clearly shows a similar embroidered fabric used as a bed covering.[32] A listing in the Santa Cruz church inventories, ca. 1787, mentions a new *colcha* given by a pious woman, intended as an *alfombra* (carpet) for the main altar.[33] The embroideries which incorporate the stylized Carmelite arms on a double-headed eagle (Figure 4 and Plate 68) are the only pictorial wool-on-wool *colcha* embroideries and the only ones, also, to incorporate religious symbols. One or all of them may, in fact, have been associated with the Chapel of Our Lady of Carmel in Santa Cruz.

On the basis of the symbol of the Carmelite *Book of Accounts* title page, which was devised between 1760 and 1780, these three textiles suggest "an 18th century age."[34] As has been pointed out, the geometric embroidery shown in Plate 67 seems, in comparison with other examples, to be earlier in date than other wool-on-wool embroideries. All of the wool-on-wool examples are natural dyed and thus could be dated pre-1850. The common suggested range for these textiles has always been 1800–1850. If Boyd's thesis regarding the 1760 Carmelite symbol is accepted, the design influence of the eighteenth-century chintz fabrics is recognized, and the seemingly older quality of the checkered textile (Plate 67) is significant, then this date range can conservatively be pushed back to 1750–1825.

Furthermore, the embroideries which incorporate the Carmelite symbol (Figure 4 and Plate 68) may have "a point of origin in or near Santa Cruz."[35] The only other wool-on-wool *colcha* embroideries with any provenience come from the San Luis Valley of Colorado. The embroidery illustrated in Plate 65 was collected in Capulín, while the textile shown in Figure 3 was purchased in Los Valdezes.[36] Since the San Luis Valley was settled by the Spanish in the 1850s, these pieces could have been woven and embroidered there, or more likely, they "could have been brought in by the colonists from northern New Mexico."[37] In any case, as far as we know, the wool-on-wool

embroideries all come from the northern part of the Rio Grande Valley. As Irene Emery has said, the production of the wool-on-wool embroideries seems to be quite "restricted in both time and space."[38]

The second style of *colcha*-type embroidery, illustrated in Plates 69 and 70 and Figure 8, "is made up of design embroidered in wool on a background of plain white cloth, usually cotton."[39] Though there has been a great deal of disagreement as to the dating of the wool-on-cotton *colcha* embroideries, it is generally accepted that they are later than the wool-on-wool examples.[40] As E. Boyd says, "it is fairly certain that embroidering on, or the use of, cotton yardage was a 19th century development in New Mexico."[41]

Although the *colcha* couching stitch continued to reign supreme with the wool-on-cotton *colcha*-type embroideries, there is a complete changeover in materials and in the way in which materials are used. A tightly woven cotton twill ground replaces the loosely woven wool *sabanilla*. Fine, plied commercial embroidery yarns come into use, replacing the thick, silky, single handspun yarns. "In a considerable number of the embroideries in this style the background material is a particular kind of soft cotton 2/1 twill of quite consistent weight, weave and width, and apparently handwoven."[42] These cotton twills were not woven in the Spanish tradition of the Rio Grande Valley, but were most probably brought to New Mexico over the Santa Fe Trail. When New Mexico became a territory of the U.S. in 1846, cottons, which had hitherto been quite rare,[43] flooded the market in New Mexico. Over the Trail, along with the trade fabrics, came the commercially prepared and, later, the synthetic-dyed yarns used in these embroideries.

Patterning of the wool-on-cotton *colcha* embroideries is very different from the distinctive forms found in the wool-on-wool examples. Almost all of the wool-on-cotton pieces seem to be framed by an outer floral border (Plates 69 and 70, Figure 8). The introduction of animal motifs is frequent, as illustrated by the deer shown in Figure 8. Common to a number of the embroideries is a central motif: either one like that in Figure 8, or a small circular motif placed at the very center of the textile.[44]

A multitude of reasons can be cited for these changes in design, practical explanations dominating. As Marianne Stoller has pointed out, "the shift to free-standing designs"[45] in the wool-on-cotton

FIGURE 8

Detail of wool-on-cotton colcha *embroidery, ca.*
1850–65, 2.12 x 1.40 m. Detail of center portion.
Illustrates the use of animal motifs and a central focus in
the design. Ground fabric: white cotton plain-weave trade
cloth. Embroidery: colcha *couching stitch, flat and*
looped stitches; commercially spun wool; natural-dyed
tans, blues, browns, and red and undyed white.
International Folk Art Foundation Collection, E. Boyd
Memorial Fund, at the Museum of International Folk Art,
a unit of the Museum of New Mexico. FA.75.28.1.

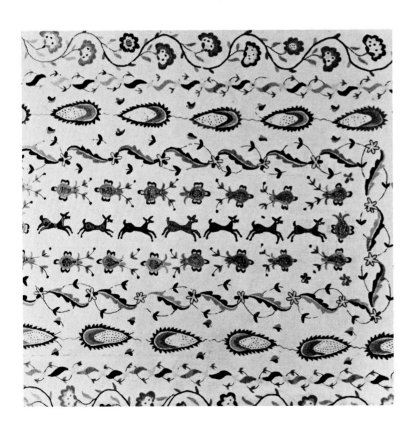

embroideries was brought about because of changes in the material used. The heavy handspun yarns were ideally suited for embroidery of the loosely woven *sabanilla,* and the weight ratio of yarns to fabric was perfect for fully covering the ground fabric. "Increasing supplies of . . . cottons, brought into the Southwest by Anglo-Americans, especially after 1846, rapidly brought the demise of *sabanilla*."[46] The silky handspun yarns would have frayed had they been used for embroidering the tightly woven twill fabrics. The new plied yarns, combined with a tightly woven ground fabric, made full coverage of the ground difficult and lent added appeal to the idea of freestanding designs.

Though there were secondary sources as well, designs of the wool-on-cotton *colcha* embroideries seem to have as their primary source the widely exported chintz fabrics of India. The story is complicated. Boyd says that "when the East India trade brought fine cottons to Europe they were received as exotic novelties, and their hand painted, block printed, or resist dyed patterns were promptly borrowed by needleworkers."[47] American crewelwork, which employs a combination of many stitches, was based on the embroidery of seventeenth-century England, which strongly reflected the Indian chintz fabrics.[48] Crewelwork of the Eastern Seaboard was brought west via the Santa Fe Trail. The textile illustrated in Plate 69 "would seem to relate stylistically to North American crewel embroidery."[49] The floral borders, the flowers themselves, the sinuous and continuous curve throughout the full length of the embroidery (Plate 69), and the stylized birds and insects (Plate 70)—all of these elements serve to illustrate the relationship of the wool-on-cotton *colcha* embroideries to eastern American crewelwork, an example of which is illustrated in Figure 9a. More significantly, the curious disembodied "C"-shaped forms which are repeated all along one side of the textile illustrated in Plate 69 and in Figure 9b are derived from floral motifs of the Indian chintz fabrics.[50] This plant form, presented as a geometric shape disassociated with the overall pattern, is a motif that recurs in a majority of the wool-on-cotton embroideries, and, as illustrated in Figure 9b, it is clear that it was derived from eastern American embroideries. Although the *colcha* couching stitch remained popular, other stitches were introduced and used in an interesting manner. Note the crosshatched effect occurring in small areas at both ends of the altar cloth illustrated in Plate 69 and

PLATE 69

Wool-on-cotton **colcha** *embroidery, ca. 1865. 2.18 x
1.40 m. Ground fabric: white cotton 2/1 twill trade cloth.
Embroidery: colcha couching stitch, flat and looped
stitches; commercially-spun wool, red, pink, light and
and dark blue, blue-green, brown, tan, natural-dyed;
white, natural-undyed. Made for a family chapel built
about 1865 by José Delores Durán at Llano de Santa
Barbara, east of Peñasco. Museum of New Mexico
Collection at the Museum of International Folk Art.
A.67.44.1.*

PLATE 70

Wool-on-cotton **colcha** *embroidery, ca. 1850. 2.01 x
0.66 m. Ground fabric: white cotton 2/1 twill trade cloth.
Embroidery: colcha couching stitch, flat and looped
stitches; commercially-spun wool; red, pink, dark blue,
browns, tans, natural-dyed; white, undyed. Said to have
been used in Cristo Rey Church, Santa Fe. Spanish
Colonial Arts Society, Inc. Collection on loan to the
Museum of New Mexico at the Museum of International
Folk Art. L.5.73.11.*

compare these sections to a similar flower detail in Figure 9c. Note also that both types of embroidery tend toward the use of the slender stem stitch for delineation of the stems. Furthermore, animals, such as the deer illustrated in Figure 8, are characteristic of American crewelwork.[51]

As mentioned above, there may be additional sources for the designs of the wool-on-cotton *colcha* embroideries. For example, these textiles seem to be somewhat closely related to certain Mexican embroideries in various museum collections.[52] Frescoes in archways dating 1762 at Misión Concepción in eastern Texas near Douglass, Nacodoches County, contain continuous floral borders quite like those depicted in the New Mexican embroideries.[53] A finely worked embroidery which may be either Texas Spanish Colonial or Mexican shows quite close affinity to the wool-on-cotton textiles.[54] And finally,

E. Boyd makes a very strong visual case for the influence of Spanish embroidery.[55] What we seem to be dealing with, as concerns the wool-on-cotton embroideries, is an international style which has, as its ultimate source, the widely exported Indian chintz fabrics.

In certain instances, the designs of the wool-on-cotton *colcha* embroideries can be seen to result from their function. The wool-on-cotton pieces seem to have been used in much the same manner as were the wool-on-wool examples. E. Boyd, however, has pointed to a shift in use: "The Anglo-American introduction of glazed windows and bedsteads created a use for curtains and counterpanes, and as a result . . . the surviving wool embroideries on cotton were made in suitable sizes and shapes for these purposes."[56] Yet *colcha* embroideries, even those which contain no religious symbols, were made specifically for church use. The textile illustrated in Plate 69 is an example. This altar cloth was made for use in a chapel. The half covering the top of the altar is framed by a border of running stems and small flowers, while larger motifs fill the center. The front panel is entirely different with a bold meander that frames large floral elements.[57]

It can be assumed that, as with the wool-on-wool embroideries, most of the wool-on-cotton textiles were made by women in the home. And again, the provenience of these pieces seems to be northern New Mexico. Though a few examples in the collections of eastern American museums suggest Mexican provenience, and though one *colcha* embroidery has come to the Museum of New Mexico from the family of Christine Lumbach in Buena Vista, Mora County,[58] the only example to have an exact provenience is the piece illustrated in Plate 69. This extremely fine altar cloth was made for the family chapel which was built around 1865 by José Delores Durán at Llano de Santa Barbara, east of Peñasco.[59] It is to be hoped that more information will come to light in the future, but at present everything indicates that wool-on-cotton *colcha* embroidery was quite strictly limited in distribution to the northern Rio Grande Valley.

During the twentieth century there have been numerous revivals of both types of *colcha* embroidery. One of these revival movements was led by Nellie Dunton, another by Rebecca James.[60] There is currently a revival of the art in the San Luis Valley. Guadalupe Salazar in Española teaches *colcha* embroidery, as does Tillie Stark in Santa Fe. Lastly,

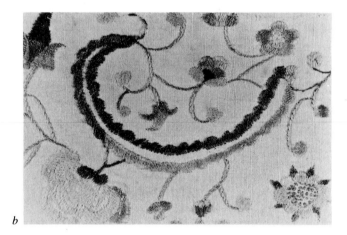

a

b

c

FIGURE 9

*Details of petticoat border, ca. 1750, found in
Connecticut. Old Sturbridge Village, 64.6.22 A and B. a.
Overall view illustrating the use of stem stitch for
fine-line curvilinear stems. b. Detail of "C"-shaped
forms. c. Detail illustrating cross-hatched effect in
the flower.*

there is a group in Taos who created the so-called Carson-type *colcha* embroidery about 1930.[61] Yet *colcha* embroidery, so admired today, was apparently not nearly so popular in former times.

In conjunction with the present project almost 2,000 textiles in over forty institutions throughout the United States have been analyzed. The survey included Rio Grande blankets, *jergas,* and *colcha* embroideries of New Mexico, and Saltillo-style *sarapes* of Mexico. Every piece that turned up was studied. Among all of these pieces there were fewer than twenty wool-on-wool *colcha* embroideries. There were a few more, over fifty, of the wool-on-cotton variety. Individuals who were very active in collecting New Mexican textiles during the 1920s and 1930s concur that whereas many hundreds of the Rio Grande blankets were collected, very few, perhaps one in one hundred of the textiles, were old style wool-on-wool *colcha* embroideries.[62]

The word *colcha* appears with some frequency in the early records. Yet given the way in which textile terms are used—coming into vogue and then going out of style, and knowing the present difficulty experienced in defining the term, it cannot be assumed that *colcha* in the documents refers to these specific types of wool embroidery. "We know of eighteenth-century bedspreads from San Juan de las Colchas (a town in Old Mexico, presumably named for one of its industries, the making of *colchas*) which were not embroidered, but brocaded, and there seems no association in Spanish of the word *colcha* with the idea of embroidery."[63] Furthermore, Minge has cited numerous references to *colchas,* most of which clearly have no relation to the New Mexican *colcha* embroideries. Only a few of the references actually describe a textile which, like the listing of *sábana de sabanilla labrada* (embroidered woolen homespun) in the 1818 inventory of the Santuario at Chimayó, was a wool-on-wool *colcha* embroidery.[64]

In 1949 Irene Emery wrote about *colcha* embroidery: "We know remarkably little about when and where in New Mexico such pieces were first made, how widespread their production may have been, whether the making of them died out at some time in the past and was later revived, or whether there has been some continuity of production of *colcha*-type embroidery in one or another of its forms up to and including the present time."[65] Today, thirty years later, there are still many unknowns. *Colcha* embroideries were used for church decoration and for bed coverings. Many pieces may have worn out; many disappeared at the time when there was an attempt to be rid of the local-style decoration in the churches. Many *colcha* embroideries may still be carefully hidden in homes as treasured family heirlooms.

With the known facts, it can only be assumed that *colcha* embroidery was a household art. These embroideries were made in the homes by women, perhaps by leisured women who were wealthy enough to be freed from the tasks of carding and spinning and so could lavish time on the making of purely decorative things.[66] Realizing how few examples of the older *colcha*-type embroideries turn up for sale, and how few appeared in our survey of museums throughout the United States, it appears that *colcha* embroidery, in former times, was indeed quite rare and unusual. As Irene Emery stated almost thirty years ago:

"The fact that so little use was made of any but this one stitch in such a comparatively large group of embroidered pieces suggests either a notably strong tradition or a much less widespread development of the craft than has generally been assumed. We may find that the use of this stitch in New Mexico—and the production of the embroideries—was more restricted in both time and space than we have been led to believe."[67] So little is known—a single note found in the church inventories seems to indicate that pious women, in a spirit of devotion, may have produced much of New Mexican *colcha* embroidery for church use.[68]

It appears that the making of *colcha* embroidery lost impetus toward the end of the nineteenth century. This is capably described by E. Boyd: "Stitchery declined in quality as did planning of patterns, which grew helter-skelter as whimsical inscriptions . . . and symbols in gaudy colors replaced handsome older designs. Crochet, patchwork, feather-stitching, and prestamped patterns for cross-stitch literally stifled creative free-hand embroidery in New Mexico by the end of the 19th century."[69]

Yet "*colcha* says 'life is . . . good and joyous.' "[70] Happily, this buoyant, free-flowing art form is now enjoying a new lease on life.

By about 1880–1900, the remarkable weaving industry instituted by the Spanish was in decline. Only a few individuals, primarily in the mountains north of Santa Fe, continued to rely upon weaving as a sole means of support. The availability of inexpensive, manufactured textiles from the eastern United States can be cited as one of the causes of this decline. Another was the shifting economic structure of the United States, as rural agrarian life made way for industrialization and urban life.

This shift in the economy had profound effects upon the Spanish arts of New Mexico. Even though art and craft traditions, which declined rapidly in other areas of the United States, were maintained in New Mexico, these traditions were often affected radically by the demands which came with increasing commercialization and changing patronage.[1]

The marketing of crafts was not retained entirely by the Spanish because Anglo-American merchants and patrons entered the field at an early date.[2] Crafts once made for domestic use began to be created primarily for purchase by tourists and curio collectors.[3] This change in patronage caused not only changes in style but in function as well. For example, the Rio Grande blanket tended to be transformed into the "Chimayó" rug.[4] Carvers made not only religious art but also secular objects. And embroiderers employed the *colcha* stitch upon place mats and doilies. The result of such shifts has been an acculturation of the arts rather than their complete demise.

Between the 1820s and 1880s the Santa Fe Trail was the highway which brought these new influences from eastern America into New Mexico. People and goods poured for the first time into the American West. The impact on the area around Santa Fe was necessarily felt owing to its unique position as a crossroads in the movements not only east and west but also north and south. In 1821 Mexico gained

Changing patterns in Southwest Spanish textiles*

CLASS	FUNCTIONAL TRADITIONAL	MODIFIED TRADITIONAL	(EXTINCTION) COMMERCIAL 1 (ANGLO TRADERS)	COMMERCIAL 11 (SPANISH WEAVERS)	COMMERCIAL 111 (ANGLO DESIGNERS)	REVIVALS	ABERRANT	REINTEGRATED ARTS
Date	1696 to 1850/60	1850/60 to 1880	1880 to 1920s	1920 to present	1930 to 1947	1930 to present	1920 to 1945	1973 to present
Intended Audience	Home use Export	Home use Export	Tourist Home use?	Tourist	Tourist/commercial sales	Anglo patrons Home use Tourist	Not applicable	Community
Market Control	Spanish	Spanish	Anglo	Spanish	Anglo	Anglo/Spanish	Not applicable	Spanish
Materials	Native	Native Synthetic dyes Some commercial wool	Commercial Some native	Commercial	Commercial	Native, some commercial	Commercial Native	Commercial
Design	Traditional Striped and Saltillo designs	Traditional Modified *Vallero* style	Some traditional Pan-Southwest Striped & Saltillo design	Some traditional Pan-Southwest	English-Scottish plaids	Recreations of traditional	Unique visions	Nostalgia scenes
Textile Types	*Jerga,* blankets, *colchas*	Blankets, *jerga*/rag rugs, *colcha*	Blankets, rugs, curtains, "scarves"	Blankets, rugs, curtains, jackets, pillows, hangings	Ties, suiting fabrics	Blankets, rugs, *colcha,* hangings, pillows, etc.	Hangings	Tapestries (embroidery of hand-drawn scenes)
Artist & Patrons	Names unknown	Names unknown	Weavers names unknown Dealers: Candelario/ Gold Fred Harvey Julius Gans McMillan	Weavers primarily anonymous Dealer/ weaving family Ortega family Trujillo family Córdova family	Weavers anon. Dealer/Designers: McCrossen Burro Weavers Knox	Patrons: Spanish Colonial Arts Society, Native Market Organizations: Artes Antiguas Vocational schools Weaving & Dyeing Workshop Individuals: David Salazar Tillie Stark Agueda Martínez Carson settlers	Celso Gallegos, Policarpio Valencia	Villanueva villagers (as organized by Carmen Orrego-Salas) Pecos quilters

*Compilation based on Graburn, 1976.

independence from Spain. New Mexico was for the first time free to open its borders to Anglos, and thus the Spanish were free to welcome commercial ventures and to oversee their operation. A major trade commodity being brought into New Mexico was textiles: "When the commonest domestic cloth, manufactured wholly from cotton, brought from two to three dollars a yard at Santa Fe, and other articles at the same ratio to cost, no wonder the commerce with the far-off market appeared to those who desired to send goods there a veritable Golconda."[5]

The effect of these newly introduced goods was not immediately destructive to traditional arts. As Drs. Wheat and Minge point out, the evidence of 1840 *guías* supports the continued existence of extremely active textile production in New Mexico at this time, twenty years after the opening of the Trail.[6] It is 1880 which marks the terminal point for the period of highly active regional textile production, as well as for a variety of other artistic endeavors, for this date represents the advent of the railroad to the American West. The effect of the railroad was to be far more profound than the first wagons to cross the Trail or the placing of the American flag upon Santa Fe's plaza in 1846. The coming of the railroad brought to an end preindustrial society in the West. Cottage industry, which disappeared in England, France, New England, and the middle western states, was to fade in New Mexico as well. With the coming of the railroad, New Mexico became inextricably tied to Western industrial society.

The period between 1820 and 1880 represents the pinnacle of artistic achievement for the Spanish in New Mexico. They were freed from colonial status and not yet ensnared by the demands of industrialization. For sixty years they were free to follow their own pursuits. During this period was to come the best of the brilliant religious folk art of the New Mexicans and the bulk of the impressive Rio Grande textile tradition.[7]

COMMERCIALIZATION

The history of Spanish weaving in the Southwest in the twentieth century is not limited only to the Spanish. Once bearers of a new culture arrive, the demands of their aesthetic and functional systems must also be satisfied.[8] The previously mentioned example, in which textiles originally designed for use as blankets were transformed for use as rugs, illustrates the type of shifts made to accommodate new users. In addition, the aesthetic demands of the newcomers included a gradual embracing of what they considered to be a "Spanish" or "Indian" style. But it was a style which had to accommodate the functional demands of Anglo-American life. Objects such as end tables, table lamps, bedsteads, and magazine racks as well as textiles were given a "Spanish" look for reasons of fashion. Over the years "Spanish" style textiles would also become available through Sears and Roebuck catalogues and modified Indian/Spanish motifs appeared on everything from rag rugs to shower curtains, thus confusing and diluting original styles and sources.

While the old Rio Grande blanket is cherished in Spanish families as an antique, contemporary textiles made by the Spanish are generally purchased by tourists who seek a representative handicraft from the Southwest. To meet this demand textiles produced in the twentieth century by Spanish people often bear designs best described as "Pan-Southwest." They are a mixture of motifs that bring to mind things both Indian and Spanish and carry a visual message of being simply southwestern (Figure 1). Such textiles fit easily into a home in Arizona, California, New Mexico, Texas, or Colorado. They are more economical than a "genuine" Navajo rug if not equally durable. The new commercial aspect to these handwoven textiles has brought materials, designs, and colors which were not present in the old, traditional Rio Grande blankets.

One of the first steps necessary for successful commercialization of the "Chimayó" was the deliberate standardization of size for individual textile types. Where blankets were previously woven in various lengths outside commercial establishments now required that a standard size be available for purchase.[9] Blankets gradually diminished in popularity since they were more expensive than mass-produced, commercial textiles, and they became less fashionable over the years. Throw or area rugs, couch throws, pillows, jackets, and occasionally curtains gained in popularity as they had higher visibility in the Anglo home. Early curio dealers and later the Chimayó establishments were able both to identify and to serve these shifting requirements. The role that traders played in the standardization of sizes, the new functions of Spanish textiles, and the use of "Pan-Southwestern" designs are not totally clear

FIGURE 1

Chimayó "scarf" by Florida Vigil, Chimayó, New Mexico, ca. 1940, one width, 66 x 42 cm. Warp: 2-ply commercial wool; weft: 4-ply commercial wool, natural-dyed indigo, cochineal, California poppy.

This small textile would have been used as a table scarf. The central diamond motif is typical of the quasi-modernistic designs which were made popular by the weaving shops in Chimayó. Both the function and design of this textile indicate that it was made for the tourist market. Like many of the weavers in Chimayó, Florida Vigil is related to one of the families which operates a weaving establishment; she is David Ortega's first cousin on his mother's side of the family. From the collection of David Ortega.

and require further research. But it appears that commercial establishments in Santa Fe in the late nineteenth and early twentieth centuries played a primary role in directing textile production to meet the demands of the tourist seeking to carry back a bit of the Southwest.

One of the early curio establishments in New Mexico was owned by the Candelario family and located on San Francisco Street in Santa Fe. This curio and general merchandise establishment was operated by Jesusito Candelario until "In 1885, Jesús hired Jake Gold to run his portion of the business, became converted to the Presbyterian faith, changed the spelling of his last name from Candelaria to Candelario, acquired an education from a mid-western divinity college and eventually became a missionary schoolmaster."[10] Gold, an easterner, ran the business from 1885 until 1903, when Candelario returned to stay with his establishment until his death in 1938.

Blanket records of the Fred Harvey Company, an enterprise which began in the curio business around 1900 (Figure 2), indicate that as early as 1901 hundreds of "Chimallo scarfs" were being sold to the company by Jake Gold for eventual distribution throughout the U.S.[11] From these ledgers also comes a terminology of three types of Spanish New Mexican weavings being purchased or sold at this time: "old" or "ancient Chimallo," "modern Chimallo," and "Chimallo scarfs."[12]

The Candelario business ledgers and correspondence, which are still extant, are a treasure for the historian seeking a glimpse of the busy days of sales and trade which succeeded the railroad.[13] An invoice dated January 8, 1910 shows the effect commercialization was having upon what the invoice calls "Chimayo" blankets. Sizes are standardized at 26" x 50", 36" x 50", 42" x 80", 55" x 80", 36" x 72", and curtains at 36" x 90".[14] Prices are fixed at a level which suggests that high production would be necessary for the craftsman to make a living. For example, a 20" x 40" blanket was purchased wholesale for $1.50. Not only standardization and rate of production but also design was being controlled through commercialization. "I want all nice and clean patterns with black and white and plenty of red in them,"[15] states an order from the Candelario store. Traders were not only purchasing finished textiles from weavers; they also were involved in the sale of materials to the weaver: "We received this morning a letter from our friend Mr. Webber, who writes under date of Nov. 17th in your behalf, advising that you are interested in a 4 ply all wool yarn of which he has sent a sample in black."[16] (Letter from Guerin Spinning Co.,

Interior of the Fred Harvey Albuquerque Indian
Building, 1905. Photograph by G. W. Hance. This
interior photo illustrates the large variety of both Indian
and Spanish antiques and tourist items which were
available to the western traveler through the Fred Harvey
Company. Museum of New Mexico Collection at the
Museum of International Folk Art.

Woonsocket, R.I., Nov. 22, 1909 to the Candelario Store.) Thus the weaver's relationship with the dealer and manufacturer was direct and dependent. High production for modest wages would necessitate the use of commercial wools. In addition, the dealer made specific requests for designs and colors which he felt were most easily marketed. The weaver, although still living and working in a rural area, was directly tied to a system which had control over his art. In such circumstances tradition quickly gives way to marketability. The effect upon many weavers and weaving areas was the end of reliance upon their art. They were not able or willing to make this change and the market for the traditional blanket was filled by machine-made products.

During this transitional period in the history of Spanish textiles there appears to be little attempt to shift textile production from cottage industry—that is, an industry whose labor force is the family working at home using their own equipment—to manufacturing. For example, the tenth U.S. Census of Manufacturers in 1880 accounts for 21 "cotton, silk, and woolen mill operatives" in New Mexico as compared to 3,124 "stockraisers and herders."[17] The direction New Mexico was taking was away from textile production, since competition with eastern mills made both cottage industry and large-scale production difficult.

The absence of fast-moving water made New Mexico an unlikely site for the development of textile factories. Rather, the late nineteenth and early twentieth centuries in New Mexico saw the rise of large-scale sheep and cattle ranching, a development which was also to have a negative effect upon the creation of the traditional Rio Grande blanket.[18]

What then was to become of textile production among the Spanish in New Mexico? Would traditional designs, techniques, and materials be lost? Would the weaver become exploited and find his art cheapened and debased? Or was it possible that in this difficult period of change, the strong human reliance upon the forces of continuity and accommodation would allow the development of another role for the handwoven textile in New Mexico?

The niche which was discovered for the "Chimayo" blanket was to be very different from the role that the Rio Grande blanket once played as primary export and household necessity. This new role served a different patron, a patron who often traveled west upon the vehicle which had wrought so many changes in New Mexican life. The tourist came west upon the railroad and returned with a souvenir, often a southwestern textile.

The train was "like a slice out of one of the eastern cities set down bodily in the midst of a perfect wilderness."[19] It brought not only a bewildering variety of new goods and a turbulent new economic system, but it also carried visitors such as the above-quoted Lord Dunraven. American and European tourists set out to view what remained of the American frontier. Not infrequently this would include a trip to the pueblos around Santa Fe as well as a visit to the historic capitol. Early tourism was strictly an upper-class affair. The expense of a western visit exceeded that of a trip to Europe.[20] Wealthy tourists, in heading west, were following a late Victorian desire for the exotic and foreign. They might well be searching for the proper ornaments to fill an "Indian Room" in their home.[21]

By 1900 increasing numbers of tourists were able to afford the trip west as travel costs became more reasonable. These tourists actively sought examples of Western Americana, be it Indian, Spanish, or cowboy. Tourism quickly became a major industry in northern New Mexico. New hotels, sightseeing services, and curio shops such as Julius Gans' Southwest Arts and Crafts, Fred Harvey Company, and McMillan's Spanish and Indian Trading Company opened to handle the new trade.

The period from 1880 to 1920, then, saw the transformation of the blanket into a tourist item. This development, while retaining some of the methods and designs of traditional blankets, incorporated a variety of new elements which clearly distinguish the new from the old. For example, the previously mentioned standardization of size, use of commercial wool, commercial cotton warps, and synthetic dyes, and a system of Pan-Southwestern design suited to tourist taste were incorporated in varying degrees depending upon the inclination of the weaver or the demands of the dealer. These textiles of 1880–1920 on the whole can be distinguished from their immediate predecessors, that is, those textiles made between 1860 and 1880. The new look of weavings made between 1880 and 1920 was a result of commercialism and accommodation to aesthetic systems which came, primarily, from outside the community. The passing of the traditional blanket and the advent of the new, of course, did not happen overnight. But after a certain point in time there were very few blankets still being made in the traditional style for traditional uses.

∧∨∧∨∧

THE WEAVER ENTREPRENEUR

Following the initial disruption of traditional life and the subsequent imposition of an Anglo economic system, a few Spanish weavers and weaving families began commercial ventures in the production of Spanish textiles for the curio or tourist trade. From 1880 to 1920, it seems that Spanish textile production primarily served the will of the Anglo-American or urban curio dealer. He ordered textiles from the weavers who in turn purchased commercial materials from him. The weaver would then sell his production back to the dealer for a modest sum. A few weavers discovered they could supplement their incomes by delivering some of their neighbors' textiles to the dealer for them. This led to the purchase of locally made textiles by a single villager for resale to the trader for profit.

This weaver was in an entrepreneurial position which was further enhanced by yet another fundamental change in modes of transportation: the availability of the automobile to the American public. With the automobile's popularity after the 1920s, not only was the buying public able to travel directly to the home of the weaver (or to the home of the weaver who had collected textiles from his weaver-neighbors) but also the weaver had more direct access to his market. With a car or truck, it was easier for the weaver with a sufficient amount of goods to carry them to the shipper and thus eliminate his reliance upon the urban dealer for sales. Although the urban dealer continued to play a vital role in marketing the production of the rural weaver, the latter, nevertheless, gained a measure of independence and control over the sales of his product and consequently was able to share in the profits of his work.

The scenario outlined above is essentially the story of Nicacio Ortega (1875–1964), Chimayó, New Mexico (Figure 3).[22] His father José Ramón Ortega (1829–1904) and grandfather Gervacio Ortega had been weavers before him. Like other weaving families such as the Trujillos, Ortizes, and Vigils of Chimayó, they lived during difficult periods of transition at the turn of the century. It can only be conjectured what discussions were held between the generations of weavers regarding the demands of the traders, the use of new materials, or the experimentation with different designs. But without the advent of private, rapid transportation, these weavers would have continued to be controlled by the urban dealer. As weavers and businessmen, families like the Ortegas and Trujillos were in a position to directly coordinate the activities of village weavers toward successful commercialism. Like the dealers before them, they continued to use wools imported from the East and Midwest. They used "Pan-Southwestern" designs and central diamond motifs and concentrated on textiles in standardized sizes.

During the Depression, 1929–39, weaving found a new impetus in communities which had lost almost all other means of income.

FIGURE 3

Blanket, Nicacio Ortega, Chimayó, New Mexico, ca. 1960, one width, 1.80 x 1.18 m. Warp and weft: 1-ply handspun undyed wool. Collection of Sallie Wagner, Santa Fe.

Chimayó, with its continued activity in weaving, relied heavily upon this income source, as evidenced in the Tewa Basin Report of 1935 which gives a picture of handicraft activities throughout the area north of Santa Fe.

Summary of weaving statistics *

	NUMBER OF WEAVERS	COMMENTS
Nambé	12	learned weaving at Santa Cruz High School
San Ildefonso	10	rag rugs
Santa Cruz	23	learned at high school, wages per hour—15¢
Puebla	1	
Cuarteles	2	
Chimayó	90–100	six blanket dealers, total sales 3,500–4,000 a year
Cundiyó	14	work on contractual basis w/Chimayó dealers
Córdova	1	part time
Truchas	10	all on contract with Chimayó dealers, earn $1/day
Angostura	3	wool purchased in Española
Barranca	1	
Chamita	2–3	some few of the families weave their own blankets
Ojo Sarco	1	
Trampas	2	
Rio Puebla District	5	twenty people in the community spin, card, and dye wools on a one-half share basis (were planning a co-op)

(Pojoaque, Chupadero/En Medio, Española, El Guache, Rio Chama, Tierra Azul, El Rito, Abiquiu, Vallecito and Rio Oso, Ghost Ranch, Leyden/Brady/Claro, Velarde, Embudo and Dixon were listed as having no weavers.)

*Compiled from *Tewa Basin Report,* 1935, Volume 2 (Weigle, ed., 1975).

FIGURE 4

Blanket, David Ortega, Chimayó, New Mexico, ca. 1960, one width, 2.06 x 1.41 m. Warp: 2-ply commercial wool; weft: 4-ply commercial wool, synthetic-dyed and undyed white. Collection of Sallie Wagner, Santa Fe.

There were 90 to 100 weavers and 7 blanket dealers in the village of Chimayó at this time. According to the report, "The seven dealers buy the wool at the rate of $1.20 to $1.45 per pound, and let it to the weavers at a rate of $1.40 to $1.60 per pound."[23]

Eighty to ninety percent of the output is sold by the dealers to business houses in New Mexico, Arizona, Colorado, and California. The sale is very uneven, the best months being October, November, and December. Since 1929 the sale has dropped off. This is the reason for the large percentage of weaving on a contractual basis. However, the sale in 1935 thus far has been better than that for the corresponding period in 1934. Most of the sales are sent out via parcel post, and the payment to the dealers is made in 30 days, or after the blankets have been sold. Many of the weavers have to wait until the blankets have been sold before receiving payment.[24]

Essentially, dealer/weavers functioned much as the early traders had, but the profits of the business remained within the community. Today, as in the past, they not only sell to passing tourists but also distribute textiles throughout the U.S. The structure of the business has remained much the same over the years, but with continued expansion. Today, David Ortega (Figure 4 and p. 187 of this publication), Nicacio's son, manages the Ortega weaving business which includes eighty active looms throughout the community with weavers who warp about 3,000 lbs. of wool a year.

Throughout the development of Spanish-owned weaving businesses the well established Anglo traders of Santa Fe continued to practice business, but they often acquired textiles from the Spanish weaving establishments for their sales in town. In the early 1930s another form of textile business developed in Santa Fe which relied upon the labor of Spanish weavers—McCrossen Handwoven Textiles. George McCrossen recollects that "They began drawing weavers from native villages like Chimayó and Santa Cruz. There is an excellent

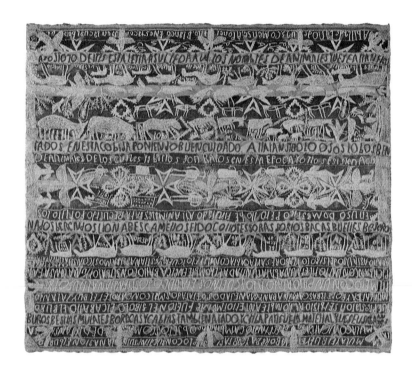

PLATE 71

Embroidery, Policarpio Valencia, Santa Cruz, New
Mexico, 1925. 1.39 x 1.64 m. Commercial cotton
bedspread ground, cotton string embroidery, synthetic
dyes. Museum of New Mexico Collection at the Museum
of International Folk Art. Gift of the Historical Society of
New Mexico. B89/13.

PLATE 72

Weaving, John R. Trujillo, Chimayó, N.M., 1976. One
width, 2.2 x 1.35 m. Commercial single-ply wool yarn in
natural colors. Museum of New Mexico Collection at the
Museum of International Folk Art. Purchased with the aid
of funds from the National Endowment for the Arts and
the International Folk Art Foundation. A.76.56.1.

PLATE 73

Weaving, October Leaves, Teresa Sagel, 1977. One
width, 1.80 x .88 m. Warp: 2-ply commercial white wool;
weft: 2-ply commercial wool. Natural dyes include apple
leaves, chile powder, cota. Museum of New Mexico
Collection at the Museum of International Folk Art.
Purchased with the aid of funds from the National
Endowment for the Arts and the International Folk Art
Foundation. A.78.21.1.

supply of native weavers with a feeling for beauty, fabrics and tradition
for painstaking craftsmanship."[25] The McCrossen business brought
looms from the East with widths standardized at 20", 38", and 60".
Weavers were engaged in making textiles designed by Preston
McCrossen, textiles which had the look of fine Scottish and English
plaids and were used as suiting and tie fabrics. According to George
McCrossen "the business started in the Depression and flew up in the
aftermath."[26] Other enterprises such as the Burro Weavers and Santa Fe
Hand Woven Fabrics entered the trade of making fine wool suiting

fabrics, again relying on Spanish weavers. In 1936 the McCrossens had seventy-eight employees and a net volume of sales of $68,186.00; by 1943 volume had grown to $145,057. The year 1943 marked a switch from the primary employment of men to women as weavers due to World War II. This successful integration of local skill with the eastern designer-craftsman came to an end by the late 1940s, evidently because of management problems as well as the growth of competing industries after the War. It should be noted that World War II, during which New Mexico lost a disproportionate number of its citizens, seems to mark the end of the formal involvement of men in weaving, with the exception of those established weaving businesses which were owned by Spanish families, such as the Ortegas and Trujillos.

.∴∴.

REVIVALS AND PATRONS

Aside from such commercial ventures as McCrossen's and Ortega's weaving establishments, the twentieth century also gave rise to revivalism in the crafts, particularly to such nearly extinct crafts as furniture-making, tinwork, *colcha* embroidery, woodcarving, and traditional weaving. Tourists eager for a bit of the West to take home with them played a role in this revival by broadening the sales potential for New Mexican crafts. But it was those Anglo settlers who came and stayed who exerted an even greater influence in the revitalization of these forms.

In the early decades of this century a new wave of Anglo migrants entered New Mexico. For many of them, New Mexico's dry climate offered hope for recovery from tuberculosis and bronchial problems. Coming on the advice of their physicians, these often wealthy patients brought with them an urban sophistication not common in New Mexico before this time. Another group—composed largely of artists and writers—journeyed to New Mexico to join friends and colleagues who had already settled there, or because they were intrigued by the area's growing reputation as a haven for artists.[27] New Mexico's light, landscape, and peoples appealed to the artistic sensibilities of these new residents. Some of them recognized the need to preserve New Mexico's

unique quality of life and art, and were among the first to attempt to save and revive native crafts.[28]

In 1922, the Pueblo Pottery Fund (later to become the Indian Arts Fund) was organized to preserve Pueblo pottery traditions. That same year the Southwest Indian Fair was established in connection with the annual Fiesta celebration.[29] Thus, the first formal efforts were directed towards the preservation of Native American crafts. But in 1925, Mary Austin and Frank Applegate founded the Spanish Colonial Arts Society, which was dedicated to the encouragement and promotion of Spanish Colonial arts.[30] And, in the decade that followed, the Society did much to awaken interest in the neglected Spanish craft traditions.

At Mary Austin's behest, beginning in 1926 and continuing through 1934, an annual exhibition and sale of Spanish crafts was held in conjunction with Fiesta. The 1928 official Fiesta program reveals that $300 in prizes were being awarded for, among other things, blankets, embroidery, hooked and braided rugs, and crocheted bedspreads.

In 1930 the Society opened the Colonial Arts Shop in Sena Plaza in Santa Fe, at first managed by weaver Helen McCrossen and later by needleworker Nellie Dunton.[31] In a February 1933 article for the magazine *Antiques,* Miss Austin boasted: "Recently the Colonial Arts Society in Santa Fe has sponsored a movement for the revival of ancient types of needlework, done with crewels on linen and cotton cloth, splendid old examples of which are still extant."[32] Miss Austin also noted that a permanent collection illustrating the best designed "authentic reproductions of old pieces" had been established. But innovation was also stimulated: "Mary Austin and Frank Applegate and a number of others have worked faithfully for the revival of these handicrafts, and with great wisdom, encouraging the people not only to copy old designs but to create new ones in the same spirit of originality and play as did their ancestors."[33] For some reason the shop never achieved solvency, and it finally closed in October 1933. Miss Austin's death in 1934 all but halted activities of the Spanish Colonial Arts Society until its revival in 1952 by the late E. Boyd.

The Society's shop was succeeded, however, by a far more successful one on Palace Avenue, subsidized and initiated by yet another member of the Spanish Colonial Arts Society, Leonora Curtin Paloheimo. This establishment, The Native Market, opened on June 16,

1934,[34] and was a Santa Fe landmark for the next six years. It was a familiar stop for all Indian Detour tour buses and a popular tourist attraction. The shop was roomy and attractive, and carried a large stock of New Mexican crafts (Figure 5). In addition, craftsmen were employed to work in public view.

Furniture, weavings, *colcha* embroideries, woodcarvings, and tinwork were all represented in the shop's inventory, but it was the textiles which were initially most heavily in demand.[35] To instruct the public on the complexities of hand textile production, spinners and weavers worked continuously in the shop:

> Weaving in the Native Market was done on two regular treadle looms, one a two-and one a four-harness loom, plus one additional loom for

extra orders. Woven fabrics were primarily made in 45-inch widths. The two-harness loom produced tapestry weave (Rio Grande blanket style), and the four-harness loom produced float weaves, which included diamond, whipcord, diagonal twill, partridge eye, herringbone, and houndstooth weaves. Traditional solid, striped, checked, and plaid patterns were woven.[36]

David Salazar, of Ribera, New Mexico, recalled that during the years he worked at the Market, from 1933 to 1936, he earned $12.00 a week. Assigned to the four-harness treadle loom, he spent most of his days weaving small blankets and mohair drapery yardage, both of which the Anglo buyers eagerly purchased.[37]

In the Native Market, only handspun natural-dyed and undyed wools were tolerated. Brilliant skeins of the wool, which was either spun in remote villages or by Doña María Martínez or her daughter Atocha on the premises, hung informally around the shop. Wool was dyed by Tillie Gabaldón Stark in a huge cauldron at the back of the store, utilizing such traditional New Mexican dyes as indigo, *cañaigre* root, chamisa, walnut hulls, brazilwood, and cochineal.[38]

Aside from the weaving produced in the Market, rugs and blankets were spun, dyed, and woven in outlying villages such as Nambé, Taos, Española, and Córdova, the latter producing all-white blankets which were very popular.[39] These products were required to meet the same stringent standards of quality as those produced in the shop. Wayne Mauzy suggested in a 1936 article on the Native Market that little of the output from the famed Chimayó weavers was represented in the Native Market inventory owing to their use of commercial dyes and yarns.[40] But it would also appear that the success of a local sales out-let—Ortega's—would have had some bearing on the availability of Chimayó weavings for other markets. In any case, policy at the Market assured that any craftsman was welcome to bring his wares to the shop, but only work which was of sufficiently high quality to pass a staff of judges was bought.[41]

While the Native Market's philosophy was to revere the traditional, it was not done at the expense of marketability. Leonora Curtin Paloheimo firmly believed that colonial designs should be adapted to serve modern needs, while retaining traditional techniques of manufacture when possible. The Spanish Colonial design dining room table and the upholstered chair were two of the Market's innovations which melded the traditional and the contemporary. Likewise, *colcha* embroidery on upholstery, drapery fabric, and napkins and tablecloths represents uses not typical of earlier times but suited to contemporary tastes.[42]

While Leonora Curtin's Native Market provided the very necessary sales outlet for the work of New Mexican craftsmen, it was the state's vocational schools which trained them. The El Rito Normal School was reported as early as 1930 as having a well established weaving department:

> With the securing of new equipment true copies of old Chimayó, old Navajo and old Spanish-Colonial rugs and blankets can be made, as well as modern adaptations of rugs; vests, table runners, blankets, and shawls. In addition to the actual weaving, rug design is taught, originality is encouraged, and the history of the old designs and methods are studied.[43]

Brice Sewell, State Director of Vocational Education and Training, pushed tirelessly to develop rural community schools which taught traditional crafts, and to garner federal monies to make this possible. Under the program spinning was taught at San José and Chupadero, weaving in Taos, and *colcha* embroidery in Puerto de Luna.

Two of Sewell's assistants, Dolores Perrault Montoya and Carmen Espinosa, had special interests in textile production. Dolores Perrault, an expert dyer and weaver, was also first manager of the Native Market, "on loan" from the vocational education department. Her mimeographed booklet on natural dyeing, one of a series prepared by the department for the use of working craftsmen, was for many years one of the few sources on the subject available to New Mexican craftsmen. In 1935 Carmen Espinosa similarly wrote a booklet on *colcha* embroidery.[44] Drawing from older examples of *colcha* embroideries in her own and Miss Curtin's collections, she provided detailed illustrations of motifs found in these pieces, including color keys. Hundreds of the pamphlets were mimeographed and sold at $1.00 apiece, often to home economics teachers throughout the state.[45]

THE "CARSON *COLCHA*"

Even prior to 1935, however, *colcha* embroidery work was undergoing a revival of sorts in Carson, New Mexico, a Mormon settlement across the river to the south of Taos. Carson had been founded in 1909 by Judge W. K. Shupe, a Mormon homesteader and Virginian by birth. He interested other Virginians in homesteading, the community grew, and by 1920 there was a population of 248 with a thriving school and church. But a continuing drought throughout the twenties discouraged some of the settlers, and many left Carson to seek work in neighboring areas. By 1930 the population had dwindled to less than 150.[46] It was during this period that Judge Shupe's son, Elmer, became involved in blanket trading on a full-time basis.[47]

It was sometime in 1930 or 1931, Elmer Shupe's sister-in-law, Frances Varos Graves, recalls, that he purchased an old wool-on-wool *colcha* embroidery in Ojo Caliente which needed repair before it could be considered saleable. As was usually the case, one of the women in the community was asked to do the repairs. Frances took the *colcha* textile, which she remembers as having a checked pattern, and taught herself the *colcha* stitch. Soon she embarked upon making one of her own design: she used the checked pattern for a border; then, remembering stories her grandfather, José Manuel Varos, had told her in childhood, she embroidered buffalos roaming the range as he had described them.[48]

Thus began a cottage industry of *colcha*-making in Carson. More Carson settlers became involved and soon there were *colcha* embroideries depicting horses and Indians, covered wagons, stagecoaches, interior scenes, saints, Penitente processions, and even variations on the Navajo chief's blanket, often with a horse or two thrown in for good measure. Involved in the *colcha* embroidery production in addition to Elmer Shupe and his sister-in-law Frances Graves, were: Frances' sister Sophie Varos Graves,[49] Mabel O'Dell (then married to yet another Graves brother), Wayne Graves, Pearl Shumate (the elder Graves sister), and Winifred Graves Shupe, Elmer's wife. As the cottage industry developed, Elmer Shupe and John

FIGURE 6

"Carson **colcha"** *embroidery, Carson, New Mexico, 1931–45. 1.96 x 1.20 m. Depiction of eight religious figures (l. to r., top to bottom; N. S. de Guadalupe, Santiago, San Isidro, San Miguel, San Antonio de Padua, N. S. de San Juan de Los Lagos, San José, Santo Niño de Atocha). Embroidered in reused wool yarns on handspun wool plain-weave ground, natural and synthetic dyes. Museum of New Mexico Collection at the Museum of International Folk Art. Gift of the heirs of the Estate of Amelia B. Hollenbeck. A.71.29.1.*

"Shorty" Shumate took control of the business end of things, such as obtaining the necessary materials and selling the finished embroideries. The others were all involved in varying degrees in making them. Some, such as Wayne Graves, who preferred Penitente scenes, and Frances and Sophie Graves, who delighted in the images of saints (Figure 6), even developed personal specialties.[50]

The "Carson *colchas*," as they were dubbed by E. Boyd, are fairly easy to distinguish from earlier examples once one is alerted to certain identifying characteristics.[51] Those which reflect an Anglo sense of pictorial composition are the easiest to spot: pictorial motifs, relatively large in size, are often central to the compositional scheme, and at times serve a narrative purpose. The human figure is often depicted. On the other hand, in early Spanish wool-on-wool *colcha* embroideries, pictorial motifs are subordinate to the overall floral design, small in size, and few in number.

In addition, the materials used in the making of Carson *colcha* embroideries were nearly all recycled. Shupe and Shumate reportedly travelled up and down the Rio Grande in search of the old woolen mattress covers known as *colchones,* made of *sabanilla.* Since, without exception, Carson *colcha* embroideries were made in the wool-on-wool style, *sabanilla* in some quantity was needed for the ground support. Frances Graves relates that the earliest Carson *colcha* embroideries utilized ravelled *sabanilla* for the embroidery yarn. But the apparent

short supply of *sabanilla* called a halt to this practice and the embroiderers took to ravelling a ragged pile of Rio Grande blankets to obtain the yarns they needed.

As one might expect, the use of such recycled materials does have telling effects on the finished pieces. Since old *sabanilla* was used for the support, one finds that the backing fabric in a Carson embroidery is often seamed in numerous and unlikely places. Likewise it is not unusual to find, since materials from older blankets were utilized, that yarns of widely varying textures and thicknesses may appear on the face of a single Carson *colcha* embroidery, some even giving evidence of previous wear. Natural and synthetic-dyed yarns were often used together with natural-undyed wools on the same piece.

Another peculiarity of the Carson *colcha* embroidery is a certain verticality in the direction of the stitches, which may have arisen because the embroiderers were self-taught. Whereas in older *colcha* embroideries one finds that the stitches follow the curves and undulations of the patterns, and that the couching stitch is used for textural interest, such an attention to detail is rare in a Carson embroidery. Consequently, some of the Carson *colcha* embroideries have a rather bland appearance when compared to early, fine examples of traditional *colcha* embroideries (Plates 65–70).

During the past forty years, the reputation of the Carson *colcha* embroidery has been downgraded. And, indeed, not all of the fifty to sixty pieces still extant and located show the same sensitivity of treatment. Since quality of embroidery and design depended entirely on the whim of the individual craftsman, the pieces varied widely. It is also a sorry fact that these *colcha* embroideries were often misrepresented as being authentic early Spanish pieces to potential buyers.[52] To be sure, some of them fairly flaunted their true identities: any supposedly Spanish-made *colcha* embroidery which depicted Los Hermanos Penitentes scourging themselves in procession, for example, would clearly have been outside the limits of both good taste and proper religious demeanor in the Spanish community. But the *colcha* embroideries sold, and apparently sold well.

The time now seems ripe for a reappraisal of the "Carson *colcha*." The embroideries are certainly interesting cultural expressions: a delightful admixture of Anglo sensibility and Spanish and Indian themes, tempered by the demands of the marketplace. Their very production offers interesting insights into the interrelationships of New Mexico's ethnic groups, and a glimpse into the hearts and minds of the makers which might otherwise have been lost. At its best, the "Carson *colcha*" is an intriguing piece of American folk art, at its worst an artless but valuable historical document. The Carson *colcha* embroidery nonetheless remains a fascinating chapter in the history of textile production in New Mexico.

NEEDLEWORK REVIVALS

Other revivals of *colcha* embroidery were sparked after the appearance in 1935 of both Carmen Espinosa's pamphlet and Nellie Dunton's book *Spanish Colonial Ornament*,[53] which included forty plates of old *colcha* embroidery designs. In the late '30s a group called El Arte Antiguo was formed in Española. About half a dozen women under the leadership of a Mrs. Cata met regularly to practice the art of *colcha* work and, on occasion, to make replacement altarcloths for the parish church. This group is still in existence, and current president María T. Luján reports that it now consists of ten members who meet once a month to stitch and socialize. But whereas in the past some of the members did their own spinning and dyeing, and used an imported hand-woven fabric from Mexico which resembled *sabanilla,* the remaining members now use only commercially available materials. They produce only a small quantity of finished work.[54]

In Taos during the 1940s, Rebecca James was taught how to do *colcha* work by Jesusita Perrault, and later encouraged by Nellie Dunton. Mrs. James' original designs included landscapes, religious themes, and floral patterns. Often employing delicate metallic yarns which she ravelled from their cotton core, her work achieved the greatest delicacy seen in the twentieth-century history of the craft (Figure 7).[55]

At the time of this writing there is little *colcha* embroidery still being made, and nearly all of it is done in the wool-on-cotton style. Frances Graves, now of Los Cordovas, N.M., is still making the wool-on-wool type, typically images of saints, and has taught a class in Taos recently. In Santa Fe, Laura Martínez Mullins (the only *colcha* embroiderer contacted who had learned the stitch from family members) now produces items only for her own use. Tillie Gabaldón Stark, who learned *colcha* embroidery at the Native Market, is an avid embroiderer who sells her work generally during the annual Spanish Market.[56] She has taught classes at the College of Santa Fe and participated in the National Folklife Festival in Washington, D.C. Most of her fine work is now done on special order. Lastly, Senaida Romero, who is primarily a tinworker, has begun to execute *colcha* embroideries which she and her husband Emilio incorporate into tin-and-glass mirrors and trinket boxes.[57] Such a use of *colcha* embroidery is nontraditional; in the past only trade cards, wallpaper, or reverse glass painting would have been seen occupying the place filled by embroidery in the Romeros' pieces. But the new tinwork items are functional and attractive, and retain a definite New Mexican feeling about them. The Romeros' popular innovations offer some hope that the *colcha* embroidery tradition may be continued.

FIGURE 7

"El Santo Niño de Atocha," **colcha** *embroidery by Rebecca Salisbury James, Taos, New Mexico, ca. 1955. 33.5 x 28.7 cm. Ground fabric: commercial cotton (?) plain weave. Embroidery: colcha couching, flat and knotted stitches, commercial wools and metallic yarns. Spanish Colonial Arts Society, Inc. Collection on loan to the Museum of New Mexico at the Museum of International Folk Art. Gift of Mason B. Wells in memory of his brother. L.5.63.24.*

Crewel embroidery was introduced into northern New Mexico through a series of workshops in 1974 which were funded by the International Folk Art Foundation. A series of six week-long embroidery workshops were held in rural locations and taught by the talented Chilean-born teacher Carmen Benavente de Orrego-Salas.[58] In these classes Mrs. Orrego-Salas taught small groups of Spanish women the basics of crewel embroidery while encouraging them to seek original subjects in their daily lives and surrounding landscape. In Pecos, a group called Artesanías de Pecos executed two large embroidered quilts. One of these, entitled "La Vida en el Valle de Pecos," is now in the collections of the Museum of International Folk Art (Figure 8).

But undoubtedly the most impressive result of the Village Workshops is a 265-foot-long embroidery in the Church of Our Lady of Guadalupe in Villanueva, N.M., a town of more than sixty families about fifty miles southeast of Santa Fe. The impetus for this embroidery was Mrs. Orrego-Salas' 1974 workshop and the suggestion of the parish priest at the time, Rev. Louis B. Hasenfass, that the women might enjoy making a few embroideries to decorate the church as a Bicentennial project. The eleven women participating in the workshop, armed only with a yardstick, pencil, and paper, met in the church to try to plan where the panels might be placed. But as excitement mounted and more and more ideas and scenes suggested themselves, the project grew into a large-scale embroidery encircling the nave, choir, and sanctuary of the church.

FIGURE 8

*"La Vida en el Valle de Pecos," crewel-embroidered
quilt* by Las Artesanías de Pecos, Pecos, New Mexico,
1974–5. 2.84 x 2.20 m. Detail of center. Ground fabric:
commercial cloth. Embroidery: variety of crewel-work
stitches, commercial wools. International Folk Art
Foundation Collection at the Museum of International
Folk Art, a unit of the Museum of New Mexico.
FA.75.32.1.

As the project developed, more women from the community were
invited to participate, until a total of thirty-six were involved. The
completed embroidery, which was dedicated on July 24, 1976, recounts
the entire history of Villanueva. Scenes range from the earliest period
predating human habitation through to the present. Depicted, among
others, are scenes of: the building of the church, the loss of lands by
Spanish families for lack of ability to communicate in English, the May
Crowning of the Virgin, rodeos and ranching, and even a panel of the
stitchers themselves at work (Figure 9). Library research and oral
history served the primary means of determining what significant events
were to be recorded. The embroidery is divided into forty-one panels,
each worked in plied wool yarns on commercial cotton and framed in
cactus-wood. This project may not be strictly a revival of a traditional
New Mexican craft; according to Graburn's analysis it is more properly

FIGURE 9

*"Father Louis and the stitchers at a prayer meeting,"
detail of the Villanueva Embroidery.* This panel designed
by Benedict Gonzales and embroidered by Antonia García
de Sena, ca. 1976. Ground fabric: commercial cloth.
Embroidery: variety of crewel-work stitches, commercial
wools. Photo by Chester Maydole, courtesy of the
Museum of New Mexico, Museum of International Folk
Art.

FIGURE 10

Celso Gallegos, *Agua Fría, New Mexico, ca. 1940.*
Photograph courtesy of George McCrossen, Santa Fe.

termed a "reintegrated" art form (p. 169), as are the Pecos quilts. However one may wish to view it, the Villaneuva Embroidery is an outstanding community arts effort which drew upon the latent skills and artistic talents of a number of rural women. The church embroidery is a source of community pride in Villaneuva, and provides some economic benefits to the village through increased tourism.[59]

ISOLATES

Not all embroideries have been associated with active groups or concerned with *colcha* embroidery.

In Graburn, one class of textiles is described as aberrant—textiles which are clearly out of the mainstream and for which there is no easy explanation. The individuals involved in the creation of these unique textiles were not weavers or embroiderers in a traditional sense. Rather, they used the medium of textiles to illuminate a personal statement or artistic vision. Their textiles were not meant to be functional nor did the artists concern themselves with the marketability of their creations. Celso Gallegos (1864–1943) and Policarpio Valencia (1854–1931) were two Spanish men working in the later decades of their lives toward a personal artistic goal.

Celso Gallegos is best known for his woodcarvings. His works are small, intimate, and frequently whimsical. They primarily represent members of the Holy Family or the saints, although a few of his secular carvings of animals are among his best. During the 1930s his work was known and collected by some of the early founders of the Spanish Colonial Arts Society, and mention is made of his embroideries.[60]

While woodcarving was frequently practiced by Spanish men, work in embroidery or rug-hooking was not. Although few of Gallegos' textiles exist, those which remain are striking testament to this man's artistic vitality. He was reputedly a kind, gentle soul who spent his life in service as a sacristan at San Ysidro Church in his home of Agua Fría, New Mexico (Figure 10). But Gallegos' work has great energy. The hooked rug shown in Figure 11 is his best known extant textile. Handspun wool, dyed with synthetic dyes of red and complementary warm oranges and yellows and contrasting blacks, are worked in looped pile on a burlap ground. Possibly the handspun wools were made available to him through the "Spanish Colonial Arts Society [which] had a shop from which they issued materials to native craftsmen to take home, work up and return to the shop for sale."[61] In any case, in both carving and his work with textiles, Gallegos' technical abilities were limited.

What is of interest is his virtuosity in the arrangement of form and color. Animal forms are handled so as to negate a firm sense of ground. They float and move over a visionary landscape of color, bright color. He used his textile as a canvas upon which he explored not only the interrelationships of form and color but texture as well. The surface is highly uneven and the textile's shape irregular. Tied wool fringe hangs down in uneven lengths, giving the textile an appearance of being untidy, though the composition is compact. Other textiles attributed to

FIGURE 11

Hooked rug, Celso Gallegos, Agua Fría, New Mexico, 1920–30. .72 x 1.18 m. Commercial burlap ground, wool embroidery, handspun wool, synthetic dyes. Museum of New Mexico Collection at the Museum of International Folk Art. Gift of Mary Cabot Wheelwright. Gift of the Historical Society of New Mexico. A.5.54.8.

Gallegos do not contain all of the attributes of this extraordinary work.[62] The embroideries are more closely related to the whimsy of his carvings. Another attributed rug/embroidery contains much of the same visual activity, except for its figure of a dog which is firmly placed in the rug's center while flowers move about it.

While the art of Celso Gallegos can be considered exceptional, the work of Policarpio Valencia must certainly be rated as monumental.[63] Little is known of his life. Brief biographies describe a man living in the rural poverty of Santa Cruz, New Mexico—more specifically El Santo

Niño, a little village at the edge of the bigger village of Santa Cruz.[64] Small though Santa Cruz is, it boasts an elegant, large adobe church built in the eighteenth century with altar decorations imported from Mexico as well as altar screens made in the nineteenth century by New Mexican *santeros*. It is a church of great age and beauty, which one can easily imagine would dominate and fill the lives of the villagers. And so it seems with Policarpio Valencia. Like Gallegos, Valencia found that textiles (Plate 71) were a medium well suited to the expression of his personal vision.

Throughout Valencia's ten known textiles runs a strong, moralistic message.[65] At times we can only guess at the textiles' meanings since the Spanish text embroidered in string upon them seems to be purposefully, perhaps even playfully, puzzling: "Here are seen likenesses of animals that in all ways resemble their real appearance. There is an adage that says the lion is not as he is painted even if by a good painter. He who painted it first did so even to the color and so it is and shall be."[66]

Covering this textile (Figure 12) are animal forms and Spanish phrases arranged in a bewildering fashion. There are messages about the fate of man and statements concerning his sins. It seems that there are layers of messages and lessons embroidered upon the heavily patched ground fabric. Most of Valencia's textiles repeat this use of embroidered language which conveys, often through the use of folk expressions, moralistic messages.

There is nothing structured about the Valencia embroideries. Lines of Spanish words come in at various angles and animal forms may punctuate a line. The play of the visual and the literary woven together successfully imparts not only great visual stimulation but a sense that an unanswered riddle is about to be solved. The answer of the riddle seems to depend not only upon an understanding of the words embroidered in cheap household string, but also upon their relationship with the other forms of the textile: the animals and the larger shapes emerge as patches. Animals and words move together as the viewer distances himself from the textile. Valencia's textiles require active involvement from the viewer. There is a compulsion to circle the textile, to go round and round it, viewing it from every angle in an effort to get at its inner meaning.

Valencia chose a variety of ground fabrics for his embroideries:

FIGURE 12

*Embroidery, Policarpio Valencia, Santa Cruz, New
Mexico, ca. 1925. 1.22 x 1.33 m. Wool ground,
commercial cotton string embroidery, buttonhole stitch.
Spanish Colonial Arts Society, Inc. Collection on loan to
the Museum of New Mexico at the Museum of
International Folk Art. L.5.54.40.*

fabric patches of denim, wool, commercial cotton bedspreads, an old
Rio Grande blanket patched with cotton, a cotton blanket, a worn rag
rug, a gored skirt. It seems that almost any ground fabric would do to
contain his embroidered messages. He used cheap cotton 4-ply string in
different colors and employed the buttonhole stitch almost exclusively
for all of the embroidery work.

One of Valencia's embroideries, perhaps his last, can be far more
easily comprehended than the rest (Figure 13). There are forty-five lines
of embroidered letters, using 4-ply cotton strings of rose, brown,
yellow, white, and blue. Around the edges and in areas where the cotton
commercial ground is absent, solid buttonhole stitch is used to fill out
the textile to an even, rectangular shape. The message of this textile is a
farewell. It is an *alabado* or hymn in which "the deceased bids farewell
to his family, his friends and the world in general."[67]

/\\.\\/\\.\\

WEAVING REVIVALS

Post-Native Market revival attempts at traditional weaving have been
surprisingly more limited than those in embroidery. Happily, both
David Ortega and John R. Trujillo, owners of the two retail operations
in Chimayó, have begun again in the last decade to encourage the
weaving of more traditional Rio Grande blanket designs in natural-dyed
and undyed wools. Commercially produced single-ply yarn called
"caracol," available from a source in southern New Mexico, was used
for these pieces until very recently. Ortega now reports that difficulty in
procuring this wool has forced a change to Icelandic wool, which his
weavers now use instead.[68] A weaving by John R. Trujillo in the
collection of the Museum of International Folk Art illustrates the banded
style currently being produced (Plate 72).

Del Sol, Inc. was a community-based project in Truchas which
also produced simple striped weavings, though of a less traditional
nature. Initiated by HELP (Home Education Livelihood Program), a
non-profit interchurch agency which channels federal and private grant
monies into rural communities, Del Sol functioned from the late 1960s
until about 1974. Rugs, pillows, purses, ponchos, and wall hangings
were woven by a dozen weavers, most of them from Truchas and nearby
Córdova, under the supervision of Alfredo Córdova.[69] A grant from the
Ford Foundation provided funds to pay these weavers a minimum wage
of $1.60 an hour for their work. Kristina Wilson designed the striped
patterns utilizing, in many cases, bright contemporary colors. The
finished product, woven of commercially available single-ply wool or

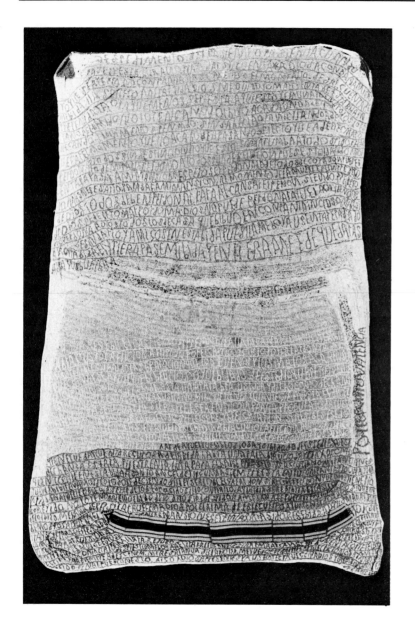

FIGURE 13

Embroidery, Policarpio Valencia, Santa Cruz, New Mexico, ca. 1930. 1.73 x 1.22 m. Cotton cloth scraps, commercial knitted belt at bottom, commercial cotton string embroidery, buttonhole stitch. Spanish Colonial Arts Society, Inc. Collection on loan to the Museum of New Mexico at the Museum of International Folk Art. L.5.54.38.

mohair, had a southwestern flavor and an affordable retail price. Outlets in New York, Los Angeles, San Francisco, Taos, Albuquerque, and Santa Fe carried Del Sol, Inc. weavings.[70]

Agueda Martínez of Medanales has taught weaving in HELP projects in Abiquiu and Hernández. Nearing eighty years of age and still weaving, Mrs. Martínez learned the craft when she married her husband Eusebio, who came from a family of weavers. Five of her seven daughters are professional weavers;[71] one of these, Cordelia Coronado, frequently teaches weaving to local women in Medanales. The designs produced are often modified Navajo types: even *Yei* and *Yeibichai* patterns may be found. Mrs. Coronado states that such treadle-loomed "Indian" rugs find a ready market.[72] Mrs. Martínez continues to weave rag rugs and traditional colonial designs along with the Indian types.

Los Tejidos Norteños is yet another outgrowth of HELP projects in northern New Mexico. This weaving group was formed in La Madera after a number of women were taught weaving by HELP instructor Connie Ortega in Española, and were then given aid for the purchase of seven looms by Ghost Ranch. The purpose of the present group, which includes seven members, is to provide information on weaving methods and materials, to facilitate purchase of materials jointly,[73] and to find retail outlets for the group's output. At present, three of the group's members, including leader María Vergara-Wilson, not only weave but do their own spinning and natural-dyeing. The emphasis at this time is on the production of traditional Rio Grande style weavings (Figure 14),

FIGURE 14

Weaving by María Vergara-Wilson, La Madera, New Mexico, 1977. 1.86 x .96 m. Warp: commercial wool yarn, 2-Z-spun-plied-S. Weft: handspun and commercial wool yarn, 2-Z-spun-plied-S. Natural and natural-dyed wool. Spanish Colonial Arts Society, Inc. Collection on loan to the Museum of New Mexico at the Museum of International Folk Art. L.5.77.5.

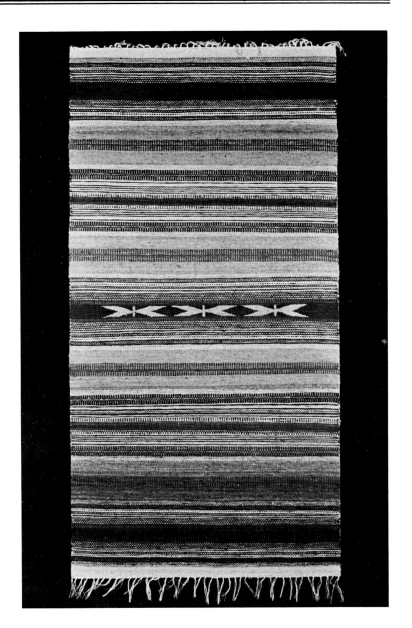

the impetus for which was the Rio Grande Dyeing and Weaving Workshops of 1976.

These workshops were cosponsored by the Museum of International Folk Art and the Los Alamos Arts Council in the hopes of inspiring contemporary Spanish New Mexican weavers to draw upon traditional Rio Grande blanket designs.[74] Twenty experienced weavers from northern New Mexico were selected to participate in two three-day workshops in Fall 1976. The first, held in Pajarito Village, concentrated on the techniques of natural wool dyeing. Weavers were provided the opportunity to experience natural dyeing firsthand (Figure 15). Some thirty pounds of wool in more than 100 vibrant shades were produced.

This wool was then utilized in a second workshop which was held at the Museum of International Folk Art, focusing upon design and weaving techniques. Numerous fine examples of old Rio Grande blankets from the museum's collections were made available for study, and analyzed from the point of view of color and motif. Participants were then encouraged to weave a small sampler based on a traditional design on the looms provided them. Finally, project coordinator Trish Spillman directed the publication of a booklet which included historical information on Rio Grande weaving, renderings of design motifs, dye recipes, samples of dyed yarns, and photographs of traditional blankets. The net result of the workshops is that the participants expressed both pleasure and surprise at being acquainted with the textile tradition of their forebears, and that several have chosen to continue weaving in more traditional modes (Plate 73).[75]

FIGURE 15

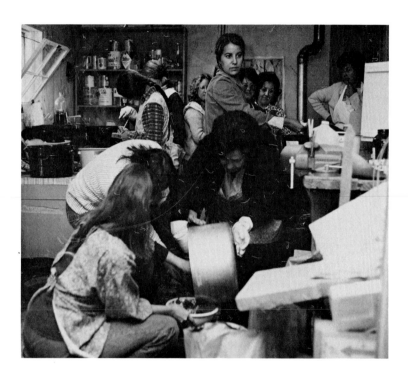

Participants of Rio Grande Textile Workshops learning principles of natural dyeing, Fall, 1976. Photo by Art Taylor. Collection of the Museum of New Mexico at Photo Archives.

CONCLUSION

The history of textile production by the Spanish in New Mexico during the twentieth century is as complex as the forces which shaped it. The effects of new cultural contacts, mass-produced imports, Anglo patrons, and revival movements were such that locally produced textiles simply did not retain the function they had had for generations in the Spanish household. Rather they became products which reflected, in part, the transformations which were occurring in the society as a whole. In the early twentieth century Spanish society in New Mexico was put to its severest test, a struggle to integrate the past with a future which would incorporate a new set of cultural values. One senses that these were, indeed, difficult times for the rural weaver. During this period, weaving in Spanish New Mexico came tragically close to extinction. Other circumstances prevented this, including the ability of weavers and weaving families to accommodate themselves and their art to changing circumstances and to maintain through their art a sense of their own cultural identity. Conscious revivals of craft traditions have also played a vital role in the maintenance of textile traditions in New Mexico since the 1930s. Today, the interest in reviving and restoring Spanish craft traditions is stronger than ever. In addition, new arts, which have no direct connection with past techniques, have been successfully integrated into Spanish communities. Revivals, commercialism, and reintegration of Spanish textiles in the twentieth century have all been essential processes in the survival and expansion of these products of a rich heritage.

APPENDICES

A THE TREADLE LOOM
NORA FISHER

In 1598, when Oñate travelled northward into New Mexico with settlers and eighty-three wagons, he brought no looms. Instead came carpenters, tools, and people who knew how to construct a complicated, indeed revolutionary, new type of machine—the treadle loom.[1] (See Figure 1.)

Pre-Spanish cultures of the Western Hemisphere had always been textile oriented, using fabrics and clothing not only as indicators of wealth, but also as ceremonial objects. Indigenous looms fell into three categories: the back-strap loom, the horizontal ground loom, and the vertical loom, the latter predominating in the Southwest.[2] All of these looms were extremely flexible and permitted the weaving of fine and complex fabrics, yet they were all designed to produce a relatively narrow textile of limited length. Pre-Columbian clothing was not tailored. A warp was made up to form the length and width of a garment piece, so the resulting fabric generally had four finished selvedges. Its size and shape were calculated before weaving for use in a given garment.

Modern observers of New Mexican Spanish weaving have judged the Spanish treadle loom—large, unwieldy, constructed of rough, hand-hewn logs—as a rather simple and clumsy instrument. In fact, the new loom brought by the Spanish was at the time a sophisticated, complex piece of machinery. Equipped with a warp beam, the treadle loom could store seemingly endless lengths of warp, and at the same time collect woven fabric on the cloth beam at the front of the loom.

Setting up and warping a loom is the most time-consuming process in weaving. Time taken by warping the treadle loom is cut to a fraction, however, because seemingly infinite lengths of yardage can easily be woven without interruption. Equally important, with the treadle loom the process of forming a shed becomes almost totally mechanized.[3] *Treadles* (foot pedals) operate *harnesses* (a set of shedding devices spanning the whole width of the loom), totally freeing the weaver's hands for the process of interlacing the weft or throwing the shuttle.

The treadle loom, brought from Europe to the Western Hemisphere by the

FIGURE 1

Treadle loom with New Mexican textiles displayed in background. Collection of Dr. and Mrs. Ward Alan Minge, Corrales, New Mexico.

Spanish, was, in fact, not indigenous to Europe. Owing to a lack of historical writing on the subject, the treadle loom's introduction to Europe is shrouded in mystery, but it probably came from the Near East.[4] It arrived in Europe around A.D. 1000 and seems to have formed "the technical basis for the tremendous expansion of the cloth trade"[5] concurrent with the growth of cities and rise of the middle class.

When the new loom appeared in Europe, it was accompanied and followed by a whole complex of tools. There were tools to facilitate yarn preparation (the spinning wheel, swift, bow, and wool cards), highly specialized machines designed to organize large quantities of prepared fiber (the rotary reel, spool rack, warping mill, and cage spools), and unusual loom parts of a new design[6] (examples are the weft-carrier or *shuttle,* the kind that can be "thrown through a shed," and the *reed,* an important implement which acts as a warp spacer and beater).[7] All of these tools were developed toward economical use of the wonderful new machine. The treadle loom, with its many accompanying tools, is above all an industrial machine. More rigid than the indigenous looms, it produces to capacity only when there is a division of labor, when a number of people are involved with the whole process: carding, spinning, dyeing, warping, weaving, finishing.

With the new loom, weaving in Europe was transformed from a woman's home-craft to an urban industry, jealously controlled by the male weavers of the cloth guilds. We have no written record concerning weaving in Europe around A.D. 1000. On the other hand, for the Europe of A.D. 1300 there are thousands of civic documents pertaining to the regulations of the cloth industry.[8] In view of the loom's impact on Europe, it seems logical to assume that it was equally important in the development of the cloth industry in New Spain.

Though there is little information concerning the introduction of the treadle loom into New Mexico, we do know that its use was well established by 1638, only forty years after Oñate's arrival. In that year the colorful and controversial Governor Luis de Rosas sent an extremely large shipment of manufactured goods, primarily textiles, to Parral, Chihuahua, for retail sale. Included in the shipment were "nineteen pieces of *sayal* containing 1900 *varas,*"[9] in other words, nineteen pieces of coarse woolen fabric, each approximately 100 meters in length. Such yardage could only have been woven on the treadle loom—only the warp and cloth beams of the treadle loom can hold such lengths of fabric.

Rosas had, indeed, established his own weaving workshop or *obraje* in Santa Fe and was accused of seizing "looms owned by private citizens in order to give his own workshop a greater monopoly over local textile production."[10] He operated a thriving business and used the treadle loom for weaving great quantities of yardage. The 1638 invoice also lists a shipment of 350 blankets and 33 drapes, most likely produced on the treadle loom.[11] This single export points to a considerable organization and division of labor in processing fibers and producing fabrics, labor which supported an extremely well established treadle-loom weaving industry in Santa Fe in the mid-1600s.

In a number of ways, however, the existing documents serve to depict a weak and disorganized New Mexican Spanish treadle-loom industry during the 16–1700s. For example, looms—hand hewn from local materials, free from metal or other imported manufactured parts—are not generally mentioned in

New Mexican wills.[12] Due to the existence of so few documents, the picture is complicated. The Pueblo Indians revolted and expelled the Spanish in 1680. Reconquest of New Mexico took place in 1693. According to the Rosas documents, as well as bans laid down by other governors,[13] the treadle-loom weaving industry was very strong in Santa Fe during pre-Revolt times. After the reconquest the nucleus of this industry seems to have been relocated in the Rio Abajo area around Albuquerque. The 1790 census describes a division of labor along ethnic lines which would presuppose an organized weaving industry, making maximum use of the treadle loom. In Albuquerque in 1790, one-third of the heads of households, almost all of them Spanish, were engaged in the weaving profession. Of the sixteen spinners listed only one was Indian, while a third of the carders were Indian.[14]

While the weaving industry flourished in the Albuquerque area, it was not reestablished in Rio Arriba around Santa Fe.[15] A report of 1803 informs us: "With respect to arts and trades, it may be said with propriety that there are none in this Province, there being no apprenticeship, official examination for master-workmen, any formality of trades-unions, or other things customary in all parts."[16] Indeed, a formal guild system never was set up in New Mexico.

To improve the quality of weaving in Santa Fe, however, the Bazán brothers were sent from Mexico City in 1807 as teachers.[17] Of interest in their contract, and noteworthy in discussing the loom, is the fact that they were given "implements . . . for the practice of their art, they having to equip . . . the necessary looms in the *Villa* of Santa Fe." Furthermore, the Bazáns needed "three pack mules" to carry these implements.[18] In 1812 Pino reported that "fine looms for cotton" had been imported by the Bazáns.[19] It can be assumed that these looms were lighter in weight than the native New Mexican looms, and constructed so as to put little strain on a fine cotton warp. As to other looms that they may have brought, we know that the frame of the treadle loom does not determine the quality of the weaving. Important, instead, are the quality of the fiber preparation tools, a strong and carefully made ratchet system to hold the fabric taut on the loom, and a precise and carefully balanced set of heddles so that a clear shed can be opened for the throwing of the shuttle.

Consider, for example, the importance of the reed as an implement for the production of fine treadle-loom woven material. Indeed, assuming the existence of finely spun yarn, it is the reed, along with the heddles, that dictates an even warp set and the warp count in the finished textile. While the average Rio Grande blanket has a warp count of only six to seven warps per 2.5 cm. (one inch), Saltillo *sarapes* of Mexico average a warp count of twelve to thirty warps per 2.5 cm. (one inch). Furthermore, the Spanish New Mexican loom was narrow, allowing for the weaving of fabrics which average only 56–70

FIGURE 2

Reeds for a treadle loom, *reeds spaced at 10, 5, and 7 per 2.5 cm. (one inch). Collection of Dr. and Mrs. Ward Alan Minge, Corrales, New Mexico.*

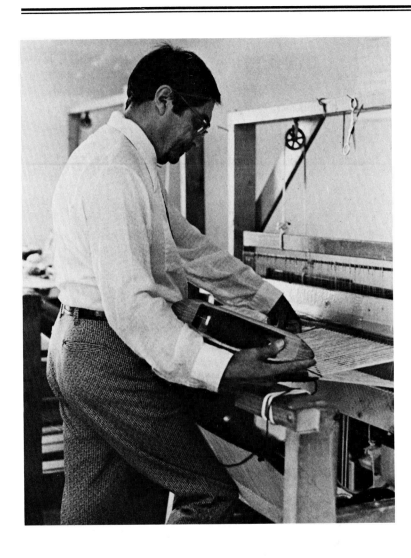

FIGURE 3

David Ortega at his loom in Chimayó. *Photo by Davis Mather.*

centimeters (22–28 inches) in width. Thinking, again, in terms of the medieval trade guilds and the type of bans that were frequently laid down in order to protect the industry, it is quite possible that a ban had been issued by the guilds in New Spain against the export of long and finely constructed loom reeds which would have restricted the width of the fabrics. The loom illustrated in Figure 1 was collected along with a wide assortment of specialized treadle loom weaving tools, which included three handmade reeds of differing fineness or dent, each designed for warp spacing of a particular type of fabric. (See Figure 2.) These particular reeds are roughly made. The frames are wood without metal parts, individual elements being lashed on with rawhide. In the late 1880s, with the advent of machine-spun cotton string warp, the typical warp count of the Rio Grande blanket changed from six to ten per 2.5 cm. (one inch). At this time, also, wider textiles began to be woven, sometimes measuring as much as 1.40 m. (55 inches). We can postulate that this is an indication that longer reeds of a finer dent, which had hitherto been unavailable from Mexican sources, were being imported from the eastern United States.

Today, though special parts have become available, the Spanish New Mexican loom has retained its traditional character as an industrial machine. (Figure 3 shows David Ortega weaving in his workshop in Chimayó.) The weaver stands on the treadles to change the shed, and a great deal of physical strength is required to beat down the weft and fully cover the warp. Certain parts of the loom have been refined, there have been many women weavers,[20] yet the loom retains the traditional form—large, sturdy, rough-hewn; it is essentially the same professional man's machine that was introduced to New Mexico by the Spanish almost 300 years ago.

Weaving requires yarns that are highly flexible, very strong, and of appropriate length. No natural fiber possesses all of these qualities in its original form, but many materials can be processed to provide them. Short fibers or filaments can be spun (simultaneous pulling out and twisting) so as to produce a very long thread or yarn and increase the strength, yet retain the necessary flexibility for weaving. Of the natural fibers, both wool and cotton yarns were spun in the Southwest, while commercial yarns of wool, cotton, silk, and linen were imported and used,[1] and some commercial wool cloths were raveled to provide fine yarns of colors otherwise not easily obtainable. Because each of these materials has its own history in the Southwest, the presence of one or more of them may help to date a textile whose history is unknown.

Virtually all handspun yarn in the Southwest—wool and cotton—is Z-spun:

> The *direction of twist* . . . is designated S or Z according to whether the trend of the spiral of the spun or twisted element conforms, when held in a vertical position, to the slant of the central portion of the letter S or the letter Z [Figure 1] . . .

> The direction of the *final twist* of a yarn is a quite definite and determinable item of description . . . In a *plied* or *re-plied* yarn the direction of the *original spin* may be more difficult to determine. Each successive twisting process usually reverses the direction of the preceding one.[2]

The Rio Grande blankets are normally characterized by single-Z-spun wefts and 2-ply (2-Z-spun-plied-S) warps.[3] This is such a hard and fast rule that any deviation from it points to a given textile as being aberrant. There are, however, certain commercially spun yarns which occur with some frequency in the Rio Grande blankets and related textiles. The most common of these are the 3-ply and 4-ply wool wefts and embroidery yarns, and the multi-ply cotton warps.

A given group of textiles generally has a known range of thread count, that is, a specific number of warps and wefts within a given unit. The unit used consistently in this publication is 2.5 cm. (one inch). The early Rio Grande

FIGURE 1

Direction of twist in a spun yarn. Adapted with
permission from Irene Emery, The Primary Structures of
Fabrics, *Diagram 1 (drawn by Nora Pickens).*

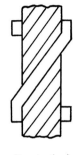

S-twist (\ )   Z-twist (/)

blankets generally have a warp count of five to seven and weft count of twenty-five to fifty per 2.5 cm. (one inch). The later blankets which contain commercial cotton warps and lumpy wool wefts have a thread count range of six to eleven warps and thirty to forty wefts per 2.5 cm. (one inch). The blankets woven using the commercially prepared wool wefts have a much higher weft count, approximately fifty per 2.5 cm. (one inch). Any deviation from the normal range is always noted with interest.

Handspun wool

Handspun wool is the principal fiber of the Rio Grande blanket and related textiles such as the wool-on-wool *colcha* embroideries, *sabanilla,* and *jerga.*

Though several varieties of sheep had been brought to the Western Hemisphere by the Spanish, it was the hardy *churro,* "suited by heredity for rocky slopes and high, dry climate,"[4] that survived the drive to New Mexico and formed the base sheep stock of the Spanish settlers.

For hand-processing, the Spanish *churro* was the ideal sheep. Its wool has a long, moderately coarse staple, nearly straight, with virtually no grease or albumen, which made it ideal for the process of hand-spinning and cleaning in a land where water was scarce and the spindle was the normal tool for making yarn. Grandstaff comments that "in common with unimproved wools, the

fleeces also contain varying quantities of kemp, . . . [an undesirable] short, coarse, opaque, nonelastic fiber. Wool of this type is well adapted for . . . weaving, since it requires little washing and can be hand-carded and spun with ease."[5] If the coarse outer fibers of the *churro* fleece were carefully hand-separated from the undercoat fibers, a fine, straight, long-staple wool resulted.[6] *Churro* sheep ranged in color from black-brown to a creamy white, and intermediate colors were produced by carding together brown and white wools, making tans and greys. With the fine silky textiles as evidence (Figure 2), we assume that this careful hand-separating of the fleeces was part of the laborious process of preparing yarns for the early Rio Grande blankets.

Throughout the centuries during which the Rio Grande blanket reigned supreme, yarn processing, which was never controlled by formal guild

FIGURE 2

Rio Grande blanket, woven of **churro wool.** *Detail of*
Plate 35.

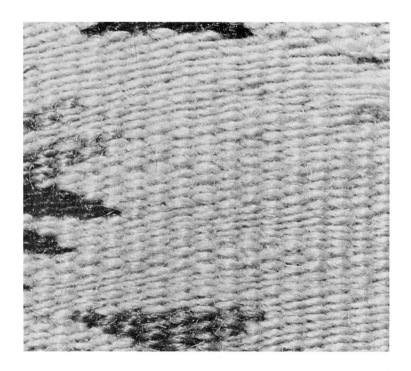

FIGURE 3

Rio Grande blanket woven of Rambouillet-Merino wool.
Detail of Chapter 8, Figure 4.

regulations, continued to be very simple and nonmechanical in nature. The treadle loom was exported from Europe along with a wide variety of associated tools, all of which were designed to facilitate the economical use of the revolutionary new machine. Yet, typical of the import of an entire complex of tools, the loom arrived in New Mexico minus the associated spinning wheel. Throughout the years, however, even into the twentieth century, the simple indigenous Indian spindle, the *malacate,* remained the principal tool for spinning the fibers to be used in the Rio Grande textiles.[7] An example of this simple tool (unusual because it includes a Majolica ceramic whorl from Mexico) is illustrated in Figure 4. It would seem that the use of the *malacate* for spinning might have hampered the increasing scale of textile production, yet spinning proceeds quickly using this simple tool. In actuality, the associated tasks of preparing the yarn for spinning are the most time consuming: clipping and sorting the wool, cleaning it, and aligning fiber strands (carding) in preparation for spinning. Both carding and spinning appear to have been daily chores performed by all members of the family, perhaps seasonally with shearing,[8] yet carding and spinning, though never controlled by guilds, were also

professions.[9] The treadle-loom-related wool cards, made of leather and fitted with metal prongs, were introduced early.

Though it is easy to spin prolifically using the simple *malacate,* it is not easy to wash, card, or spin the fine improved wools which are normally greasy and kinky. *Churro* yarns naturally tend to be smooth; that is, the long individual fibers generally were combed parallel to each other, producing a yarn with a hard, clean, shiny appearance. In contrast, Merino wool produces a yarn of somewhat fuzzy, matted, bumpy, and dull appearance. Merino has a very short, kinky fleece, heavy with grease and albumen, and is so difficult to process by the hand methods of the Southwest that, when Rambouillet Merino were introduced in 1859, and crossed with *churro,* the quality of both spinning and weaving deteriorated rapidly. This change in quality of fiber is clearly illustrated by comparing Figures 2 and 3.

Increasingly, from about 1870 on, handspun wool yarns in southwestern weaving degenerated in quality, and, combined with cotton twine warps and poor quality synthetic dyes that did not take well on the greasy wool, resulted in a period of generally poor weaving. After 1900, commercial wool was used in better quality rugs and blankets; and by the 1930s, sheepbreeding experiments for the Navajo had provided, again, a better "native" wool.

FIGURE 4

Whorl for* malacate *(spindle), glazed majolica. *The ceramic dates this to the Puebla Polychrome Period, 1650–90. (Cordelia P. Snow, personal communication.) Museum of New Mexico Collection at the Laboratory of Anthropology. 43304/11.*

Handspun cotton

When the Spanish arrived in New Mexico, introducing their tiny *churro* sheep, they found the Pueblo Indians, well versed in textile production, weaving primarily with the locally grown cotton. Handspun native cotton (*Gossypium hopi*, A.D. 1 to present) was apparently introduced from Mexico into the southern part of the Southwest about the time of Christ, and by A.D. 700 had spread into the northern part.[10] Cotton replaced or supplemented several native fibers, such as yucca and *apocynum,* for nonloom textiles, and quickly became the standard fiber for cloth-weaving among the prehistoric Pueblo Indians.

Cotton was prepared for use by first removing the fiber from the boll and picking the seeds from the mass. Then the fiber was placed on loose sand or between the folds of a blanket and beaten lightly with a fanlike beater to produce a fluff or pad ready for spinning. Spinning was accomplished by means of the *malacate.*

The tuft of cotton fiber was attached to the tip of the spindle which was then twirled by the right hand, thus twisting the fiber as it was being pulled out by the left hand to form a thread or yarn for weaving.

Handspun cotton yarn found only limited use by the Spanish. There is an unusual group of six Rio Grande blankets in which a handspun Z-spun cotton weft is combined with natural-dyed tapestry-woven wool.[11] There are so few of these textiles that they are really "mavericks among many hundreds"[12] of recorded Rio Grande blankets. Though cotton is today extensively cultivated in southern New Mexico, this fiber played only a minimal role in the development of Rio Grande weaving.

Commercial cotton twine (1880 to present) may have been introduced as early as the 1860s, but by about 1880 the Pueblo, Navajo, and Spanish weavers commonly used it for warps. About 1900, cotton twine warps were discouraged for larger fabrics but continued to be used as warp for pillow tops and curio runners and for saddle blankets, where cotton is superior to wool because it neither shrinks nor loses its strength when wet. The Pueblos continue to use cotton twine as warp in most of their cotton fabrics and as weft in many of them.

Raveled yarn

Commercial wool cloth of various weaves and qualities was a standard import in New Mexico from 1598 on. Much of the cloth was woven in Mexico, but some came from Europe. Coarse wool cloth, including *sayal, bayeta, bayetón,* and *jerga,* was also woven in commercial establishments in Santa Fe and Albuquerque.[13] Some of these early cloths were raveled by southwestern weavers to obtain colored yarns, which were then incorporated into their own textiles. They were used by the Spanish in small decorative figures, by the Navajo for both figures and backgrounds, and by the Pueblos primarily for embroidery threads. There is historical evidence that the Navajo were using raveled yarn in 1788, and it was in fairly common use by all southwesterners throughout most of the 1800s.

Bayeta is the term usually applied to early raveled yarns, and since *bayeta* is the Spanish equivalent for English baize, it is generally thought that English baize was the cloth raveled to obtain *bayeta* yarn.[13] In Spanish, however, *bayeta* is applied to a variety of flannellike cloths and does not specifically designate English baize. Because of this, it seems best to designate the raveled yarns by their physical characteristics.

Early raveled yarn (1750–1865) was produced from fine cloth, with threads about .35mm. in diameter, dyed red with lac or cochineal. Both Z- and S-spun yarns were used until about 1825, after which S-spun dominates until about 1865.[15] Until 1821, the cloth raveled came through Mexico or was produced locally, but by 1826, virtually all cloth came over the Santa Fe Trail, and much of it appears to have been American in origin. Because of their fineness, yarns were usually used paired or tripled, laid parallel to each other and not plied.

Late raveled yarn (1865–75) is usually termed *American flannel.* Almost all was raveled from wool cloths or blankets, and tends to be fuzzy and soft. Some of the earlier cloths were presumably dyed with cochineal, but most were synthetic-dyed in various shades of orange-red. The yarns are highly variable in diameter, ranging from .30 mm. to 1.10 mm. with most either .50 or .90 mm., which reflects the wide variety of fabrics being raveled. The smallest were used in groups of three to five, and sometimes as bundles with as many as nine threads. Intermediate sized yarns might be used paired or as singles, while the larger yarns were used as singles. These coarser yarns were used primarily by the Navajos, and most were raveled from a cloth specifically termed *bayeta,* supplied to the Navajo as part of their annuity issue by the U.S. Army.

Revival raveled yarn (1895–1900) was used in a few Navajo blankets woven for collectors at this time, as copies of Classic blankets. It was low quality synthetic-dyed plain-weave *bayeta* carried by Hubbell and other traders on the Reservation. Yarns in this group resemble those of the .55 mm.-diameter American flannel, and are recognizable primarily from the blanket design.

Respun raveled yarn (1865 to ca. 1880) was made from cloth that did not ravel cleanly into separate yarns. These fibers were recarded and respun to produce a handspun yarn. Bits of red cloth were frequently carded together with white native wool to produce a carded pink yarn very characteristic of the 1865 to 1880 period.[16]

Cloth strips (1870 to ca. 1880) were made from cloths that did not ravel well. These fabrics were cut into narrow strips and used as wefts. Some were made into a thick roll, but others were woven in such a way that the short, cut ends extended from the surface so as to resemble terrycloth in texture and appearance.[17]

Commercial wool yarns

Commercial plied yarns, like commercial cloth, were standard items of supply and trade during Spanish Colonial times. There is little evidence that they were used in weaving at that time, but they were utilized in embroidery. After Mexico won its independence from Spain in 1821, the source of supply changed, and these yarns were imported across the Santa Fe Trail. During the 1800s commercial yarns were used much as raveled cloth had been used, for small spots of color by the Spanish weavers, for embroidery by the Pueblos, and for both decorative elements and backgrounds by the Navajo.

Saxony yarn (1800 to 1865) was a fine, 3-ply yarn spun from the wool of Saxony Merino sheep and dyed with natural dyes. Saxony yarns were produced in Saxony, Germany, but also in England and France, and in New England. After 1821, Saxony yarns were imported across the Santa Fe Trail. They were widely used by the Spanish for color accents, and about mid-century, by the Navajos for general weaving. Some early writers on Navajo weaving confused Saxony with retwisted *bayeta* threads.[18]

Early Germantown yarn (1864 to 1875) is often confused with Saxony. Like Saxony, it is a 3-ply yarn, but it is dyed with synthetic dyes, in a wide range of colors that tend to be dull in appearance. The wool tends to be harsher in feel, as well, and the yarn is coarser than Saxony. It was introduced in 1864 as part of the annuity for the Navajo at Bosque Redondo, great quantities being issued in subsequent years.[19]

Germantown yarn (1875 to present) is 4-ply. It was introduced about 1875 and rapidly replaced the earlier 3-ply variety. Like its predecessor, it was synthetic-dyed, but in an even wider range of colors. Although its use for blankets and rugs was discouraged after 1900, it continued to be used in pillow tops and runners until 1935. The Pueblos continue to use Germantown for embroidery and brocade weaving.[20]

C FABRIC STRUCTURE
NORA FISHER

A woven textile is composed of *"interworked elements"*[1] arranged in a structure which, in effect, holds the fabric together. "Those who have for some years tried to correlate textile terms used in different parts of the world have been thwarted by the conflicting, inconsistent, and often inadequate terms in any one language."[2] Because widely varying terminology is used by handweavers, anthropologists, archaeologists, historians, ethnologists, art historians, and interior and fashion designers—and all of these professions are represented by our contributing authors—the practical descriptive terminology suggested by Irene Emery in *The Primary Structures of Fabrics* is used throughout this publication.

Including only variations of *"simple interlacing,"*[3] specifically *plain* and *float weaves,* the structures of southwestern Spanish textiles are not complicated. It is necessary, nevertheless, to describe the varieties involved.

"The simplest possible interlacing of warp and weft elements produces *plain weave* . . . . If the warp and weft elements are equally spaced and either identical or approximately equal in size and flexibility, the *plain weave* can be described as *balanced*."[4] (See Figure 1.) A number of the simple Rio Grande yardage fabrics such as *sayal* and *sabanilla* are, or are thought to have been, *balanced plain weave*.[5]

"If . . . the wefts are sufficiently numerous and sufficiently compacted to completely cover the warps, the fabric is *weft-faced*."[6] (Figure 2) In contrast with the yardage fabrics, the Rio Grande blankets are all *weft-faced plain weave*. The vast majority are woven with weft stripes. Among this group of fabrics, a large percentage were woven *double-width*. Irene Emery has clearly explained this method, which is used for weaving a wide fabric on a narrow loom:

If the weft is continuous but always interweaves twice (over and back) with the warps of one layer before shifting to the other layer, the two layers of the fabric will be joined by the common weft only along one edge and, when removed from the loom, will spread flat and form a single *simple-weave* fabric double the width that was set up in the loom. Thus, it is only the construction method that is *double,* not the finished fabric. If the method of construction is known it is entirely reasonable to describe and classify such a fabric as *double-woven,* or as *double-width*.[7]

FIGURE 1

"Balanced plain weave, *warp and weft equal in size, spacing and count." Reprinted with permission of Irene Emery, from* The Primary Structures of Fabrics, *Figure 85.*

FIGURE 2

"Weft-faced plain weave." *Reprinted with permission of Irene Emery from* The Primary Structures of Fabrics, *Figure 87.*

FIGURE 3

Paired warps *at the center of a* double-width weft-faced plain-woven *Rio Grande blanket. Detail of Plate 5.*

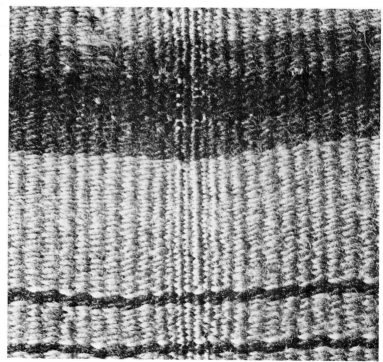

FIGURE 4

"**Slit tapestry weave,** *showing vertical and diagonal boundaries between color areas." Reprinted with permission of Irene Emery from* The Primary Structures of Fabrics, *Figure 93.*

FIGURE 5

"***Diagrammatic construction of a* tapestry weave** *join showing* single dovetailing." *Reprinted with permission of Irene Emery from* The Primary Structures of Fabrics, *Figure 96.*

The *double-woven weft-faced plain weave* Rio Grande blankets can easily be identified, for they are characterized by a group of heavier, *paired* warps at the exact center of the textile. (Figure 3)

The Rio Grande blankets which contain motifs (Plates 18–58) are *tapestry-woven.* Irene Emery has this description of the technique:

> *Weft-faced plain weave* identifies the weave when it lacks the special characteristic of discontinuous-weft patterning. It is when that characteristic is added that *weft-faced plain weave* becomes *tapestry weave.*[8]

> *Tapestry weaving* generally involves two fundamental principles: hiding the warp with closely packed wefts to secure solid color, and weaving independent wefts back and forth each in its own pattern area.[9]

> Inasmuch as there are few if any wefts that extend the full width of a tapestry-woven fabric, the structural feature that is most significant in distinguishing between varieties of *tapestry weave* is to be found at the meeting point of the wefts of laterally adjacent areas. According to the nature of the connection, or lack of connection, between areas, *tapestry weave* is called *slit, dovetailed . . .* or *interlocked.*[10]

For the most part, *tapestry-woven* Rio Grande blankets are characterized by a lack of "structural connection between laterally adjacent areas." They are *slit tapestry.* As is clearly illustrated in Figure 4, when a diagonal line is being woven, there need not be a "structural connection" between areas in order to form a firmly constructed fabric. To produce vertical lines and avoid vertical slits in Rio Grande blanket design, *single dovetailing* (Figure 5) and, rarely,

FIGURE 6

"Diagrammatic construction of **single interlocking** *between warps."* Reprinted with permission of Irene Emery from The Primary Structures of Fabrics, Figure 100.

FIGURE 7

Detail of Rio Grande blanket, shown in Plate 35. *Close-up of* tapestry weave.

FIGURE 8

Detail of Rio Grande blanket. Close-up of eccentric tapestry weave. *The Denver Art Museum. 1969–208.*

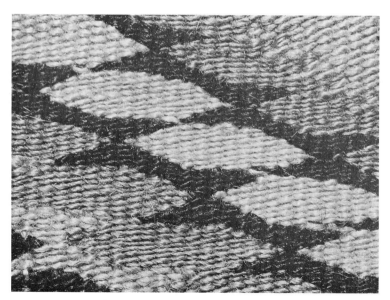

FIGURE 9

Detail of **jerga.** *Close-up of 2/2 twill weave. Chapter 14, Figure 3.*

FIGURE 10

Ojo de perdiz jerga. *Close-up of* diamond twill weave. *Detail of Chapter 14, Figure 4.*

FIGURE 11

End finish, *Rio Grande blanket. Detail of Plate 35.*

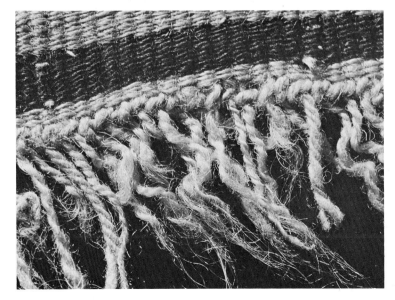

single interlocking (Figure 6) are used.[11] Occasionally, also, *eccentric,* or *nonhorizontal*[12] wefts appear in tapestry-woven Rio Grande blankets. The close-up details shown in Figures 7 and 8 illustrate the variations of *tapestry weave* most commonly used in the Rio Grande blanket.

The Rio Grande *jerga* and a very few examples of *sabanilla* are classified structurally as *float weaves—twill weaves,* to be specific.[13] As illustrated by the *jerga* details shown in Figures 9 and 10, *"Twill weaves* are *float weaves* characterized by a diagonal alignment of floats . . . the primary structural differences between *twill weaves* pertain to two basic factors: the numerical span of the floats and the direction of the diagonals. The numerical designation of a twill gives its basic *float span ratio*—for example, 2/1, 3/1, 2/2."[14] Reversing the direction of the *twill* diagonal can "create patterns of diagonals"[15] such as the *diamond twill* illustrated in Figure 10.

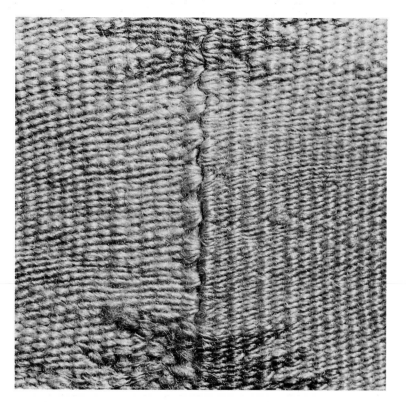

FIGURE 13

Center seam, Rio Grande blanket. Detail of Plate 35.

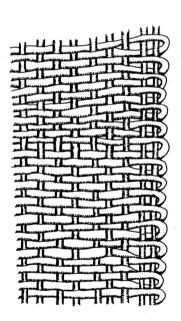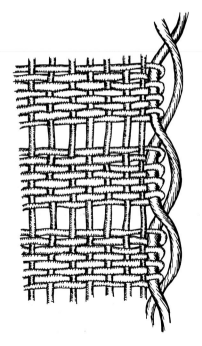

FIGURE 12

Selvedges: left, Rio Grande; right, Navajo system. Drawn by Nora Pickens.

Structures of the Rio Grande textiles are *simple weaves*. In like manner, the finishing touches given these textiles are simple. The warps of the Rio Grande blankets normally seem to have been cut and finished with simple knots, such as that shown in Figure 11. Figure 12 illustrates the simple woven selvedge of the Rio Grande blanket as compared to the twined side selvedge of the Navajo blanket (the vertical Navajo loom produces a textile with four selvedges, almost always reinforced by twining which results in corner tassels.)[16] As Figure 13 illustrates, the seaming of two loom widths was generally accomplished using a very simple *running stitch.*[17]

D NATURAL AND SYNTHETIC DYES
DOROTHY BOYD BOWEN AND TRISH SPILLMAN

The early Rio Grande blankets are distinguished by natural colors and dyes—soft whites and undyed browns, the rich dark and medium blue of indigo, the blue-red of cochineal, warm red to yellow-tan, and the sunny golden yellow from various plants. With these colors some of the finest Rio Grande blankets were produced. Today, 150 years later, there remains a liveliness and richness of color unique to these natural-dyed blankets.

It would be naive to think that the Spanish used natural colors and dyes because of their preference for the natural tones over the colors of synthetic dyes. Before 1860 only natural dyes were available. It is almost impossible for us to imagine the difficulty that color presented to the Spanish colonists before the introduction of prepackaged commercial synthetic dyes. Natural dyeing is a long, involved process and, since the best dyestuffs are not native to this area, the colonists had to import them from Mexico and South America—a very expensive undertaking. Indigo and red dyes have been noted as trade items, gifts to Indians, and as supply items found in the Presidial Company in Santa Fe from

as early as 1802. The red is referred to as *vermellón*.[1] It was sold in packets and may have been a vermilion pigment (cinnabar or mercuric sulfide) or, as indicated by contemporary dictionaries, a red dye (cochineal).

The textile industry of New Mexico never reached the same high degree of technical excellence and specialization found in Mexico. In New Spain separate guilds with rigid specific *Ordenanzas* existed for weavers of silk, cotton, wool, etc., as well as for dyers of the separate fibers. There is no historical information that would indicate the existence of a guild system for wool dyeing in New Mexico. The 1790 census of the Albuquerque area listed other phases of weaving as professions but did not mention dyeing. It was, therefore, probably a project of the home, with the women doing most of the work. The Bazán brothers were hired for their weaving skills; since they came from Mexico where the highly structured weaving guild systems existed, their ability to dye wool was at best a secondary skill. They likely adapted the Pueblo methods and materials for dyeing, some of which will now be described.

Prior to the dyeing process, wool must be thoroughly washed to remove the grease and dirt. The Spanish have long used the yucca, *amole* (*Yucca* spp.), as

207

"soap" for their laundry as well as for washing wool. The root of the yucca is dug, broken into small pieces, crushed, and left in the sun to dry. An excellent lather is formed when the small pieces are stirred into cold water. Hot water is then added to the soapy water.[2]

Since wool does not have an affinity for most dye solutions, it is necessary to mordant the wool. In this process the mordant fixes the dye on the wool fibers.[3] In addition to mordants, urine, which was used as a detergent and solvent by the early colonists, was collected in large copper vats and left to ferment.[4] Many trees such as juniper, oak, and wild cherry and other plants are rich in tannic acid, which acts as a mordant so that when parts of these are used in a dye, an additional mordant is not required.

During the natural-dye revival period of the 1930s, the most common mordant was alum. A native alum (alunogen) is found in New Mexico. According to Tillie Stark, who did the dyeing for the Native Market in Santa Fe, alum was the most frequently used mordant, with tin used less frequently. Acidifying agents such as nitric acid and cream of tartar were used less frequently.[5] Today, another popular mordant is potassium dichromate, or chrome.

Each mordant affects the color of the dye differently. When four skeins of wool, each with a different mordant, are entered into the same dye pot at the same time, the result is four distinct colors. Note Plate 73, a contemporary, natural-dyed hanging, which has at least five different shades from the one dye pot of cota (Thelesperma spp.). This is primarily due to the four mordants: tin, alum, chrome, and iron. The fifth color is the result of an afterbath in the tin mordant.

The material from which the dye pot is made can also affect the color of the wool. Initially, the Spanish and Pueblos used large highly fired clay pots for dyeing.[6] When available, copper pots were also used for dyeing.[7] An iron pot will darken the color and an aluminum pot will dull the color. An earthern pot will not affect the clarity of the dyes.

Indigo (Indigofera spp.) has been known as the world's most important dyestuff for four thousand years.[8] When the Spanish arrived in the New World in 1512, the Indians were using an indigo.[9] In New Mexico, indigo was imported in lump form via Mexico, but the species is not known.

Lumps of indigo are insoluble in water, so a different solvent was required. According to oral tradition, copper pots placed at each end of a village were used to collect children's urine. Fermented urine provided a reducing agent and a mild alkali, which acted to convert the indigo to its soluble state. The wool was then placed in the dye bath overnight, after which it was dried without wringing and later rinsed until the water was clear.[10] As it comes from the dye pot a coppery blue-green, the indigo-dyed wool oxidizes in the air back to the original blue color. Various shades of blue could be obtained depending upon the length of time the wool spent in the dye pot and the strength of the solution.

Indigo was also used as an overdye: yellow wool was dipped into indigo to produce green. As early as 1884 Matthews noted Navajo use of indigo over natural yellow.[11] Four of the five natural-dyed green yarns from Rio Grande blankets analyzed by Saltzman were confirmed to be indigo over natural-dyed yellow.[12] An early example of this color appears in Plate 18.

Indigo was also used with natural brown to make it darker and richer, as, for example, in the darkest areas of the blanket illustrated in Plate 47.

It is interesting to note indigo as a stock article of trade and to compare its value with other trade articles. A ledger from 1854 indicates merchandise brought by wagon train from Missouri to Mariano Yrisarri's store at Ranchos de Albuquerque. Forty-eight pounds of indigo at $1.10 lb. may be compared with the other nonmanufactured imported goods such as coffee for 10¢ lb., almonds at 13¢ lb., sugar at 6¢ lb., and nutmeg at $1.40 lb., the only price comparable with that of indigo. As a typical manufactured item, a flintlock rifle for $4.00 is listed.[13]

Indigo was perhaps the most widely used imported dye from 1800 to 1870, and its presence is one of the most distinguishing characteristics of the old Rio Grande blankets. During this period, the finest weaving was produced. Almost every early blanket reviewed in this publication contains indigo, usually as the predominant color. Even with the introduction of commercially dyed yarns and some of the early synthetic colors, natural indigo continued to compete with synthetic indigo until after World War I.

Brazil was a common dyestuff of New Spain and was also imported for use on local handspun wool.[14] It was obtained from various species of red dyewood trees. The first red dyewood was the heartwood of *Caesalpinia sappan* (now known as Sappan wood), which was used in Europe during the Middle Ages. The Portuguese discovered a similar red wood in Brazil and named the territory for the dyewood. This New World brazil is *Caesalpinia brasiliensis*.[15] The third source of brazilwood dye was a shrub grown in Nicaragua, Colombia, and Venezuela—*Haematoxylon brasiletto*.[16] The export of this latter dye began about 1848 and continued until World War I. Its color range was red to purple, but was highly fugitive, which may account for the range in color within the so-called brazilwood dyes. In a majority of Rio Grande blankets the red has faded to a golden tan, so it is possible that this fugitive brazilwood found its way to the northern New Mexico dye pots. Historical accounts mention *palo brasil* being used as a dye in colonial New Mexico. Because of the apparent importance of brazilwood as a Spanish dye, Saltzman analyzed fibers with reputed brazilwood dye from six Rio Grande blankets.[17] He established that in these particular blankets the dye was neither brazilwood, mountain mahogany, logwood, nor *cañaigre,* but was unable to identify the dyestuff. In the blanket illustrated in Plate 8 Saltzman felt that the dye was probably a red wood, slightly different from his standard for brazilwood.

The Chacón reference to *palo brasil* imported "from the outer country" by dyers in 1803 is translated as "brazil stick."[18] According to Don Eulogio Gallegos, an octogenarian weaver and dyer in the 1930s, brazilwood arrived in remote northern New Mexico villages in the form of split logs two feet long.[19] This practice may have resulted in references to "logwood," which could have been the origin of confusion that has arisen between these two dyes. There are some similarities. Both were transported in log form, both had to have the reddish heartwood chipped or rasped away before it could be used, and the dampened, chipped wood was left to ferment a few days for each dye. True logwood (*Haematoxylon campechianum,* also called "campeche wood") produces black, blue, purple, and silver-grey in contrast to the red dye of brazilwood, and does not appear in any of the Rio Grande samples analyzed by Saltzman.

The only two imported dyes used by Don Eulogio Gallegos were reported to have been brazilwood and indigo. Native plants provided the rest of his colors. Basically, the same indigenous dye plants have been used by Navajo and Spanish, often using the same recipe. One cannot assume, however, that because the Navajo used a particular dye the Spanish did also. Mr. Gallegos provided a tie to earlier times; he was an older man, "patriarch in whom memory and direct hearsay together span easily a century of time," weaving in 1930 on a loom a hundred years old in a remote village, Tierra Azul, near Abiquiu.[20] Although weaving in the twentieth century, he used dyes and materials of the nineteenth century. This suggests the possibility of other remote weavers continuing to weave traditional designs of indigo and brazilwood, which could account for some of the indigo blankets found in excellent condition in northern New Mexico. As late as 1914 James wrote that the older dyers of Chimayó still used "Brazil sticks" when asked to dye wool for a "native color" blanket, despite the general replacement of that color by packaged synthetic dyes.[21]

A native hardwood tree which is said to produce a similar color to that of brazilwood is the native mountain mahogany (*Cercocarpus* spp.). E. Boyd thought that mountain mahogany rather than brazilwood was used locally, but Saltzman's tests of natural-dyed tan fibers did not indicate the presence of this native material. Mention should be made, however, of Mrs. Bryan's *Navajo Native Dyes,* for therein appear more recipes for mountain mahogany than for any other dye plant. Twelve different colors are obtained by using the bark of the root by itself, in combination with other plant materials, or as an afterbath dye in combination with prickly pear.[22]

The third important imported dye is cochineal, which was the most expensive. Cochineal is the female insect *Dactylopius coccus,* which lives on the prickly pear cactus (*Opuntia cochenillifera*) in Mexico. The female insect must be harvested while heavy with eggs. After picking, the insects are steamed, dried, and ground into a powder which is the dye.[23]

To dye with cochineal the wool may be left unmordanted, but different mordants and chemicals may be used to obtain various shades of red ranging from orange-red to blue-red to dark brown-red. By examining the Mexican *Ordenanzas* (guild regulations for weavers and dyers) much can be learned about the common usage of cochineal dye. In the eighteenth century, we find mention of *morado de grana* (mulberry cochineal), *leonado de grana* (tawny cochineal), *envinado de grana* (wine-hued cochineal), and *tinto en grana o encarnado* (color in cochineal or red).[24] Cochineal is also referred to as *carmesí,* which is a blue-red hue. These brilliant cochineal hues are still unfaded in the fine Saltillo *sarapes* from the early nineteenth century. In the *Ordenanzas de Tinte de Paños, 1738, 1760–1,* we read that to dye twenty pounds of wool yarn and a cloth seventy-four to seventy-five *varas* long required ten pounds of cochineal.[25]

Unlike indigo and brazil, cochineal appears mainly in imported commercially dyed factory-spun yarn. Only the highest quality blankets contained this cochineal-dyed yarn, and it was used sparingly. At some point, however, the Spanish may have used cochineal to dye their native handspun wool. The blanket in Plate 22 contains a 1-ply handspun wool weft dyed with cochineal. Documents record the importation of pounds of *carmesí* (cochineal) into New Mexico in the 1830s.[26] There are still old-time New Mexican dyers who have jars of cochineal sitting on their shelves. Cochineal was also used in the 1930s at the Native Market.[27]

An unexpected result of the Saltzman dye analysis is the discovery of the use of an early red dye, lac or gum-lac, an insect dye known for centuries. In the Rio Grande textiles it occurs only on yarn that appears to be either handspun or raveled.[28] Lac has been used in India for thousands of years. It was also exported to England and to the United States, where its cheaper cost made it popular as a substitute for the slightly more brilliant cochineal, until both were supplanted by synthetic dyes.[29] There is, thus, some question as to how lac-dyed yarns arrived in New Mexico—at an early date by way of the Manila Galleon or at a much later date over the Santa Fe Trail.

Mention should be made of the surprising discovery in Rio Grande blankets of another red, red-orange, and brown dye: madder. Madder *(Rubia tinctorium),* one of the older dye materials, has been known for centuries. The description of madder production in the nineteenth century includes pulverizing the roots of the plant. This powder form was not completely satisfactory due to the possible adulteration with brick dust, mahogany wood, and other mineral substances.[30] Madder may or may not have been imported to the Spanish colonies. There are fourteen species of a related genus—*Galium,* native to New Mexico, seven of which are found in the upper Rio Grande area.[31] Madder was certainly much less expensive than either cochineal or indigo. An American dye journal in 1831 lists the following prices per pound for the six most popular dyes:

Quercitron	$ .06
Fustic	.06
Logwood	.06
Madder	.18¾
Indigo	2.25
Cochineal	5.00–5.50[32]

Saltzman identified a soft, warm red and a brown-red as a madder-like dye (not *Rubia tinctorium,* but probably a local *Galium* species) in the blanket shown in Plate 53. This verifies the use of a madder-like dye, probably a local plant, in the area of Abiquiu in the 1870s.

The yellow dyes from the early blankets and *colchas* were not identified by Saltzman as being from the common imported dyestuffs such as weld, fustic, quercitron, or saffron. Nor were they from any native plant material which traditionally produces a bright, clear yellow. (See Saltzman index, note 5, for complete yellow listings.) The most common color extracted from plants is yellow in varying shades, but in using the comparison method, it is possible to determine only what a yellow is not, rather than what it is. Without positive identification at this writing, the authors have turned to historical data which mention yellow-producing dye plants.

There is one reference to "saffron for dyeing" in a California-bound ship's cargo list of 1822, which proves that saffron was being imported by the California Spanish people as a dyestuff.[33] Saffron had been cultivated in Spain from the time of the early Arab occupation and was common all over Europe by the sixteenth century.[34]

Chamisa (Chrysothamnus spp.) "is one of the oldest known of the indigenous dyes."[35] The brilliant yellow blossoms of this rabbit brush dot the roadsides and arroyos in brilliant array in the fall. The blossoms are gathered fresh and either used immediately or left to dry. The yellow, when used fresh, is brighter than the dye from the dried flowers.

Another clear, bright yellow comes from the *yerba de la víbora (Gutierrezia* spp.) or snakeweed. This plant is also important to the Spanish for medicinal purposes.[36] (The Spanish relied on the land and its vegetation for numerous medicinal and superstitious remedies as well as food. Much knowledge about the healing properties of certain plants has passed from one generation to the next.)

Cañaigre (Rumex hymenosepalus) is a native dock which grows extensively along the roadsides in New Mexico. It is said to have multiple uses, including cleansing the mouth, tanning hides, and dyeing wool in orange, gold, or rust. The roots, dug in the fall after the top foliage has died, are sliced and then dried for later use. The high percentage of tannic acid present eliminates the need for mordanting.[37]

Capulín, or chokecherry *(Prunus melanocarpa),* from the San Luis Valley is another native plant of multiple purpose—it is used for jam, jelly, wine, and stomach medicine. It is said to have been used as a dye in the San Luis Valley during the synthetic dye period. Unfortunately, spectrophotometry did not identify *capulín* dye among the reds tested, so its use cannot be verified. Perhaps, since *capulín* is rich in tannin, it was used in conjunction with some other natural dyestuff which has now been forgotten.

The last dye to be mentioned is known primarily as a tea to the Spanish, Indian, and Anglo. *Cota,* Navajo tea *(Thelesperma megapotamicum*—syn. *gracile),* grows from one to two feet tall. The flowers and stems are gathered in the late summer and may be used fresh or dried. Shades ranging from orange, deep gold, and bronze to rust are obtained from this versatile plant depending upon the mordant used. *Cota,* one of the more popular dye plants among contemporary craftsmen, was used most effectively by Teresa Sagel in the textile in Plate 73.

It is a mistake to assume that these natural dyes do not fade. Frequently, the original color will fade or change from a warm red to a cool red. While the intensity of natural dyes tends to lessen, however, the early synthetic dyes used in Rio Grande blankets faded and ran badly. Although many of the natural dyes in the early blankets have faded and changed, the character of the blankets has not been altered visually as much as those treated with synthetic dyes.

Once synthetic dyes became available in the late 1860s, the use of natural dyes quickly declined. What once took hours of preparation could now be done in minutes with the packaged dyes. The riotous colors of the later synthetic-dyed blankets contrast sharply with the somber rich tones of the natural-dyed blankets.

Much has been written concerning the discovery, development, and dissemination of synthetic dyes. Although a thorough discussion of the subject is beyond the scope of this publication, mention should be made of the earliest "aniline" or coal tar dyes which are commonly found along with natural dyes in blankets woven between 1860 and 1900.

The first coal tar dye was Mauve, discovered by the English chemist Perkin in 1856. An early synthetic dye of similar color appears in the blankets in Plates 25, 26, and 51. Another early synthetic dye was Methyl violet, discovered in 1861 by Lauth; it was widely distributed and may appear in the blankets in

Plates 26, 28, 40, and 51. Early blue dyes were Lyons blue (1860), Alkali blue (1862), and Diphenylamine blue (1866). By 1869 Alizarin, the main component of madder, had been synthesized, and by 1872 Methyl green had been discovered.[38]

Two of the blankets analyzed by Saltzman may contain Orange II, which was discovered in 1876 by Roussin.[39] One of these is the wedge-weave "servant blanket" shown in Plate 2.

Indigo was not chemically synthesized until 1880, and not marketed until 1897.[40] Since the earlier synthetic blues mentioned above were pale and faded badly, New Mexico dyers apparently continued using natural indigo long after synthetic dyes had replaced madder, cochineal, and brazil.

The revival of the use of natural dyes in the 1930s has been mentioned. Tillie Stark, under the direction of Leonora Curtin Paloheimo, was responsible for the dyeing of wool for weaving and needlework at the Native Market. She has said that barrels of brazilwood chips and cochineal and cartons of powdered indigo were imported for dyeing. The local vegetation used for dyeing was *chamisa, cañaigre,* and walnut hulls.[41]

There is once again a revived interest in using natural dyes. One dye pot will often yield a variety of shades and hues which, when woven, blend together in pleasing combinations. The handspun, hand-dyed yarn is finding favor with many weavers who have studied the old Rio Grande blankets. Several weavers from the 1976 Rio Grande Dyeing and Weaving Workshops at the Museum of International Folk Art tried to reproduce some of the old designs and colors using the synthetic dyed yarns, but they soon discovered that the lengthy process of natural dyeing produced yarns with a subtlety and quality not found in yarns dyed with the inexpensive synthetic dyes available to the mass market.

Through the years many myths have sprung up concerning the use of dyes by the Spanish in the Rio Grande area. *Palo brasil* (brazil stick), *vermellón* (vermilion—cinnabar or cochineal), *añil* (indigo), *carmesí* (cochineal), and native plants are all mentioned in the documents as dyes used in the coloring of textiles.[1] Other dye sources are cited in the more recent literature,[2] and contemporary craftsmen use many dyes in addition. Thus, many individuals have attempted to guess what dyes were used in the early textiles. It has been proven many times, however, that visual identification of dyes is not reliable.

Positive identification of natural dyes used in historic or prehistoric textiles requires interdisciplinary cooperation of museum people, chemists, botanists, biologists, and dyers. In our study of southwestern Spanish textiles we have been fortunate to have had the expertise, spirited interest, and enthusiasm of Max Saltzman, chemist, and Gail Tierney, ethnobotanist, as well as the practical experience of Trish Spillman and other local weavers, most especially, the late Mable Morrow.

Saltzman contracted with us to perform thirty analyses. In actual fact, due to his native curiosity, he has contributed a total of fifty-five analyses. This group of analyses constitutes an important body of specific facts concerning southwestern Spanish dyeing, and the first effort toward positive identification of dyes used by the Spanish in the southwestern United States.

Max Saltzman is now a Research Specialist in the Institute of Geophysics and Planetary Physics at the University of California at Los Angeles. He is a consultant in the field of color technology and the appropriate use of colorants in industry and Adjunct Professor of Chemistry (Color Science) at Rensselaer Polytechnic Institute, Troy, New York where he still participates in the program of teaching and research. Before his retirement in 1973 after almost thirty years in the dye and pigment industry with Allied Chemical, he was Manager of Color Technology for Allied Chemical Corporation's Specialty Chemical Division. Starting in 1948, he developed techniques for the identification of organic pigments, based on the early work of Formanek and others, using the technique of solution spectrophotometry. In the early 1960s, at the request of Dr. Junius Bird of the American Museum of Natural History, he successfully applied these same techniques to the identification of colorants used in the textiles of pre-Columbian Mesoamerica (for Mr. Peter Gerhard) and Peru (for Dr. Mary Elizabeth King, then at the Textile Museum). The methods used for the identification of organic pigments in industrial materials proved to be equally useful for the identification of the red, blue, and purple dyed and painted fabrics of pre-Columbian Central and South America. In 1975, with the aid of a grant from the Munsell Color Foundation, a dye identification laboratory was established at the University of California at Los Angeles to work with the textiles of pre-Columbian Peru.

At that time, almost twenty years ago, Saltzman wrote two articles describing his method and, with two coauthors, made a plea for cooperation between industry and the arts. The technique used to make positive identification of dyes is chemical "spectrophotometric transmittance curves of solutions of pigments in . . . solvents."[3] The dye is dissolved in a solution, and a spectrophotometric curve of "the *qualitative* nature of the color of the solution"[4] is obtained by using an instrument known as a spectrophotometer. The curve is then compared with known reference standards. Although expertise and continuity of experience are necessary, the technique is relatively simple and the equipment is neither complicated nor expensive.

The technique is simple, yet we lack known reference standards. We need continued cooperation among botanists, dyers, museum people, and chemists. Saltzman and his associates wrote about this problem in 1963:

> The key to the proper use of this method lies in preparation of a file of known materials to be used for comparison with the curves of unknown materials.[5]

> The dyes or pigments used may have been of botanical or animal origin and we may or may not have authentic samples of these. If we do not have authentic known samples, we can only supply a negative analysis; that is, we can only state that the dye or pigment is not one with which we are familiar.[6]

It takes knowledge, skill, and time to obtain an authentic sample. A botanist—a biologist in the case of animal materials—must collect, identify, and authenticate a sample of the dye from the plant or animal source. That sample must then be processed; that is, the fiber must be dyed by a person who is willing to work under clinical conditions, documenting each step of the dyeing process. The dye in the yarn is then dissolved in a solvent, and a curve is obtained on the spectrophotometer, producing a reference standard.

The aim of Saltzman, Keay, and Christensen in 1963 was to promote cooperation between industry and the arts. They spoke of a central location where analysis could be done, then communicated and shared, with reference standards available to all interested laboratories. Fifteen years later Saltzman is still lobbying for cooperation between industry and the arts. We still do not have a proper working set of reference standards. Red dyes (which come from a few select sources) and indigo (which is a single chemical compound) are easy to identify. Yellows, tans, and browns come from innumerable plant sources, and we simply do not have the necessary reference standards for positive identification of these dyes. Saltzman, still focused on identifying pre-Columbian Peruvian dyes, is involved in a cooperative project which is aimed at pinpointing just exactly what plants were used for dyeing over 2,000 years ago in Peru.

For the museum person there is a slight drawback in the use of spectrophotometry for the analysis of dyes. The technique does involve the destruction of a small amount of sample. As Saltzman phrased it, "the amount of material to be used in the identification is a function of the importance . . . of this identification."[7] We feel that the careful removal of a few centimeters of yarn from a specimen is warranted in order to build up a body of knowledge concerning dyes and dyeing. Indeed, we feel fortunate that Saltzman has been willing to leave his Peruvian interests for a short while and take a brief sojourn in New Mexico, focusing on positive identification of the dyes of the southwestern United States.

The analysis of fifty-five Rio Grande blanket and *colcha* embroidery samples has provided much new and surprising information. We discovered much more cochineal than we had suspected. Fifteen of the samples submitted contained cochineal, encompassing a wide range of color from yellow-red to dark blue-red. Interestingly, all of these samples of cochineal-dyed yarn are commercially prepared 3- and 4-ply yarn.[8] We had not expected to find madder- or lac-dyed yarn in southwestern Spanish textiles. Both turned up: two shades of madder-type dye were found in a servant blanket woven in the Abiquiu area,[9] and lac appeared in three samples, every time we attempted to identify cochineal in a single handspun or raveled Z-spun yarn. Synthetic-dyed reds appeared several times in fabrics that also contained cochineal, or in fabrics that we felt should contain cochineal. We had expected to find indigo and, indeed, it did turn up in six of seven samples submitted.

Due to a lack of proper reference standards, positive identification of the red-brown, yellow, and tan dyes is impossible at this point. Yet negative results gives us a chance to examine old myths. Brazilwood, logwood, and mountain mahogany have been mentioned in documents and recent literature as popular dyes of the Spanish.[10] In fact, these three dyes, which produce very different colors, have been spoken of in New Mexico as being one and the same dye.[11] None of the three were found in the dye analysis. The dye used for the distinctive so-called "brazilwood" red-brown found in a specific group of bands-and-stripes blankets remains to be identified.[12] We do have a clue. The least faded of the "brazilwood" samples did prove to be some type of red wood dye.[13]

Indeed, the famous "brazilwood" referred to in the documents may have been a highly fugitive form of red wood dye. Perhaps someday we will have a reference standard to identify it. In the meantime we are lucky to have found one pristine unfaded sample that points toward verifying the use of a red wood dye. Some nine reference standards were used for the yellow dyes; five of these are extremely popular dyes in the Southwest today.[14] We have not been able to identify any yellows—twelve samples were submitted with no positive results.

Follow-up projects are needed. We need to provide reference standards by hiring botanists to collect materials and dyers to work under carefully controlled clinical conditions. In the meanwhile we are fortunate to have been told that we can no longer point to a color and glibly state that it is obvious that it must be *chamisa-*, *chamizo-*, or snakeweed-dyed.

We submitted two yarns from two separate textiles which we thought might be *cañaigre*-dyed. Far more illuminating, these two dyes turned out to be related to Orange II, an early synthetic dye—a bit of information which allows us to pinpoint dates for these two important pieces.[15]

Indeed, the dye analysis has given us a great deal of information; in fact, the results of the analysis and its implications are referred to in every paper of this publication. But there is probably even more information to be gleaned from careful examination and comparison of the details of this extensive dye analysis.

DYE ANALYSIS

UCLA #	ACCESSION CAT. NUMBER	OWNERSHIP	COLOR	MAKE-UP	NATURAL DYES	SYNTHETIC DYES	COMMENTS
D–32–1	FA.67.43.3	IFAF	Faded purple	3-ply		N.I.[1]	Plate 54
D–32–2	26103/12	SAR	Purple	1-ply		N.I.[1]	
D–32–3	A.5.57.10	MNM	Red-Brown	1-ply	Madder[2]		Plate 53
D–32–4	A.5.57.10	MNM	Red	1-ply	Madder[2]		Plate 53
D–32–5	FA.67.16.1	IFAF	Red	3-ply	Cochineal[3]		Plate 37
D–32–6	FA.67.43.3	IFAF	Red-Orange	3-ply		N.I.[1]	Plate 54
D–32–7	FA.67.43.3	IFAF	Red	3-ply	Cochineal[3]		Plate 54
D–32–8	L.5.52.32	SCAS	Red	1-ply		N.I.[1]	
D–32–9	L.5.56.35	SCAS	Red	1-ply		N.I.[1]	
D–32–10	L.5.58.41	SCAS	Red	3-ply	Cochineal[3]		Plate 65
D–32–11	L.5.58.41	SCAS	Tan	1-ply	N.I.[1]		Not brazil.[4] Plate 65
D–32–13	L.5.62.68	SCAS	Bright orange	1-ply		N.I.[1]	Plate 30
D–32–14	L.5.62.68	SCAS	Orange	1-ply		N.I.[1]	Plate 30

1. N.I. means that the dye, natural or synthetic, could not be identified.

2. Madder. The control used was *Rubia tinctorium.* The example analyzed is a dye of the general family of madder-like plants *Rubiaceae, Rubia* sp., not necessarily *Rubia tinctorium* L. Since there are fourteen species of the closely related *Galium* native to New Mexico, seven of which are found in the upper Rio Grande area, this dye may have been from one of these native plants.

3. Cochineal. The control used was *Dactylopius coccus* (formerly known as *Coccus cacti*). The dyestuff is composed of dried bodies of insects, *Dactylopius coccus*, which flourish on the host plant, *Opuntia coccinellifera.* Cochineal is generally thought to have been imported from Mexico. It is worth noting, however, that varieties of the insect grow on the host plants, popularly known as nopal or prickly pear cactus, at least as far north as Boulder, Colorado.

4. Controls used for the red-brown-tan colors were: brazilwood *(Caesalpinia brasiliensis)*; logwood *(Haematoxylon campechianum* L.); mountain mahogany *(Cercocarpus* spp., dye sample courtesy of Mrs. Spillman, not verified by a botanist); *cañaigre (Rumex hymenosepalus);* and chokecherry *(Prunus* spp.). Many barks and woods, all sources of tannins, provide brown and tan dyestuff.

UCLA #	ACCESSION CAT. NUMBER	OWNERSHIP	COLOR	MAKE-UP	NATURAL DYES	SYNTHETIC DYES	COMMENTS
D–32–15	L.5.62.85	SCAS	Faded red	3-ply	Cochineal[3], plus unknown yellow[5]		Plate 38
D–32–16	L.5.62.85	SCAS	Red	3-ply	Cochineal[3], plus unknown yellow[5]		Plate 38
D–32–17	T.318	SAR, SF	Orange	1-ply		Probably Orange II[6]	Plate 16
D–32–18	18088	UC	Orange	1-ply		Maybe Orange II[6]	Plate 2
D–32–19	18088	UC	Pink	1-ply		N.I.[1]	Plate 2
D–32–20	18088	UC	Orange-Pink	1-ply		N.I.[1]	Plate 2
D–33–22	L.5.58.41	SCAS	Yellow	1-ply	N.I.[1]		Similar to D–33–23 Plate 65
D–33–23	L.5.62.68	SCAS	Yellow	1-ply	N.I.[1]		Similar to D–33–22 Plate 30
D–33–24	L.5.62.69	SCAS	Yellow-Brown	1-ply	N.I.[1]		Similar to D–33–25 and D–33–27
D–33–25	L.5.62.69	SCAS	Yellow	1-ply	N.I.[1]		Similar to D–33–24 and D–33–27
D–33–27	26119/12	MNM	Yellow	1-ply	N.I.[1]		Similar to D–33–24 and D–33–25
D–33–29	L.5.62.69	SCAS	Green (Grey-Green)	1-ply			Cannot identify[7] No indigo
D–33–30	26119/12	MNM	Blue-Green	1-ply	Indigo[8], plus unknown yellow[5]		
D–33–31	18088	UC	Yellow-Brown	1-ply	N.I.[1, 5]		Unknown yellow Plate 2
D–33–32	A.63.8.1	MNM	Red	3-ply	Cochineal[3]		
D–33–33	L.5.62.83	SCAS	Pink	3-ply		N.I.[1]	Plate 51
D–33–34	L.5.62.83	SCAS	Orange-Red	3-ply	Cochineal[3], plus unknown yellow[5]		Plate 51
D–33–35	L.5.62.83	SCAS	Blue-Red	3-ply	Cochineal[3]		Plate 51
D–33–36	L.5.61.79	SCAS	Red-Brown	1-ply		N.I.[1]	
D–33–38	A.5.57.35	MNM	Tan	1-ply			Cannot identify[7]

5. Controls used for the yellow colors were: rabbit brush locally called *chamisa* (*Chrysothamnus nauseosus* or *Chrysothamnus* spp.); calliopsis (*Coreopsis tinctoria* or native *Coreopsis cardaminifolia*); saffron (*Crocus sativus* L.); snakeweed (*Gutierrezia* spp.); *chamizo* or four-winged salt bush (*Atriplex canescens*); safflower (*Carthamus tinctorius*); dock or *cañaigre* (*Rumex* spp.); weld (*Reseda luteola* L.); fustic (*Morus tinctoria,* formerly known as *Chlorophora tinctoria);* and osage orange (*Maclura pomifera*).

Since many plants yield a yellow dye, and few standards are available, it is extremely difficult to identify the plant origins of the yellow dyes.

6. Orange II is a very early synthetic dye discovered in 1876, color index number 15507 or 15510. D–32–17 gives a better analysis than D–32–18; therefore, the less certain statement on D–32–18.

7. *Cannot identify* means just that. We cannot even state if it is natural or synthetic or even if it is a dyed fiber as contrasted with a naturally colored one.

8. Indigo. The control used was *Indigofera tinctoria* L. (See Tierney, 1977, p. 33: "*Indigofera suffruticosa,* a native of Mexico and the West Indies [may have been popular species in New Mexico], though the product of several species might have been used.")

UCLA #	ACCESSION CAT. NUMBER	OWNERSHIP	COLOR	MAKE-UP	NATURAL DYES	SYNTHETIC DYES	COMMENTS
D–33–39	L.5.62.83	SCAS	Blue-Green	1-ply	Indigo[8]		Plus unknown yellow,[5] but only by inference. No yellow was extracted. Indigo may have been used on a natural-undyed tan. Plate 51
D–33–40	A.64.27.2	MNM	Blue	1-ply	Indigo[8]		
D–34–41	A.64.27.2	MNM	Green	1-ply	Indigo[8], plus unknown yellow[5]		
D–34–43	A.5.54.6	MNM	Green	1-ply	Indigo[8], plus unknown yellow[5]		
D–34–45	A.5.54.6	MNM	Blue	1-ply	Indigo[8]		
D–34–46	3761	Taylor	Red	3-ply	Cochineal[3]		
D–34–47	3772	Taylor	Red	3-ply	Cochineal[3]		
D–34–48	3772	Taylor	Red, Z-spun	1-ply	Lac[9]		
D–34–49	3773	Taylor	Red	3-ply	Cochineal[3]		Plate 62
D–34–50	18088	UC	Red-Brown	1-ply	Not brazil[4]		N.1., may be natural or synthetic. Plate 2
D–34–51	L.5.62.73	SCAS	Dark brown	1-ply	Not brazil[4]		N.1., may be natural or synthetic. Similar to D–34–52. Plate 46
D–34–52	L.5.62.70	SCAS	Red-Brown	1-ply	Not brazil[4]		N.1., may be natural or synthetic. Similar to D–34–51. Plate 9
D–34–54	L.5.62.84	SCAS	Red	3-ply	Cochineal[3]		Plate 40
D–34–55	L.5.62.84	SCAS	Dark red	3-ply	Cochineal[3]		Plate 40
D–34–56	L.5.62.98	SCAS	Red	3-ply	Cochineal[3]		Plate 55
D–34–58	L.70.3.39	FH	Red	3-ply		N.1.[1]	Plate 56
D–34–59	L.70.3.39	FH	Brown-Red	3-ply		N.1.[1]	Plate 56
D–34–60	L.71.17.2	FH	Brown-Red	1-ply	Maybe a red dye wood[10]		Plate 8
D–35–61	L.5.61.81	SCAS	Light red	1-ply (20thC.)	Cochineal[3]		
D–35–62	L.5.62.71	SCAS	Light red	1-ply		N.1.	Unknown—probably synthetic, Plate 10
D–35–67	T.380	SAR, SF	Red	1-ply	Lac[9]		
D–35–68	1969–208	DAM	Red, Z-spun	1-ply	Lac[9]		
D–35–69	L.70.3.35	FH	Red	1-ply	Lac[9]		
D–67–75	60–220–032	Lowe	Red	1-ply	Cochineal[3]		Plate 22
D–67–76	L.5.62.74	SCAS	Red	1-ply	Lac[9]		Plate 61

9. Lac. The control used as lac or gum-lac (*Laccifer lacca,* formerly known as *Coccus lacca.* See Rita J. Adrosko, *Natural Dyes and Home Dyeing,* pp. 28–30). The sample analyzed is an insect pigment of the family that includes cochineal, lac (from India) and kermes (from the Mediterranean basin). It is *not* cochineal and is very close to lac. We do not have any sample of kermes. Our best opinion on both chemical and historical grounds is that it is lac.

10. This is not brazilwood, but may be a red dye wood related to brazilwood. See note 4 above.

Alnus tenuifolia
VERNACULAR: alder, *aliso*
PART USED: inner bark dark red and spongy—easily removed
COLOR: red
REFERENCE: Dennis, 1939

Atriplex canescens
VERNACULAR: four-wing salt-bush, *chamiso (zo), chamisa (za), cenizo, blanco*
PART USED: bark combined with mountain mahogany
COLOR: reddish

REFERENCE: Dennis, 1939

Berberis fremontii
VERNACULAR: barberry, *algerita, palo amarillo*
PART USED: berries
COLOR: purple
REFERENCE: Dennis, 1939

PART USED: roots
COLOR: yellow
REFERENCE: Sedillo-Brewster, 1935

Betula occidentalis
VERNACULAR: western birch, *abedul*
PART USED: bark
COLOR: red-brown
REFERENCE: Dennis, 1939

217

Carthamus tinctorius (introduced)
VERNACULAR: safflower, *azafrán (asafrán)*
PART USED: probably blossom
COLOR: yellow
REFERENCE: Dennis, 1939

Celtis spp.
VERNACULAR: hackberry, *palo duro, palo blanco*
PART USED: perhaps the berries
COLOR: red
REFERENCE: Dennis, 1939

Cerocarpus montanus
VERNACULAR: mountain mahogany, *palo duro*
PART USED: root—combined with salt-bush
COLOR: red
REFERENCE: Dennis, 1939

Chrysothamnus spp. (all New Mexico species)
VERNACULAR: rabbit-bush, *chamiso (zo), chamisa (za)*
PART USED: immature flowers, mature flowers, dried flowers
COLOR: lemon yellow, green-yellow, dull yellow
REFERENCE: Dennis, 1939, Sedillo-Brewster, 1935

Coreopsis cardaminiflora
VERNACULAR: tickseed
PART USED: blossoms
COLOR: red
REFERENCE: Dennis, 1939

Coreopsis tinctoria (introduced)
VERNACULAR: calliopsis, *berros*
PART USED: blossoms
COLOR: reddish
REFERENCE: Morrow, 1966

Cowania mexicana
syn. *C. stansburiana*
VERNACULAR: cliff rose, *romero cedro*
PART USED: leaves and stems
COLOR: brown, tan in combination with *Juniperus* spp.
REFERENCE: Dennis, 1939

Crocus sativas (introduced)
VERNACULAR: saffron, *azafrán (asafrán)*
PART USED: blossoms
COLOR: lemon yellow
REFERENCE: Sedillo-Brewster, 1935

Delphinium scaposum
VERNACULAR: larkspur, *espuela de caballero*
PART USED: petals
COLOR: blue
REFERENCE: Dennis, 1935

Ephedra trifurca
VERNACULAR: Mormon tea, *cañutillo*
PART USED: probably the stems
COLOR: "This plant is sometimes substituted for *Alnus tenuifolia* bark in making pale red dye."
REFERENCE: Dennis, 1939

Equisetum spp.
VERNACULAR: horsetail rush, *carricillo (carisillo), canolilla, cola de caballo, cañutillo*
PART USED: probably the stems and cones
COLOR: green
REFERENCE: Morrow, 1966, #24

Helenium hoopesii
VERNACULAR: sneezeweed, *yerba del lobo*
PART USED: flowers and juniper ash
COLOR: yellow
REFERENCE: Dennis, 1939

Heuchera spp.
VERNACULAR: alum root
PART USED: stems
COLOR: pinkish tan
REFERENCE: Dennis, 1939

Hymenoxys richardsonii
syn. *H. metcalfei*
VERNACULAR: Colorado rubber weed, *pingue, pinhué, pinguay*
PART USED: blossom
COLOR: yellow
REFERENCE: Dennis, 1939

Juglans major
VERNACULAR: walnut, *nogal, hojas de nogal, nuez*
PART USED: hulls and twigs
COLOR: hulls—yellow-brown, twigs—light brown
REFERENCE: Dennis, 1939

Juniperus spp.
VERNACULAR: juniper, *cedro, bellota de sabina, tascate, cuipa de sabina, cedro colorado*

COLOR: brown, tan
REFERENCE: Dennis, 1939

Juniperus monosperma
VERNACULAR: one-seeded juniper, *cedro, alamciga de sabina, sabina, rama de sabina*
PART USED: bark and berries
COLOR: green
REFERENCE: Dennis, 1939

Larrea tridentata
syn. *Covillea tridentata, C. glutinosa*
VERNACULAR: creosote bush, *gobernadora, guamis, wame gobernadora, hediondilla, goma de senora, hediodia*
PART USED: charcoal from bush
COLOR: green-blue
REFERENCE: Dennis, 1939

Mirabilis sp. (probably *M. multiflora*)
VERNACULAR: four o'clock, *maravilla*
PART USED: petals
COLOR: light brown, sometimes purple
REFERENCE: Dennis, 1939

Pinus edulis
VERNACULAR: *piñon,* pinyon
PART USED: gum in combination with *Rhus* sp.
COLOR: black
REFERENCE: Dennis, 1939

Potentilla fruticosa
syn. *Dasiphora fruticosa*
VERNACULAR: bush cinquefoil, *rosillo*
PART USED: probably the flower
COLOR: yellow
REFERENCE: Sedillo-Brewster, 1935

Populas nigra (introduced)
VERNACULAR: Lombardy poplar, *álamo de Italia*
PART USED: leaves
COLOR: green-yellow
REFERENCE: Colton, 1965

Prunus spp.
VERNACULAR: wild cherry, *capulín*
PART USED: leaves
COLOR: green
PART USED: roots

COLOR: purple
REFERENCE: Dennis, 1939

Prunus americana
VERNACULAR: wild plum, *ciruela*
PART USED: roots
COLOR: red
REFERENCE: Dennis, 1939

Prunus persica (introduced)
VERNACULAR: peach, *durazno*
PART USED: leaves
COLOR: yellow
REFERENCE: Colton, 1965

Psilostrophe tagetina
VERNACULAR: paper flower
PART USED: blossoms
COLOR: yellow
REFERENCE: Dennis, 1939

Pterospora andromeda
VERNACULAR: pine drops
PART USED: fruit
COLOR: tan
REFERENCE: Colton, 1965

Rhus trilobata
syn. *R. aromatica*
VERNACULAR: squaw-bush, skunk-bush, *lemita*
PART USED: twigs, leaves with piñon and minerals
COLOR: black
REFERENCE: Dennis, 1939

Rumex hymenosepalus
VERNACULAR: *cañaigre, cañaigra, caña agria*
PART USED: roots
COLOR: yellow-brown, orange
REFERENCE: Sedillo-Brewster, 1935

Tagetes micrantha
VERNACULAR: bitterball, *anisillo*
PART USED: fruit?
COLOR: yellow
REFERENCE: Morrow, 1966, #3 & 4

Thelesperma megapotamicum
syn. *T. gracile*
VERNACULAR: Indian tea, Navajo tea, *cota, té, té de los Navajos*

PART USED: whole plant
COLOR: yellow, green
REFERENCE: Morrow, 1966

Verbesina encelioides
syn. *Ximenesia exauriculata*
VERNACULAR: crownbeard, *añil del muerto*
PART USED: petals
COLOR: yellow
REFERENCE: Dennis, 1939

Zinnia grandiflora
syn. *Crassina pumila*
VERNACULAR: desert zinnia, *cinco llagas*
PART USED: petals
COLOR: yellow
REFERENCE: Dennis, 1939

The main sources for this list are the master's dissertations by Mela Sedillo-Brewster and Mary Dennis, probably the most complete concerning the early use of dye plants in this area. For the scholarly, they detail the original references not generally available and not mentioned here.

Although out of our geographical zone, some dye plants in Mary Colton's book were introduced into our area by the Spanish Colonials (peach, for instance). Another, pine-drops, has a verbal tradition of being an early dye plant in northern New Mexico, and, indeed, it is still sought after.

A Checklist of the Angiosperms and Gymnosperms of New Mexico, Arizona Flora, and the *Flora of New Mexico* were used to bring the nomenclature of the plants up to date. The early synonyms, however, are included with the list in case anyone wishes to go back to the original references.

The vernacular names were acquired mostly through the medicinal plant books; it seems that many dye plants are also *remedios.*

NOTES

ABBREVIATIONS USED FOR NAMES OF INSTITUTIONS

AMERIND	The Amerind Foundation, Inc.; Dragoon, Arizona
AMNH	American Museum of Natural History; New York City, New York
ASM	Arizona State Museum, University of Arizona; Tucson, Arizona
CC	The Colorado College; Colorado Springs, Colorado
CSHS	State Historical Society of Colorado; Denver, Colorado
DAM	The Denver Art Museum; Denver, Colorado
DENISON	Denison University Gallery; Granville, Ohio
DE YOUNG	Fine Arts Museums of San Francisco, de Young Memorial Museum; Golden Gate Park, San Francisco, California
DMNH	Denver Museum of Natural History; Denver, Colorado
EL PASO	El Paso Centennial Museum; El Paso, Texas
FH	Fred Harvey Fine Arts Collection; Phoenix, Arizona
FIELD	Field Museum of Natural History; Chicago, Illinois
HEARD	Heard Museum of Anthropology and Primitive Art; Phoenix, Arizona
HISTORY	History Division, a unit of the Museum of New Mexico; Santa Fe, New Mexico
HSA	Hispanic Society of America; New York City, New York
HSNM	Historical Society of New Mexico; Santa Fe, New Mexico
IFAF	International Folk Art Foundation; Santa Fe, New Mexico
KIT CARSON	Kit Carson Memorial Foundation; Taos, New Mexico
LAB	Laboratory of Anthropology, a unit of the Museum of New Mexico; Santa Fe, New Mexico
LACM	Los Angeles County Museum of Natural History; Los Angeles, California
LOWE	Lowe Art Museum, University of Miami; Coral Gables, Florida
LOWIE	Lowie Museum of Anthropology, University of California; Berkeley, California
MA	Museum of Albuquerque; Albuquerque, New Mexico
MCNAY	McNay Art Institute; San Antonio, Texas
MAI	The Museum of the American Indian, Heye Foundation; New York City, New York
MAXWELL	Maxwell Museum of Anthropology, University of New Mexico; Albuquerque, New Mexico
MNA	Museum of Northern Arizona; Flagstaff, Arizona
MNM	Museum of New Mexico; Santa Fe, New Mexico
MOIFA	Museum of International Folk Art, a unit of the Museum of New Mexico; Santa Fe, New Mexico
MPM	Milwaukee Public Museum; Milwaukee, Wisconsin
MR	The Millicent Rogers Museum; Taos, New Mexico
NELSON	William Rockhill Nelson Gallery and Atkins Museum of Fine Arts; Kansas City, Missouri
NTM	Navajo Tribal Museum; Window Rock, Arizona
PANHANDLE	The Panhandle-Plains Historical Museum; Canyon, Texas
PEABODY	Peabody Museum of Archaeology and Ethnology, Harvard University; Cambridge, Massachusetts
SAR	School of American Research, Santa Fe, and Collections of the School of American Research in the Museum of New Mexico
SCAS	Spanish Colonial Arts Society, Inc.; Santa Fe, New Mexico
SDMM	San Diego Museum of Man; San Diego, California
TAYLOR	The Taylor Museum, Colorado Springs Fine Arts Center; Colorado Springs, Colorado
TM	The Textile Museum; Washington, D.C.
UCM	University of Colorado Museum; Boulder, Colorado
UMP	The University Museum of the University of Pennsylvania; Philadelphia, Pennsylvania
USNM	Smithsonian Institution, National Museum of History and Technology, Department of Cultural History; Washington, D.C.
WITTE	The San Antonio Museum Association, Witte Memorial Museum; San Antonio, Texas
YALE	Yale University Art Gallery; New Haven, Connecticut

CHAPTER 1

1. See Nora Fisher, pp. 192 ff. of this publication for discussion of the impact of the treadle loom.

2. Lansing B. Bloom, "A Trade Invoice of 1638," p. 242.

3. Lansing B. Bloom, "Early Weaving in New Mexico," p. 230.

4. Edward Norris Wentworth, *America's Sheep Trails*, p. 419.

5. H. G. Ward, *Mexico in 1827*, p. 424.

6. Manuel Carrera Stampa, *Los Gremios Mexicanos*, pp. 335–37.

7. Santa Fe, State Records Center and Archives, Spanish Archives of New Mexico (hereafter SRCA, SANM II), April 14, 1977, cited in Bloom, "Early Weaving," pp. 230–31.

8. Santa Fe, SRCA, SANM II, Dec. 18, 1789, Roll 12, Frame 238.

9. New Mexico is customarily divided into two sections: the Rio Arriba north of La Bajada Hill and the Rio Abajo south of La Bajada.

10. Virginia Langham Olmstead, transl. and compil., *Spanish and Mexican Colonial Censuses of New Mexico: 1790, 1823, 1845*, pp. 1–128.

11. See Dorothy Boyd Bowen, pp. 96-97 and 140 ff. of this publication.

12. Olmstead, pp. 1–128.

13. Santa Fe, SRCA, SANM II, Aug. 28, 1803, Roll 15, Frame 84. Note: Herbs we referred to as *yerba* rather than the more literate *hierba* throughout this publication.

14. Abelardo Carrillo y Gariel, *El Traje en la Nueva España*, p. 31.

15. Santa Fe, SRCA, SANM II #2249c, 2250, 2255, 2315, 2335, 2565, cited in Bloom, "Early Weaving," pp. 234–38.

16. Pedro Bautista Pino, *Three New Mexico Chronicles*, p. 36.

17. Archer Butler Hulbert, ed., *Southwest on the Turquoise Trail*, p. 84.

18. Ibid., p. 91.

19. Ibid., p. 179.

20. John Adam Hussey, "The New Mexico-California Caravan of 1847–1848," pp. 1–2.

21. Ibid., p. 12.

22. Franco Brunello, *The Art of Dyeing in the History of Mankind*, p. 279.

23. Wentworth, pp. 237–38.

24. Ibid.

25. Marianne Stoller, p. 150 of this publication.

26. See Charlene Cerny and Christine Mather, p. 168 ff. of this publication.

CHAPTER 2

1. Bailey W. Diffie, *Latin-American Civilization, Colonial Period*, pp. 387, 389; Clarence Henry Haring, *Trade and Navigation Between Spain and the Indies in the Time of the Hapsburgs*, pp. 126–27.

2. George Parker Winship, *The Colorado Expedition*, pp. 378–79, 487, 501; Ralph Emerson Twitchell, *The Spanish Archives of New Mexico*, vol. 1, p. 175.

3. Albert H. Schroeder and Don S. Matson, *A Colony on the Move*, pp. 11, 33, 48, 68.

4. George P. Hammond and Agapito Rey, *Don Juan de Oñate, Colonizer of New Mexico 1595–1628*, vol. 5, pp. 44, 143–44, 215–16, 240, 300–301. Concerning the treadle loom see Nora Fisher, p. 192 ff. of this publication.

5. Hammond and Rey, *Don Juan de Oñate*, pp. 108, 141, 218–19.

6. George P. Hammond and Agapito Rey, *The Rediscovery of New Mexico*, pp. 82–83, 85, 129, 131, 135, 137, 142.

7. Ibid., pp. 185, 191–93, 220, 223.

8. Hammond and Rey, *Don Juan de Oñate*, pp. 508–9, 512–13, 593, 603.

9. Ibid., pp. 610, 630, 641, 650, 653, 692–93.

10. He found several pueblos occupied by Jumanos near the Salinas (vicinity of Quivira National Monument) east of the Rio Grande, the four principal ones being called: Atripuy, Genobey, Quelotatrey, and Patastrey. See Frederick Webb Hodge, *Handbook of American Indians North of Mexico*, 1912.

11. Hammond and Rey, *Don Juan de Oñate*, pp. 610, 630, 641, 650, 653, 692–93.

12. Ibid., p. 695, Fray Juan de Escalona to the Viceroy, 1 October 1601.

13. France V. Scholes, "Royal Treasury Records, 1596–1683," pp. 10–11.

14. Ibid., pp. 11–13. This is an early indication that looms were constructed by local carpenters along with other household furnishing.

15. Frederick Webb Hodge, George P. Hammond, and Agapito Rey, *Fray Alonso de Benavides' Revised Memorial of 1634*, p. 169.

16. Ibid., p. 102. This must be one of the earliest documentary references to Pueblo Indians working with wool. Lansing B. Bloom conjectured that the Indians began learning about wool with the Coronado expedition (1540) and further that they "certainly did so when sheep in larger numbers were brought in by Juan de Oñate and the first colonists in 1598." See Lansing B. Bloom, "Early Weaving in New Mexico," p. 229. Recent scholarship supports the use of sheep by these explorers and early colonists for food. The author's guess is that the Pueblos began receiving instruction in sheep raising and working with wool once the friars were able to begin missions and had received adequate numbers of sheep and cattle. The earliest missions were started in the mid-1620s about coincident with Benavides' office as *custos*.

17. France V. Scholes, *Troublous Times in New Mexico*, pp. 48–49.

18. Ibid., pp. 12, 26, 59.

19. Ibid., pp. 34, 36, 44–45, 111–12.

20. Ibid., p. 53. Order prepared by Governor Don Diego (Dionisio) Peñalosa Briceño y Berdugo, 7 January 1664, Santa Fe, State Records Center and Archives, Spanish Archives of New Mexico (hereafter SRCA, SANM II), January 1664; Frank D. Reeve, *History of New Mexico*, vol. 1, pp. 174, 188–89. Note: In locating archival documents in SRCA refer to dates of documents listed at end of note entries, rather than to subject listings or specific dates, which are meant to amplify the text. (For example, see "January, 1664" above rather than "Order prepared by Governor . . . Peñalosa . . ." or "7 January 1664.")

21. Charles Wilson Hackett, *Revolt of the Pueblo Indians of New Mexico and Otermín's Attempted Reconquest, 1680–1682*, vol. 8 of CCCP, vol. 1, pp. 207; vol. 2, p. 269.

22. Reeve, pp. 173–75, 184–89.

23. France V. Scholes, "Church and State in New Mexico, 1610–1650," p. 300, n. 6; p. 306, n. 25. See Fisher, p. 193 of this publication.

24. Scholes, *Troublous Times*, pp. 110–13.

25. Ibid., p. 231.

26. Reeve, pp. 173, 185, 192.

27. Hackett, pp. 74, 82, 206–8. The last citation is letter of Antonio de Otermín to the Viceroy, Paso del Río del Norte, 20 October 1680.

28. Ibid., pp. 166, 169, 173, 176, 180–81. Declaration of Maestre de Campo Pedro de Leiva, sixty-eight years of age, San Lorenzo, 20 October 1681;

Declaration of Maestre de Campo Francisco Gómez, Lieutenant General, fifty-three years of age, San Lorenzo, 21 October 1681; Testimony of Sargento Mayor Sebastián de Herrera, forty-four years of age, San Lorenzo, 21 October 1681; Declaration of Diego López Sambrano, San Lorenzo, 21 October 1681.

29. Twitchell, pp. 395, 397, 399, 405, 409; J. Manuel Espinosa, *First Expedition of Vargas into New Mexico 1692*, pp. 33–34.

30. Lists showing how De Vargas distributed supplies from Mexico, 1 May 1697, in Santa Fe, SRCA, SANM II, March 28, 1696.

31. Fray Francisco de Vargas petitions the Governor for guards to protect the friars at the missions, 28 March 1696, and case involving two sheep at Pueblo of Tesuque, 5 June 1697, in Santa Fe, SRCA, SANM II, March 28, 1696, and June 5, 1697–March 10, 1698.

32. Governor de Vargas' Inventory, 20 April 1704, in Santa Fe, SRCA, SANM II, April 20, 1704.

33. Reeve, p. 311 ff.; Tibo J. Chávez, *El Río Abajo*, pp. 21–31.

34. Twitchell, p. 378; Citizens of Albuquerque petition the Governor and Captain General to sell wool and lambs, 13 September 1737, in Santa Fe, SRCA, SANM II, September 13, 1737; petition to the Governor of New Mexico by citizens of Albuquerque who wish to sell sheared wool, 22 May 1744, in Santa Fe, SRCA, SANM II, May 22, 1744; permission granted by Governor Don Joachín Codallos y Rabal on 22 May 1744 to sell Francisco de Vargas and Don Manuel de Anaya Villagran "para tierra afuera," in Santa Fe, SRCA, SANM II, June 16, 1745; petition to Governor of New Mexico by citizens of Albuquerque to sell wool, 16 June 1745, in Santa Fe, SRCA, SANM II, June 16, 1745; permission granted on 16 June 1745, in Santa Fe, SRCA, SANM II, June 16, 1745.

35. Case involving illegal trade with the French, 1723, in Santa Fe, SRCA, SANM II, March 21,

1724. Marc Simmons, *New Mexico, A Bicentennial History*, pp. 80–81.

36. Prosecution of Miguel de Salazar for illegal trade with Comanches, 1739, in Santa Fe, SRCA, SANM II, June 11–20, 1739.

37. List of goods confiscated from four Frenchmen detained in the presidio at El Paso on 1 December 1750, 3 February 1751, in Santa Fe, SRCA, SANM II, February 3–March 12, 1751.

38. Alfred Barnaby Thomas, ed. and transl., *Teiodoro de Croix and the Northern Frontier of New Spain, 1776–1783*, p. 48.

39. Alfred Barnaby Thomas, *Forgotten Frontiers*, p. 33. See also *Father Juan Agustín de Morfi's Account of Disorders in New Mexico, 1778*, transl. and ed. Marc Simmons.

40. Ibid., p. 114.

41. Ibid., p. 164, 212.

42. Ibid., pp. 180–82.

43. Governor Juan Bautista de Anza prohibits New Mexicans to travel without a permit, 24 April 1784, in Santa Fe, SRCA, SANM II, April 24, 1784.

44. Report by Governor Jacobo Ugarte y Loyola to the viceroy on economic conditions in New Mexico, 25 October 1788, in Santa Fe, SRCA, SANM II, October 25, 1788.

45. Governor Ugarte y Loyola to Governor Fernando de la Concha, Santa Fe, 18 December 1789, in Santa Fe, SRCA, SANM II, December 18, 1789.

46. Inventory of goods belonging to the deceased Indian Phelipe, Isleta, 7 January 1730, in Santa Fe, SRCA, SANM II, January 7, 1730. Alcalde of Albuquerque investigates disposal of these goods.

47. Inventory of the estate of the Indian María Calabacita, Pueblo of Santo Domingo, 18 May 1744, in Santa Fe, SRCA, SANM II, May 18, 1744.

48. Suit of Rosa García de Noriega, wife of Ben-

tura Romero vs. Juan de Tafoya over sheep, Jurisdiction of Albuquerque, 13 August–16 September 1767, in Santa Fe, SRCA, SANM II, August 13–September 16, 1767.

49. Gifts to Allied Indians, Santa Fe, 28 August 1787 through 31 December 1788, in Santa Fe, SRCA, SANM II, August 28, 1787–December 31, 1788. The Spanish Archives in Santa Fe contain numerous similar lists. Of the many *casos* in the collection of the author only a few of the small ones are tin-lined for cooking.

50. Draft letter prepared by Pedro de Nava regarding Apache raid on Acoma, November, 1799, in Santa Fe, SRCA, SANM II, November 20, 1799.

51. Eleanor B. Adams and Fray Angélico Chávez, *The Missions of New Mexico 1776,* pp. 50, 56–57, 87, 94, 142, 164, 186, 188, 205, 303. Letter of Fray Silvestre Vélez de Escalante to Fray Fernando Antonio Gómez, Zuni, 18 August 1775.

52. Thomas, pp. 96, 98–99, 100–101, 107–8, 111.

53. Adams and Chávez, pp. 30, 36–37, 150, 241–46, 249; Inventories in the Estate of Domingo Martín, Santa Cruz, 18 May 1740, in Santa Fe, SRCA, SANM II, May 18, 1740; Inventory in the Estate of Don Joseph Reaño, Santa Fe, 18 July 1744, in Santa Fe, SRCA, SANM II, November 24, 1743–November 4, 1744; Inventory in the Estate of Juana Luján, Rancho de San Antonio, 15 July 1761–22 August 1761, in Santa Fe, SRCA, SANM II, July 15–August 22, 1761; María Joachina Mestas, Atrisco, Jurisdiction of Albuquerque, 2 April–14 November 1772, in Santa Fe, SRCA, SANM II, April 2–November 14, 1772. Complaint of Matheo Joseph Pino of San Clemente vs. Mariano Martín over *partido* contract, 16 July 1763, in Santa Fe, SRCA, SANM II, April 25–May 25, 1767; complaint of Don Joseph Reaño to the Governor and Captain General over bad handling of sheep at Ojo Caliente, 2 November 1740, in Santa Fe, SRCA, SANM II, October 31–November 8, 1740. Most of the suits evolve in the Jurisdiction of Albuquerque especially in the years 1750–70, Santa Fe, SRCA, SANM II.

54. In the 1790 Census of New Mexico, Santa Fe, SRCA, SANM II, November 20, 1790, ranch owners were carefully singled out; these constituted a large percentage of men and their wives who used the titles of Don or Doña and who had servants.

55. Throughout this chapter, spelling of family names ending in "s" has been retained as found in the documents and no attempt has been made to standardize them according to academic usage.

56. New Mexico Census for 1790, Santa Fe, SRCA, SANM II, November 20, 1790.

57. Bloom, pp. 234, 237; Twitchell, pp. 453–54, 454n.

58. New Mexico relieved of *alcabala* for ten years, *Bando* of 24 September 1796, Santa Fe, SRCA, SANM II, September 24, 1796; Report on Economic Conditions in New Mexico prepared by Miguel Romero, Francisco Peres Serreno, Juan Rafael Ortiz, José Pino, Miguel Quintana, José Rafael Sarracino, Pedro Bautista Pino, José Mariano de la Peña, and Antonio J. Ortiz, 17 June 1805, in Santa Fe, SRCA, SANM II, June 17, 1805.

59. This traditional head covering for women and girls in New Spain was never produced commercially in New Mexico in Spanish Colonial times nor during the Mexican Period, 1821–46. *Rebozos* were imported even during the Mexican Period when restrictions on trade produced greater exchange of *efectos del país.*

60. Inventory of the Estate of Francisco Afán de Rivera, Santa Fe, 13 March 1726, in Santa Fe, SRCA, SANM II, February 5, 1729–March 6, 1736.

61. Inventory of the Estate of the Indian Phelipe, Isleta, 7 January 1730, in Santa Fe, SRCA, SANM II, January 7, 1730.

62. Weaving, materials, and animals described in *Visita* of Don Joachín Codallos y Rabal, 20 June–20 October 1745, in Santa Fe, SRCA, SANM II, June 20–October 20, 1745.

63. Materials and Animals in the Estate of the Indian María Calabacita, Pueblo of Santo Domingo, 18 May 1744, in Santa Fe, SRCA, SANM II, May 18–23, 1744.

64. Suit of Phelipe Tafoya, Resident of Santa Fe, against D. Juan Joseph Moreno, Santa Fe, 19 July 1764, in Santa Fe, SRCA, SANM II, July 19–26, 1764.

65. Inventory of the Estate of Juana Luján, Nuestra Señora de Soledad, Rancho de San Antonio, 15 July 1761–22 August 1761, in Santa Fe, SRCA, SANM II, July 15–August 22, 1761.

66. Inventory of the late Juan Miguel Alvarez de Castillo, in the home of Diego Antonio Sanches, Fuenclara, Jurisdiction of Albuquerque, 18 March–22 April 1765, in Santa Fe, SRCA, SANM II, March 18–April 22, 1765.

67. Debts of the Prisoner Mariano Baca, Prisoner in the Jail, Santa Fe, 1 August 1767, in Santa Fe, SRCA, SANM II, August 1, 1767–November 22, 1768.

68. Testament of Matheo Joseph Pino, Santa Fe, December 7, 1768, in Santa Fe, SRCA, SANM II.

69. Donations of goods or money to build a local defense fund.

70. War contributions, Santa Fe, 18 November 1799; war contributions from San Carlos de Alameda and other places, 1809; both in Santa Fe, SRCA, SANM II, November 18, 1799.

71. It is unclear just what *vermellón* was: vermilion (cinnabar, a pigment) or a dye (most likely cochineal). Dictionaries of the period do use the term *vermellón* to describe cochineal and also to refer to bright red color.

72. This Spanish or Indian term appears elsewhere but the meaning is lost, though it probably refers to a burlap-type fabric which was used to wrap *tercios,* shipping bundles.

73. Inventory of Presidial Company, Santa Fe, 18 April 1815; the account of the soldier Antonio Chaves, no day, 1815; both in Presidial Company Papers, Santa Fe, SRCA, SANM II, April 18–December 31, 1815.

74. Inventory of the Presidial Company Store and Granary, Santa Fe, 30 June 1817, in Presidial Company papers, Santa Fe, SRCA, SANM II, January 1–December 1, 1817; see also weaving and other items delivered to Captain Don Valentín Moreno by order of Señor Gobernador Interino Don José Manrique, by First Lieutenant Don Ysidro Rey, Santa Fe, no day, 1812, in Presidial Company Records, Santa Fe, SRCA, SANM II, March 1–December 1, 1812.

75. Contributions to troops from Sonora and Vizcaya now in New Mexico, Santa Fe, no day, 1818, in Santa Fe, SRCA, SANM II, September 18–November 16, 1818; contributions for redemption of captives, 1820–21, in Santa Fe, SRCA, SANM II, June 30–July 22, 1822.

76. Gifts to Allied Indians, Santa Fe, 28 August–31 December 1788, in Santa Fe, SRCA, SANM II, August 28, 1787–December 31, 1788; 1801, in Santa Fe, SRCA, SANM II, October 31, 1801; 1807, in Santa Fe, SRCA, SANM II, October 31, 1807; 20 November 1811, in Santa Fe, SRCA, SANM II, November 20, 1811; and 31 October 1815, in Santa Fe, SRCA, SANM II, July 10–October 31, 1815. A few similar lists are also in Santa Fe, SRCA, SANM II.

77. Adams and Chávez, inventories *passim*.

78. New Mexico Church Inventories, 1796, in Santa Fe, SRCA, SANM II, April 11–September 1, 1796.

79. See Fisher, p. 166 of this publication.

80. E. Boyd, *Popular Arts of Spanish New Mexico*, pp. 68–69.

81. Materials donated for the chapel Nuestra Señora del Rosario, Santa Fe, 31 August 1808, in Santa Fe, SRCA, SANM II, August 31, 1808.

82. Expenses for utilities and other services to the *Ayuntamiento* for the Villa de Albuquerque, 9 December 1814, in Santa Fe, SRCA, SANM II, December 9–10, 1814.

83. 1790 Census of New Mexico, in Santa Fe, SRCA, SANM II, November 20, 1790. See also Fisher, p. 194 of this publication.

84. Bloom, pp. 232–33. It is generally agreed that the Navajo did not fabricate silver jewelry until a much later date; thus the jewelry described here was probably not of Indian manufacture.

85. Ibid., pp. 233–34. Economic conditions of New Mexico as reported by Governor Don Fernando de la Concha, Santa Fe, 28 August 1803, in Santa Fe, SRCA, SANM II, August 28, 1803. See also Fisher, p. 144 of this publication.

86. Contract with Bazán brothers, 3 September 1805, Santa Fe, SRCA, SANM II, September 3, 1805; received in Santa Fe, 30 May 1806, in Santa Fe, SRCA, SANM II, May 30, 1806; Bazán brothers accounts to build machines, Santa Fe, 1 July 1809, in Santa Fe, SRCA, SANM II, July 1, 1809. *Alcaldes* of Santa Fe report on disciples of Bazán, Santa Fe, 31 August 1809, in Santa Fe, SRCA, SANM II, August 31, 1809. Bloom, pp. 234–38. The copper may have been for dye pots.

87. Pedro Bautista Pino, *Three New Mexico Chronicles*, p. 223.

88. Boyd, pp. 200–201, 204–5. The late E. Boyd believed she found several blankets made by the son of Ignacio, Joaquín Bazán.

89. Josiah Gregg, *Commerce of the Prairies* (1967), Chapter 1 is an excellent overview of this trade.

90. Arancel General Interno e Instrucción para Gobierno de las Aduanas Marítimas en el Comercio Libre del Imperio Mexicano, Mexico, 1821, in Santa Fe, State Records Center and Archives, Mexican Archives of New Mexico (hereafter SRCA, MANM), December 15, 1821. Circular exempting New Mexico from paying duty on *efectos nacionales* for seven years, Ministerio de Hacienda, Circular No. 27, 24 October 1823, in Santa Fe, SRCA, MANM, January 14–December 24, 1823. The Hacienda renewed the tax exemption as needed and the embargos continued in more or less the same form; see Hacienda Embargo of 1829, Santa Fe, SRCA, MANM, January 3–December 13, 1829.

91. Census for August and September 1822, in Santa Fe, SRCA, MANM, August–September 1822; Census—Plan que Arreglar la Estadística, Cochití and Santa Cruz de la Cañada, February 1823, in Santa Fe, SRCA, MANM, February, 1823. Unfortunately, most of these censuses are lost. The census made no distinction for ranchers, and craftsmen were lumped under one heading—*artesanos*.

92. See inventories for 1829 in Santa Fe, SRCA, MANM, July 10–21, 1829.

93. Ward Alan Minge, "Last Will and Testament of Severino Martinez," pp. 33, 38, 46.

94. *Guía* for D. Ermenigildo Chaves to Chihuahua, Durango, and Mexico City, Santa Fe, 28 July 1831, in Santa Fe, SRCA, MANM, January 1–December 31, 1831.

95. *Guías* for 1832 in Santa Fe, SRCA, MANM, January 23–September 1, 1832. *Guía* no. 97 for Mariano Chaves, Los Padillas, 12 July 1832, in Santa Fe, SRCA, MANM, January 23–September 1, 1832.

96. *Guías* nos. 2 through 24, Santa Fe, 16–31 August 1835, in Santa Fe, SRCA, MANM, August 16, 1835–October 26, 1840.

97. *Guías* nos. 20 through 35, Santa Fe, August 1837, in Santa Fe, SRCA, MANM, January 10–November 8, 1837.

98. *Guías*, Libros de Guías Departmental, Año de 1844, in Santa Fe, SRCA, MANM, January 1–December 2, 1844.

99. Gregg, pp. 134–35; see Fisher, p. 197 of this

publication. This is a fine description of the Spanish *churro* sheep. Wool for an average blanket would have cost 30–40 cents.

100. Gregg, p. 193.

101. Pino, pp. 317–18.

102. Myra Ellen Jenkins and Ward Alan Minge, *Record of Navajo Activities Affecting the Acoma-Laguna Area, 1746–1910,* pp. 50, 58, 60–62, 65, 69, 72, 80, 89.

103. Gregg, p. 193; Lieutenant Colonel W. H. Emory and Lieutenant J. W. Abert, *Notes of a Military Reconnaisance, from Fort Leavenworth, in Missouri, to San Diego, in California, Including Part of the Arkansas, Del Norte, and Gila Rivers,* Executive Document No. 41, Thirtieth Congress–First Session, 1848, pp. 34–35.

104. New Mexico Census Records for 1822, in Santa Fe, SRCA, MANM, August–September, 1822; Official contributions and money from various *alcaldías* in 1825, in Santa Fe, SRCA, MANM, January 11–December 30, 1825; New Mexico Census Records for 1829, in Santa Fe, SRCA, MANM, November, 1829. Gregg, p. 111.

105. Gifts to Jicarillas, Santa Fe, 22 September 1825; Gifts to Utes, Santa Fe, 1 August 1825, Gifts to *Indios Aliados* (unidentified), Santa Fe, 10 October 1825, Gifts to Navajos, Santa Fe, 20 December 1825, all in Santa Fe, SRCA, MANM, February 1–December 20, 1825; Goods given to *Indios Aliados* (unidentified), Santa Fe, 14 April 1826, Gifts to Comanches, Santa Fe, 19 August 1826, Gifts to Navajos and Jicarillas, Santa Fe, 30 August 1826, Gifts to Utes, Santa Fe, 12 July and 12 September 1826, all in Santa Fe, SRCA, MANM, February 1–December 31, 1826; Gifts for Allied Indians in New Mexico, purchased in Chihuahua by Captain Don Juan José Arocha at the bequest of Señor Comisionado General Don José Manuel de Terluaga, Chihuahua, 11 June 1827, all in Santa Fe, SRCA, MANM, January 1–December 16, 1827.

106. Inventory of goods belonging to Pedro Ar-

mendaris in House of Francisco Ortiz, Santa Fe, 13 October 1822, in Santa Fe, SRCA, MANM, February 12–September 9, 1823.

107. *Guía* for William B. Giddings to Chihuahua and Sonora, Santa Fe, 16 August 1831, in Santa Fe, SRCA, MANM, January 1–December 31, 1831.

108. *Guía* no. 52 for Michael Woods, Santa Fe, 15 August 1834, in Santa Fe, SRCA, MANM, January 1–December 2, 1834; Manifests of goods brought from the United States to Santa Fe by William Hawk, 20 July 1834, in Santa Fe, SRCA, MANM, July 20–December 30, 1835, and by Robert W. Morris, 21 August 1834, in Santa Fe, SRCA, MANM, July 20–December 30, 1835; Manifests of goods brought from the United States to Santa Fe by Joe Sutton and Josiah Gregg, 21 July 1835, in Santa Fe, SRCA, MANM, July 20–December 30, 1835; Manifest for goods brought from the United States by Eugene Leitendorfer, n.d., 1846, Hacienda Records. For other manifests and *guías,* consult Santa Fe, SRCA, MANM for the years 1829–46. Prussian blue, like vermilion, is a pigment, not a dye. Both pigments have been positively identified on New Mexican Spanish *santos,* see Rutherford J. Gettens and Evan H. Turner, "The Materials and Methods of Some Religious Paintings of Early Nineteenth-Century New Mexico," p. 5.

109. Compiled from *Guías* for the years 1838; 1840; 1844. These records are incomplete. See Santa Fe, SRCA, MANM, January 30–November 6, 1838; February 25–October 26, 1840; January 1–December 2, 1844.

110. Gregg, pp. 148, 149–51, 193.

111. Emory and Abert, pp. 34–35.

112. Minge, *passim.*

113. Inventory and appraisal of personal property of Lieutenant Colonel Blas de Hinojos, Santa Fe, 17 July 1835, in Santa Fe, SRCA, MANM, July 8, 1835–January 20, 1836; Inventory and Estate of Albino Pérez, Santa Fe, 1 March–26 September 1838, in Santa Fe, SRCA, MANM, March 1–

September 26, 1838; Appraisal of the Articles in the Will of Manuel Márquez y Melo, Santa Fe, 30 June 1827, in Santa Fe, SRCA, MANM, June 30, 1827.

114. Emory and Abert, p. 39. Prized possessions of this family were gilded mirrors, a couch, and foreign goods.

115. Susan Shelby Magoffin, *Down the Santa Fe Trail and Into Mexico,* p. 154.

116. Estate of Cura Tomás Terrazas, n.d., Santa Fe, in Santa Fe, SRCA, MANM, December 10–May 27, 1827; articles purchased at the store by members of the Presidial Company, 9 July 1827, in Santa Fe, SRCA, MANM, January 1–December 15, 1827; Inventory of Presidial Soldier, Santa Fe, 1829, in Santa Fe, SRCA, MANM, January 1–December 31, 1829; Will of Tomás Madrid, Santa Fe, 27 January 1830, in Santa Fe, SRCA, MANM, January 27, 1830.

117. Gregg, p. 148; donations of *manta de Indio* to soldiers in Santa Fe, November and December 1821, in Santa Fe, SRCA, MANM, September 1–December 31, 1821.

118. Unlike the 1790 census, those of the Mexican Period described numerous other occupations but no weavers.

119. Certainly, with seventy-one looms, there must have been craftsmen in Albuquerque.

120. Census of the Villa de San Felipe Neri de Albuquerque, 10 September 1822, Census of Pueblo del Paso del Rio del Norte, August 1822, Census of Pueblo de San Buenaventura de Cochití, August 1822, Census of Santa Cruz de la Cañada, August 1822, all in Santa Fe, SRCA, MANM, August–September, 1822; Plan que Arreglar la Estadística, 12 February 1823, Estado que manifiesta el número de Vienes que tiene la Jurisdiccion de la Villa de Sta. Cruz de la Cañada 15 February 1823, all in Santa Fe, SRCA, MANM, February 1823. Cf. Virginia Langham Olmstead, transl. and compil., *Spanish and Mexican Colonial Censuses of New Mexico,* p. 37.

121. Census reports for 1823, in Santa Fe, SRCA, MANM, February, 1823.

122. Census for Sabinal, 23 November 1829, Census for Santo Tomás de Abiquiu, 28 November 1829, Censuses for Cochití, Santo Domingo, Peña Blanca, Cañada de Cochití, and Bajada, 17 November 1829; all in Santa Fe, SRCA, MANM, November, 1829.

123. Census for the Barrios of Guadalupe, San Francisco, San Miguel, and Torreón, Santa Fe, 1841, in Santa Fe, SRCA, MANM, undated census, 1841. No other information survives from this remarkable and thorough work.

124. Declaration made to Governor Mariano Martínez by José Ignacio Trujillo, resident of San Antonio de Carnué, 26 July 1844, Santa Fe, SRCA, MANM, January 17–December 26, 1844; Certification made by the Juez of the Jurisdiction of Sandia, 3 September 1844, Santa Fe, SRCA, MANM, Hacienda Records, 1844; Manifest to export *Efectos del País* to Chihuahua and Tierra Caliente made by Juan de Batia (X), 3 September 1844 (describing blankets woven by his peon), in Santa Fe, SRCA, MANM, January 1–December 2, 1844.

CHAPTER 3

1. Kate Kent, "The Cultivation and Weaving of Cotton in the Pre-historic Southwestern United States," pp. 462, 467, 468, 486–89.

2. George P. Hammond and Agapito Rey, *Narratives of the Coronado Expedition, 1540–1542,* pp. 171–76.

3. France V. Scholes, "Church and State in New Mexico, 1610–1650," pp. 297–333. See Nora Fisher, p. 192 ff. of this publication.

4. Charles Avery Amsden, *Navajo Weaving, Its Technique and Its History* (1934 ed.), p. 127.

5. Fray Alonso de Benavides, *The Memorial of Fray Alonso de Benavides,* p. 44.

6. Charles W. Hackett, *Historical Documents Relating to New Mexico, Nueva Vizcaya and Approaches Thereto, to 1773,* p. 382.

7. W. W. Hill, "Some Navajo Culture Exchanges During Two Centuries (with a translation of the early eighteenth century Rabal manuscript)," pp. 395–415.

8. See Trish Spillman, p. 62 ff. of this publication.

9. The warp/weft ratio refers to the thread count, the specific number of warps and wefts within a given unit. This is an important characteristic in distinguishing types of textiles. See Nora Fisher and Joe Ben Wheat, p. 196 of this publication.

10. Pedro Bautista Pino, *Three New Mexico Chronicles,* p. 133.

11. E. Boyd, *Popular Arts of Spanish New Mexico,* pp. 200–17, *passim.* See Dorothy Boyd Bowen, p. 142 of this publication.

12. Josiah Gregg, *Commerce of the Prairies,* Max L. Moorhead, ed. (1954), p. 148.

13. Santa Fe, MANM, 1840–1841 (Roll 28), *passim.* See Minge, p. 26 of this publication.

14. Gregg, *Commerce,* ed. Moorhead, p. 148.

15. For discussion of Indian servitude see Marianne Stoller, p. 42 of this publication.

16. Two of these were woven in the San Luis Valley (Plate 2, and Stoller, p. 44 ff., Figure 1, of this publication). The third was collected in Torreón and may currently be at the Southwest Museum in Los Angeles. The fourth is shown in Plate 53 and discussed by Bowen, p.123 of this publication.

17. For a discussion of the continuation of Indian servitude after 1846, see Stoller, p. 44 , n. 52 of this publication.

18. Santa Fe, SRCA, Records of the Office of Indian Affairs, Frank McNitt Collection, National Archives, T21, Roll 7, RG75, 1866–67.

19. Weaving in the San Luis Valley continued after 1900, see Stoller, p. 50 of this publication; the decline of weaving in the Rio Abajo took place earlier.

CHAPTER 4

1. Research on weaving in the San Luis Valley was initially undertaken as part of a project sponsored by the Virginia Neal Blue Resource Centers for Colorado Women under grants from the Four Corners Regional Commission in 1974 and 1975, and appreciation is extended to both agencies for providing the opportunity. Most of the research that appears in this paper, however, was done independently or extracted from data collected on a research grant sponsored by the Faculty Research and Development Fund, The Colorado College, to whom sincere thanks are also extended.

Many people have assisted in providing information and assistance in this research, and my warmest gratitude is offered them: Mrs. Celia Vigil Abernathy, Mr. Zach Bernal, Mrs. Elvira Borrego, Dr. Eva Borrego, Mr. Marcus Durán, Mr. and Mrs. Maclovio Gallegos, Mr. and Mrs. Castelar García, Mr. Julián Lobato, Mr. and Mrs. Frank Martínez, Mrs. Sam Montoya, Mr. Joe Morrow, Miss Gladys Robinson, Mrs. Joyce Romero, Mr. Elmer Shupe, Mr. and Mrs. Eben Smith, Mrs. E. L. Stoller, Dr. Britt Story, Dr. Frances L. Swadesh, Mrs. Tina Valdez, Mr. and Mrs. Patrick Vigil, Mrs. Dorothy Wilson, Sister Michelle Wittenrongel, Mrs. Charles H. Woodard, Mrs. Elaine Woodard, Mr. John Yaple, and Mr. Nesrala Zegob, Jr. Dr. Myra Ellen Jenkins and Mr. Richard Salazar of the New Mexico State Records Center, Miss Julie Eddy and Dr. George Fagan of The Colorado College Library, Miss Kee DeBoer, formerly of that library, the librarians at the Colorado State Historical Society Library, the Western History Library, and the Denver Public Library, and, most especially, Mrs. C. E. Moeny of the Colorado Room, Adams State College Library, provided the kind of help that only good archivists and librarians can. Miss Laura Lippman, Research Assistant, Department of Anthropology, The Colorado College, laboriously extracted the data used from the U.S. Census records and some from the Archives of the Archdiocese of Santa Fe (AASF). Miss Nora Fisher has been patient and encouraging in leading this project, as well as most generous in sharing her knowledge of textiles. Finally, and most significantly, this work is dedicated to the memory of E. Boyd, who taught me, as she did so many, most of what we know about Hispanic arts and crafts of the Southwest.

2. Edward H. Spicer, "Plural Society in the Southwest," p. 24.

3. D. W. Meinig, *Southwest: Three Peoples in Geographical Change 1600–1970,* p. 25.

4. See Colin B. Goodykoontz, "The People of Colorado," for population figures.

5. The history of Colorado is well told in Leroy R. Hafen, ed., *Colorado and Its People,* and more recently in Carl Ubbelohde, Maxine Benson, and Duane A. Smith, *A Colorado History.* That of Spanish Colonial New Mexico is covered by Ward Alan Minge, p. 8 ff. of this publication; for its Territorial Period see Robert W. Larson, *New Mexico's Quest for Statehood, 1846–1912.* Howard Roberts Lamar, *The Far Southwest 1846–1912,* provides a broader coverage of the entire Southwest area between 1842 and 1912, and Meinig gives a geographical view of its entire history.

6. Frances Leon Swadesh, *Los Primeros Pobladores,* is the best source on Ute-Hispano relations in the Chama, San Juan, and San Luis Valleys.

7. Purnee A. McCourt, "The Conejos Land Grant of Southern Colorado," pp. 37–38.

8. Guy Herstrom, "Sangre de Cristo Grant," and others give Narciso's age as twelve or thirteen.

Baptismal records, however, report his baptism on October 30, 1827 (AASF B–47, Taos; Fray Angélico Chávez, "New Names in New Mexico, 1820–1850," p. 296, lists all the Beaubien children).

9. Herstrom, pp. 76–86.

10. Primarily those collected under the Colorado Writer's Project by C. E. Gibson in 1933–34, when some of the children of original settlers were still alive. At State Historical Society of Colorado Library, Denver; hereafter referred to as Denver, CSHS, CWP with document numbers.

11. Denver, CSHS, CWP Doc. 349/28.

12. A typescript of this document is in Robert N. Anderson, "Guadalupe, Colorado," Appendix 1. Whether this colony persisted then without interruption in settlement cannot be ascertained. The Guadalupe colonists of 1854 make no mention of it, or of others which oral records claim were made at Los Cerritos and Servilleta prior to 1854. (Marianne Stoller, untitled MS forthcoming, reviews these records.)

13. Olibama Lopez Tushar, *The People of ''El Valle,''* pp. 13, 47.

14. The only documentation for this persistent oral report is from the Book of Marriages from Taos which records the marriage on January 14, 1850, of José Salomé Jaques from San Acacio and (originally) Abiquiu to María Antonia Nora Vigil from Sangre de Cristo [Desmontes] (AASF, Book of Marriages, Taos, 1845–56; M–41, #252). Jaques may not have stayed, however; he is listed as one of the original settlers of San Luis de Culebra in 1851 (Denver, CSHS, CWP Doc. 349/247–B).

15. E. C. Van Diest, "Early History of Costilla County," p. 141.

16. M. L. Crimmins, "Fort Massachusetts, First United States Military Post in Colorado," p. 128.

17. Delfino Salazar, "A Brief Historical Review," pp. 102–3.

18. Family history and genealogies are corroborated by documentary evidence in AASF, Books of Marriages and Baptism for Taos and Arroyo Hondo.

19. See Herbert Brayer, *William Blackmore,* vol. 1.

20. Stoller, MS.

21. Luther Bean, *Land of the Blue Sky People,* 1964; Stoller MS; Nicholas G. Morgan, "Mormon Colonization in the San Luis Valley."

22. Marianne Stoller, "Traditional Hispanic Arts and Crafts in the San Luis Valley of Colorado."

23. See Dorothy Boyd Bowen, p. 123, Plate 53 of this publication for documentation of a *criada* blanket from the Abiquiu area.

24. L. R. Bailey, *Indian Slave Trade in the Southwest,* is the most comprehensive study of Indian servitude in the Southwest, but Leroy R. and Ann W. Hafen, *Old Spanish Trail,* are specific on the Old Spanish Trail while Swadesh has superior discussions on the interpersonal relations between Indians and Spanish for the area of our concern. In the earlier New Mexican documents the term *criado (-a)* is not used; instead, the terms *sirviente* and *indio(a)* are used to describe Indian servants.

25. See Joe Ben Wheat, p. 29 ff. of this publication.

26. Hafen and Hafen, p. 100.

27. The imposition of duty on the woven blankets by California authorities ended the Old Spanish Trail traffic, ironically just before the Treaty of Guadalupe Hidalgo made both New Mexico and California part of the United States (Hafen and Hafen, p. 194).

28. Edward Norris Wentworth, *America's Sheep Trails,* pp. 128, 131; and Hafen and Hafen, p. 182.

29. Hafen and Hafen, pp. 178–79.

30. Ibid., p. 187. Hafen and Hafen suggest that the figures may be a little inflated.

31. Hafen and Hafen, pp. 171, 189, 271.

32. See John Upton Terrell, *The Navajos,* pp. 182–91.

33. Denver, CSHS, CWP, Doc. 349/44.

34. These figures, compiled from the household censuses for these years, are somewhat arbitrary because the area included varies. In 1860 and 1870 the entire Valley is represented; 1880, however, includes Conejos and Costilla counties but not Saguache (created in 1867, but included in 1870 here), Rio Grande, or Hinsdale (both created in 1874). Also excluded from the 1880 figures for Conejos and Costilla counties are railroad and tie camp workers, since they were mostly transients. Ethnic determination follows that of the Census records (category "Race"); again there is variation for Hispanos and Anglos not only by year but also by census taker. Some marked "M" or "Mex" and "W"; subsequently, the "M"'s were marked over with "W"'s in many cases. Combining last name with state or country of origin, however, made it possible to distinguish these two ethnic categories with some confidence. These figures were compiled by Laura Lippman, Research Assistant in the Department of Anthropology, The Colorado College. It was not possible to carry the figures to the turn of the century, as would be desirable, because the data sheets for 1890 were burned in a fire at the National Archives, and because the Archives has not yet released the 1900 sheets for public use.

35. The complete list, with owner, location, age, tribal affiliation, etc., is published by D. Eugene Combs, "Enslavement of Indians in the San Luis Valley of Colorado," pp. 22–29.

36. See Marianne Stoller, p. 44 of this publication.

37. Emilia Gallegos Smith, "Reminiscences of Early San Luis," p. 25.

38. Denver, CSHS, CWP, Docs. 349/14, 19, and 27–B.

39. "He [informant Ramón Ruybal, whose family settled at Mesitas in 1856 when he was two years old] describes the trip as follows: over the Cumbres to Dulce, across the Coraque, through the Canado [sic] del Cabresto, over the Mesa de la Fragua, through Canalla [sic] de la Jara, and past what is known as the Martínez Ranch to Cañada del Ojo a la Cueva where the people lived." (Denver, CSHS, Doc. 349/19.)

All but the last-named place are shown on Swadesh's map (1974, pp. xxiv–v), making it possible to establish Largo or Gobernador Canyons as the likely destinations. The account also notes that the Indians were living in cliff dwellings in the caves (i.e., were "camping" in prehistoric dwellings), and were very timid and without weapons. Swadesh suggests that these last two characteristics are far more descriptive of Paiutes than Navajos, and small bands of Paiutes—also raided by the Utes for captives—were known in the same area at the same time (Swadesh, personal communication). Head's census does report five "Pah-Utes" in the San Luis Valley in 1865.

40. "Time-Event Chart in the San Luis Valley," p. 11; also Bailey, pp. 121–22. Actually, it is unlikely that the Hispanos were "fooled" into thinking the Hopi were Navajos. Their long and intimate acquaintance with Indians of the Southwest gave them expert knowledge and awareness of tribal and linguistic differences.

41. Smith, p. 24–25. There are no reports that Navajo women and girls were used as herders by their Hispano owners, although they traditionally perform these roles in their own culture.

42. Combs, pp. 22–29. For discussion of Navajo women weaving, see Stoller, p. 50 ff. of this publication.

43. In 1853, José Darío Gallegos and María Eulogia Valdez were *padrinos* for a baptism; their residence was given as Plaza de la Santísima Trinidad [de Arroyo Seco, a *plaza* a few miles northeast of Taos] (AASF, Arroyo Hondo, B–1, #1075).

44. "San Luis Store Celebrates Centennial," p. 258.

45. Denver, CSHS, CWP, Doc. 349/27–B.

46. In the late 1860s, when the three were told they were free, Refugio disappeared. Apparently Antonia married an Army Lieutenant at Fort Garland, and their descendants still live in the Valley (Combs, p. 4).

47. Ibid., pp. 3–4.

48. Ibid., p. 4.

49. Baca and his wife, María Simonia [also Simoneta] Valdez, are listed as *padrinos* (god parents) at a wedding in 1850 when their residence is also given as the *plaza* of Santísima Trinidad [de Arroyo Seco] (AASF, Book of Marriages, M–41, #276).

50. Baca descendants interviewed by the present writer also volunteered this name and claimed that Siriaco was Indian, not "Mexican" as listed in the census. Informants reported that Siriaco and Encarnación were Navajos, Guadalupe a Ute (Combs, p. 4). Siriaco married a local Hispana and had children; he left the Bacas and worked for many years for an Anglo doctor in San Luis. Guadalupe is also reported to have had a son and to have died in 1925; Baca gave her a lot of land to live on which she left to Juan Antonio's great grandson, Luis Gallegos (Combs, p. 4). Encarnación is said to have died in the flu epidemic of 1917–18.

51. "Time-Event Chart," p. 9.

52. Since the Spanish system of slavery differed markedly from the Anglo, the Emancipation Proclamation was not always interpreted by people of the Valley as applying to their *criados.* One of Combs' informants expressed their feelings: "The people who had Indians thought that the Emancipation Proclamation concerned only the South and the Negro. They did not feel that it applied to them. This was a different situation." (Combs, p. 8.) The passage by Congress of an act forbidding peonage in the Territory of New Mexico (and elsewhere) in 1867 prompted these official declarations of freedom (Thirty-Ninth Congress, Second Session).

53. The Beryl G. and Charles H. Woodard Collection of textiles was given to the Colorado State Historical Society Museum in 1963, following Mr. Woodard's death. Colonel Woodard was born in Kansas and grew up in Trinidad, Colorado; he graduated from The Colorado College in 1911 and took his law degree at Boston University. In 1915 he started practicing law in Alamosa, Colorado, then served in World War I and returned to Alamosa where he practiced for twenty-five years; in 1936 he opened an office in Colorado Springs and split his time between the two until he entered the Air Force in 1941 and the office in Alamosa was permanently closed. During his years in the Valley he became very interested in Rio Grande textiles, and in the '20s and '30s began buying them because he saw that the craft was dying or dead and no one else seemed to care about them. He bought primarily through an agent, Pete Lucero, but sometimes people brought old blankets to him directly or he bought in family homes. Although some blankets were from New Mexico, the majority were purchased in the San Luis Valley where they were supposedly made (information kindly supplied by Mrs. Woodard, 1975). The Woodard Collection consists of more than fifty Rio Grande textiles, accompanied by descriptions and notes on weavers, locations, etc. (referred to here as the Woodard MS). After the Colorado State Historical Society Museum received the collection, E. Boyd, then Curator of Spanish Colonial Art at the Museum of New Mexico, was invited to study and describe them; her work is referred to here as the Boyd MS. Mr. Joe Morrow, Curator of CSHSM, and Mrs. Woodard kindly gave permission to use both of these manuscripts.

54. Denver, CSHS, Woodard Collection, Woodard MS, Boyd MS.

55. Denver, CSHS, Woodard MS.

56. Denver, CSHS, Boyd MS, p. 19. Note that Boyd mistakenly used the word *Merino* in describing *churro* wool; the word *churro* has been substituted throughout.

57. Denver, CSHS, CWP, Doc. 349/27–B. In 1859 María Esquipula Vigil, daughter of Juan Miguel Vigil and Guadalupe Bageyas (Vallejos?) of the Plaza de la Culebra, was married (AASF, Book of Marriages, Arroyo Hondo, M–42, #771). If Juan Miguel Vigil is the same man, his first wife must have died, for a descendant identifies his great-grandmother as María Rosa Vargas. In the 1880 census Juan M. Vigil is listed as a fifty-year-old farmer, and his wife, Rosa, as fifty-two. Their grandson, Fred Vigil, who was born in 1874 and died in 1971, was a lifelong resident of San Luis.

58. Denver, CSHS, Woodard MS, Boyd MS.

59. Tushar, p. 39.

60. Ibid., p. 47.

61. Ibid., p. 38.

62. Denver, CSHS, Woodard MS, Woodard correspondence.

63. Denver, CSHS, Boyd MS, p. 35.

64. See Stoller, p. 44 of this publication.

65. Denver, CSHS, Woodard MS; Boyd MS, p. 18. Pablo García is listed in Conejos County in the 1870 census; he was twenty-eight years old and a prosperous farmer, according to the property valuation given in that census.

66. Denver, CSHS, Boyd MS.

67. Denver, CSHS, Woodard MS. See also Spillman, p. 70 of this publication.

68. Denver, CSHS, Boyd MS.

69. Three Esquibel brothers, Juan, Ramón, and Rafael, were among the second group of settlers (i.e., probably in the mid-to-late-1850s) in the *plazas* of San Pedro y San Pablo, and were famous for the horses which they raised. Félix was the descendant of one of these men, perhaps Juan, who is listed in the 1880 census, and he died not too long prior to Vigil's research in 1956 (Charlie A. Vigil, "History and Folklore of San Pedro and San Pablo,

Colorado," p. 12). At one time he operated a store in San Pablo. The Esquibels had Indian *criados,* as did quite a few other people in San Pablo and San Pedro according to the 1870 and 1880 censuses; one Rita Eisquvel [sic] is listed as a laundress, twenty-one years old in 1880, living in an independent household.

70. Miss Gladys Robinson, personal communication, 1975.

71. These brothers were the sons of Juan María García and Pablita Martínez, who are said to have come from San José, New Mexico, and settled near Manassa (at Los Cerritos) in 1852, subsequently moving to La Servilleta, a *plaza* a little further up the Conejos River, because it afforded better protection from the Indians (Denver, CSHS, CWP, Doc. 349/14). Juan María García is said to have owned Indian slaves; in one incident reported by his son, Epimenio, he traded a burro for an Indian boy sick with smallpox whose owner was going to kill him just as he would a sick sheep or calf. Another time, according to the same record, he obtained a small Indian girl for two goats. Epimenio's cousin was stolen by Indians and grew up with them, marrying the son of the man who stole her. Librado García and his loom are pictured in Lester Griswold, *Handicraft,* 8th ed., p. 248.

72. It is appropriate here to apologize for any weaver overlooked or for any incorrect information inadvertently included, and to earnestly request any reader having more information on weavers in the San Luis Valley to contact the author. Additional textiles from the San Luis Valley in the exhibit include Plates 4 and 25.

73. If the census report is correct, Damián would have been ninety-six or ninety-seven at his death; the census-taker, however, seems more likely to have made mistakes than family and community members.

74. Since the project was federally financed, its products could not be sold, but were used in the decoration of local schools, the V.A. facility of

Monte Vista, etc.; amazingly enough, not one single piece from this project could be found in any of these institutions—or traced—thirty-five years later.

75. Most information on this project was supplied by Miss Gladys Robinson, who went to some effort to review old records, dig out materials, and refresh her memory on my behalf. Her efforts are much appreciated.

76. "Nathaniel P. Hill Inspects Colorado," p. 267.

77. Ibid., p. 273.

78. Tushar, pp. 39 and 41.

79. For further discussion of the treadle loom see Fisher, p. 192 of this publication.

80. Stoller MS.

81. See also Tushar, p. 26.

82. Tushar, p. 33.

83. Vigil, p. 16.

84. Tushar, p. 33.

85. "Time-Event Chart," p. 19.

86. Marcus Durán, personal communication.

87. See Nora Fisher and Joe Ben Wheat, p. 197 ff. of this publication.

88. Private Land Claims, U.S. Surveyor General; microfilm, SRC, Report #143, File #1.

89. Wentworth, p. 563.

90. Ibid., p. 564.

91. Jas. A. Kelly, "Sheep Raising and Feeding," pp. 6–8.

92. Wentworth, p. 368.

93. Frank A. White, *La Garita,* p. 27.

94. Miss Gladys Robinson, personal communication.

95. Denver, CSHS, CWP, Doc. 349/4.

CHAPTER 5

1. Franz Huning, *Traders on the Santa Fe Trail,* pp. 24–25.

2. For methods of dating, see chart.

3. Edward Norris Wentworth, *America's Sheep Trails,* pp. 235–36. According to the Daughters of the Utah Pioneers (December, 1977), several of the Mormon wives were Scandinavian weavers. This may explain the Four Corners provenience of several Scandinavian textiles, NTM T–20 and MAI 19/3011. The former was identified as a Navajo "slave blanket" by Charles Amsden. The latter (MAI 19/3011) was later copied by a Navajo weaver (MAI 19/3010). Both Scandinavian pieces are woven in the double interlocking tapestry weave with warp of a plant fiber which appears to be flax.

CHAPTER 6

1. A breakdown of the 408 striped blankets in U.S. museum collections was established according to dyes and materials used. This encompasses two large categories: early blankets of natural wool and imported natural dyes, and the later synthetic-dyed blankets. Dyes were used as a criterion because continuous design-oriented groupings did not exist, except within certain dye types.

2. It is logical to assume different levels of expertise in weaving. Beginners probably wove band-and-stripe blankets, while advanced weavers wove the more complex Saltillo designs. See also Nora Fisher, p. 201 ff. of this publication.

3. Four-harness looms have been used for weaving striped blankets as well as *jerga,* as can be seen in the earliest examples right up to the twentieth century ones. See Trish Spillman, p. 146 ff. of this publication.

4. Max Saltzman, p. 216 of this publication, UCLA, D–35–62 (L.5.62.71) dye not identified, unknown, probably synthetic.

5. See Charlene Cerny and Christine Mather, p. 180 ff. of this publication. Shupe is a trader in Taos, N.M.

6. Additional examples of blankets with tricolor beading which may also be of San Luis Valley provenience include IFAF FA.67.43.1, MR BL 55. Personal communication, Elmer Shupe, November, 1977.

7. Documentation concerning the Woodard Collection textiles is available in Denver, CSHS.

8. Personal communication, Elmer Shupe, March, 1977.

9. For further discussion of wool types see Nora Fisher and Joe Ben Wheat, p. 197 ff. of this publication.

10. For a description of the technical differences among Navajo, Pueblo, and Spanish blankets see Joe Ben Wheat, p. 31 ff. of this publication. For illustrations of Navajo striped blankets, see Mary Hunt Kahlenberg and Anthony Berlant, *The Navajo Blanket,* Plates 25, 26, 32, and 43.

11. See E. Boyd, *Popular Arts of Spanish New Mexico,* pp. 175–76.

12. For the dye analysis see Saltzman, pp. 214-16 of this publication, UCLA D–32–11 (L.5.58.41), D–34–50 (U.C. 18088), D–34–51 (L.5.62.73), D–34–52 (L.5.62.70), D–34–60 (FH L.71.17.2). There has been a confusion among brazilwood, logwood, and mountain mahogany as possible dye sources. None of these disparate dyes, in fact, were used to produce this red-brown. See Bowen and Spillman, p. 208 of this publication.

13. L.77.101.1 Personal communication from the lender, Edward B. Grothus, Los Alamos.

14. Personal interviews with local Spanish families have failed to turn up further information concerning the use of the so-called "wedding blanket." For a further discussion of the wedding blanket and utility blanket types, see Boyd, p. 196. This terminology may reflect a confusion with the Hopi wedding blanket. For a description of the Hopi wedding blanket see Frederic H. Douglas, "Main Types of Pueblo Cotton Textiles," pp. 168–69.

15. The buttonhole stitch edgings are not part of the original blanket.

16. Harry Percival Mera, *Spanish-American Blanketry*, Plate 20.

CHAPTER 7

1. José R. Benítez, *El Traje y El Adorno en México, 1500–1910*, p. 141.

2. Ibid.

3. Kate Kent, "The Cultivation and Weaving of Cotton in the Pre-historic Southwestern United States," pp. 605–9. For further discussion of the origins of the *sarape* in Mexico see Donald and Dorothy Cordry, *Mexican Indian Costumes*, and Patricia Rieff Anawalt, "Pan-Meso American Costume Repertory at the Time of Spanish Contact."

4. For further discussion of looms see Nora Fisher, p. 192 ff. of this publication.

5. Charles Gibson, *Tlaxcala in the 16th Century*, p. 151.

6. Ibid., pp. 154–55.

7. Ibid., pp. 183–86.

8. Vito Alessio-Robles, *Coahuila y Texas en la Epoca Colonial*, pp. 134–35.

9. Ibid., p. 608.

10. Ibid.

11. Jacques Revault, *Designs and Patterns from North African Carpets and Textiles, passim.* Indi-

viduals currently pursuing research concerning Portuguese, Spanish, and North African motifs and symbolism include, among others, Schuyler V. R. Cammann, University of Pennsylvania, Philadelphia, and Ed Wade, Peabody Museum, Cambridge, Massachusetts.

12. E. Boyd, *Popular Arts of Spanish New Mexico*, p. 190.

13. One must go back into archeological time to find Chinese weaving with serrate diamonds similar to those which form the basis of Saltillo weaving design. William Willetts, *Chinese Art*, pp. 257–61; Schuyler Cammann, personal communication to Nora Fisher, December, 1976, asserted that there was no Chinese influence in Saltillo *sarape* design. For a thorough study of Chinese influence in colonial Peru, see Schuyler Cammann, "Chinese Influence in Colonial Peruvian Tapestries."

14. These observations are based on the author's examination of textiles in the Mexico National Museum of Anthropology in 1974.

15. Warp-patterned fabrics, which are relatively easy to weave on the back-strap loom, are very difficult to accomplish on the highly mechanized treadle loom. When the treadle loom appears in an area weft-faced fabrics are likely to turn up: the occurrence of weft ikat, for example, is related to the use of tapestry weave; see Fisher, p. 139 ff. of this publication.

16. Alessio-Robles, p. 392.

17. Ibid.

18. Max L. Moorhead, *New Mexico's Royal Road*, p. 45.

19. Aduana, *Guías* to Mexico, Santa Fe, SRCA, MANM, January 30–November 6, 1838.

20. Lansing B. Bloom, "Early Weaving in New Mexico," *passim;* France V. Scholes, "Church and State in New Mexico, 1610–1650," p. 300 n. 6, p. 306 n. 25. Fisher, p. 193 of this publication.

21. Virginia Langham Olmstead, transl. and com-

pil., *Spanish and Mexican Colonial Censuses of New Mexico: 1790, 1823, 1845, passim.* Also see Minge, p. 21 of this publication.

22. Pedro Bautista Pino, *Three New Mexico Chronicles*, pp. 35–36.

23. Ibid.

24. Boyd, pp. 204–5. The main problem in adopting Saltillo-derived motifs in Rio Grande weaving must have been in making the necessary design adjustments to allow for the use of coarser New Mexico yarns.

25. Alessio-Robles, *passim.*

26. Aduana, *Guías* to Mexico, Santa Fe, SRCA, MANM, January 30–November 6, 1838.

27. Josiah Gregg, *Commerce of the Prairies*, ed. Max L. Moorhead (1954), pp. 147–48.

28. See Dorothy Boyd Bowen and Trish Spillman, p. 207 ff. of this publication.

29. See Nora Fisher and Joe Ben Wheat, p. 199 ff. of this publication.

CHAPTER 8

1. For a discussion of tapestry weave, see Nora Fisher, p. 203 ff. of this publication.

2. Harry Percival Mera, *Spanish American Blanketry*.

3. E. Boyd, *Popular Arts of Spanish New Mexico*, p. 187 ff.

4. CSHS E.2018.42.

5. Edward Norris Wentworth, *America's Sheep Trails*, pp. 332–33. See Stoller, p. 45 , n. 53 of this publication.

6. SCAS L.5.72.29.

7. See Joe Ben Wheat, p. 32 of this publication.

8. Lowe 70.220.034.

9. See Anthony Berlant and Mary Hunt Kahlenberg, *Walk in Beauty,* Plates 2, 6, 23, 24, 34, 35, and 36; see also Charles Avery Amsden, *Navajo Weaving, Its Technique and Its History* (1934 ed.), Plates 38, 48, 64, 74, 75, 91, 98.

10. UMP NA 9101, Taylor numbers 2286, 1907, and 445, and MNM A.8.57.9.

11. MNM A.8.57.9.

12. FH L.71.17.7.

13. MAI 17/7285.

14. MNM L.5.62.87.

15. Taylor 3794, Lowie 2/10751, and LACM A–5141–16.

16. CSHS E.2018.19.

17. See Marianne Stoller, p. 40, chart   of this publication.

18. AMNH 65/3315.

19. Lowie 2/10751.

20. SAR, SF T.445, LACM A–5141–209, LACM A–5141–12 (Plate 23), and MAI 1/3990.

21. Field 1825.

22. Taylor 3751, MAI 1/3997, and Lowe 61.073.008.

23. Stoller states that Pablo García, a 28-year-old farmer, is listed in the 1870 Conejos County Census. Stoller, p. 46 , n. 65 of this publication.

24. Taylor 2280, 2483, MR BL 4, AMNH 65/3316 (Figure 5), and MAI 2607 and 2608.

25. Taylor 2280.

26. MAI 2608 and MR BL 4.

27. Sagel is a young weaver from Española, N.M.

28. CSHS E.2018.32, Lowe 60.220.036, MAI 1/3995, and UMP NA 3480.

29. UMP NA 3480.

30. Taylor 2283.

31. MAI 6/4007, ASM E.2727, and LACM A–5141–20.

32. LACM A–5141–20.

33. CSHS E.2018.6.

34. For use of the term *Frazadas de Rio Abajo bordeadas* see Ward Alan Minge, p. 25 of this publication.

CHAPTER 9

1. MAI 16/9714, MR BL 59, AMNH 65/3320, and SCAS L.5.62.97.

2. LACM A–5141–14 and A–5141–11.

3. Taylor 3793 and SDMM 25909.

4. See Anthony Berlant and Mary Hunt Kahlenberg, *Walk in Beauty,* Figure 45, Plates 52 and 54.

5. SCAS L.5.62.89 (Figure 5), CSHS E.2018.24, and MNM A. 64.5.2.

6. CSHS E.2018.24.

7. SAR, SF T.320.

8. SAR 45320/12 and MNM A.64.20.2.

9. MNM A.67.12.1.

10. Accession Records, Museum of New Mexico, A.5.57.10.

11. Mrs. Cleofas M. Jaramillo, *Romance of a Little Village Girl,* pp. 94–95, and Obituary, *Santa Fe New Mexican,* May 28, 1920, p. 6, col. 3.

12. United States Census, 1860, Rio Arriba County, New Mexico, p. 215. The age of Juliana is corroborated by the 1850 New Mexico Territorial Census, vol. 2, Rio Arriba and Santa Ana Counties, p. 28.

13. Joe Ben Wheat, p. 33 ff. of this publication.

14. SAR, SF T.327, Lowe 61.073.013, Taylor 3756, and UC WTXC–2.

15. Marianne Stoller, p. 43 ff. of this publication.

CHAPTER 10

1. Joe Ben Wheat, "Spanish-American and Navajo Weaving, 1600 to Now," p. 205.

2. E. Boyd, *Popular Arts of Spanish New Mexico,* p. 193. E. Boyd's source for information concerning Patricia Montoya was Elmer Shupe of Taos, who must have told her the story some twenty years ago. Years earlier, Mr. Shupe's father had told him about Patricia Montoya, a girl with "deformed feet," whose family had made the loom with a hand-operating shedding device. Mr. Shupe obtained additional information from a neighbor who was of the Montoya family and repeated this story to me, word for word, on December 6, 1977. Another Taos native, Juanita Jaramillo, a greatniece of Patricia Montoya, has traced the history of her family. There were at least five Montoya sisters: Patricia, Doloritas, and Martina, who were weavers, and Juanita and Petrita, who assisted in wool preparation. Juanita Jaramillo, interviewing her great-aunt in Trampas, was given to understand that Patricia Montoya may have had a broken nose or hare lip but was not otherwise deformed or crippled (personal communication, February 10, 1978). Cf. Juanita Jaramillo, "Rio Grande Weaving: A Continuing Tradition," pp. 14–15. Patricia Montoya is thought to have been born about 1860. She could not have been a master weaver by the age of five or ten. A thorough search of the 1870 and 1880 U.S. Censuses for Taos County has not confirmed the existence of Patricia Montoya. Further study of the baptismal records of the AASF may turn up more information, however.

3. In all cases, provenience data for the *Vallero* blankets comes from a secondary source. Though a number of these textiles are attributed to Peñasco,

Trampas, and even Patricia Montoya, not one is associated with reliable firsthand collection data.

4. Harry Percival Mera, *Spanish-American Blanketry,* Plates 17–19.

5. Ibid., Plate 18.

6. The eight-pointed star was eventually adopted as a popular motif of Navajo blanket weaving (George Wharton James, *Indian Blankets and Their Makers,* p. 36, Figure 19), and it certainly was also common in Mexico.

7. Wheat, p. 205.

8. Carrie Hall and Rose G. Kretsinger, *The Romance of the Patchwork Quilt in America,* p. 55.

9. Ibid., p. 55. "This is of French origin. The LeMoyne brothers were given a grant of land in 1699 known as Louisiana and in 1718 they founded the city of New Orleans. In the New England states the name was shortened to *Lemon Star.*"

10. See Mildred Davison and Christa C. Mayer-Thurman, *Coverlets, A Handbook of the Collection of Woven Coverlets in the Art Institute of Chicago,* Plates 62, 64, 65, 95, 99, 113, and 140.

11. Charles Avery Amsden, *Navajo Weaving, Its Technique and Its History* (1964 ed.), Plate 114.

12. Carleton L. Safford and Robert Bishop, *America's Quilts and Coverlets,* pp. 266, 267, 268, 272, 273.

13. Ibid., pp. 139–41.

14. SCAS L.5.69–15. (This section concerning pictorials was written by Dorothy Boyd Bowen.)

15. Ramón Mena, "El Zarape," pp. 394–98.

16. Wheat, p. 205.

CHAPTER 11

1. Alfred Bühler, "The Origin and Extent of the Ikat Technique," p. 1607.

2. Incidentally, weft ikat does in fact occur in Mexico. Its occurrence, however, is very rare and the pieces bear no resemblance to the blankets under discussion. See Ellin F. Grossman, "Textiles and Looms from Guatemala and Mexico."

3. E. Boyd, "Ikat Dyeing in Southwestern Textiles"; E. Boyd, *Popular Arts of Spanish New Mexico,* p. 204. For discussion of the Bazán brothers, see pp. 22, 76, 142, and 194 of this publication.

4. Verbal communication, Katharine Jenkins, Berkeley, California, November 5, 1977.

5. Irmgard Johnson, Mexico City, Mexico, letter July 1, 1977. María Teresa Pomar, Directora, Museo Nacional de Artes y Industrias Populares, Mexico, visited the Museum of International Folk Art, December 4, 1977. She was shown, without comment, the textile illustrated in Figure 1. Her response is of interest: "It can't be Mexican, what about Guatemalan?"

6. Boyd, "Ikat Dyeing"; Boyd, *Popular Arts,* p. 199 ff.

7. AMNH 65/4602.

8. Jon Erickson, Curator of Collections, The Heard Museum, personal communication, November, 1977. Bernard Fontana, Ethnologist, Arizona State Museum, Tucson, letter December, 1977.

9. Heard NA SW SPR–9.

10. Bühler, p. 1605.

11. Letter from Alfred Bühler, Museum für Völkerkunde, Basel, Switzerland, November 16, 1977.

12. Alfred Bühler, *Ikat, Batik, Plangi;* Jack Lenor Larsen, *The Dyer's Art.*

13. Larsen, *Dyer's Art,* p. 191.

14. Lila M. O'Neale, *Textiles of Highland Guatemala,* p. 10.

15. Ibid., p. 26.

16. Letter (November 9, 1977) from Edwin Shook,

Director, Monte Alto Project, Miami Museum of Science, living in Antigua, Guatemala. Letter from Carlos Elmenhorst, collector, Guatemala, June 11, 1978.

17. See Ward Alan Minge, p. 20 of this publication.

18. Stephan F. Borhegyi, "The Miraculous Shrines of Our Lord of Esquipulas in Guatemala and Chimayó," p. 87.

19. Boyd, *Popular Arts,* pp. 352, 353, 395.

20. Personal communication, Myra Ellen Jenkins, Chief, Historical Service Division, New Mexico State Record Center and Archives, January 25, 1978.

21. Marianne Stoller, personal communication, 1978. Research is in progress. The suggestion that the weft ikats might be linked to the presence of the Guatemalan cult of Our Lord of Esquipulas in Chimayó came from Stoller, who has done some research on the subject of the Esquipulas cult and is in the process of accumulating more data. In an attempt to follow through on the theory the author interviewed Myra Ellen Jenkins (New Mexico State Records Center and Archives, January 25, 1978) and Fray Angélico Chávez (O.F.M., Santa Fe, January 26, 1978). No concrete information surfaced, though, as Chávez reiterated, the name *Molleno* (The person credited with the *santos* of Our Lord of Esquipulas) is not New Mexican in origin. The name cannot be tied specifically to Guatemala, however.

22. Letter from Alfred Bühler, November 16, 1977.

23. See Joe Ben Wheat, p. 75 ff. of this publication; Nora Fisher, p. 192 ff. of this publication.

CHAPTER 12

1. E. Boyd, "Rio Grande Blankets Containing Hand Spun Cotton Yarns," and Harry Percival Mera, *The Alfred I. Barton Collection of Southwestern Textiles,* p. 99.

2. FH L.70.3.36, SCAS L.5.62.74, IFAF FA. 64.21.1., Taylor 3772 and 3773 (Plate 62), Lowe 65.050.107, and MNA 2203/E.1870. An eighth piece which is more questionable in origin is SCAS L.5.70.35. The extremely high thread count and indigo-dyed handspun cotton weft appear to disqualify this textile as Rio Grande.

3. MNA 2203/E.1870, FH L.70.3.36, SCAS L.5.62.74, and Taylor 3772 and 3773.

4. Taylor 3772 and 3773. A small area of apparently raveled Z-spun yarn in 3772 has been identified by Saltzman as lac (D–34–48D). This would tentatively date these two pieces before 1825.

5. MNA 2203/E.1870.

6. E. Boyd, *Popular Arts of Spanish New Mexico*, pp. 200–201. Belén is about thirty-five miles north of Lémitar, and Tomé is perhaps another ten miles north of Belén, on the Rio Grande.

7. Fray Angélico Chávez, *The Origins of New Mexico Families*, p. 147.

8. According to Mela Sedillo-Brewster, cotton was raised in Lemitar until about 1930, and in 1935 some people were still carding and spinning their own cotton. She described two handspun "home-dyed" handwoven cotton blankets seen in one home, and in another home saw several pounds of carded cotton being spun for blankets. Sedillo-Brewster, p. 49. Since there is no mention of wool, the cotton presumably was dyed, probably with synthetic packaged dyes, unlike any of the blankets described in this article.

9. Lowe 65.050.107. This blanket contains 2-ply handspun wool warp; weft is 1-ply handspun wool (natural-dyed green and cochineal wool and white cotton carded together to form pink) and 3-ply commercial wool (natural-dyed tan and cochineal).

10. See Ward Alan Minge, p. 10 ff. of this publication and Joe Ben Wheat, p. 29 ff. of this publication.

11. Lansing B. Bloom, "Early Weaving," p. 234.

citing Santa Fe, SRCA, SANM II, December 16, 1803.

12. Missions of the "Custodia" of the Conversion of Saint Paul, Report made by Fray Josef Benito Pereyro of Santa Clara, December 30, 1808. Santa Fe, SRCA, SANM II, April 14, 1792, translated by Public Survey Office, p. 10.

13. Don Ignacio Ricardo Bazán asked, in February, 1807, to marry Juana Apolonia Gutiérrez of Pajarito, just south of Albuquerque. Though their daughter was baptized in Santa Fe in 1809, she married a man from Tomé and apparently settled there. Joaquín Alejandro Bazán, son of Don Ignacio, married a native of Belén and died there at age sixty-four in 1871. Chávez, *Origins*, pp. 146–47.

CHAPTER 13

1. *Manta* is not included in this discussion because throughout the Western Hemisphere the Spanish word *manta* has assumed a wide variety of definitions. Certainly *manta* was a common fabric used for tribute and tax payment. Certainly, also, it is known to have been a product of the New Mexican Pueblo Indian loom. Today, in Mexico, *manta* is treadle-loom woven commercial cotton. We cannot be certain that *manta* was ever a product of the Spanish treadle loom in New Mexico, however. E. Boyd covered this subject in detail, referring to the sixteenth-century Mexican documents which had been cited by Abelardo Carrillo y Gariel (1959) E. Boyd, *Popular Arts of Spanish New Mexico*, pp. 233–36.

2. Nora Fisher, p. 193 ff. of this publication.

3. Marianne Stoller, p. 49 of this publication. Also, for uses of handwoven yardage in the San Luis Valley see Stoller, pp. 48-52 of this publication.

4. Boyd, *Popular Arts*, p. 188.

5. Fisher, p. 193 of this publication.

6. Information on color of Franciscan habit courtesy of Friar Lino Gómez Canedo, O.F.M., Academy of American Franciscan History, Washington, D.C. Information concerning the use of *sayal* in Mexico provided by Abelardo Carrillo y Gariel, *El Traje en la Nueva España*, pp. 33, 206.

7. See Fisher, p. 201 of this publication for definition of plain weave.

8. Pedro Bautista Pino, *Three New Mexico Chronicles*, p. 35.

9. Boyd, *Popular Arts*, p. 177.

10. Ibid., pp. 177–81. E. Boyd described excavated fragments which may, indeed, be examples of handwoven New Mexican *bayeta*. See also Fray Angélico Chávez, "The Unique Tomb of Fathers Zarate and de la Llana in Santa Fe," p. 101. Note: *Bayeta* woven in New Mexico is not to be confused with the imported fabric of the same name, generally considered to be English in origin. See also Joe Ben Wheat, "Spanish-American and Navajo Weaving 1600 to Now," p. 214, regarding the probability of an eastern American origin for *bayeta* after 1812.

11. Irene Emery, "Wool Embroideries of New Mexico," p. 149. *Sabanilla*, commonly used both in English and Spanish, is difficult to define. Irene Emery presents a clear and inclusive discussion of the whole range of ways that this term is used in Spain, and in both English and Spanish in New Mexico. Emery, "Wool Embroideries," pp. 147–51.

12. Stoller, p. 50 of this publication.

13. Olibama López Tushar, *The People of "El Valle,"* pp. 42–43; Mrs. Cleofas M. Jaramillo, *Shadows of the Past*, p. 48.

14. See Fisher, p. 153 ff. Plates 65–68 of this publication.

15. Leroy R. Hafen, *The Overland Mail, 1849–1869*, pp. 136–42; on New Mexico: Sytha Motto, *Old Houses of New Mexico and the People Who*

Built Them, p. 53. The wool mill built by Samuel Watrous in 1879 operated until 1884. It was a financial success, producing blankets, rugs, carpets, and *sarapes.* On Utah: Edward Norris Wentworth, *America's Sheep Trails,* p. 235. In the mid-1860s a wool mill was established at Parley's Creek Canyon. In spite of numerous attempts, we have not discovered what types of fabrics were woven in these mills.

CHAPTER 14

1. E. Boyd, *Popular Arts of Spanish New Mexico,* p. 182.

2. Governor de Vargas' Inventory, 20 April 1704, in Santa Fe, SRCA, SANM II, April 20, 1704.

3. Pedro Bautista Pino, *Three New Mexico Chronicles,* p. 120.

4. Franz Huning, *Traders on the Santa Fe Trail,* p. 24.

5. Archer Butler Hulbert, ed., *Southwest on the Turquoise Trail,* pp. 155–61. The separate measurements may indicate differing qualities of fabric.

6. War Contributions, Santa Fe, 18 November 1799, in Santa Fe, SRCA, SANM II, November 18, 1799; see also Minge, pp. 13, 19 of this publication.

7. Susan Shelby Magoffin, *Down the Santa Fe Trail and Into Mexico,* p. 154.

8. Personal communication, Mr. John Yaple, Curator Emeritus, Millicent Rogers Museum, April 1977.

9. Personal communication, Alan Vedder, February 14, 1978. A twill weave saddle blanket was purchased by Vedder from a man who said it had been made thirty years ago (1930s) by his family.

10. Mildred Stapley, *Popular Weaving and Embroidery in Spain,* p. 2.

11. Dr. Minge obtained many of his room-size *jerga* from older homes where layers of linoleum were being torn up. Under these superimposed layers, *jerga,* in remarkable condition, was discovered. Perhaps a wealth of *jerga* still remains protected by linoleum!

12. Marianne Stoller, p. 45 of this publication.

13. See Stoller, p. 51 of this publication.

CHAPTER 15

1. Marianne Stoller, "Hispanic Arts and Crafts of the San Luis Valley," p. II–9.

2. Irene Emery, "Wool Embroideries of New Mexico: Some Notes on the Stitch Employed"; Irene Emery, "Wool Embroideries of New Mexico: Notes on Some of the Spanish Terms."

3. E. Boyd, *Popular Arts of Spanish New Mexico,* p. 210.

4. Marianne Stoller, p. II–12.

5. Jacqueline Enthoven, "The Bokhara Stitch and Colcha Embroidery," p. 37.

6. Emery, "Wool Embroideries . . . Stitch Employed," p. 344.

7. For further discussion of *sabanilla,* see Nora Fisher, p. 144 ff. of this publication.

8. See Appendix E, UCLA D32–10, p. 214 of this publication.

9. See Appendix E, UCLA D32–11, p. 214 of this publication.

10. E. Boyd, MNM records, A.5.54.9. A likely source for this checkered design may be a type of checkered tapestry-woven *sarape* from Querétaro, IFAF FA.70.37.14.

11. Nelson 63–52, Taylor 3737, TM 1965.59.1.

12. SCAS L.5.60.5 and SCAS L.5.60.6 are the two textiles made of cotton sacking and knitting yarn. Closely related are MNM P.10.52.2 and MAI 17/7295.

13. SCAS L.5.63.5.

14. Also MAI 7/685, a badly damaged textile displaying a double-headed eagle at either end.

15. Boyd, *Popular Arts,* p. 213.

16. Santa Fe, SRCA, Archives of the Archdiocese of Santa Fe, *Book of Accounts,* Books XXIV and XXXIX, Santa Cruz (Box 1), 1761–1818. Typically, the Carmelite arms would be presented in a shield-shaped form rather than a heart-shaped form. The Carmelite arms contain a cross, represented as being on top of Mount Carmel, with a star in the bottom center of the Mount and two stars in the field at either side of the cross which represent Saint Theresa of Avila and Saint John of the Cross. Normally the two stars are not connected by a crescent-shaped form at the bottom of the cross but, instead, float in the field at either side of the cross. Fray Angélico Chávez, personal communication, February 7, 1978. Cover of the *Ordo for the Recitation of the Divine Office and Celebration of Mass, 1977,* Carmelite Priory, London, 1976, courtesy of the Carmelite Monastery, Santa Fe, New Mexico.

17. John Irwin and Katharine B. Brett, *Origins of Chintz,* p. 19. Irwin and Brett have devoted many years to a study of the Indian textile trade. The subject is extremely complex, involving numerous documents and a great deal of reciprocal influence. The leaves in the Indian chintz fabrics, for example, may in fact be sixteenth-century Flemish verdure tapestries as their design source. Leaves and related motifs similar to those illustrated in Plate 66 inspired chair covering made by WPA *colcha* workers in the 1930s. (Personal communication, Concha Ortiz y Pino de Kleven. July 2, 1978.)

18. Irwin and Brett, p. 69, Figures 29 and 30, Plates 28B and 62B.

19. Ibid., p. 1.

20. Ibid.

21. Ibid.

22. Joe Ben Wheat, "Spanish Weaving Terms Used in the Documents." In the course of research, Joe Wheat has compiled this list which gives us easy reference to the names of imported fabrics.

23. Irwin and Brett, p. 1, n.2.

24. Wheat, p. 11.

25. Boyd, *Popular Arts,* p. 218.

26. William Lytle Schurz, *The Manila Galleon,* p. 361.

27. Cordelia P. Snow, Santa Fe, personal communication, January 23, 1978. See note on file (Library, Museum of International Folk Art) which details references concerning these excavations of Ming Dynasty (ca. 1644) and Ching Dynasty, K'ang-hsi era (1622–1722) porcelains.

28. Schurz, p. 362.

29. Ibid., p. 32.

30. Ibid.

31. Ibid., p. 137.

32. Abelardo Carrillo y Gariel, *El Traje en la Nueva España,* Figure 62 and Figure 60.

33. Santa Fe, SRCA, AASF, Accounts, XXXXVI, Santa Cruz (Box 1), 1782–95, post 1787. The three pictorial embroideries are those illustrated in Figure 4, Plate 68, and MAI 7/685, not illustrated. See note 13.

34. Boyd, *Popular Arts,* p. 213.

35. Ibid. Though the Carmelite lay organization gained wide popularity throughout northern New Mexico, Santa Cruz remained its center.

36. MNM records, SCAS L.5.58.41, MNM A.5.54.10.

37. Stoller, p. II–17.

38. Emery, "Wool Embroideries . . . Stitch Employed," p. 344.

39. Emery, "Wool Embroideries . . . Spanish Terms," p. 143.

40. Boyd, *Popular Arts,* pp. 214–20.

41. Ibid., p. 218.

42. Emery, "Wool Embroideries . . . Spanish Terms," p. 143. Others have asserted that this fabric is definitely machine-made, but the selvedges do have an uneven quality which may indicate that it was handwoven. It is very difficult, with a fabric such as this cotton twill, to distinguish between the hand- and machine-woven. Furthermore, it is also difficult to define just what is meant by the term *handwoven* with this type of fabric.

43. Boyd, *Popular Arts,* p. 217.

44. Cf. Taylor 5093.

45. Stoller, pp. II–13; also II–16, II–18.

46. Stoller, p. II–16.

47. Boyd, *Popular Arts,* p. 216.

48. *Crewel* yarn is defined as twisted, plied, worsted (straight long-staple) wool yarn. See Catherine A. Hedlund, *A Primer of New England Crewel Embroidery,* p. 5.

49. Letter from Donald King, Keeper, Department of Textiles, Victoria and Albert Museum, November 25, 1977. Donald King also states that Plate 68 might show some relationship to Portuguese embroidery, and Plate 65 to North American bed rugs. He sent three photos of Portuguese embroideries to be used for comparative purposes; one contains birds that relate to those in Plate 68, while the other two use a variation of the couching stitch. On file, Library, Museum of International Folk Art.

50. Irwin and Brett, Plates 22, 58, 61, 63B, etc.

51. Hedlund, pp. 2, 3, 18.

52. MNM 2677, MNM A.63.4.2, Taylor 1623.

53. Personal communication, Dorothy Bowen, 1977. Photos and documentation on file at the Museum of International Folk Art.

54. Witte, 30–4114–93G.

55. Boyd, *Popular Arts,* p. 215, Figure 133.

56. Ibid., p. 220.

57. E. Boyd, Museum of New Mexico records. Due to the fact that the Catholic Church decrees that an altar must be left bare, use of a cloth in this manner is unusual. This regulation was apparently waived, however, in the case of private family chapels. (Personal communication, Father Cuesta.) Several other wool-on-cotton *colcha* embroideries illustrate a similar divided design: Taylor 3789 and 5094.

58. Museum of New Mexico records, MNM A.76.66.1.

59. Museum of New Mexico records, MNM A.67.44.1. The chapel has since been destroyed.

60. See Charlene Cerny and Christine Mather, p. 182 ff. of this publication.

61. For further details regarding these revival embroideries, see Cerny and Mather, p. 180 ff. of this publication.

62. Elmer Shupe, personal communication, March 18, 1977; María Chabot, Albuquerque, personal communication, May 10, 1977.

63. Emery, "Wool Embroideries . . . Spanish Terms," p. 151.

64. Ward Alan Minge, pp. 18 etc, of this publication. (Reference to the inventory in the Santuario is on p. 20.)

65. Emery, "Wool Embroideries . . . Stitch Employed," p. 339.

66. Laura Martínez Mullins, personal communication, December 15, 1977. She is the only Spanish woman presently known to have learned *colcha* work directly from her family. Her comments reinforced our suspicion that *colcha* work may have been the leisure-time product of the wealthier class.

67. Emery, "Wool Embroideries . . . Stitch Employed," p. 344.

68. See note 33 above.

69. Boyd, *Popular Arts,* p. 218.

70. Stoller, p. II–9.

CHAPTER 16

1. Charles Briggs, "To Talk in Different Tongues," pp. 37–51. An enlightening discussion of the effects which patronage had upon one man's art.

2. The term *Anglo* or *Anglo-American* in New Mexico refers to all non-Indian non-Spanish people.

3. Nelson H. H. Graburn must be cited for his innovative work on the arts of acculturation. The chart is based in part on discussion in his introduction to *Ethnic and Tourist Arts.*

4. This shift in function for the blanket was certainly not the only transformation made, nor were all woven textiles made for, or used as, rugs. But, this particular transformation has been the most enduring. Items such as couch throws, car robes, baby blankets, draperies, table runners and scarves, coats, vests, neckties, and bedspreads were more subject to the rigors of fashion. The earliest noted reference to a "Chimallo rug" is 1901, Santa Fe, Museum of International Folk Art, Fred Harvey Company Blanket Books. By the 1930s, with the more active involvement of Anglo patronage and the establishment of vocational schools, Spanish New Mexican weavings were frequently suggested for use as rugs; see: Wayne Mauzy, "Santa Fe's Native Market," p. 70; John E. Lawler, "Spanish-American Normal School," p. 28; Ina Sizer Cassidy, "Art and Artists of New Mexico," May, 1941, p. 23; Ina Sizer Cassidy, "Art and Artists of New Mexico," September, 1940, pp. 44–45.

5. Col. Henry Inman, *The Old Santa Fe Trail,* p. 44.

6. See Ward Alan Minge, pp. 25-26 , Joe Ben Wheat, p. 32 of this publication. These incomplete *guías* record that 20,000 textiles were exported from New Mexico in a single year. This high rate of production in 1840 indicates the great importance weaving had in the New Mexican economy prior to the 1880s.

7. Comment based upon lecture by George A. Kubler, "The Arts: Fine and Plain." Winterthur Conference on American Folk Art, November 11, 1977.

8. Graburn, Introduction.

.9. For specific sizes, see p. 171 of this publication.

10. Gene F. Doyle, "Candelario's Fabulous Curios," p. 5.

11. Santa Fe, Museum of International Folk Art, Fred Harvey Blanket Books, 1900–39.

12. Ibid.

13. History Library of the Museum of New Mexico, Candelario Business Correspondence, 1909–10, M72–5/20 Box 11.

14. Ibid.

15. Ibid.

16. Ibid.

17. Department of the Interior, Census Office, 1883, pp. 728, 740.

18. See Nora Fisher and Joe Ben Wheat, p. 197 ff. of this publication for discussion concerning decline of quality in wools.

19. Earl Pomeroy, *In Search of the Golden West,* p. 65, quoting Lord Dunraven's *Past Times and Pastimes* (London: Hodder & Stoughton, Ltd., 1922), vol. 1, pp. 72–73.

20. Pomeroy, p. 65, quoting Lord Dunraven, pp. 7–9.

21. William Seale, *The Tasteful Interlude,* pp. 21, 238, 239.

22. Neil M. Clark, *The Weavers of Chimayo,* unpaginated.

23. Marta Weigle, ed., *Hispanic Villages of New Mexico,* p. 90.

24. Ibid., p. 91.

25. George McCrossen, "The Handweaving Phenomenon in the Southwest During the Two Decades Between 1930–1950," p. 29.

26. Ibid., p. 22.

27. Erna Fergusson, *New Mexico,* pp. 366–78.

28. See Briggs for an interesting discussion of the relationship between Anglo patrons and Spanish craftsmen during this period.

29. Betty Toulouse, "Pueblo Pottery Traditions, Ever Constant, Ever Changing," pp. 24–26.

30. Santa Fe, Spanish Colonial Arts Society, from the original Certificate of Incorporation of the Spanish Colonial Arts Society, Inc., 1929.

31. The shop was also known by the name of "Spanish Arts Shop."

32. Mary Austin, "Spanish Colonial Furnishings in New Mexico," p. 49. Nowhere else in the literature of this period was any other mention made of this *colcha* embroidery revival effort. It seems evident, however, that Nellie Dunton, herself an avid *colcha* stitcher, would have played some role. See Fisher, p. 153 ff. of this publication for a detailed description of the *colcha* stitch.

33. "Fiesta Event: The Spanish Colonial Arts Society," pp. 105–6.

34. Sarah Nestor, *The Native Market of the Spanish New Mexican Craftsmen,* p. 18.

35. Ibid., p. 25.

36. Ibid.

37. Interview with David Salazar, Santa Fe, Winter, 1977. It should be noted that Salazar, born in 1901, learned to weave upon his own initiative, in part by observing the aged sheepherder and weaver Bartolo Rael of La Ciénega shortly before his death in 1912. Salazar at seventy-six is still weaving today, lives in Ribera, New Mexico, and is the last known weaver to be making *jerga*. He still spins and dyes all his own yarns, and uses only natural dyes, including cochineal, as well as un-dyed wools.

38. Interview with Tillie Gabaldón Stark, Santa Fe, December 15, 1977. See Tierney, pp. 217 ff. of this publication for suggested botanical names of these plants; see also Dorothy Boyd Bowen and Trish Spillman, p. 207 of this publication.

39. Mauzy, p. 70, and Nestor, p. 25.

40. Mauzy, p. 70.

41. Mary W. Coan, "Handicraft Arts Revived," p. 13.

42. Mauzy, p. 69.

43. Lawler, p. 28.

44. [Carmen Espinosa] NM Dept. of Vocational Education. *NM Colonial Embroidery*.

45. Interview with Carmen Espinosa, Albuquerque, May 10, 1977.

46. Muriel Haskel, "The Mormon Church West of the Rio Grande," pp. 1–4.

47. Elmer Shupe, in an interview in Taos on March 17, 1977, relates that as early as 1904, when his father was the Singer Sewing Machine agent and living in Mariana, he would take old blankets in trade for sewing machines. Shupe actually began dealing in blankets ca. 1922, which he recalls as a "bad year" in Carson. That year he took a job with the railroad in Alamosa, Colorado and in his spare time would ride on his bicycle purchasing blankets in nearby villages. But in 1927 he was laid off for two weeks. He spent a week buying and selling blankets full-time, and cleared a hefty $800.00 profit. Thus began his career as a blanket trader.

48. Interview with Frances Graves, Los Córdovas, New Mexico, March 17, 1977. This old checked

colcha may well be the one represented in Plate 67 which was purchased from Elmer Shupe in 1954.

49. These two Spanish sisters had married the two Mormon Graves brothers.

50. Frances Graves expressed her distaste for the Penitente pieces which Wayne Graves made, stating she felt it was "wrong" to do these. She continues to do *colcha* embroidery today, still preferring to execute images of saints to other themes.

51. Santa Fe, MNM accession records. See also Boyd, *Popular Arts*, p. 214.

52. Such avid collectors as Florence Dibell Bartlett and Mary Cabot Wheelwright purchased many of these wool-on-wool embroideries for prices in the hundreds of dollars, at a time when older pieces were selling for $500 to $800 apiece. During the Depression, such a purchase would have involved a sizeable investment on the part of the buyer—and a not insignificant stimulus to the struggling Carson economy.

53. Nellie Dunton, compil. *The Spanish Colonial Ornament and the Motifs Depicted in the Textiles of the Period of the American Southwest, Compiled and Arranged by Nellie Dunton*.

54. Telephone interview with María T. Luján, December 15, 1977.

55. Rebecca James, *The Colcha Stitch*, contains illustrations of the work of Rebecca James.

56. The Spanish Market was revived in 1965 by the late E. Boyd under the aegis of the Spanish Colonial Arts Society. It is now held in late July of each year under the portal of the Palace of the Governors. It is gratifying to note that while in 1965 only sixteen craftsmen participated, in 1977 thirty were admitted. There is also a growing interest on the part of younger craftsmen, particularly in the areas of woodcarving and weaving.

57. The Romeros also use strips of woven textiles, which they purchase from Ortega's Weaving Shop in Chimayó, in much the same manner.

58. Mrs. Orrego-Salas, who lives in Bloomington, Indiana, initiated a crewel embroidery project in Ninhue, Chile in 1971. The charming naive embroideries produced by that village have attracted considerable attention in Chile and the United States and continue to be a source of income for the Ninhueños. Crewelwork, in contrast to *colcha* work, involves the use of many stitches and is always worked using a plied woolen yarn.

59. Santa Fe, Library, Museum of International Folk Art, slides, tapes, and transcripts documenting the Villaneuva Embroidery, 1976.

60. Helen Cramp, "The Old Santo Maker," pp. 29, 46; and E. Boyd, "Celso Gallegos—A Truly Spontaneous Primitive Artist," pp. 215, 216.

61. Unpublished accession records at the Museum of International Folk Art, Santa Fe, for MNM A.5.59.22.

62. Collections at the Museum of International Folk Art, Santa Fe: SCAS L.5.72.4, MNM A.5.59.22, SCAS L.5.70.11, SCAS L.5.70.12.

63. See Irene Emery, "Samplers Embroidered in String," pp. 35–51, for a more complete discussion of some of the technical aspect of Valencia's work as well as transcriptions of embroideries. Emery did an outstanding job of unearthing the true identity of this artist.

64. E. Boyd Collection, Santa Fe, SRCA.

65. Collections at the Museum of International Folk Art, Santa Fe: MNM B89/13, MNM B89/48, A.8.54.1, MNM A.9.54.28M, MNM A.5.54.3, MNM A.9.54.59M, SCAS L.5.53.39, SCAS L.5.54.40; one Policarpio Valencia in Fred Harvey Collections at the Heard Museum, Phoenix, Arizona.

66. Museum of International Folk Art, accession number A.9.54.28M.

67. E. Boyd Collection, Santa Fe, SRCA, from information provided to E. Boyd by Dr. Rubén Cobos, University of New Mexico.

68. Telephone interview with David Ortega, December 28, 1977.

69. In 1971 Alfredo Córdova opened his own weaving shop in Truchas. At the time of this writing he, his wife Gabrielita, and son Harry weave banded and Pan-Southwestern designs for sale in the shop.

70. Walter Briggs, "Truchas Weaves for the World," p. 32.

71. Epifania Archuleta, Cordelia Coronado, Luisa García, Gertrudes Manzanares, and Georgia Serrano.

72. Interview with Cordelia Coronado, Medanales, Winter, 1976.

73. A revolving fund for materials has been provided by the Society of Friends in Santa Fe, which enables the weavers to buy materials.

74. These workshops were made possible by grants from the Los Alamos Arts Council, the New Mexico Arts Commission, and the National Endowment for the Arts.

75. For a more complete description of these workshops, see Trish Spillman, "Rio Grande Weaving and Dyeing Workshop," pp. 14–24.

APPENDIX A

1. A loom is a machine for *weaving* (interlacing a set of warp threads with a set of weft threads). A loom holds the warp taut, and usually incorporates a *shedding device,* by means of which the warp threads can be separated into groups and then pulled apart to form an opening or shed, through which the weft passes or is "thrown" when wound on a shuttle. The 1977 Irene Emery Textile Roundtable at the Textile Museum in Washington, D.C., was devoted entirely to the subject of the loom. There are innumerable definitions of this machine. Cf. Irene Emery, *The Primary Structures of Fabrics,* p. 75; Kate Kent, "The Cultivation and Weaving of Cotton in the Prehistoric Southwestern United States," p. 483; and Marta Hoffmann, *The Warp-Weighted Loom,* p. 5.

2. Kent, pp. 483–89.

3. See note 1 above.

4. Hoffmann, p. 336.

5. Ibid., p. 258.

6. The first European illustration of the treadle loom, ca. A.D. 1200, was identified because distinctive new design loom parts were included in the drawing. Hoffmann, pp. 259–61.

7. Ibid., pp. 259–96. As is usually the case with the introduction of a whole complex of tools, certain of the indigenous tools were retained and adopted by the Spanish. Most noteworthy, the *malacate,* or Pueblo Indian spindle, has continued to be used even in the twentieth century, while the spinning wheel was extremely slow to gain popularity in New Mexico. For further discussion of spinning and the *malacate* see Nora Fisher and Joe Ben Wheat, p. 198 ff. of this publication.

8. Hoffmann, p. 258 ff.

9. Lansing B. Bloom, "A Trade Invoice of 1638," p. 244, translating an invoice found in Parral, Chihuahua, Mexico. A *vara* is a short meter or yard, measuring approximately 84 cm. (33 inches). For a more detailed description of *sayal* see Nora Fisher, pp. 144 ff. of this publication.

10. France V. Scholes, "Church and State in New Mexico, 1610–1650," p. 307, n.25; Ibid., p. 300, n.6, citing Petition of Francisco de Salazar, July 5, 1641, A.G.I., Patronato 247, Ramo 7. Most of the laborers in the workshop were Indians, including Mexican Indians (Ibid., p. 300, n.6e).

11. Bloom, "Trade Invoice," pp. 244–45. The shipment also included buffalo hides, chamois, candles, clothing, and many types of processed textiles. Of the textiles, we have good reason to assume that the 50 hangings or *reposteros* and the 126 small blankets or *mantas* were of Pueblo Indian manufacture (Scholes, p. 300, n.6). While Lansing Bloom was the first to translate the 1638 invoice (Bloom, "Trade Invoice,") E. Boyd, *Popular Arts of Spanish New Mexico,* pp. 188–89. Joe Ben Wheat should be credited with placing this information in perspective—acknowledging *sayal* production as the proof of the treadle loom and mentioning Rosas' confiscation of looms (Wheat, personal communication, 1977).

12. Harry Percival Mera, *Spanish-American Blanketry,* p. 22; Boyd, *Popular Arts,* p. 188. As Mera notes, some wills between 1750 and 1800 described looms. For further comments on the lack of information in the documents concerning looms see Minge, p. 12 ff. of this publication.

13. Lansing B. Bloom, "Early Weaving in New Mexico," p. 229. In 1664 Governor Briceño forbade the church "to employ Indian women in spinning, weaving *mantas,* stockings, or any other things without express license from me or from him who may govern in my place." The governor was seeking control over the church, but he was at the same time protecting a vested interest in the textile industry.

14. Virginia Langham Olmstead, transl. and compil., *Spanish and Mexican Colonial Censuses of New Mexico, 1790, 1823, 1845.*

15. Ibid.

16. Bloom, "Early Weaving," p. 233, citing Santa Fe, SRCA, SANM II, August 28, 1803.

17. For mention of looms built by the Bazáns see Minge, p. 22 of this publication.

18. Bloom, "Early Weaving," p. 235, citing Santa Fe, SRCA, SANM II, September 3, 1805.

19. Pedro Bautista Pino, *Three New Mexico Chronicles,* p. 36.

20. For references to women weavers, see pp. 45, 49, 123, and 178 of this publication. Women were known to have woven not only blankets, but also almost all of the *sabanilla* and lighter weight fabrics. Today, though the big Spanish loom is essentially a man's tool, women may even outnumber men as weavers.

APPENDIX B

1. Silk yarns were imported widely during colonial times, probably for use by the Spanish for embroidery. Silk was rarely used in weaving, but two Navajo blankets of silk are known, both collected in the early 1860s. They are woven from 3-ply commercial silk yarn, dyed with natural dyes in a wide variety of colors. Silk also appears in some fine Saltillo *sarapes*. Three other Navajo blankets, dating about 1895 to 1900, were woven from single-ply floss silk yarn, dyed with synthetic dyes. While linen was widely used for warps in Saltillo weaving, it has been noted in southwestern weaving in only two or three Navajo blankets dating about 1860.

2. Irene Emery, *The Primary Structures of Fabrics,* p. 11.

3. Although a variety of abbreviations and symbols exist for the description of yarn twist, for the sake of clarity all descriptions in this publication are written out. Thus, a single-ply yarn is referred to as 1-ply, Z-spun, or single-Z-spun; a 2-, 3-, or multiply yarn is referred to as a 2-ply, 3-ply, multi-ply, or, in full, for example 3-Z-spun-plied-S. As demonstrated, hyphens are employed throughout to delineate the description of an individual yarn unit. Cf. Emery, *Primary Structures,* p. 13 for further discussion of this subject. In the Southwest, the presence of S-spun yarn indicates that the yarn is raveled from commercial cloth.

4. Jean M. Burroughs, "From Coronado's Churros," p. 9. Cf. Charles Wayland Towne and Edward Norris Wentworth, *Shepherd's Empire,* p. 4; E. Boyd, *Popular Arts of Spanish New Mexico,* pp. 189, 192, 193. Joe Wheat was the first to point out that there has been a great deal of confusion in identifying the type of wool used by the early Spanish. Joe Ben Wheat, "Spanish-American and Navajo Weaving, 1600 to Now," p. 201, n.10. It was not Merino. Closely related to the Rambouillet, Merino is an "improved" wool, extremely fine, kinky, greasy, and difficult to hand process.

5. James O. Grandstaff, *Wool Characteristics in Relation to Navajo Weaving,* p. 4. The small Navajo sheep is descended from the Spanish *churro.* Due to the obvious coarsening of Navajo weaving, "a study was made by the United States Department of Agriculture, in cooperation with the Department of the Interior, at the Southwestern Range and Sheep Breeding Laboratory, Fort Wingate, N.M., from 1937 to 1939, to determine the physical characters of Navajo wool that make it particularly adapted to hand-weaving by Navajo women." (Grandstaff, p. 34). Grandstaff describes the careful comparison of wool characteristics of a variety of the earlier Navajo textiles with that of the new improved Rambouillet. In the choice of available wools, Spanish weaving seems to parallel Navajo weaving.

6. See Grandstaff, p. 23.

7. The "Mexicans" along the Rio Grande were using the spinning wheel at least by the 1880s. Washington Matthews, "Navajo Weavers," p. 376.

8. Marianne Stoller, p. 49 of this publication.

9. See Dorothy Boyd Bowen, p. 6 of this publication.

10. See Gail Tierney, "Plants for the Dyepot," p. 30. See also Kate Kent, "The Cultivation and Weaving of Cotton in the Prehistoric Southwestern United States," *passim,* for full discussion of prehistoric cotton cultivation in the Southwest.

11. See Bowen, p. 140 ff. of this publication. Native cotton was first supplemented and then largely replaced in the 1930s by commercial cotton batting purchased at the trading posts. Commercial wool cards, introduced by the Spanish, had long since replaced the whipping technique for ginning cotton, but the same technique was used for spinning the commercial batting. Among the Pueblos, handspun cotton continued to be the primary material for ceremonial garments such as kilts, kachina sashes, wedding blankets, and embroidered dance shawls. Today, handspun yarn of native cotton or cotton batting is used by the Hopi for weaving and by some other Pueblos in minor ceremonial ways.

12. Boyd, *Popular Arts,* p. 201.

13. See Nora Fisher, p. 144 ff. of this publication.

14. For a related discussion of the use of raveled yarns see Anthony Berlandt and Mary Hunt Kahlenberg, *Walk in Beauty,* p. 51 ff.

15. Saltzman's identification of *lac* Z-spun yarn, apparently raveled, in Taylor 3772 would date this cotton blanket before 1825.

16. The blanket in Plate 51 contains carded pink handspun yarn.

17. The blanket in Bowen, p. 97, Figure 7 of this publication, contains bundled strips of what appears to be cochineal-dyed fabric.

18. Saxony yarn appears in the blankets in Plates 23, 37, 38, 39, 40, 51, 54, 55, and 62 of this publication.

19. This yarn appears in the blankets in Plates 40, 51, 54, 55, and 56 of this publication.

20. Four-ply Germantown yarn appears in Plates 41, 42, 49, 55, and 56 of this publication.

APPENDIX C

1. Irene Emery, *The Primary Structures of Fabrics,* p. 17. Note: Irene Emery, *The Primary Structures of Fabrics,* is quoted extensively throughout this appendix.

2. Ibid., p. vii.

3. Ibid., p. 75.

4. Ibid., p. 76.

5. Nora Fisher, p. 144 ff. of this publication.

6. Emery, *Primary Structures,* p. 77.

7. Ibid., p. 156.

8. Ibid., p. 88.

9. Ibid., p. 78.

10. Ibid., p. 79.

11. Ibid., pp. 80–81.

12. Ibid., pp. 82–83. Frequently the effect of *eccentric tapestry weave* is achieved in the Rio Grande blankets by the subsequent addition of small embroidered inserts. (See Plates 14, 61, and 62.)

13. Emery, *Primary Structures*, p. 92. "In *simple interlacing* [of one set of wefts with one set of warps] any deviation from the consistent alternation which characterizes *plain weave* necessarily produces warp and weft floats." "*Float:* any portion of a warp or weft element that extends unbound over two or more units of the opposite set on either face of a fabric." (Ibid., p. 75.)

14. Ibid., p. 92. For *twill weave,* "a minimum of three warp groupings is essential (four, for warp and weft floats of equal span)." Thus, all four harnesses of the treadle loom were used for the production of the *twill-woven* fabrics.

15. Ibid., p. 92.

16. Many Rio Grande blankets have been extensively repaired. Navajo weavers were frequently employed as repairers. Thus, Navajo-style selvedge cords and related corner tassels are frequently found to have been added to Rio Grande blankets. One must take care to realize that this is the result of repair work.

17. See Emery, *Primary Structures*, p. 234.

APPENDIX D

1. Ward Alan Minge, pp. 20, 22, 24 of this publication.

2. Mela Sedillo-Brewster, "New Mexican Weaving and the Practical Vegetable Dyes from Spanish Colonial Times," p. 23.

3. Mordant was originally believed to corrode the fibers, allowing them to accept the color. It was later found that mordants fix the dye. R. L. M. Allen, *Colour Chemistry,* p. 6.

4. Governor Chacón reported in 1803 that urine was used in dyeing with native herbs. Santa Fe, SRCA, SANM II, August 28, 1803.

5. Conversation with Tillie Stark, Dec. 15, 1977, recorded on tape, Library, Museum of International Folk Art, Santa Fe, New Mexico.

6. Personal communication, Joe Ben Wheat, February 21, 1977.

7. Of the many New Mexican *cazos* (copper pots) in the collection of Ward Alan Minge, all of the large ones are untinned.

8. W. A. Vetterli, "The History of Indigo," pp. 3066–67.

9. Joseph Bruyas, "Les Procédes de Teinture de L'Amérique Précolombienne," p. 429.

10. Sedillo-Brewster, p. 30.

11. Washington Matthews, "Navajo Weavers," p. 376.

12. MNM 26119/12, MNM A.64.27.2, MNM A.5.54.6, and SCAS L.5.62.69. Indigo, but no yellow, appeared in the dull blue-green of SCAS L.5.62.83.

13. E. Boyd, *Popular Arts of Spanish New Mexico*, pp. 317–26.

14. In eighteenth-century New Spain, brazil was known to produce several hues depending on the mordant: *morado de brasil* (mulberry brazil), *leonado de brasil* (tawny brazil), *encarnado de brasil* (red brazil), and *envinado de brasil* (wine-hue brazil). Abelardo Carrillo y Gariel, *El Traje en la Nueva España*, p. 35.

15. Franco Brunello, *The Art of Dyeing in the History of Mankind,* p. 337.

16. Rita J. Adrosko, *Natural Dyes and Home Dyeing,* p. 26. *Haematoxylon* is normally referred to as logwood—this is the exception.

17. SCAS L.5.58.41, HSNM A.5.57.35, SCAS L.5.62.70, SCAS L.5.62.73, UC 18088, and FH L.71.17.2. See also Fisher, pp. 212-14 of this publication.

18. Santa Fe, SRCA, SANM II, Aug. 28, 1803. Translation by Myra Ellen Jenkins.

19. Charles Avery Amsden, *Navajo Weaving, Its Technique and Its History,* p. 89.

20. Ibid.

21. George Wharton James, *Indian Blankets and Their Makers,* p. 30.

22. Nonabah G. Bryan, *Navajo Native Dyes, passim.*

23. Adrosko, p. 24. For the definitive study of cochineal see R. A. Donkin, *Spanish Red,* 1977.

24. Abelardo Carrillo y Gariel, *El Traje en la Nueva España,* p. 35.

25. Manuel Carrera Stampa, *Los Gremios Mexicanos,* p. 171.

26. Minge, p. 26 of this publication.

27. Conversation with Tillie Stark, December 15, 1977.

28. UCLA D–34.48, D–35–67, D–35–69 and D–67–76. It has also been identified by Saltzman in a Navajo textile in the collection of the University of Colorado Museum.

29. Adrosko, pp. 28–30.

30. Ibid., pp. 21, 23.

31. William C. Martin and Edward F. Castetter, *A Checklist of Gymnosperms and Angiosperms of New Mexico,* p. 160.

32. Adrosko, p. 8.

33. Hubert Howe Bancroft, *California Pastoral,* p. 466.

34. Brunello, p. 149.

35. L. S. M. Curtin, *Healing Herbs of the Upper Rio Grande,* p. 57.

36. Tibo J. Chávez, *New Mexican Folklore of the Rio Abajo,* p. 32.

37. Gail Tierney, "Plants for the Dyepot," pp. 29, 31.

38. See Brunello, p. 301, for a more complete chronological list of the early synthetic dyes. Samples from Plate 51 do not dissolve in alcohol and are not likely to be either the rare Mauve or more common Methyl violet. Saltzman (personal communication, June 25, 1978).

39. SAR, SF 7236/12 and UC 18088.

40. Brunello, p. 293.

41. Conversation with Tillie Stark, December 15, 1977.

APPENDIX E

1. See Dorothy Boyd Bowen and Trish Spillman, pp. 207-11 of this publication; Minge, pp. 20-22, 24 of this publication.

2. See Gail Tierney, p. 217 ff. of this publication.

3. Saltzman, "Color Matching via Pigment Identification," p. 4.

4. Ibid., p. 5.

5. Saltzman, *et al.,* "The Identification of Colorants in Ancient Textiles," p. 243.

6. Ibid.

7. Ibid., p. 247.

8. The last test included a cochineal-dyed 1-ply yarn (Plate 22, D67–75).

9. See Bowen and Spillman, pp. 209-10 of this publication, and Bowen, p. 123, Plate 53 of this publication.

10. See Bowen and Spillman, p. 207 ff. of this publication.

11. E. Boyd, *Popular Arts of Spanish New Mexico,* p. 175, Plate 12.

12. See Trish Spillman, p. 66 of this publication.

13. Saltzman, p. 216, n. 10 of this publication.

14. See Bowen and Spillman, p. 210 ff. of this publication and Saltzman, p. 214, n. 1, 5, and 7 of this publication.

15. Saltzman, p. 215, D–32–17, D–32–18, and p. 215, n. 6 of this publication.

PUBLIC COLLECTIONS OF TEXTILES RESEARCHED

INSTITUTION	CITY/STATE	ABBREVIATION	RIO GRANDE BLANKETS	OTHER RIO GRANDE TEXTILES*	MEXICAN TEXTILES	MISCELLANEOUS**	TOTAL
Northeastern United States							
Peabody Museum of Archaeology and Ethnology, Harvard University	Cambridge, Mass.	Peabody	22	—	20	2	44
Yale University Art Gallery	New Haven, Conn.	Yale	5	4	—	—	9
American Museum of Natural History	New York City, New York	AMNH	33	—	93	—	126
Hispanic Society of America	New York City, New York	HSA	—	—	2	—	2
Museum of the American Indian, Heye Foundation	New York City, New York	MAI	63	10	63	3	139
Middle Atlantic and Southern United States							
The University Museum of the University of Pennsylvania	Philadelphia, Pennsylvania	UMP	19	—	9	—	28
Smithsonian Institution, National Museum of History and Technology Department of Cultural History***	Washington, D.C.	USNM	3	5	2	—	10
The Textile Museum	Washington, D.C.	TM	9	5	35	2	51
Lowe Art Museum	Coral Gables, Florida	Lowe	37	2	1	—	40
Midwestern United States							
Denison University Gallery	Granville, Ohio	Denison	—	—	10	—	10
Milwaukee Public Museum	Milwaukee, Wisconsin	MPM	7	—	—	—	7
Field Museum of Natural History	Chicago, Illinois	Field	8	—	34	—	42
William Rockhill Nelson Galley and Atkins Museum of Fine Arts	Kansas City, Missouri	Nelson	—	1	—	—	1
Texas							
El Paso Centennial Museum	El Paso, Texas	El Paso	6	—	3	—	9
McNay Art Institute	San Antonio, Texas	McNay	18	—	3	—	21

*Includes *jerga, colcha, sabanilla,* etc.

**Mainly includes fabrics mistakenly attributed to Southwest Spanish, such as German-made imitations of Saltillo *sarapes.*

***This indicates Spanish textiles only within one department. Additional textiles in other departments of the Smithsonian.

INSTITUTION	CITY/ STATE	ABBREVIATION	RIO GRANDE BLANKETS	OTHER RIO GRANDE TEXTILES*	MEXICAN TEXTILES	MISCELLANEOUS**	TOTAL
Panhandle-Plains Historical Museum	Canyon, Texas	Panhandle	1	—	1	—	2
The San Antonio Museum Association, Witte Memorial Museum	San Antonio, Texas	Witte	—	—	16	1	17
Colorado							
The Colorado College	Colorado Springs, Colorado	CC	1	—	—	—	1
The Denver Art Museum	Denver, Colorado	DAM	21	1	4	—	26
Denver Museum of Natural History	Denver, Colorado	DMNH	34	2	12	—	48
State Historical Society of Colorado	Denver, Colorado	CSHS	64	12	6	3	85
The Taylor Museum, Colorado Springs Fine Arts Center	Colorado Springs, Colorado	Taylor	112	31	32	—	175
University of Colorado Museum	Boulder, Colorado	UCM	13	2	—	—	15
New Mexico							
Maxwell Museum of Anthropology, University of New Mexico	Albuquerque, New Mexico	Maxwell	23	4	10	1	38
Museum of Albuquerque	Albuquerque, New Mexico	MA	7	4	2	—	13
Museum of New Mexico	Santa Fe, New Mexico	MNM					
Museum of International Folk Art, MNM	Santa Fe, New Mexico	MNM	59	47	12	8	126
Gift of the Historical Society of New Mexico, MNM at MOIFA	Santa Fe, New Mexico	MNM	11	16	—	—	27
International Folk Art Foundation on loan to MNM, MOIFA	Santa Fe, New Mexico	IFAF	9	7	11	4	31
Spanish Colonial Arts Society, Inc., on loan to MNM, MOIFA	Santa Fe, New Mexico	SCAS	62	63	9	1	135
Collections of the School of American Research in the MNM [MOIFA]	Santa Fe, New Mexico	SAR	—	2	—	—	2
Laboratory of Anthropology, MNM	Santa Fe, New Mexico	LAB	54	—	—	—	54

INSTITUTION	CITY/ STATE	ABBREVIATION	RIO GRANDE BLANKETS	OTHER RIO GRANDE TEXTILES*	MEXICAN TEXTILES	MISCELLANEOUS**	TOTAL
Collections of the School of American Research in the MNM [LAB]	Santa Fe, New Mexico	SAR	49	2	—	—	51
History Division, MNM	Santa Fe, New Mexico	History	10	5	—	—	15
School of American Research, Santa Fe	Santa Fe, New Mexico	SAR, SF	51	6	—	—	57
Kit Carson Memorial Foundation	Taos, New Mexico	Kit Carson	18	10	—	—	28
The Millicent A. Rogers Museum	Taos, New Mexico	MR	22	8	—	—	30
Arizona							
The Amerind Foundation, Inc.	Dragoon, Arizona	Amerind	11	—	9	—	20
Arizona State Museum, University of Arizona	Tucson, Arizona	ASM	8	1	11	5	25
Fred Harvey Fine Arts Collection	Phoenix, Arizona	FH	28	4	15	3	50
Heard Museum of Anthropology and Primitive Art	Phoenix, Arizona	Heard	22	13	5	—	40
Navajo Tribal Museum	Window Rock, Arizona	NTM	5	—	1	1	7
Museum of Northern Arizona	Flagstaff, Arizona	MNA	21	1	11	1	34
California							
Los Angeles County Museum of Natural History	Los Angeles, California	LACM	26	1	17	—	43
San Diego Museum of Man	San Diego, California	SDMM	23	—	7	—	30
Lowie Museum of Anthropology, University of California	Berkeley, California	Lowie	5	—	43	—	48
Fine Arts Museums of San Francisco, de Young Memorial Museum	Golden Gate Park, San Francisco, California	de Young	9	—	3	—	12

PLATE LIST

*NOTE: Throughout the publication, unless a dye analysis number is attached, the designation of "natural" or "synthetic" dyes is a product of educated guesswork. Asterisks indicate that some dye analysis has been performed. See Appendix E, Dye Analysis, for further details.

23. Los Angeles County Museum of Natural History, William Randolph Hearst Collection — A.5141.12 (L77.96.1)

24. Lowe Art Museum — 60.220.033 (L.77.97.2)

25. Beryl G. and Charles H. Woodard Collection, Colorado Historical Society — E.2018–15 (L.77.102.4)

26. Beryl G. and Charles H. Woodard Collection, Colorado Historical Society — E.2018–1 (L.77.102.1)

"Saltillo leaf" bands

27. Museum of New Mexico Collection at the Museum of International Folk Art — A.65.67.3

28. Spanish Colonial Arts Society, Inc. Collection on loan to the Museum of New Mexico at the Museum of International Folk Art — L.5.62.78

Combination Saltillo motif bands

29. Los Angeles County Museum of Natural History, William Randolph Hearst Collection — A.5141.19 (L.77.96.2)

30. Spanish Colonial Arts Society, Inc. Collection on loan to the Museum of New Mexico at the Museum of International Folk Art — L.5.62.68*

Saltillo design systems
"Lightning" pattern

31. Spanish Colonial Arts Society, Inc. Collection on loan to the Museum of New Mexico at the Museum of International Folk Art — L.5.62.97

32. Fred Harvey Fine Arts Collection on loan to the Museum of New Mexico at the Museum of International Folk Art — L.71.17.3

33. From the Collections of the University Museum of the University of Pennsylvania — NA 4989 (L.77.98.1)

34. From the Collection of Al Packard, Santa Fe — L.77.87.1

Basic Saltillo pattern

35. Spanish Colonial Arts Society, Inc. Collection on loan to the Museum — L.5.63.4

of New Mexico at the Museum of International Folk Art

36. Museum of New Mexico Collection at the Museum of International Folk Art — A.65.67.2

37. International Folk Art Foundation Collection at the Museum of International Folk Art — FA.67.16.1*

38. Spanish Colonial Arts Society, Inc. Collection on loan to the Museum of New Mexico at the Museum of International Folk Art — L.5.62.85*

39. Los Angeles County Museum of Natural History, William Randolph Hearst Collection — A.5141.212 (L.77.96.3)

40. Spanish Colonial Arts Society, Inc. Collection on loan to the Museum of New Mexico at the Museum of International Folk Art — L.5.62.84*

41. Museum of New Mexico Collection at the Museum of International Folk Art — A.60.21.3

42. Collections of the School of American Research in the Museum of New Mexico — 45314/12

Basic Saltillo pattern
without central lozenge

43. Lowe Art Museum — 65.050.127 (L.77.97.3)

44. Spanish Colonial Arts Society, Inc. Collection on loan to the Museum of New Mexico at the Museum of International Folk Art — L.5.70.6

45. The Taylor Museum, Colorado Springs Fine Arts Center — 5074 (L.77.93.10)

Central diamond, corner slashes,
no side borders

46. Spanish Colonial Arts Society, Inc. Collection on loan to the Museum of New Mexico at the Museum of International Folk Art — L.5.62.73*

47. From the Collection of Mr. and Mrs. Larry Frank, Arroyo Hondo, New Mexico — L.77.105.1

Concentric diamonds

48. Museum of New Mexico Collection at the Museum of International Folk Art — A.66.41.1

49. School of American Research, Santa Fe — T.438
50. Museum of New Mexico Collection at the Museum of International Folk Art — A.5.56.40

Other diamond designs

51. Spanish Colonial Arts Society, Inc. Collection on loan to the Museum of New Mexico at the Museum of International Folk Art — L.5.62.83*
52. Spanish Colonial Arts Society, Inc. Collection on loan to the Museum of New Mexico at the Museum of International Folk Art — L.5.62.79

Saltillo-derived designs, servant blanket

53. Museum of New Mexico Collection at the Museum of International Folk Art — A.5.57.10*

Vallero-style blankets

54. International Folk Art Foundation Collection at the Museum of International Folk Art — FA.67.43.3*
55. Spanish Colonial Arts Society, Inc. Collection on loan to the Museum of New Mexico at the Museum of International Folk Art — L.5.62.98*
56. Fred Harvey Fine Arts Collection on loan to the Museum of New Mexico at the Museum of International Folk Art — L.70.3.39*
57. The Taylor Museum, Colorado Springs Fine Arts Center — 5087 (L.77.93.12)
58. Museum of New Mexico Collection at the Museum of International Folk Art — A.71.20.1

Weft ikat blankets

59. International Folk Art Foundation Collection at the Museum of International Folk Art — FA.64.21.1
60. Collection of Frank Packard, on loan to the Museum of New Mexico, Laboratory of Anthropology — 36329/12

Blankets containing handspun cotton yarn

61. Spanish Colonial Arts Society, Inc. Collection on loan to the Museum of New Mexico at the Museum of International Folk Art — L.5.62.74

62. The Taylor Museum, Colorado Springs Fine Arts Center — 3773* (L.77.93.9)

OTHER RIO GRANDE TEXTILES

Jergas

63. Spanish Colonial Arts Society, Inc. Collection on loan to the Museum of New Mexico at the Museum of International Folk Art — L.5.62.95
64. Beryl G. and Charles H. Woodard Collection, Colorado Historical Society — 2018.51 (L.77.102.6)

Colcha embroideries
Wool-on-wool

65. Spanish Colonial Arts Society, Inc. on loan to the Museum of New Mexico at the Museum of International Folk Art — L.5.58.41*
66. Fred Harvey Fine Arts Collection on loan to the Museum of New Mexico at the Museum of International Folk Art — L.70.3.38
67. Museum of New Mexico Collection at the Museum of International Folk Art — A.5.54.9
68. International Folk Art Foundation Collection at the Museum of International Folk Art — FA.67.43.4

Wool-on-cotton

69. Museum of New Mexico Collection at the Museum of International Folk Art — A.67.44.1
70. Spanish Colonial Arts Society, Inc. Collection on loan to the Museum of New Mexico at the Museum of International Folk Art — L.5.73.11

TWENTIETH-CENTURY NEW MEXICAN WEAVING AND EMBROIDERY

71. Museum of New Mexico Collection at the Museum of International Folk Art — B 89/13
72. Museum of New Mexico Collection at the Museum of International Folk Art — A.76.56.1
73. Museum of New Mexico Collection at the Museum of International Folk Art. Purchased with the aid of funds from the National Endowment for the Arts and the International Folk Art Foundation — A.78.21.1

GLOSSARY

Alfombra: Floor covering; woven or pile carpet.

Algodón: Cotton.

Añil: Indigo, a plant dye. *(See* Appendices D and E.)

Baize: Generally a commercial woolen or cotton fabric napped to imitate felt. The Spanish term *bayeta* is one possible translation for baize.

Bayeta: Variety of simple yardage woven on the treadle loom in New Mexico. *(See* Chapter 13.) Yarn raveled from an imported commercial cloth, baize, was also used to make *bayeta.(See* Appendix B.)

Bayetón: Variety of simple yardage woven on treadle loom in New Mexico, generally heavier than *bayeta.*

Brazilwood: One of several red dyewoods. *(See* Appendices D and E.)

Calico: Lightweight plain weave cloth commonly used for chintz painting and named for the seaport of Calicut on the southwest coast of India; the most common import to New Mexico.

Campeche Cloth: Treadle-loom woven fabric of Mexico imported to New Mexico at an early date.

Cañaigre: A plant dye. *(See* Appendices D and F.)

Capulín: Chokecherry, possibly used as a dye. *(See* Appendices D and E.)

Card, To: To cleanse, untangle, and collect together fibers preparatory to spinning, by the use of a card (instrument for carding fibers that generally consists of bent wire teeth set closely in rows in a thick piece of leather fastened to a back).

Chamiso: Rabbit brush, a plant dye. *(See* Appendices D and F.)

Chintz: Printed calico from India, or imitations from other designated areas.

Churro: Common sheep of Spain.

Cochineal: An insect dye. *(See* Appendices D and E.)

Colcha: Bedcovering.

Colcha Embroidery: The term *colcha* has now been extended in English to include New Mexican embroideries which utilize a couching stitch called the *colcha* stitch. *(See* Chapter 15.)

Colchón: Mattress.

Cota: Indian tea, a plant dye. *(See* Appendices D and F.)

Criado(a): Indian captive adopted into a Spanish family and treated as a servant.

Eccentric Tapestry Weave: Weave in which wefts are not at right angles to the warp. *(See* Appendix C.)

Faja: Belt.

Flannel: Fabric with a napped surface.

Float Weave: Weave with floats (any portion of a weft or warp element that extends over two or more units of the opposite set). The float weave that occurs in Rio Grande blankets is twill weave. *(See* Appendix C.)

Frazada: Blanket.

Fulling: The process of shrinking and thickening(wool cloth) by moisture, heat, and pressure.

Germantown Yarn: Commercially prepared yarn. *(See* Appendix B.)

Guías: Passports which frequently contain cargo lists.

Harness: A device for raising and lowering warp threads in a loom, to form a shed. A loom can have two or more harnesses.

Heddle: One of the sets of parallel cords or wires that compose the harness used to control warp threads on a loom.

Indiana: The most common cloth imported into New Mexico, usually chintz or calico, identical to *indianilla.*

Indianilla: See indiana.

Indigo: Añil, a plant dye. *(See* Appendices D and E.)

Jerga: Spelled variously *gerga, herga, xerga.* Generally twill-woven fabric used primarily for floor covering and also under mattresses and for packing material and clothing.

Lac: An insect dye. *(See* Appendices D and E.)

Logwood: A dye related to the red dyewoods. *(See* Appendices D and E.)

Loom: A machine for weaving. *(See* Appendix A.)

Loom, Backstrap: A loom indigenous to the Western Hemisphere.

Loom, Treadle: A loom with beams which are used for storing long lengths of warp and cloth, and treadles which control the warp threads. Brought to the Western Hemisphere by the Spanish. *(See* Appendix A.)

Loom, Vertical: A loom indigenous to the Western Hemisphere, best known example of which is the Navajo loom.

Madder: A plant dye. *(See* Appendices D and E.)

Manta: Variously defined as a shawl, an Indian dress, a fabric commonly used as tribute or tax payment, treadle-loom-woven commercial cloth, or unbleached sheeting. A term whose meaning has changed over the years.

Merino: Rambouillet-Merino sheep were introduced in 1859, and crossed with the *churro.*

Mordant: A substance that fixes the dye on the wool fibers.

Mountain Mahogany: Possibly used as a dye. *(See* Appendices D and E.)

Napped: Brushed or fulled.

Obraje: Weaving workshop.

Ojo de Perdiz: Diamond or partridge eye; in Rio Grande weaving, found in *jerga.*

Ordenanzas: Guild regulations for weavers and dyers.

Plain Weave: The simplest possible interlacing of warp and weft elements to form a fabric. *(See* Appendix C.)

Ply: One of the strands in a yarn. A 2-, 3-, or 4-ply yarn consists of that many single elements twisted together. *(See* Appendix B.)

Rebozo: Shawl; traditional headcovering for women and girls imported from Mexico to New Mexico.

Reed: A device on a loom resembling a comb and used to space warp yarns evenly.

Sábana: Sheet.

Sabanilla: Variety of simple yardage woven on the treadle loom in New Mexico, usually of handspun wool. *(See* Chapters 13 and 15.)

Saltillo: A city in Mexico known for its beautiful *sarapes.*

Santero: A maker of wooden images of saints.

Sarape: A blanket or shawl worn by men.

Saxony Yarn: Commercially prepared yarn. *(See* Appendix B.)

Sayal: Variety of simple yardage woven on the treadle loom in New Mexico, harsh in quality and not finished in any way. Originally a sackcloth-type fabric used by the Franciscans for their habits. *(See* Chapter 13.)

Selvedge: Woven edge of a fabric, self edge.

Serge: A durable twill-weave fabric.

Servant Blanket: Blanket woven by an Indian captive who had been adopted by a Spanish family. *(See* Chapters 3 and 4.)

Shed: The passageway between the threads of the warp through which the shuttle is thrown, made by raising and lowering the alternate warp threads (controlled by harnesses) so as to form an opening.

Shuttle: A device used in weaving for interlacing weft with warp, by passing weft threads between warp from one side of the cloth to the other.

Slave Blanket: *See* Servant Blanket.

Spinning: The process of simultaneously drawing out and twisting fibers into a continuous strand.

Spindle: A weighted stick or tool used for spinning. In the Southwest, the indigenous spinning tool is the *malacate.*

Tápalo: Woman's shawl.

Tapestry Weave: Weft-faced plain weave fabric in which weft threads do not run from selvedge to selvedge but form the pattern, each one being woven back and forth over the warp threads only where its particular color is needed. *(See* Appendix C.)

Telar: Loom, treadle loom.

Treadle: Foot pedal on the treadle or harness loom.

Twill Weave: A textile structure in which wefts float (pass over or under two or more warp threads), frequently producing diagonal lines on the fabric surface. *(See* Appendix C.)

Vara: A short meter or yard, measuring approximately 84 cm. or 33 in.

Vermellón: Vermilion; red pigment of either mercuric sulfide or cinnabar; a dye (most likely cochineal or lac); bright red.

Warp: Set of yarns extending lengthwise on a loom. *(See* Appendices A and C.)

Wedge-Weave: Navajo eccentric tapestry-weave technique; pulled-warp weave. *(See* Plate 2.)

Weft: The set of yarns interlaced with the warp. *(See* Appendices A and C.)

Yerba: Plant; weed; herb.

BIBLIOGRAPHY

BOOKS

ADAMS, ELEANOR B., AND CHAVEZ, FRAY ANGELICO. *The Missions of New Mexico 1776: A Description by Fray Francisco Atanasio Domínguez, With Other Contemporary Documents*. Albuquerque: University of New Mexico Press, 1956.

ADROSKO, RITA J. *Natural Dyes and Home Dyeing*. New York: Dover, 1971.

AHLBORN, RICHARD EIGHME. "Comments on Textiles in Eighteenth-Century Spanish New Mexico." In *Imported and Domestic Textiles in 18th-Century America*. Edited by Patricia L. Fiske. Paper presented at Irene Emery Roundtable on Museum Textiles, 1975 Proceedings.

ALESSIO-ROBLES, VITO. *Coahuila y Texas en la Epoca Colonial*. Mexico: n.p., 1938.

ALLEN, R. L. M. *Colour Chemistry*. London: Nelson, 1971.

AMSDEN, CHARLES AVERY. *Navajo Weaving, Its Technique and Its History*. Santa Ana: Fine Arts Press, 1934.

———. *Navajo Weaving, Its Technique and Its History*. Chicago: Rio Grande Press, 1964.

BAILEY, L. R. *Indian Slave Trade in the Southwest*. Los Angeles: Westernlore Press, 1966.

BANCROFT, HUBERT HOWE. *California Pastoral: The Works of Hubert Howe Bancroft,* vol. 34. San Francisco: The History Co., 1888.

BEAN, LUTHER. *Land of the Blue Sky People*. Revised edition. Alamosa: Ye Olde Printe Shoppe, 1964.

BENAVIDES, FRAY ALONSO DE. *The Memorial of Fray Alonso de Benavides, 1630*. Translated by Mrs. Edward E. Ayer. Albuquerque: Horn and Wallace, 1965.

BENITEZ, JOSE R. *El Traje y El Adorno en México, 1500–1910*. Guadalajara: n.p., 1947.

BERLANT, ANTHONY, AND KAHLENBERG, MARY HUNT. *Walk in Beauty: The Navajo and Their Blankets*. Boston: New York Graphic Society, 1977.

BOYD, E. *Popular Arts of Spanish New Mexico*. Santa Fe: Museum of New Mexico Press, 1974.

BRAYER, HERBERT O. *William Blackmore: The Spanish-Mexican Land Grants of New Mexico and Colorado, 1863–1878*. 2 vols. Denver: Bradford-Robinson, 1949.

BRIGGS, CHARLES L. "To Talk in Different Tongues: The 'Discovery' and 'Encouragement' of Hispano Woodcarvers by Santa Fe Patrons, 1919–1945." In *Hispanic Crafts of the Southwest*. Edited by William Wroth. Colorado Springs: Taylor Museum of the Colorado Springs Fine Arts Center, 1977.

BRUNELLO, FRANCO. *The Art of Dyeing in the History of Mankind*. Vicenza: Neri Pozza Editore, 1973.

BRYAN, NONABAH G. *Navajo Native Dyes; Their Preparation and Use*. Washington: United States Department of the Interior, Bureau of Indian Affairs, 1940.

BUHLER, ALFRED. *Ikat, Batik, Plangi; Reserve-musterunge aus Vorderasien, Zentralasien, Sudosteurope und Nordafrika*. Basel: Pharos-Verlag Hansrudolf Schwabe, A. G., 1972.

CALENDAR OF THE MICROFILM EDITION OF THE MEXICAN ARCHIVES OF NEW MEXICO, 1821–46. Santa Fe: State of New Mexico Records Center. 1821–46.

CALENDAR OF THE SPANISH ARCHIVES OF NEW MEXICO, 1621–1821. Santa Fe: State of New Mexico Records Center. 1621–1821.

CARRERA STAMPA, MANUEL. *Los Gremios Mexicanos: La Organización General en Nueva España, 1521–1861.* Mexico: 1954.

CARRILLO Y GARIEL, ABELARDO. *El Traje en la Nueva España.* México: Instituto Nacional de Antropología e Historia, 1959.

CHAVEZ, FRAY ANGELICO. *The Origins of New Mexico Families.* Santa Fe: William Gannon, Publisher, 1954.

———. *Archives of the Archdiocese of Santa Fe 1678–1900.* Publications of the Academy of American Franciscan History, Bibliographical Series, vol. 3. Washington: Academy of American Franciscan History, 1957.

CHAVEZ, TIBO J. *New Mexican Folklore of the Rio Abajo.* Portales: Bishop Printing Co., 1972.

———. *El Rio Abajo.* Pampa Print Shop, n.d.

CLARK, NEIL M. *The Weavers of Chimayó.* Santa Fe: Vergara Printing Co., 1953.

COLTON, MARY-RUSSEL FERRELL. *Hopi Dyes.* Northern Arizona Flagstaff Bulletin No. 41. Flagstaff: Northland Press, 1965.

CORDRY, DONALD AND DOROTHY. *Mexican Indian Costumes.* Austin: University of Texas Press, 1968.

CURTIN, L. S. M. *Healing Herbs of the Upper Rio Grande.* Santa Fe: Laboratory of Anthropology, 1947.

———. *Healing Herbs of the Upper Rio Grande.* Los Angeles: Southwest Museum, 1965.

DAVISON, MILDRED, AND MAYER-THURMAN, CHRISTA C. *Coverlets, A Handbook of the Collection of Woven Coverlets in The Art Institute of Chicago.* Chicago: The Art Institute of Chicago, 1973.

DICKEY, ROLAND F. *New Mexico Village Arts.* Albuquerque: University of New Mexico Press, 1949.

DIFFIE, BAILEY W. *Latin-American Civilization, Colonial Period.* Harrisburg: Stackpole Sons, 1947.

DONKIN, R. A. *Spanish Red: An Ethnogeographical Study of Cochineal and the Opuntia Cactus.* Transactions of The American Philosophical Society, 67, part 5 (1977). Philadelphia: The American Philosophical Society.

DOUGLAS, FREDERICK H. *Main Types of Pueblo Cotton Textiles.* Norman Feder, November, 1977. (A reprint of the 1940 Denver Art Museum Department of Indian Art Leaflets 92–93.)

DUNTON, NELLIE, compil. *The Spanish Colonial Ornament and the Motifs Depicted in the Textiles of the Period of the American Southwest, Compiled and Arranged by Nellie Dunton.* Philadelphia: H. C. Perleberg, 1935.

EMERY, IRENE. *The Primary Structures of Fabrics.* Washington: The Textile Museum, 1966.

[ESPINOSA, CARMEN] New Mexico Department of Vocational Education. *Vegetable Dyes Bulletin.* Santa Fe, 1935.

ESPINOSA, J. MANUEL. *First Expedition of Vargas Into New Mexico 1692,* 10, Coronado Cuarto Centennial Publications. Albuquerque: University of New Mexico Press, 1940.

FERGUSSON, ERNA. *New Mexico.* New York: Alfred A. Knopf, 1951.

———. *New Mexico's Royal Road.* N.p., n.d.

FONTANA, BERNARD L.; FAUBERT, EDMOND J. B.; AND BURNS, BARNEY T. *The Other Southwest. Indian Arts and Crafts of Northwestern Mexico.* Phoenix: Heard Museum, 1977.

FORBES, R. J. *Studies in Ancient Technology,* 4. Leiden: E. J. Brill, 1964.

FORD, KAREN COWAN. *Las Yerbas de la Gente: A Study of Hispanic-American Medicinal Plants.* Museum of Anthropology, University of Michigan, #60. Ann Arbor: University of Michigan Press, 1975.

GIBSON, CHARLES. *Tlaxcala in the 16th Century.* Stanford: Stanford University Press, 1967.

GIBSON, CHARLES E., JR. *Alamosa, Conejos, and Costilla Counties: Interviews Collected During 1933–34 for the State Historical Society of Colorado by Civil Works Administration Workers.* Typescripts. Denver: State Historical Society of Colorado, n.d.

GOODYKOONTZ, COLIN B. "The People of Colorado." In *Colorado and Its People,* 2, edited by Leroy R. Hafen, pp. 77–120. New York: Lewis Historical Publishing Co., 1948.

GRABURN, NELSON H., ed. *Ethnic and Tourist Arts: Cultural Expressions from the Fourth World.* Berkeley: University of California Press, 1976.

GRANDSTAFF, JAMES O. *Wool Characteristics in Relation to Navajo Weaving.* Washington: U.S. Dept. of Agriculture, Technical Bulletin no. 790, 1942.

GREGG, ANDREW K. *New Mexico in the 19th Century: A Pictorial History.* Albuquerque: University of New Mexico Press, 1968.

GREGG, JOSIAH. *Commerce of the Prairies.* Edited by Max L. Moorhead. Norman: University of Oklahoma Press, 1954.

———. *Commerce of the Prairies.* Lincoln: University of Nebraska Press, 1967.

GRISWOLD, LESTER. *Handicraft.* 8th Ed. Colorado Springs: Out West Printing and Stationery Co., 1942.

GROVE, PEARCE S.; BARNETT, BECKY J.; AND HANSEN, SANDRA J., eds. *New Mexico Newspapers: A Comprehensive Guide to Bibliographic Entries and Locations.* Albuquerque: University of New Mexico Press, 1975.

HACKETT, CHARLES WILSON. *Historical Documents Relating to New Mexico, Nueva Vizcaya and Approaches Thereto, to 1773.* Washington: Carnegie Institution of Washington, 1937.

————. *Revolt of the Pueblo Indians of New Mexico and Otermín's Attempted Reconquest, 1680–1682.* Coronado Cuarto Centennial Publications, 1540–1940, vol. 8. Albuquerque: University of New Mexico Press, 1970, 2d Printing.

HAFEN, LEROY. *The Overland Mail, 1849–1869.* Cleveland: Arthur H. Clark, 1927.

————, ed. *Colorado and Its People.* 2 vols. New York: Lewis Historical Publishing Co., 1948.

HAFEN, LEROY R., AND ANN W. *Old Spanish Trail: Santa Fe to Los Angeles.* Glendale: Arthur H. Clark Co., 1954.

HALL, CARRIE, AND KRETSINGER, ROSE G. *The Romance of the Patchwork Quilt in America.* New York: Bonanza Books, 1935.

HAMMOND, GEORGE P., AND REY, AGAPITO. *Narratives of the Coronado Expedition, 1540–1542.* Coronado Cuarto Centennial Publications, 1540–1940, vol. 2. Albuquerque: University of New Mexico Press, 1940.

————. *Don Juan de Oñate, Colonizer of New Mexico 1595–1628.* Coronado Cuarto Centennial Publications, 1540–1940, vol. 5. Albuquerque: University of New Mexico Press, 1953.

————. *The Rediscovery of New Mexico.* Coronado Cuarto Centennial Publications, 1540–1940, vol. 3. Albuquerque: University of New Mexico Press, 1966.

HARING, CLARENCE HENRY. *Trade and Navigation Between Spain and the Indies in the Time of the Hapsburgs.* Cambridge: Harvard University Press, 1918.

HARPER, ALLAN G.; CORDOVA, ANDREW R.; AND KALERVA, OBERG. *Man and His Resources in the Middle Rio Grande Valley.* Albuquerque: University of New Mexico Press, 1943.

HARVEY, BYRON. *The Fred Harvey Fine Arts Collection.* Phoenix: The Heard Museum, 1976.

HEDLUND, CATHERINE A. *A Primer of New England Crewel Embroidery.* Sturbridge: Old Sturbridge Village, 1963.

HERSTROM, GUY. "Sangre de Cristo Grant." In *The 1960 Brand Book of the Denver Posse of the Westerners,* vol. 16. Edited by Guy M. Herstrom. Boulder: Johnson Publishing Co., 1961.

HILL, ALBERT F. *Economic Botany.* 2d ed. New York: McGraw-Hill, 1952.

HODGE, FREDERICK WEBB. *Handbook of American Indians North of Mexico.* Washington: Government Printing Office, 1912.

HODGE, FREDERICK WEBB; HAMMOND, GEORGE P.; AND REY, AGAPITO. *Fray Alonso de Benavides' Revised Memorial of 1634: With Numerous Supplementary Documents Elaborately Annotated.* Coronado Cuarto Centennial Publications, 1540–1940, vol. 4. Albuquerque: University of New Mexico Press, 1945.

HOFFMANN, MARTA. *The Warp-Weighted Loom.* Oslo: Norsk Folkemuseum, Universitets-forlaget (Studia Norvegica, no. 14), 1964.

HULBERT, ARCHER BUTLER, ed. *Southwest on the Turquoise Trail: The First Diaries on the Road to Santa Fe.* Colorado Springs: The Stewart Commission of Colorado College, and Denver: Denver Public Library, 1933.

HUNING, FRANZ. *Traders on the Santa Fe Trail: Memoirs of Franz Huning, With Notes by His Granddaughter, Lina Fergusson Browne.* Albuquerque: Calvin Horn, University of Albuquerque, 1973.

INMAN, COL. HENRY. *The Old Santa Fe Trail: The Story of a Great Highway.* Topeka: Crane & Co., 1909.

IRWIN, JOHN, AND BRETT, KATHARINE B. *Origins of Chintz.* London: Her Majesty's Stationery Office, 1970.

JAMES, GEORGE WHARTON. *Indian Blankets and Their Makers.* Chicago: McClurg and Co., 1914.

JAMES, REBECCA. *The Colcha Stitch: Embroideries by Rebecca James.* Santa Fe: Museum of International Folk Art, 1963.

JAMES, THOS. *Three Years Among the Indians and Mexicans.* St. Louis: Missouri Historical Society, 1916.

JARAMILLO, JUANITA. "Rio Grande Weaving: A Continuing Tradition." In *Hispanic Crafts of the Southwest.* Edited by William Wroth. Colorado Springs: The Taylor Museum of the Colorado Springs Fine Arts Center, 1977.

JARAMILLO, MRS. CLEOFAS M. *Shadows of the Past.* Santa Fe: Seton Village Press, 1941.

————. *Romance of a Little Village Girl.* San Antonio: Naylor Co., 1955.

JENKINS, MYRA ELLEN, AND MINGE, WARD ALAN. *Record of Navajo Activities Affecting the Acoma-Laguna Area, 1746–1910.* Santa Fe: Acoma-Laguna Exhibit no. 530 in Land Claims Commission Docket 229, 1961.

JETER, JAMES, AND JUELKE, PAULA MARIE. *The Saltillo Sarape, An Exhibition Organized by the Santa Barbara Museum.* Santa Barbara: New World Arts, 1978.

KAHLENBERG, MARY HUNT, AND BERLANT, ANTHONY. *The Navajo Blanket.* New York: Praeger Publishers in association with the Los Angeles County Museum of Art, 1972.

KEARNEY, THOMAS H., AND PEEBLES, ROBERT H. *Arizona Flora.* Berkeley and Los Angeles: University of California Press, 1964.

KUBLER, GEORGE A. *The Shape of Time: Remarks on the History of Things.* New Haven: Yale University Press, 1962.

LAMAR, HOWARD ROBERTS. *The Far Southwest 1846–1912.* New York: W. W. Norton & Co., 1970 (1966).

LARSEN, JACK LENOR. *The Dyer's Art: Ikat, Batik, Plangi.* New York: Van Nostrand Reinhold, 1976.

LARSON, ROBERT W. *New Mexico's Quest for Statehood, 1846–1912*. Albuquerque: University of New Mexico Press, 1968.

MAGOFFIN, SUSAN SHELBY. *Down the Santa Fe Trail and Into Mexico: The Diary of Susan Shelby Magoffin, 1846–47*. Edited by Stella M. Drumm. New Haven: Yale University Press, 1926.

MARTIN, WILLIAM C., AND CASTETTER, EDWARD F. *A Checklist of Gymnosperms and Angiosperms of New Mexico*. Albuquerque: University of New Mexico, 1970.

MATTHEWS, WASHINGTON. "Navajo Weavers." In *Third Annual Report of the Bureau of Ethnology*. Washington, 1884.

MEINIG, D. W. *Southwest: Three Peoples in Geographical Change 1600–1970*. New York: Oxford University Press, 1971.

MERA, HARRY PERCIVAL. *Pueblo Indian Embroidery*. Santa Fe: Laboratory of Anthropology, vol. 4, 1943.

————. *The Alfred I. Barton Collection of Southwestern Textiles*. Santa Fe: San Vicente Foundation, 1949.

MOORHEAD, MAX L. *New Mexico's Royal Road*. Norman: University of Oklahoma Press, 1958.

MORFI, FATHER JUAN AGUSTÍN DE. *Father Juan Agustín de Morfí's Account of Disorders in New Mexico, 1778*. Translated and edited by Marc Simmons. Santa Fe: Historical Society of New Mexico, 1977.

MOTTO, SYTHA. *Old Houses of New Mexico and the People Who Built Them*. Albuquerque: Calvin Horn, 1973.

MURILLO, GERARDO. *Las Artes Populares en México*. México: Editorial Cultura, 1922.

MYRICK, DAVID F. *New Mexico Railroads: An Historical Survey*. Golden: Colorado Railroad Museum, 1970.

NESTOR, SARAH. *The Native Market of the Spanish New Mexican Craftsmen; Santa Fe, 1933–1940*. Santa Fe: The Colonial New Mexico Historical Foundation, 1978.

OLMSTEAD, VIRGINIA LANGHAM, translator and compiler. *Spanish and Mexican Colonial Censuses of New Mexico: 1790, 1823, 1845*. Albuquerque: New Mexico Genealogical Society, 1975.

O'NEALE, LILA M. *Textiles of Highland Guatemala*. Washington: Carnegie Institute of Washington, Publication 567, 1945.

OSBORNE, LILLY DE JONGH. *Guatemalan Textiles*. New Orleans: Tulane University, 1935.

OTHON DE MENDIZABAL, MIGUEL. "La Evolución de la Industria Textil." In *Obras Completas*, vol. 3. Mexico: 1946–47.

PARISH, WILLIAM J. *The Charles Ilfeld Company: A Study of the Rise and Decline of Mercantile Capitalism in New Mexico*. Cambridge: Harvard University Press, 1961.

PINO, PEDRO BAUTISTA. *Three New Mexico Chronicles: The* Exposición *of Don Pedro Bautista Pino, 1812; The* Ojeada *of Lic. Antonio Barreiro, 1832; and* The Additions *by Don José Agustín de Escudero, 1849*. Translated, with introduction and notes, by H. Bailey Carroll and J. Villasana Haggard. Albuquerque: The Quivira Society, 1942.

POMEROY, EARL. *In Search of the Golden West*. New York: Alfred A. Knopf, 1957.

REEVE, FRANK D. *History of New Mexico*. Vol. 1. New York: Lewis Historical Publishing Co., 1961.

REVAULT, JACQUES. *Designs and Patterns from North African Carpets and Textiles*. New York, 1973.

RITTENHOUSE, JACK A. *The Santa Fe Trail. A Historical Bibliography*. Albuquerque: University of New Mexico Press, 1971.

SAFFORD, CARLETON L., AND BISHOP, ROBERT. *America's Quilts and Coverlets*. New York: E. P. Dutton & Co., 1972.

SAHAGUN, FRAY BERNARDINO DE. *General History of the Things of New Spain*. Books 8, 9, 10. Santa Fe: The School of American Research and the Museum of New Mexico, 1954, 1959, 1961.

SCHOLES, FRANCE V. *Troublous Times in New Mexico 1659–1670*. Albuquerque: University of New Mexico Press, 1942.

SCHROEDER, ALBERT H., AND MATSON, DON S. *A Colony on the Move: Gaspar Castaño de Sosa's Journal 1590–1591*. Santa Fe: The School of American Research, 1965.

SCHURZ, WILLIAM LYTLE. *The Manila Galleon*. New York: E. P. Dutton and Co., 1939.

SEALE, WILLIAM. *The Tasteful Interlude: American Interiors Through the Camera's Eye, 1860–1917*. New York: Praeger Publishers, 1975.

SIBLEY, G. C. *The Road to Santa Fe, 1825–7*. Albuquerque: University of New Mexico Press, 1952.

SIMMONS, MARC. *New Mexico, A Bicentennial History*. New York, Nashville: W. W. Norton & Co., American Association for State and Local History, 1977.

SPICER, EDWARD H. "Plural Society in the Southwest." In *Plural Society in the Southwest*. Edited by Edward H. Spicer and Raymond H. Thompson. New York: Interbook, a publication of the Weatherhead Foundation, 1972.

STAPLEY, MILDRED. *Popular Weaving and Embroidery in Spain*. New York: William Helburn, 1924.

START, LAURA E. *The McDougall Collection of Indian Textiles from Guatemala and Mexico*. Oxford: Oxford University Press, 1948.

STOLLER, MARIANNE L. "Traditional Hispanic Arts and Crafts in the San Luis Valley of Colorado." In *Hispanic Crafts of the Southwest*, edited by William

Wroth. Colorado Springs: The Taylor Museum of the Colorado Springs Fine Arts Center, 1977.

———. Untitled *MS*. Forthcoming.

SWADESH, FRANCES LEON. *Los Primeros Pobladores*. Notre Dame: University of Notre Dame Press, 1974.

TEJADA, MIGUEL M. LERDO DE. *Comercio Exterior de México desde la Conquista Hasta Hoy, 1853*. Mexico, 1967.

TERRELL, JOHN UPTON. *The Navajos*. New York: Harper and Row, 1972 (1970).

THOMAS, ALFRED BARNABY. *Forgotten Frontiers: A Study of the Spanish Indian Policy of Don Juan Bautista de Anza, Governor of New Mexico, 1777–1787*. Norman: University of Oklahoma Press, 1932.

———., ed. and transl. *Teodoro de Croix and the Northern Frontier of New Spain, 1776–1783*. Norman: University of Oklahoma Press, 1941.

TILLEY, MARTHA. *Three Textile Traditions*. Colorado Springs: The Taylor Museum, 1967.

TOWNE, CHARLES WAYLAND, AND WENTWORTH, EDWARD NORRIS. *Shepherd's Empire*. Norman: University of Oklahoma Press, 1946.

TUSHAR, OLIBAMA LOPEZ. *The People of "El Valle."* Denver: Private Publication, 1975.

TWITCHELL, RALPH EMERSON. *The Leading Facts of New Mexico History*. 5 vols. Cedar Rapids: Torch Press, 1911–17.

———. *The Spanish Archives of New Mexico*. Vol. 1. Cedar Rapids: Torch Press, 1914.

UBBELOHDE, CARL; BENSON, MAXINE; AND SMITH, DUANE A. *A Colorado History*. Boulder: Pruett Publishing Co., 1972.

U.S. DEPARTMENT OF THE INTERIOR, CENSUS OFFICE. *Report on the Manufactures of the United States at the Tenth Census, June 1, 1880*. Washington: U.S. Government Printing Office, 1883.

VELAZQUEZ DE LA CADENA, MARIANO; GREG, EDWARD; AND IRIBAS, JUAN L. *The Revised Velázquez: A New Pronouncing Dictionary of the Spanish and English Languages*. Englewood Cliffs: Prentice-Hall, 1973.

WARD, H. G. *Mexico in 1827*. London: Henry Colburn, 1828.

WEIGLE, MARTA, ed. *Hispanic Villages of New Mexico*. Santa Fe: The Lightning Tree—Gene Lyon, 1975. (A reprint of vol. 2 of the 1935 Tewa Basin Study with Supplementary Materials.)

WEIGLE, PALMY. *Ancient Dyes for Modern Weavers*. New York: Watson-Guptill, 1974.

WENTWORTH, EDWARD NORRIS. *America's Sheep Trails*. Ames: Iowa State College Press, 1948.

WHITE, FRANK A. *La Garita*. La Jara: Cooper Printing Co., 1971.

WILLETTS, WILLIAM. *Chinese Art*. Baltimore: Pelican Books, 1958.

WINSHIP, GEORGE PARKER. *The Coronado Expedition*. Fourteenth Annual Report of the Bureau of American Ethnology, 1896.

WOOTON, E. O., AND STANDLEY, PAUL C. *Flora of New Mexico*. Contributions of the United States Herbarium. Vol. 19. Washington, D.C.: Washington Printing Office, 1915.

WOOTON, E. O., AND STANDLEY, PAUL C. *Flora of New Mexico*. Vol. 7, *U.S. Flora*. Edited by J. Cramer. Washington: U.S. Government Printing Office, 1972 (reprint).

ARTICLES

AUSTIN, MARY. "Spanish Colonial Furnishings in New Mexico." *Antiques* 23, no. 2 (1933): 46–49.

BARKER, RUTH LAUGHLIN. "The Craft of Chimayo." *El Palacio* 28, no. 6 (1930): 161–73.

BLOOM, LANSING B. "Early Weaving in New Mexico." *New Mexico Historical Review* 2, no. 3 (1927): 228–38.

———. "A Trade Invoice of 1638." *New Mexico Historical Review* 10, no. 3 (1935): 242–48.

BORHEGYI, STEPHAN F. "The Miraculous Shrines of Our Lord of Esquipulas in Guatemala and Chimayo." *El Palacio* 60, no. 3 (1953): 83–111.

BOYD, E. "Celso Gallegos—A Truly Spontaneous Primitive Artist." *El Palacio* 60, no. 5 (1953): 215–16.

———. "Ikat Dyeing in Southwestern Textiles." *El Palacio* 68, no. 3 (1961): 185–89.

———. "Rio Grande Blankets Containing Hand Spun Cotton Yarns." *El Palacio* 71, no. 4 (1964): 22–28.

BRIGGS, WALTER. "Truchas Weaves for the World." *New Mexico Magazine* 47, no. 8 (1969): 32.

BRUYAS, JOSEPH. "Les Procédes de Teinture de L'Amérique Précolombienne." *Teintex* 35, no. 7 (1970): 420–32.

BUHLER, ALFRED. "The Ikat Technique." *Ciba Review*, no. 44 (1942): 1586–96.

———. "Dyes and Dyeing Methods for Ikat Threads." *Ciba Review*, no. 44 (1942): 1597–1603.

———. "The Origin and Extent of the Ikat Technique." *Ciba Review*, no. 44 (1942): 1604–11.

BURROUGHS, JEAN M. "From Coronado's Churros." *El Palacio* 83, no. 1 (1977): 9–13.

CAMMANN, SCHUYLER. "Chinese Influence in Colonial Peruvian Tapestries." *Textile Museum Journal* 1, no. 3 (1964): 21–34.

CARLSON, ALVAR WARD. "New Mexico's Sheep Industry 1850-1900: Its Role in the History of the Territory." *New Mexico Historical Review* 44, no. 1 (1969): 25–49.

CASSIDY, INA SIZER. "Art and Artists of N.M.: N.M. Crafts Center." *New Mexico Magazine* (September, 1940): 25, 44, 45.

———. "Art and Artists of New Mexico: Handcrafts Center." *New Mexico Magazine* (May, 1941): 23, 35–36.

———. "Art and Artists of N.M.: N.M. Crafts Center." *New Mexico Magazine* (November, 1949): 26, 49.

———. "Art and Artists of N.M.—Statewide Craft Exhibit." *New Mexico Magazine* (November, 1952): 35, 47.

———. "Art and Artists of N.M.—New Mexico Wholesale Crafts." *New Mexico Magazine* (January, 1955): 22, 39.

CHAVEZ, FRAY ANGELICO. "The Unique Tomb of Fathers Zarate and de la Llana in Santa Fe." *New Mexico Historical Review* 15, no. 2 (1940): 101.

———. "New Names in New Mexico, 1820–1850." *El Palacio* 64, nos. 9–10 (1957): 291–318.

CLARK, ANNA NOLAN. "Art of the Loom." *New Mexico Magazine* 16, no. 11 (1938): 9–11, 35–36.

COAN, MARY W. "Handicraft Arts Revived." *New Mexico Magazine* 13, no. 2 (1935): 13, 14–15.

COMBS, D. GENE. "Enslavement of Indians in the San Luis Valley of Colorado." *The San Luis Valley Historian* 5, no. 1 (1973): 1–20.

CONNER, VEDA NEVILLE. "The Weavers of Chimayó." *New Mexico Magazine* 29, no. 8 (1951): 19, 41, 43.

CRAMP, HELEN. "The Old Santo Maker." *New Mexico Magazine* 9, no. 1 (1931): 20, 46.

CREWS, MILDRED F. "Needlework Heritage." *New Mexico Magazine* 40, nos. 11 and 12 (November and December, 1962): 44–47.

CRIMMINS, M. L. "Fort Massachusetts, First United States Military Post in Colorado." *The Colorado Magazine* 15 (1938): 128–35.

DOYLE, GENE F. "Candelario's Fabulous Curios." *The Denver Westerners Monthly Roundup* 24, no. 9 (1968): 3–13.

DUSENBERG, WILLIAM H. "Woolen Manufacture in New Spain." *The Americas* 4 (1947): 223–34.

EMERY, IRENE. "Wool Embroideries of New Mexico: Some Notes on the Stitch Employed." *El Palacio* 56, no. 11 (1949): 339–45.

———. "Wool Embroideries of New Mexico: Notes on Some of the Spanish Terms." *El Palacio* 57, no. 5 (1950): 143–52.

———. "Samplers Embroidered in String." *El Palacio* 60, no. 4 (1953): 35–51.

EMORY, LT. COL. W. H., AND ABERT, LT. J. W. "Notes of a Military Reconnaisance from Fort Leavenworth, in Missouri, to San Diego, California . . ." Made in 1846–47 with the advanced guard of the Army of the West. Report of the Secretary of War, 30th Congress, Exec. Doc. 41, Washington, 1848.

ENTHOVEN, JACQUELINE. "The Bokhara Stitch and Colcha Embroidery." *Needle Arts* 7, no. 3 (1976): 27–28.

"FIESTA EVENT: THE SPANISH COLONIAL ARTS SOCIETY." *El Palacio* 29, no. 2 (1930): 105–6.

GETTENS, RUTHERFORD J., AND TURNER, EVAN H. "The Materials and Methods of Some Religious Paintings of Early Nineteenth-Century New Mexico." *El Palacio* 58, no. 1 (1951): 3–16.

GROSSMAN, ELLIN F. "Textiles and Looms from Guatemala and Mexico: The Elsie McDougall Collection." *Handweaver and Craftsman* 7, no. 1 (1955): 6–11.

HILL, W.W. "Some Navajo Culture Exchanges During Two Centuries (with a translation of the early eighteenth century Rabal manuscript)." *Smithsonian Miscellaneous Collections* 100 (1940), Washington, D.C.

HURT, AMY PASSMORE. "Chimayó, The Village Time Has Blest." *New Mexico Magazine* (November, 1934): 10–12, 43, 45.

HUSSEY, JOHN ADAM. "The New Mexico-California Caravan of 1847–1848." *New Mexico Historical Review* 18, no. 1 (1943): 1–16.

JONES, CHARLES IRVING. "William Kronig, New Mexico Pioneer: From His Memoirs of 1849–60." *New Mexico Historical Review* 19, nos. 3 and 4 (1944): 185–224, 271–311.

KELLY, JAS. A. "Sheep Raising and Feeding." *Souvenir of the San Luis Valley* (1906): 6–8.

KENT, KATE. "The Cultivation and Weaving of Cotton in the Prehistoric Southwestern United States." *American Philosophical Transactions,* New Series, 47, pt. 3 (1957).

LAWLER, JOHN E. "Spanish-American Normal School." *New Mexico Highway Journal* 8, no. 10 (1930): 26–28.

LAWRENCE, ELEANOR FRANCES. "Mexican Trade Between Santa Fe and Los Angeles, 1830–1848." *California Historical Society Quarterly* 10 (March, 1931): 27–39.

"LOS TEJIDOS NORTEÑOS." *Interweave* 1, no. 4 (1976): 15.

McCOURT, PURNEE A. "The Conejos Land Grant of Southern Colorado." *The Colorado Magazine* 52, no. 1 (1975): 34–51.

MARTINEZ, JOHNNY. "The History Makers of Villaneuva." *New Mexico Magazine* 53, no. 12 (1975): 16–17.

MAUZY, WAYNE. "Santa Fe's Native Market." *New Mexico Magazine* 40, nos. 13, 14, 15 (March 25, April 1–8, 1936): 65–73.

MENA, RAMON. "El Zarape." *Anales del Museo Nacional de Arqueología, Historia y Etnografía* 3, Cuarta Epoca (1925): 373–98.

MINGE, WARD ALAN. "Last Will and Testament of Severino Martinez." *New Mexico Quarterly* 33, no. 1 (1963): 35–56.

MORGAN, NICHOLAS G. "Mormon Colonization in the San Luis Valley." *The Colorado Magazine* 27, no. 4 (1950): 269–93.

MURDOCH, ALLAN. "Looms of the Mountains." *The Santa Fean* 2 (Summer, 1942): 7–9.

"NATHANIEL P. HILL INSPECTS COLORADO." *The Colorado Magazine* 33, no. 4 (1956): 241–76.

THE NEW MEXICAN. Obituary, May 28, 1920: 6, col. 3.

ORREGO-SALAS, CARMEN B. DE. "The Villanueva Tapestry." *Needle Arts* 8, no. 4 (1977): 8–9.

POLESE, RICHARD L., AND SACHSE, JAMES M. "New Mexico's Sheep Industry Today: New Promise for a Timeless Resource." *El Palacio* 83, no. 1 (1977): 25–27.

"SAN LUIS STORE CELEBRATES CENTENNIAL." *The Colorado Magazine* 34, no. 4, (1957): 256–62.

SALTZMAN, MAX. "Color Matching via Pigment Identification." *Dyestuffs* 43, no. 3 (1959): 1–9. Reprint.

SALTZMAN, MAX; KEAY, A. M.; AND CHRISTENSEN, JACK. "The Identification of Colorants in Ancient Textiles." *Dyestuffs* 44, no. 6 (1963): 241–51.

SCHOLES, FRANCE V. "Church and State in New Mexico, 1610–1650: Chapter 5: The Administration of Luis de Rosas, 1637–1641." *New Mexico Historical Review* 11, no. 4 (October, 1936): 297–333.

———. "Royal Treasury Records, 1596–1683." *New Mexico Historical Review* 50, nos. 1, 2 (1975): 5–23, 139–64.

SEWELL, BRICE H. "A New Type of School." *New Mexico School Review* 15, no. 2 (1935): 49–50.

———. "Fine Furniture—Handmade." *New Mexico Magazine* (May, 1939): 27.

SMITH, EMILIA GALLEGOS. "Reminiscences of Early San Luis." *The Colorado Magazine* 24, no. 1 (1947): 24–25.

SPILLMAN, TRISH. "Rio Grande Weaving and Dyeing Workshop." *El Palacio* 83, no. 1 (1976): 14–24.

STAMM, ROY ALLEN. "October in Cordova." *New Mexico Magazine* (October, 1935): 14–15, 38.

TIERNEY, GAIL. "Plants for the Dyepot." *El Palacio* 83, no. 3 (1977): 28–35.

"TIME-EVENT CHART OF THE SAN LUIS VALLEY." *The San Luis Valley Historian* 1, nos. 1, 2, 3 (1969).

TOULOUSE, BETTY. "Pueblo Pottery Traditions, Ever Constant, Ever Changing." *El Palacio* 82, no. 3 (1976): 14–47.

TRUMBO, THERON MARCOS. "The Gifts of Chimayó." *New Mexico Magazine* 25, no. 2 (1947): 19, 33, 35.

VAN DIEST, E.C. "Early History of Costilla County." *The Colorado Magazine* 5, no. 4 (1928): 140–43.

VETTERLI, W. A. "The History of Indigo." *Ciba Review,* no. 85 (1951): 3066–71.

WENTWORTH, EDWARD NORRIS. "The Advent of Sheep in New Mexico." *New Mexico Stockman* 4, no. 11 (1939): 3, 21.

WHEAT, JOE BEN. "Spanish-American and Navajo Weaving, 1600 to Now." *Collected Papers in Honor of Margery Ferguson Lambert.* Papers of the Archaeological Society of New Mexico, 3 (1976): 199–226.

WOOLFORD, WITHERS. "Revival of Native Crafts." *New Mexico Magazine* (September, 1931): 9, 24–26.

MANUSCRIPTS

ANAWALT, PATRICIA RIEFF. "Pan-Mesoamerican Costume Repertory at the Time of Spanish Contact." Ph.D. dissertation, University of California, Los Angeles, 1975.

ANDERSON, ROBERT N. "Guadalupe, Colorado: A Social and Economic History of Early Community." Master's thesis, Adams State College, 1966.

BRAZIL, BLAS., JR. "A History of the Obrajes in New Spain." Master's thesis, University of New Mexico, 1962.

DENNIS, MARY. "Plants and Animals Used As Sources of Dye, Paint, and Skin Dressing in the Southwest." Master's thesis, University of New Mexico, 1935.

HASKEL, MURIEL. "The Mormon Church West of the Rio Grande." Carson, N. M. Unpublished WPA material available at History Division, Museum of New Mexico.

JENKINS, KATHARINE DREW. "An Analysis of the Saltillo Style Mexican Sarapes." Master's thesis, University of California, n.d.

LA FORCE, JAMES CLAYBURN. "The Development of the Spanish Textile Industry 1750–1800." Ph.D. dissertation, University of California, 1965.

MARTINEZ, REYES N. "The Weaver of Talpa." *New Mexico Writers' Project.* Unpublished manuscript, History Division, Museum of New Mexico, Santa Fe.

McCROSSEN, GEORGE. *The Handweaving Phenomenon in the Southwest During the Two Decades between 1930–1950: Being the History of McCrossen*

Handwoven Textiles, Inc., Library of the Museum of International Folk Art, Santa Fe.

MERA, HARRY PERCIVAL. *Spanish-American Blanketry; Its Relationship to Aboriginal Weaving in the South West*. Santa Fe: School of American Research. Unpublished manuscript. 1947–51.

SALAZAR, DELFINO. "A Brief Historical Review." In *A Hundred Years of Irrigation in Colorado*. Colorado Irrigation Centennial Committee. Mimeographed, 1951: 101–104.

SEDILLO-BREWSTER, MELA. "New Mexican Weaving and the Practical Vegetable Dyes from Spanish Colonial Times." Master's thesis, University of New Mexico, 1935.

STOLLER, MARIANNE. "Hispanic Arts and Crafts of the San Luis Valley." In *Determining the Feasibility of Developing a Craft Business Enterprise for Rural Low Income U.S. Citizens Living in the San Luis Valley*. 11 (August, 1974): 9–23. Final Report submitted to the Four Corners Regional Commission. A project of the Colorado Commission on the Status of Women. The Virginia Blue Resource Centers for Women.

TURNER, ROBT. P., JR. "The Cotton Textile Industry of New Spain." Master's thesis, University of New Mexico, 1967.

VIGIL, CHARLIE A. "History and Folklore of San Pedro and San Pablo, Colorado." Master's thesis, Adams State College, 1956.

WHEAT, JOE BEN. "Spanish Weaving Terms Used in the Documents." Unpublished manuscript, on file at the Museum of International Folk Art, Santa Fe, 1977: 1–20.

UNPUBLISHED MATERIALS AND DOCUMENTS

The unpublished material in this publication consists for the most part of references to be found in the New Mexico State Records Center and Archives, Santa Fe, New Mexico, which contains the Spanish, Mexican, and Territorial Archives of New Mexico as well as U.S. Census reports and the microfilmed Archives of the Archdiocese of Santa Fe. The specific documents are listed in the chapter notes, with short descriptions and inclusive dates which correspond to those in published guides, such as Twitchell, *The Spanish Archives of New Mexico*, Vols. 1 and 2; *Calendar of the Spanish Archives of New Mexico, 1621–1821; Calendar of the Microfilm Edition of the Mexican Archives of New Mexico, 1821–46;* and Chávez, *Archives of the Archdiocese of Santa Fe, 1678–1900,* all in the *Books* section of the Bibliography. In addition the Colorado State Historical Society holds the Woodard and the Boyd manuscripts which deal with the Beryl G. and Charles H. Woodard collection of textiles as well as the typescript records of the Colorado Writer's Project, 1933–34, which was coordinated by Charles Gibson.

Also on file in libraries at the Museum of International Folk Art and the History Division of the Museum of New Mexico are business records, correspondence, taped interviews, and other primary source materials used in writing and compiling this publication. Accession records and records of the Spanish Textile Tradition project are held at the Museum of International Folk Art in Santa Fe.

INDEX